UNLOCKING
POTENTIAL

Identifying and Serving Gifted
Students From Low-Income Households

UNLOCKING
POTENTIAL

EDITED BY

Tamra Stambaugh, Ph.D., &
Paula Olszewski-Kubilius, Ph.D.

Routledge
Taylor & Francis Group

NEW YORK AND LONDON

Library of Congress Cataloging-in-Publication Data

Names: Stambaugh, Tamra, editor. | Olszewski-Kubilius, Paula, editor.
Title: Unlocking potential : identifying and serving gifted students from
    low-income households / Tamra Stambaugh, Ph.D., and Paula
    Olszewski-Kubilius, Ph.D.
Description: Waco : Prufrock Press Inc., 2020. | Includes bibliographical
    references. | Summary: "This edited book, written by authors with
    extensive experience in working with gifted students from low-income
    households, focuses on ways to translate the latest research and theory
    into evidence-supported practices that impact how schools identify and
    serve these students"-- Provided by publisher.
Identifiers: LCCN 2020036321 (print) | LCCN 2020036322 (ebook) |
Subjects: LCSH: Gifted children--Identification. | Gifted
    children--Education--United States. | Children with social
    disabilities--Education--United States.
Classification: LCC LC3993.2 .U57 2020 (print) | LCC LC3993.2 (ebook) |
    DDC 371.95--dc23
LC record available at https://lccn.loc.gov/2020036321
LC ebook record available at https://lccn.loc.gov/2020036322

First published in 2020 by Prufrock.Press Inc.

Published in 2021 by Routledge
605 Third Avenue, New York, NY 10017
2 Park Square, Milton Park, Abingdon, Oxon OX14 4RN

Routledge is an imprint of the Taylor & Francis Group, an informa business.

© 2020 by Taylor & Francis Group

Cover design by Allegra Denbo and layout design by Shelby Charette

ISBN: 9781032144665 (hbk)
ISBN: 9781646320806 (pbk)

DOI: 10.4324/9781003239383

Table of Contents

Foreword

This book on the implications of poverty for talent development offers important recommendations for educators and policymakers on what needs to occur in reforming gifted programs and services to reach students from low-income households more effectively. Chapters are very well-balanced in respect to the psychological issues and concepts that affect this population, as well as the educational issues that impact pathways to social mobility and life success. It is also a well-researched volume that draws on research across and beyond education, sharing insights from sociologists, psychologists, and economists whose work is critical to understanding the scope of the problem within the American educational system. Key stakeholder groups are acknowledged and addressed as potential barriers as well as facilitators of learning. These groups include parents, teachers, counselors, and the students themselves.

Translation of research into practice is emphasized in the book, especially in chapters that acknowledge the power of interventions of out-of-school programs and services, in-school curriculum interventions, and educational policies that promote acceleration and other modes of curriculum flexibility. Of particular interest is the focus on the long-term educational trajectories that track students from low-income backgrounds across early childhood, middle childhood, and secondary levels in respect to understanding the intersections of development, aptitudes, and individual differences. Concerns for university education also suggest that the development of these learners in the subtleties of both social and cognitive skill sets is crucial to negotiating ever more challenging environments that may lack the personal support students may have enjoyed earlier.

As a team, the editors of the volume bring a wealth of both research and practical expertise on the topic under study. Olszewski-Kubilius has almost 40 years of consistent and outstanding work in addressing the needs of students from low-income backgrounds through designing out-of-school program experiences and implementing a research program that provides answers to important questions related to these learners and their needs. Her longitudinal research to assess how these students perform beyond middle school and what the impacts are of specific interventions at earlier and later stages of development is groundbreaking and important for educators to understand in crafting successful interventions. Stambaugh's record of achievement in working with these learners is equally impressive, especially at the level of sustained practice. Her work has traversed local, state, national, and university levels in addressing the problem for more than 30 years. She has worked diligently in developing curriculum and program services to meet the needs of these learners at precollegiate levels and has translated that work through professional development and materials for teachers and other educators.

I know this book will help thousands of educators searching for answers to developing talent in children from low-income households. It provides important contemporary research and applications of that research in effective practice. No population deserves to benefit from gifted education and talent development mechanisms more than those high-aptitude learners from low-income backgrounds.

—Joyce VanTassel-Baska, Ed.D., Jody and Layton Smith
Professor Emerita of Education and Founding Director,
Center for Gifted Education at William & Mary

CHAPTER 1

Poverty, Academic Achievement, and Giftedness: *A Literature Review*

Paula Olszewski-Kubilius,
Tamra Stambaugh, and Susan Corwith

Poverty affects educational opportunity, upward mobility, and even basic health and security. It also significantly affects the opportunities for children with talent to develop and manifest their abilities in creative productive achievement in adulthood. In this chapter, we review the demographics of poverty in the U.S. followed by a brief review of the effects of poverty on general educational achievement. We complete this chapter with a review of how poverty affects talent development and what can be done about it, previewing subsequent chapters that explore important aspects of talent development for students from poverty in more depth.

Definitions of Poverty

Poverty is a social construct that is complex and multifaceted. Poverty can be defined in economic terms; for example, student poverty is typically operationalized in educational research within the U.S. as whether or not a student qualifies for free or reduced lunch. In other research, poverty is conceptualized more broadly, encompassing measures of other aspects of potential social and economic disadvantage (Burney & Bielke, 2008; Engle & Black, 2008), including levels of parental education, parental occupation, and learning resources within the home (e.g., number of books) or community. Carnevale et al. (2019) noted that family socioeconomic status (SES) that considers household income, parental education, and parental occupational prestige is a "more accurate reflection than income of the advantages and disadvantages that impact a child's chances for academic and economic success" (p. 5). For example, some occupations may not have high economic capital but strong social capital (e.g., educators). New immigrants who are well educated and considered professionals within their home countries but cannot work in the fields or at the level for which they are educated and trained may have limited finances for summer programs or private schools; however, they can provide an intellectually rich home and stress higher education. Additionally, among families classified as low income, there are degrees of poverty; poverty that is enduring and generational is much more deleterious in its effects on children than poverty that is episodic, such as the result of a temporary job loss (Michelmore & Dynarski, 2017).

Family income does not tell the whole story; children of mothers who were low income but had higher levels of education had higher levels of math knowledge (numbers and shape, relative size, ordinal sequence, addition, and subtraction) and reading skills (letter and sound recognition) upon entry into kindergarten (U.S. Department of Education, 2000), supporting the important role of early, informal teaching and exposure by parents to school readiness and achievement.

Additionally, Sampson (2002) found that families with lower incomes and levels of education can be diverse in terms of values and expectations for their child's school achievement. Low-income families of high-achieving Black students had what he called "middle-class values" toward education, including stressing educational achievement, setting times for study and homework at home, and facilitating their child's participation in extracurricular and outside-of-school activities. These parents communicated a positive view of the future and reinforced an internal locus of control. Families of low-achieving children communicated different beliefs about the future and/or verbally endorsed similar values but did not follow through with consonant supportive actions.

Major predictors of resiliency include connections to caring family members and adults in the community, intelligence and problem-solving skills, hope and optimism, and strong executive skills (Masten, 2001), and these factors can be present in families despite lower family incomes.

The Demographics and Geography of Poverty Among Children in the U.S.

According to the National Center for Children in Poverty (Jiang et al., 2016), in the U.S. 41% of all children under 18 years of age, 15.4 million children, and 44% of children under the age of 9 live in low-income families ("poor" is defined as below 100% of the federal poverty threshold [FPT], and "near poor" is between 100% and 199% of the FPT). Younger children are more likely to be in low-income families than older children (43% to 44% for children under age 12, and 37% for children ages 12–17). More children live in poverty than adults.

Rates of children from low-income families vary by race and ethnicity, with Hispanic children comprising the largest share of young children living in low-income families (36%; Jiang et al., 2016). In the U.S., African American, Native American, and Hispanic children come from disproportionally poor and low-income households, with 64% of African American children, 65% of Native American children, 61% of Hispanic children, 31% of White children, and 28% of Asian American children living in poverty. However, it is worth noting that there is variability in poverty rates within ethnic/racial groups as well—for example, within and between new immigrants and families who have been in the U.S. for generations (Burney & Cross, 2006; Kitano, 2006). Still, poverty and ethnicty/race are clearly linked in the U.S.

Poverty rates also vary substantially by geographic region, with higher rates of children in low-income households residing in the South (48%) than in the West (43%), and with the Midwest (42%) and Northeast (37%) housing the lowest percentages of low-income families (Jiang et al., 2016). According to testimony by Kneebone (2017) of the Brookings Institute to the House Ways and Means Committee, Subcommittee on Human Resources, the geography of poverty has changed in the United States. Poverty has typically been associated with large urban centers or rural areas, and it has historically been concentrated there. Poverty grew in the 2000s due to the recession, increasing in rural and urban areas by 20%, but also increasing in other regions—specifically small metropolitan areas and the suburbs. Suburbs around all major cities of the U.S. constituted 48% of the increase in families living below the poverty line between 2000 and 2015. The largest demographic group in the suburban poor is non-Hispanic Whites. According to research by the Economic Policy Institute using national data sets, the percentage of children in the U.S. on free and reduced lunch has increased rapidly between the mid 1990s and 2013 as well; in 2013, more than half of the eighth graders in U.S. public schools were on free and reduced lunch (Carnoy & Garcia, 2017). These rates of low-income families in the U.S. are only increasing. In a trend analysis study by the Nielsen Company using the U.S. Census Bureau data (Anderson, 2009), it was hypothesized that between the years 2020 and 2050 those living in poverty will increase significantly as those who are considered upper middle class, affluent, or wealthy decrease in numbers, thus predicting that the majority of individuals in the U.S. will be in the lower middle to poor income range. If this trend continues as predicted, it will have a direct impact on the economy, including the job market, spending, and U.S. competitiveness (Anderson, 2009).

Poverty and Its Effects

Research documents the many consequences of poverty, specifically the adverse effects of poverty on learning and achievement outcomes (Ellis et al., 2017; Lacour & Tissington, 2011; Moore et al., 2009). At the most fundamental level, poverty can affect children's health due to less availability of enough food, nutritious food, and medical care that can impact brain development. According to Hair et al. (2015), students from low-income backgrounds showed more diminished gray matter and scored lower on standardized tests than their wealthier counterparts. In another study, Hanson and colleagues (2015) found that brain development in students from low-income households was not as significant from infancy into primary school when compared to those not in poverty. The amount of time a student lived in poverty also impacted their future trajectories, negatively impacting the level of academic performance and adult productivity over time (Hair et al., 2015). Additionally, children from low-income households had reduced brain surface when compared to students of families that made $150,000 or more (Noble et al., 2015).

Other negative effects of poverty are mediated through family and community dynamics, such as a less enriching home environment, harsh and controlling parenting, a lack of maternal responsiveness, parental stress, and fewer community institutions that provide support (Engle & Black, 2008). It was speculated that "poverty and the conditions that often accompany it—violence, excessive noise, chaos at home, pollution, malnutrition, abuse and parents without jobs—can affect the interactions, formation, and pruning of connections in the young brain" (Hayasaki, 2016, para. 13). As such, early opportunities are critical for children who come from low-income families or communities.

Research shows that the effects of poverty on the educational achievement of children begin at birth, and deleterious effects on cognitive growth start in children's early environments. Differences in exposure to language and vocabulary (Hart & Risley, 2003) and informal exposure to the natural world (Curran & Kellogg, 2016; Morgan et al., 2016) in children's early environments have been documented. Such disparities significantly impact children's readiness for school, put them behind at the start of school for their academic growth, and persist and grow as children proceed through school (Fernald et al., 2013; Morgan et al., 2016).

Family income affects housing options and consequently neighborhood safety and access to community and educational resources that can promote optimal child development (Engle & Black, 2008; Pew Research Center, 2015). Poverty also affects educational opportunity (e.g., school choice, availability of early childhood education) and school quality (e.g., fewer advanced classes, less experienced teachers, higher teacher turnover; Aaronson et al., 2007; Rivkin et al., 2005). Poverty limits the financial and person power resources available within the family to support learning beyond the school day, such as trips to museums, participation in cultural events, and extracurricular or summer programs (Snellman et al., 2015). Poverty can also impact students' aspirations, including whether or not they view a future for themselves that includes higher education and professional careers, as a result of limited access to peer and/or adult mentors and professionals who can assist with educational paths and career development (Snellman et al., 2015).

Achievement, Excellence, and Opportunity Gaps

Educational achievement gaps between groups of children in the U.S. have been a major focus of policy and reform efforts (e.g., No Child Left Behind Act). Reardon (2011), using data from 19 nationally representative studies, examined the history of achievement gaps in the U.S. and concluded that the income gap in educational achievement, defined as the difference between children whose families were at the 90th versus the 10th percentile of family income, has widened and is now twice as large as the Black-White achievement gap. Although this chapter focuses on the impact of low income on educational achievement for gifted children, racial disparities in educational achievement exist above and beyond the impact of income (Levy et al., 2016), and implicit bias and stereotypes impact educational opportunity and achievement (Carnevale et al., 2019). For example, some of the largest ethnic/racial minority achievement gaps exist at the highest socioeconomic levels (Miller, 2004). Racism negatively and independently affects identification and educational opportunities and outcomes for children from ethnic/racial minority groups, including gifted children (see Ford, 2011; McBee, 2010). Therefore, similar effects can exist regardless of income if access and opportunity are not provided.

The achievement gap between lower and higher income children is present at school entry and persists as children progress through school (Carnevale et al., 2019). In a 2009 policy brief, researchers from the College Board (Barton & Coley, 2009) identified the following factors contributing to achievement and, ultimately, opportunity gaps: the rigor of the school curriculum, the quality of training and the experience levels of teachers, class size, teacher absence and turnover, access to instructional technologies within and outside of school, parental participation in school events, parental reading to children, excessive television viewing, and summer achievement losses. Their research showed that the disparities on these factors between children from higher income backgrounds and those from lower income backgrounds had not changed since an earlier study in 2003 (Barton & Coley, 2009).

Growing income disparities within the U.S. likely contribute to widening opportunity gaps and are reflected in another significant factor affecting achievement gaps—the differential investments of families from higher and lower income levels in educational opportunities for their children. Kornrich and Furstenberg (2013) studied data from the Consumer Expenditure Survey and found that families in the top two deciles of income spend 5 to 7 times more on their children's education than families in the lowest two deciles. High-quality day care and early education were among the most prominent family investments. There were also wide differences in family expenditures on enrichment activities. In 2005–2006, 20% of parents from the highest income categories spent $7,500 more than families in the bottom 20% on enrichment activities such as music lessons (Duncan & Murnane, 2011).

Lack of both formal and informal learning opportunities in the summer is cited as a major contributor to achievement gaps; research shows that two thirds of the achievement gap between lower and higher income students in grade 9 can be attributed to disparities in summer learning opportunities (i.e., access beyond the school day to enriched opportunities) that accumulate over time (McCombs et al., 2017).

The National Assessment of Educational Progress (NAEP), often called the nation's report card, has documented the achievement of different groups of students in the U.S. since 1990. This research has shown large and persistent achievement gaps between students who do and do not qualify for the federal free and reduced lunch program (National Center for Education Statistics, n.d.) since its inception. Recent NAEP data showed that the gaps in test performance in mathematics and reading at grades 4 and 8 between students who are eligible for free and reduced lunch and students who are not eligible remained relatively stable from 2013 to 2017.

Moreover, higher achieving, lower income students lose ground in school. Feinstein (2003) conducted a longitudinal study tracking academic achievement from preschool to age 10 and found that students from low-income backgrounds who were in the top quartiles of achievement initially declined over time, while the wealthier participants maintained their high achievement. Similarly, children from wealthier families who were in the lowest quartiles of achievement evidenced greater gains and ended up outperforming the students from low-income families who started out in the highest quartiles.

These early and persistent achievement disparities have significant consequences for adulthood. A kindergartner who comes from a high-SES family and with test scores in the bottom 50% has a 7 in 10 chance of reaching high SES in adulthood, while a kindergartner from a low-SES family with test scores in the top 50% has only a 3 in 10 chance of being high SES by the age of 25 (Carnevale et al., 2019).

Degree of poverty affects the size of achievement gaps, with wider gaps for children who have experienced persistent economic disadvantage as evidenced by eligibility for free and reduced lunch for multiple years, compared to students who are occasionally or intermittently eligible (Michelmore & Dynarski, 2017). To illustrate this point, Michelmore and Dynarksi (2017) examined student achievement data from the state of Michigan and from the Early Childhood Longitudinal Study. They estimated that, in math achievement, children who were persistently disadvantaged economically scored .94 standard deviation units below students who were never eligible for free and reduced lunch, and .23 standard deviation units below students who were occasionally eligible.

The findings regarding achievement gaps are similar for students who score in the upper quintiles of performance. Plucker and colleagues (2010, 2013) brought attention to a facet of achievement gaps that has historically been ignored—differences in achievement between subgroups of children at the highest levels of achievement, or what the authors termed "excellence gaps." Based on their analysis of NAEP as well as state-level achievement data, these authors found that although there have been increases in the percentages of students scoring at advanced levels, particularly on NAEP from 1996 to present, there are still wide gaps between students who qualify for free and reduced lunch and those who do not. For example, based on NAEP (National Center for Education Statistics, n.d.) data, 3% of fourth graders on free and reduced lunch scored at the highest level of achievement on NAEP reading compared to 15% of students not on free and reduced lunch. For eighth graders, these corresponding percentages in reading are 3% versus 7% and in math are 3% versus 15%. Also, Plucker et al.'s (2010, 2013) analysis shows that schooling does not close these excellence gaps, as they continue throughout elementary school and even widen in math. These differences in high levels of achievement are consequently reflected in gaps in students qualifying for gifted services. A study of gifted education practices conducted with 2,000 school districts across the U.S. by Callahan et al. (2014) found that 50% of the districts surveyed reported much lower percentages of students from poverty in their programs compared to these students' representation in the district population. In fact, less than 18% of the districts reported percentages for gifted students from low-income backgrounds that mirrored percentages for the district overall.

The Trajectories of Gifted Students From Low-Income Backgrounds

A child from a high-SES family is more likely to maintain high achievement scores throughout schooling than a child from a low-SES family (Carnevale et al., 2019). There are important and varied issues at each level of schooling to be considered, as the effects of poverty accumulate over time and significantly affect the development of children's talent. The trajectories of students' talent development paths can be significantly impacted by a lack of opportunity, identification, and access.

Paths in Elementary School

Although children from higher income households are more likely to start school with achievement levels in the top 25% compared to those from lower income households (72% vs. 28%; Wyner et al., 2007), there are large numbers of children who qualify for free and reduced lunch who do score at these levels. However, more of these children will fall out of the top quartile by grade 5 compared to their more economically advantaged peers (44% vs. 21%). A similar finding of loss of talent was obtained by the Fordham Institute (Xiang et al., 2011). A large sample of students with achievement levels at the 90th percentile or above on the Northwest Evaluation Association reading or math subtest was tracked from grades 3 to 6 to determine if students remained in the top decile of achievement. Results showed that students from high-poverty schools were underrepresented among high achievers overall, and their proportions declined over time. Although most students' achievement did not fall below the 70th percentile, declines at these levels could impact students' qualification for gifted services, which typically use cutoff scores of 90% to 95% on achievement tests (Xiang et al., 2011).

Paths in Middle School

Children from lower income households who are good candidates for advanced and accelerated programming are less likely than peers from higher income families to receive these services in middle school. Loveless (2009) studied the use of tracking within schools, particularly in mathematics. Although tracking has a troubled history within U.S. schools, it has recently seen a resurgence, according to Loveless, particularly in mathematics. Loveless examined NAEP data and found that, in general, middle schools serving students with economic disadvantages were less likely to offer tracked math classes in middle school—specifically early access to algebra—and, as expected, Hispanic and Black middle school students from low-income families were much less likely to be placed in tracked mathematics classes even if available compared to their White and Asian American peers with more opportunities. Specifically, 25% of these students were placed in a course lower than algebra in eighth grade despite scoring at the 90th percentile or above in math on the NAEP test. According to Loveless, although the research on the effects of tracking on the achievement of students is equivocal, it is most positive for academically talented learners who receive an accelerated or enriched curriculum. He concluded that high achievers in low-income schools do not have the same opportunities or resources to access advanced curriculum and are more likely to be in schools that support detracking, which could serve as a barrier to future success and access.

Achievement in middle school is an important contributor to continued achievement in high school, particularly for success in the ninth grade, a critical transition year for all students. Allensworth et al. (2014) studied the trajectories of middle school students into high school in a large urban school district with a poverty rate of 86%. They found that middle school grades were the best predictor of high school grades, and high grades in core subjects contributed to successful trajectories in high school, ultimately leading to enrollment at selective institutions of higher education. However, even students with high middle school grades experienced some decline when transitioning into ninth grade; students with GPAs in the top quartile saw a decline of .6 GPA unit from eighth to ninth grade, and 40% of students who had As or Bs in middle school and scored at the level of "exceeds standards" on the mandatory state test earned a C or lower in ninth-grade math. Similarly, Xiang et al. (2011) found that students from high-poverty schools were more likely to lose their high flyer status (top 10% on achievement in reading or math) as they moved from sixth to ninth grade. Lower grades and achievement can affect students' eligibility for honors-level or other advanced classes in high school.

Allensworth et al. (2014) and Rosenkranz et al. (2014) pointed to two important contributors for students' falling grades from middle to high school: a decline in class attendance and a lack of appropriate amounts of time invested in studying. The researchers attributed these to significantly less support from teachers in terms of monitoring and structuring homework and assignments and in efforts to encourage or motivate students—in other words, an expectation of increased independence on the part of students and ownership for their learning. The researchers' studies of student perceptions revealed that certain teacher behaviors were regarded as helpful to a successful transition to high school and maintenance of high grades, including providing individual attention around specific academic problems, monitoring student work and giving regular feedback to students about how to improve their grades, and explaining concepts clearly. Strong academic performance in middle school combined with supportive teachers and environments in high school enable students from low-income backgrounds to maintain high achievement and stay on upward trajectories of achievement.

Paths in High School

Research shows that achievement patterns for students are largely set by the time they enter high school (Carnevale et al., 2019). The Education Trust (Bromberg & Theokas, 2014) published the report "Falling Out of the Lead: Following High Achievers Through High School and Beyond" based on data from the Educational Longitudinal Study of 2002. For this report, Bromberg and Theokas compared the trajectories of subgroups of high-achieving students (defined as scoring at 75th percentile or above on a reading and math test given to all high school sophomores). They found that lower percentages of students from low-income backgrounds enter high school scoring in the top quartile in achievement in math or reading compared to students from higher income backgrounds (10% vs. 50%). Still, the authors noted that these higher achieving students from low-SES backgrounds represent a sizeable group of academically able students nationwide—more than 60,000 students. Students from low-income backgrounds who score in the top 25% in reading and math achievement are less likely to take advanced mathematics courses or Advanced Placement (AP) classes during high school or be enrolled in an International Baccalaureate (IB) program compared to their more economically advantaged academic peers—29% versus 42% for taking calculus, and 50% versus 70% for taking at least one AP course, for students from lower income backgrounds versus those from higher income backgrounds, respectively. Although a component of these disparities is the availability of advanced classes in students' schools, the study found that higher achieving students from low-income backgrounds are less likely to take calculus even when it is offered (36%) compared to their more advantaged peers (45%). Likely, the lack of understanding on students' part of the importance of advanced classes for paths toward higher education, as well as low expectations on the part of educators and poor counseling and advising, contribute to the underrepresentation of these students in advanced classes.

There are many documented benefits of taking AP classes and exams. Research shows that students who score a 3 or higher on an AP exam earn higher grades in college, perform well in subsequent classes in the same content area, take more college classes in the discipline, and have higher graduation rates (College Board, 2014). The Education Trust study (Bromberg & Theokas, 2014) showed, however, that higher achieving students from lower income backgrounds are less likely to pass AP exams compared to higher achieving peers from higher achieving backgrounds. As students started high school with comparable levels of achievement, the lower AP test performance is likely due to poorer instruction within their AP classes and, perhaps, differences in outside-of-school learning opportunities that provide preparation for advanced classes.

Differential learning opportunities within the schools of high-achieving students from lower income backgrounds are also implicated in their performance on college entrance exam. These students are less likely to take the SAT or ACT tests than their more advantaged peers, thereby limiting their access to more selective institutions of higher education. Additionally, students from lower income backgrounds who begin high school as high achievers earn SAT scores that are 100 points lower on average than those of students from higher SES backgrounds (Bromberg & Theokas, 2014).

Paths in Higher Education

Research shows that high-achieving students from low-income backgrounds who attend more selective institutions of higher education have better outcomes, including higher graduation rates, higher rates of continuing on to graduate school, and higher first salaries (Giancola & Kahlenberg, 2016). However, based on data from three national longitudinal studies, high-achieving students from low-income backgrounds are more likely to attend less selective colleges than their peers from high-income backgrounds (21% versus 14%), a phenomenon referred to as "under-matching" (Wyner et al., 2007). Giancola and Kahlenberg (2016), using data from the U.S. Department of Education's

Education Longitudinal Study of 2002, found that high-achieving students (top quartile) from high-income families were 3 times more likely to enroll in a selective institution of higher education than similarly high-achieving students from lower income families (24% vs. 8%). Additionally, students from lower income backgrounds were less likely to graduate from college (49% vs. 77%) and less likely to earn a graduate degree (29% vs. 47%; Wyner et al., 2007).

Factors that contribute to undermatching include the perception by students and families that they cannot afford selective institutions (even though out-of-pocket expenses can decrease with the selectivity of the higher education institution due to more generous financial aid), as well as poor or inadequate counseling and advising regarding college options and costs (Giancola & Kahlenberg, 2016). Additionally, many children from low-income families lack exposure to higher SES adults in professional occupations, affecting their expectations for higher education and tacit knowledge about educational paths (Carnevale et al., 2019).

Opportunity to Learn: A Central Construct

> In the interaction between nature and nurture, the education system plays a critical role and can act as a lever: with adequate resources, schools can influence students' development of skills and abilities and, ultimately, their socioeconomic mobility through advanced educational attainment. Thus, education policy can make the difference between whether children fulfill their potential or fall by the wayside. (Carnevale et al., 2019, p. 3)

Clearly, the opportunities for achievement and talent development along the K–12 paths for low- versus high-income families are not equal. Many of the factors documented in research boil down to differences in students' opportunities to learn—including preschool, community programs, advanced classes, gifted programs, and quality of instruction within classes. Schmidt et al. (2015) conducted a cross-national study using PISA (Programme for International Assessment) data to assess the relationship between opportunity to learn in math, SES, and mathematics achievement. Relying on student reports to measure their familiarity with algebra and geometry concepts and exposure to formal mathematics instruction in school, the authors used a variety of data analytical strategies to assess the contributions of various factors. Their results showed that opportunity to learn had a strong and direct relationship to SES and accounted for one third of the relationship between SES and mathematical achievement. Importantly and somewhat surprisingly, these researchers also found that within the U.S. there were greater differences in opportunity to learn within schools than between schools. Essentially half of the within-school relationship between SES and mathematics literacy was accounted for by differences in opportunities to learn that occurred within school, implicating differences in the content and level of the curriculum, the quality of instruction, and access of students to advanced courses and high-quality instruction. Adelson et al. (2016) found similar results for the subject of reading based on statewide data for Kentucky, also implicating differences within school in opportunities to learn for students.

The Psychology of Poverty

Laurin et al. (2019) attempted to parse the psychology of low-socioeconomic status. They noted that a child born into a family from the highest income level is twice as likely to live at that level as an adult compared to a child born into a family at the lowest income level, and this finding is true across countries, including the U.S. (Jäntti et al., 2006). Using expectancy value theory, they cited the importance of three beliefs to upward social mobility: believing that one has the skills and supports needed for success, believing that one will be rewarded for exceptional performance, and valuing the reward. Many factors affect these beliefs, including perceptions of stereotype threat, cultural values and orientation, self- and group-serving cognitions, identity-affiliation concerns, and direct experiences. As a result, individuals' motivation to strive to achieve in order to improve their social status can be seriously impacted. Thus, although motivation is an individual factor that is critical to achievement and talent development, it is seriously impacted by structural and psychological factors (Laurin et al., 2019). The psychological aspects of poverty as they impact gifted children will be elaborated in subsequent chapters in this book.

How Can the Effects of Poverty Be Curbed to Focus on Developing Talents?

Clearly, if talent is to be developed, then students must have opportunities to practice and showcase their talents. The timing of when a student enters a field matters and impacts their future trajectory. Motivation, emotional strength, and access to opportunities and mentors also matter (Subotnik et al., 2017). Many times, students from low-income households are unable to take advantage of or be exposed to ways to showcase or develop their talents. Schools must provide ways to identify, cultivate, and promote strengths in all students, especially those from low-income households. When gifted services are cut due to lack of funding or accusations of elitism, many times it is the students from low-income households who suffer the most, as they are more dependent on schools for services than students from more advantaged families who can access outside-of-school programming. In order to mitigate some of the problems previously discussed, alternative ways of identifying and serving gifted students from low-income households are required. We provide a cursory overview here to set the stage for some of the best practices recommended in the literature. The subsequent chapters in this book will provide in-depth discussion about each of these recommendations.

1. **Educators must identify talent in alternative and more inclusive ways in order to cultivate it.** Multiple measures for identification (instead of one test score, composite score, or measure), local norms, universal screeners, domain-specific assessments and performance-based tasks, and challenging curriculum have all been shown to be effective ways to increase the number of students from low-income households who are identified and served (Olszewski-Kubilius & Corwith, 2018), along with less reliance on teacher referrals, which have been found to be an unnecessary gatekeeper. Discussions of identification systems, policies, and specific methods are found in Chapters 3 and 4, including specific information about the pros and cons of various methods as well as assessment approaches, policies, procedures, and systems for best identifying students from low-income households.

2. **The recognition of context, culture, and individual differences matters in allowing students to play to their strengths.** Taking into account students' culture, context, values, priorities, and backgrounds is important for identifying and serving gifted students. Understanding who students are as individuals, as well as the groups with whom they identify, supports culturally responsive, strength-based identification and allows for stronger connections with families and greater support for students. Historically, students from low-income backgrounds have been underrepresented in gifted programs, as have students from racial and ethnic minorities (see Peters & Engerrand, 2016). Students from low-income backgrounds come from all racial groups, and students from ethnic/racial minority backgrounds may be less likely to be identified and served regardless of income or even high achievement. Race and SES combine to reduce the chances of identification and participation, particularly for African American students from low-income backgrounds. Research also indicates that underrepresentation for students from low-income households persists even within states that

specifically define identification procedures to address underrepresentation and varies widely from school to school (McBee, 2010). Chapter 2 addresses this issue through a strength-based lens and highlights factors contributing to underrepresentation as well as intersections between income and ethnicity/race. The final chapter of this book examines this construct through student voices, and includes individuals from a variety of backgrounds and levels of poverty who reflect upon their experiences.

3. **Specialized opportunity-based interventions are necessary for students to fill in learning gaps resulting from lack of opportunity and develop higher level skills.** Warne et al. (2013), in a study of diversity within gifted programs in Utah, showed that much of the disparity in the identification and participation of students from racial, ethnic, and socioeconomic minorities in gifted programs in the state was due to these students' lower academic achievement scores. Therefore, preidentification programs that involve providing some services prior to formal identification allow students to "catch up" and show their advanced abilities, interest, and motivation. Lessons learned when designing out-of-school programs in this manner are discussed in Chapter 8, while identification systems are outlined in Chapter 3. The use of curriculum as an equalizer for this type of programming is also alluded to in Chapters 5 and 7, with leadership considerations outlined in Chapter 12.

4. **Out-of-school programs matter for talent development.** How students spend their outside-of-school time also impacts their trajectory (Csikszentmihalyi et al., 1993) and future creative production (Subotnik et al., 2011). Research supports the importance of school-based extracurricular activities for children's development, particularly to prevent the summer slide that affects children from lower income backgrounds more than children with more opportunities and contributes to achievement gaps (McCombs et al., 2017). Participation in extracurricular activities allows for the development of supportive social networks of academically oriented peers, and increased social capital via mentors, coaches, and teachers (Snellman et al., 2015). They can also facilitate the development of important psychosocial skills, such as collaboration skills via team sports and leadership skills via school clubs. Research shows that participation in extracurricular activities has positive effects on youths, such as higher test scores and lower dropout rates, as well as higher occupational and educational attainment, political and civic engagement, and overall better mental

and physical health. (Snellman et al., 2015). The role of participation in outside-of-school and extracurricular activities may be underappreciated in terms of its effect on youth development, particularly in the development of talent. Extracurricular programs found effective in developing talent are discussed in Chapter 8.

5. **Family relationships and community assets matter.** Students from low-income households may be more likely to have families that are wary of school systems or afraid that the students may outsmart or outgrow them. Parents may also fear that education or special programming will take their children away from the family and their communities, especially if the children are first generation college students or have responsibilities for taking care of younger siblings or other household duties. Family bonds are present for all families, but may be especially tight for students from low-income households, as everyone must work together in order to "make ends meet." Schools that become community centers, view the family as an asset and as a partner in education, and take the time to understand the context and culture of the students they serve tend to have higher attendance, more family involvement, and higher achievement gains. What occurs for students outside of formal schooling is also important. This can include informal learning at home through family outings, access to books and music, supplies to make art, and other educational materials; opportunities to explore and learn about one's natural environment through play and access to parks; and opportunities to gain important skills through participation in informal recreational activities. Thoughtful educators can identify and tap into family strengths to build support for high achievement and persistence. Chapter 11 explains ways that schools can engage families and community assets as well as national foundations to garner strengths and utilize community resources to support talent development.

6. **The explicit teaching of inner strength and habits of achievement matters.** Many researchers have promoted the idea that giftedness requires more than high intellectual or cognitive abilities, including "noncognitive" characteristics such as motivation and creativity (Gágne, 2005; Renzulli, 2005), psychosocial skills (Subotnik et al., 2011), and even the ability to capitalize on chance (Tannenbaum, 2003). The deliberate teaching of psychosocial skills important in talent development, including perseverance, healthy risk-taking, and managing emotions and stress, contributes to a student's successful management of a long trajectory, and these skills are even more important for students from

backgrounds that may include stressful circumstances and significant obstacles. Obstacles include low expectations from teachers, potential peer isolation, and lack of knowledge about paths toward higher education and careers. Thus, counselors must be attuned to the special needs of gifted students from low-income backgrounds. These issues are addressed in depth in Chapters 9 and 10.

7. **Systems and policies matter.** Systemic approaches that are vertically and horizontally aligned and comprehensive allow the most opportunity for making lasting change. It is unfortunate when a student from a low-income household can access services in one grade but not another due to a lack of articulation across grade levels. Moreover, if systems are disjointed such that identification and services do not match, or students are identified but not provided appropriate levels of challenge or scaffolding to fill in gaps, or students are not given opportunities to show their talents, they are less likely to thrive. Different programs are needed for students who already demonstrate high levels of accomplishment and achievement, and for students who possess potential but do not necessarily achieve at high levels given lack of opportunity. Using or creating identification practices to find more children with advanced learning potential goes hand-in-hand with designing programs to turn that potential into actual achievement. There are several effective program models that have increased the achievement of high-potential students from low-income households so as to enable them to qualify for subsequent advanced courses and gifted programs. Chapter 12 provides specific information about how schools can connect identification, curriculum, services delivery models, professional development, and data management systems into a cohesive and evidence-supported continuum of services that allows seamless support for students from low-income households as they transition from early childhood through high school and into college.

8. **Curriculum and instruction matter.** There are many Javits grants and other special projects focused on curriculum and instruction as a way to identify students from low-income and historically underrepresented backgrounds. There are noted curricula found effective with students from low-income households and other underrepresented students in gifted education. These curricula have several features in common, such as scaffolded approaches, explicit modeling and teaching of habits of the discipline, conceptual thinking, and real-world applications or relevant, hands-on approaches to learning (Stambaugh & Chandler, 2012). Effective curricula capitalize on student strengths,

such as problem solving and creative thinking, while also supporting gaps in learning by modeling habits of professionals. Additional information about special projects, models, instructional strategies, and curricula examples are discussed in Chapters 5, 6, and 7.

9. **Professional development matters.** Educators' beliefs about the very nature of giftedness and talent affect the referral process at the most fundamental level. Many identification systems include teacher referrals or teacher nominations in order for students to be eligible for further assessment for gifted services. Often these beliefs include that giftedness is a fixed characteristic demonstrated by effortless learning and above-grade-level achievement. A key issue for the identification of gifted children from poverty is whether educators believe that gifted potential can exist in the absence of high accomplishment and if that potential can be observed and discerned in some fashion. National data show that educators are largely untrained in gifted education and, in particular, the characteristics of culturally and economically diverse gifted students (National Association for Gifted Children & Council of State Directors of Programs for the Gifted, 2015). The use of challenging curriculum to spot talent that may not be revealed on tests (Robinson et al., 2018) increases identification, promotes the development of gifted pedagogy for a broader range of students, and capitalizes upon gifted students' strengths. Curriculum and instructional techniques and Javits projects focused on curriculum interventions with students from low-income and diverse backgrounds cite professional development as a fundamental prerequisite for successful implementation. Teachers need to match instruction to students' needs and context while using effective pedagogical strategies and resources to identify and promote student strengths and talents. Many chapters in this book discuss the importance of a cohesive professional development plan that includes modeling of expected tasks, domain-specific models, reflection, accountability with support, and contextual understanding and tailoring of instruction to one's particular context. Professional development considerations are assumed for all approaches addressed in each chapter as a central tenet for promoting awareness, expertise, and ultimately success in supporting this unique population of students and their families.

Fundamentally, if gifted education is to increase the talent development of more students, particularly students from poverty, it must embrace a broadened vision of gifted education—a vision that places greater emphasis on talent development and cultivation of ability along with identification and recognition of high achievement. This means nurturing skills, considering those skills within the context of a child's opportunities, and moving the child forward in ways that support ongoing learning and access. By acknowledging these individual differences, educators can support students to reach their full potential and curb some of the detrimental effects of poverty that diminish talented students' trajectories.

References

Aaronson, D., Barrow, L., & Sander, W. (2007). Teachers and student achievement in the Chicago Public High Schools. *Journal of Labor Economics, 25*(1), 95–135. https://doi.org/10.1086/508733

Adelson, J. L., Dickinson, E. R., & Cunningham, B. C. (2016). A multigrade, multiyear statewide examination of reading achievement: Examining variability between districts, schools, and students. *Educational Researcher, 45*(4), 258–262. https://doi.org/10.3102/0013189X16649960

Allensworth, E. M., Gwynee, J. A., Moore, P., & de la Torre, M. (2014). *Looking forward to high school and college: Middle grade indicators of readiness in Chicago public schools*. The University of Chicago Consortium on Chicago School Research.

Anderson, D. (2009). *The United States in 2020 a very different place*. The Nielsen Company. https://www.nielsen.com/us/en/insights/article/2009/the-united-states-in-2020-a-very-different-place

Barton, P. E., & Coley, R. J. (2009). *Parsing the achievement gap II: Policy information report*. Educational Testing Service.

Burney, V. H., & Beilke, J. R. (2008). The constraints of poverty on high achievement. *Journal for the Education of the Gifted, 31*(3), 171–197. https://doi.org/10.4219/jeg-2008-771

Burney, V. H., & Cross, T. L. (2006). Impoverished students with academic promise in rural settings: 10 lessons from Project Aspire. *Gifted Child Today, 29*(2), 14–21. https://doi.org/10.4219/gct-2006-200

Bromberg, M., & Theokas, C. (2014). *Falling out of the lead. Following high achievers through high school and beyond*. The Education Trust.

Callahan, C. M., Moon, T. R., & Oh, S. (2014). *National surveys of gifted programs: Executive summary: 2014*. University of Virginia, National Research Center on the Gifted and Talented. https://www.nagc.org/sites/default/files/key%20reports/2014%20Survey%20of%20GT%20programs%20Exec%20Summ.pdf

Carnevale, A. P., Fasules, K. L., Quinn, M. C., & Campell, K. P. (2019). *Born to win, schooled to lose: Why equally talented students don't get equal chances to be all they can be*. Center on Education and the Workforce, Georgetown University.

Carnoy, M., & Garcia, E. (2017). *Five key trends in U.S. student performance*. Economic Policy Institute. https://www.epi.org/publication/five-key-trends-in-u-s-student-performance-progress-by-blacks-and-hispanics-the-takeoff-of-asians-the-stall-

of-non-english-speakers-the-persistence-of-socioeconomic-gaps-and-the-dam
aging-effect

College Board. (2014). *The 10th annual AP report to the nation*. https://research.college
board.org/programs/ap/data/nation/2014

Csikszentmihalyi, M., Rathunde, K., & Whalen, S. (1993). *Talented teenagers: The roots
of success and failure*. Cambridge University Press.

Curran, F. C., & Kellogg, A. T. (2016). Understanding science achievement gaps by
race/ethnicity and gender in kindergarten and first grade. *Educational Researcher,
45*(5), 273–282. https://doi.org/10.3102/0013189X16656611

Duncan, G. J., & Murnane, R. J. (Eds.). (2011). *Executive summary: Whither opportunity? Rising inequality, schools, and children's life chances*. Russell Sage Foundation.
https://www.russellsage.org/sites/all/files/Whither%20Opportunity_Executi
ve%20Summary.pdf

Ellis, B. J., Bianchi, J., Griskevicius, V., & Frankenhuis, W. E. (2017). Beyond risk
and protective factors: An adaption-based approach to resilience. *Perspectives on
Psychological Science, 12*(4), 561–587. https://doi.org/10.1177/1745691617693054

Engle, P. L., & Black, M. M. (2008). The effects of poverty on child development and
educational outcomes. *Annals of the New York Academy of Science, 1136*(1), 243–
256. https://doi.org/10.1196/annals.1425.023

Feinstein, L. (2003). Inequality in the cognitive development of British children in
the 1970 cohort. *Economica, 70*(277), 73–97. https://doi.org/10.1111/1468-0335.
t01-1-00272

Fernald, A., Marchman, V. A., & Weisleder, A. (2013). SES differences in language
processing skill and vocabulary are evident at 18 months. *Developmental Science,
16*(2), 234–48. https://doi.org/10.1111/desc.12019

Ford, D. Y. (2011). *Multicultural gifted education* (2nd ed.). Prufrock Press.

Gágne, F. (2005). From gifts to talents: The DMGT as a developmental model. In R. J.
Sternberg & J. E. Davidson (Eds.), *Conceptions of giftedness* (2nd. ed., pp. 98–119).
Cambridge University Press. https://doi.org/10.1017/CBO9780511610455.008

Giancola, J., & Kahlenberg, R. D. (2016). *True merit: Ensuring our brightest students
have access to our best colleges and universities*. The Jack Kent Cooke Foundation.
https://www.jkcf.org/research/true-merit-ensuring-our-brightest-students-ha
ve-access-to-our-best-colleges-and-universities

Hair, N. L., Hanson, J. L., Wolfe, B. L., & Pollak, S. D. (2015). Association of child poverty, brain development, and academic achievement. *JAMA Pediatrics, 169*(9), 822–
829. https://doi.org/10.1001/jamapediatrics.2015.1475

Hanson, J. L., Hair, N., Shen, D. G., Shi, F., Gilmore, J. H., Wolfe, B. L., & Pollak, S. D. (2015).
Correction: Family poverty affects the rate of human infant brain Growth. *PLoS ONE
10*(12), Article e0146434. https://doi.org/10.1371/journal.pone.0146434

Hart, B., & Risley, T. R. (2003). The early catastrophe: The 30 million word gap by age 3.
American Educator, 27(1), 4–9.

Hayasaki, E. (2016). *How poverty affects the brain*. Newsweek. https://www.newsweek.
com/2016/09/02/how-poverty-affects-brains-493239.html

Jäntti, M., Roed, K., Naylor, R., Bjorklund, A., Bratsberg, B., Raaum, O., Osterbacka, E.,
& Eriksson, T. (2006). *American exceptionalism in a new light: A comparison of intergen-*

erational earnings mobility in the Nordic countries, the United Kingdom and the United States (No. 1938). Institute for the Study of Labor.

Jiang, Y., Ekono, M., & Skinner, C. (2016). *Basic facts about low-income children: Children under 18 years, 2014.* National Center for Children in Poverty. http://www.nccp.org/publications/pub_1145.html

Kitano, M. (2006). Poverty, diversity, and promise. In J. VanTassel-Baska & T. Stambaugh (Eds.), *Overlooked gems: A national perspective on low-income promising learners* (pp. 31–35). National Association for Gifted Children.

Kneebone, E. (2017). *The changing geography of US poverty.* The Brookings Institution. https://www.brookings.edu/testimonies/the-changing-geography-of-us-poverty

Kornrich, F., & Furstenberg, F. (2013). Investing in children. Changes in parental spending on children 1972–2007. *Demography, 50,* 1–23. https://doi.org/10.1007/s13524-012-0146-4

Lacour, M., & Tissington, L. D. (2011). The effects of poverty on academic achievement. *Educational Research and Reviews, 6*(7), 522–527.

Laurin, K., Engstron, H. B., & Alic, A. (2019). Motivational accounts of the vicious cycle of social status: An integrative framework using the United States as a case study. *Perspectives on Psychological Science, 14*(2), 107–137. https://doi.org/10.1177/1745691618788875

Levy, D. J., Heiseel, J. A., Richeson, J. A., & Adam, E. K. (2016). Psychological and biological responses to race-based social stress as pathways to disparities in educational outcomes. *American Psychologist, 71*(6), 455–473. https://doi.org/10.1037/a0040322

Loveless, T. (2009). *Tracking and detracking: High achievers in Massachusetts middle schools.* Thomas B. Fordham Institute. https://fordhaminstitute.org/national/research/tracking-and-detracking-high-achievers-massachusetts-middle-schools

Masten, A. S. (2001). Ordinary magic: Resilience processes in development. *American Psychologist, 56*(3), 227–238. https://doi.org/10.1037/0003-066x.56.3.227

McBee, M. (2010). Examining the probability of identification for gifted programs for students in Georgia elementary schools: A multilevel path analysis. *Gifted Child Quarterly, 54*(4), 283–297. https://doi.org/10.1177/0016986210377927

McCombs, J. S., Augustine, C. H., Schwartz, H. L., Bodilly, S. J., Mcinnis, B., Lichter, D. S., & Cross, A. B. (2017). *Making Summer count: How summer programs can boost children's learning.* Rand Education.

Michelmore, K., & Dynarski, S. (2017). The gap within the gap: Using longitudinal data to understand income differences in educational outcomes. *AERA Open, 3*(1). https://doi.org/10.1177/2332858417692958

Miller, L. S. (2004). *Promoting sustained growth in the representation of African Americans, Latinos, and Native Americans among top students in the United States at all levels of the education system* (RM04190). University of Connecticut, The National Research Center on the Gifted and Talented.

Moore, K. A., Redd, A., Burkhauser, M., Mbwana, K., & Collins, A. (2009). *Children in poverty: Trends, consequences and policy options.* Child Trends.

Morgan, P. L., Farkas, G., Hillemeier, M. M., & Maczua, S. (2016). Science achievement gaps begin very early, persist, and are largely explained by modifiable factors. *Educational Researcher, 45*(1), 18–35. https://doi.org/10.3102/0013189X16633182

National Association for Gifted Children & Council of State Directors of Programs for the Gifted. (2015). *2014–2015 state of the states in gifted education: Policy and practice data.* https://www.nagc.org/sites/default/files/key%20reports/2014-2015%20State%20of%20the%20States%20%28final%29.pdf

Noble, K. G., Houston, S. M., Brito, N. H., Bartsch, H., Kan, E., Kuperman, J. M., Akshoomoff, N., Amaral, D. G., Bloss, C. S., Libiger, O., Schork, N. J., Murray, S. S., Casey, B. J., Change, L., Ernst, T. M., Frazier, J. A., Gruen, J. R., Kennedy, D. N., Van Zijl, P. V., . . . Sowell, E. R. (2015). Family income, parental education and brain structure in children and adolescents. *Nature Neuroscience, 18,* 773–778. https://doi.org/10.1038/nn.3983

National Center for Education Statistics. (n.d.). *NAEP data explorer.* https://www.nationsreportcard.gov/ndecore/xplore/NDE

Olszewski-Kubilius, P., & Corwith, S. (2018). Poverty, academic achievement, and giftedness: A literature review. *Gifted Child Quarterly, 62*(1), 37–55. https://doi.org/10.1177/0016986217738015

Peters, S. J., & Engerrand, K. G. (2016). Equity and excellence: Proactive efforts in the identification of underrepresented students for gifted and talented services. *Gifted Child Quarterly, 60*(3), 159–171. https://doi.org/10.1177/0016986216643165

Pew Research Center. (2015). *Parenting in America: Outlook, worries, aspirations are strongly linked to financial situation.* https://www.pewsocialtrends.org/2015/12/17/parenting-in-america

Plucker, J. A., Burroughs, N., & Song, R. (2010). *Mind the (other) gap! The growing excellence gap in K–12 education.* Center for Evaluation and Education Policy, Indiana University.

Plucker, J. A., Hardesty, J., & Burroughs, N. (2013). *Talent on the sidelines: Excellence gaps and America's persistent talent underclass.* Center for Education Policy Analyses, University of Connecticut.

Reardon, S. F. (2011). The widening academic achievement gap between the rich and the poor: New evidence and possible explanations. In G. J. Duncan & R. J. Murnane (Eds.), *Whither opportunity? Rising inequality, school and children's life chances* (pp. 91–116). Russell Sage Foundation.

Renzulli, J. S. (2005). The three-ring conception of giftedness: A developmental model for promoting creative productivity. In R. J. Sternberg & J. E. Davidson (Eds.), *Conceptions of giftedness* (2nd ed., pp. 246–279). Cambridge University Press. https://doi.org/10.1017/CBO9780511610455.015

Rivkin, S. G., Hanushek, E. A., & Kain, J. F. (2005). Teachers, schools, and academic achievement. *Econmetrica, 73*(2), 417–458. https://doi.org/10.1111/j.1468-0262.2005.00584.x

Robinson, A., Adelson, J. L., Kidd, K. A., & Cunningham, C. M. (2018). A talent for tinkering: Developing talents in children from low-income households through engineering curriculum. *Gifted Child Quarterly, 62*(1), 130–144. https://doi.org/10.1177/0016986217738049

Rosenkranz, T., de la Torre, M., Stevens, W. D., Allensworth, E. M (2014). *Free to fail or on-track to college. Why grades drop when students enter high school and what adults can do about it.* The University of Chicago Consortium on Chicago School Research.

Sampson, W. A. (2002). *Black student achievement: How much do family and school really matter?* Scarecrow Press.

Schmidt, W. H., Burroughs, N. A., Zoido, P., & Houang, R. T. (2015). The role of schooling in perpetuating educational inequality: An international perspective. *Educational Researcher, 44*(7), 371–386. https://doi.org/10.3102/0013189X15603982

Snellman, K., Silva, J., Frederick, C. B., & Putnam, R. D. (2015). The engagement gap: Social mobility and extracurricular participation among American youth. *The Annals of the American Academy of Political and Social Science, 657*(1), 194–207. https://doi.org/10.1177/0002716214548398

Stambaugh, T., & Chandler, K. L. (2012). *Effective curriculum for underserved gifted students.* Prufrock Press.

Subotnik, R. F., Olszewski-Kubilius, P., & Worrell, F. C. (2011). Rethinking giftedness and gifted education: A proposed direction forward based on psychological science. *Psychological Science in the Public Interest, 12*(1), 3–54. https://doi.org/10.1177/1529100611418056

Subotnik, R. F., Olszewski-Kubilius, P., & Worrell. F. C. (2017). Talent development as the most promising focus of giftedness and gifted education. In S. I. Pfeiffer, E. Shaunessy-Dedrick, & M. Foley-Nicpon (Eds.), *APA handbook on giftedness and talent* (pp. 231–245). American Psychological Association.

Tannenbaum, A. J. (2003). Nature and nurture of giftedness. In N. Colangelo & G. A. Davis (Eds.), *Handbook of gifted education* (3rd ed., pp. 45–59). Allyn & Bacon.

U.S. Department of Education. (2000). *America's kindergartners* (NCES 2000-070). National Center for Education Statistics.

Warne, R. T., Anderson, B., & Johnson, A. O. (2013). The impact of race and ethnicity on the identification process for giftedness in Utah. *Journal for the Education of the Gifted, 36*(4), 487–508. https://doi.org/10.1177/0162353213506065

Wyner, J. S., Bridgeland, J. M., & DiIulio, J. J., Jr. (2007). *Achievementrap: How America is failing millions of high-achieving students from lower-income families.* Jack Kent Cook Foundation & Civic Enterprises.

Xiang, Y., Dahlin, M., Cronin, J., Theaker, R., & Durant, S. (2011). *Do high flyers maintain their altitude? Performance trends of top students.* Thomas B. Fordham Institute. https://fordhaminstitute.org/national/research/do-high-flyers-maintain-their-altitude-performance-trends-top-students

Intersections of Culture, Context, and Race With Poverty: *Implications for Services for Gifted Learners From Low-Income Backgrounds*

Dante D. Dixson

As outlined throughout this book, poverty has been shown to have an insidious effect on students living up to their full academic potential. However, in order to fully understand how poverty affects academic talent development, one must also consider the context that surrounds poverty during talent development. Both poverty *and* its context likely result in deleterious effects on academic potential, not just poverty alone (see Olszewski-Kubilius & Corwith, 2018, for a review). Several of the more prominent contextual factors that have been shown to interact with poverty are race, English proficiency, and geography (Kettler et al., 2015; Schmidt et al., 2015).

For example, the National Center for Education Statistics (2017b) reported that almost a third of African American (33.7%) and Hispanic (28%) school-age children lived in poverty in the United States, compared to about a 10th of

European American (11.4%) and Asian American (10.9%) school-age children. Further evidence regarding the complicated relationship between poverty and race, English proficiency, and geography include the statistics that English language learners (ELLs) and urban families have poverty rates 20% to 60% higher than their native English speaking (12.3% vs. 15.1%) and rural/suburban counterparts (10% vs. 16%; Fontenot et al., 2018). These statistics make it clear that there is considerable overlap among families that have a low income, are from ethnic/racial minority backgrounds, live in urban areas, and have children who are ELLs. Thus, when trying to mitigate the effects of poverty on students living up to their full academic potential, examining all of these interrelated factors is imperative, as the relationship between poverty and talent development might change depending on these other factors, possibly necessitating a different remedy.

In this chapter, I review how poverty interacts with race, English language proficiency, and geography within the context of gifted and talented education (GATE) and the subsequent implications for talent development. I begin each section with a discussion of the importance of a contextual factor (i.e., race, English language proficiency, or geography) within the context of GATE and then review how the factor interacts with poverty in hindering students of that group from being identified as academically gifted or from receiving GATE services. I conclude the chapter with discussions of how these factors as a whole relate to poverty within the context of GATE, as well as the importance of taking these factors into account as a field when identifying these students for GATE programs or providing GATE services to them.

Race

Race within the context of GATE has been well studied (see Worrell & Dixson, 2018, for a review). Most studies indicate that a potentially gifted student's race has implications for the likelihood that the student will be identified as academically gifted and subsequently receive appropriate support to develop their academic potential (Carman & Taylor, 2010; Elhoweris et al., 2005; McBee, 2010). For instance, in a nationally representative sample of more than 21,000 students, Grissom and Redding (2016) found that even after controlling for standardized test scores, gender, socioeconomic status, teacher characteristics, and classroom characteristics, African American and Hispanic students were identified as academically gifted at rates of 44% and 84% the rate of European American students, respectively. In addition, Grissom and Redding found that Asian American students were identified at 111% the rate of European American students. Thus, race is an important factor within GATE.

African American and Hispanic Students

As can be inferred from Grissom and Redding (2016), the two ethnic groups that are most adversely affected by current GATE identification and programing methods are African American and Hispanic students. If one assumes that racial groups should be represented in GATE programs in proportion to their representation in public schools, African American students are underrepresented by about 48% (19% public school representation and 10% GATE representation), and Hispanic students are 36% underrepresented (25% public school representation and 16% GATE representation; Ford, 2014; Office for Civil Rights, 2012; Worrell & Dixson, 2018).

Although the reasons for underrepresentation are highly debated, some of the most well-known that have empirical support are: (a) racism—African American and Hispanic students are discriminated against solely because of their race (Elhoweris et al., 2005; Grissom & Redding, 2016); (b) lack of opportunity—African American and Hispanic students have significantly fewer opportunities to demonstrate their academic potential/talent in front of GATE gatekeepers (Card & Giuliano, 2015; McBee, 2006); and (c) achievement gaps—African American and Hispanic students score significantly lower on the exact measures (e.g., standardized test, school grades) used to determine eligibility into GATE programs (Reeves & Halikias, 2017; Worrell, 2007; Worrell & Dixson, 2018). One study that is commonly cited to exemplify the hardship of being African American or Hispanic within GATE is Elhoweris et al. (2005). In this study, Elhoweris and colleagues had teachers read a vignette of a student with characteristics typical of the academically gifted (e.g., advanced thinker, creative, etc.). All of the vignettes were identical except for the presented race of the student; one group of teachers was told the student was African American, one group was told the student was European American, and the last group was not given any information about the student's race. Elhoweris and colleagues found that teachers were meaningfully less likely to refer students for GATE testing or support their placement in a GATE program when students were described as African American, compared to European American students (Hedges's g = .39 for referral and .30 for placement recommendation) or when ethnicities were not given at all (g = .44 for referral and .30 for placement recommendation).

Poverty Versus Race

A common discussion among scholars and school administrators has been whether race or poverty is the primary driver of various groups being underrepresented in GATE programs. Several studies shed light on this debate, with the general conclusion being that the literature is mixed. Although some studies indicate that poverty and socioeconomic status play a larger role than race in some groups being underrepresented in GATE (e.g., Carman & Taylor, 2010; Olszewski-Kubilius & Corwith, 2018; Peters & Engerrand, 2016), other studies indicate that race plays the larger role (e.g., Elhoweris et al., 2005; Grissom & Redding, 2016; Kettler & Hurst, 2017). For example, Nicholson-Crotty et al. (2016) found in a nationally representative of more than 20,000 students that African American students were almost 3 times (2.88) more likely to be assigned to GATE programming when they had an African American teacher compared to a European American teacher after controlling for socioeconomic status and a host of other factors (e.g., location, education, test scores, gender), implying that race plays a huge role over socioeconomic status and poverty. In contrast, Warne et al. (2013) conducted an assessment of GATE representation across race in a sample of about 14,000 academically gifted students. They found that after controlling for socioeconomic status, African American students were identified at about the same rate as European American students (92.9% the rate of European American students), while Hispanic students were identified at a slightly higher rate (1.25 times the rate of European American students).

The likely reality is that both race and poverty are large factors in students being identified as academically gifted, and the relative importance of each varies depending on the context. Several studies support this conclusion (e.g., Elhoweris et al., 2005; McBee, 2006, 2010; Peters & Engerrand, 2016; Worrell & Dixson, 2018; Worrell et al., 2019). Given this conclusion and the fact that a considerable proportion of ethnic/racial minority groups live in poverty (National Center for Education Statistics, 2017b), there are several ramifications that GATE personnel should consider with regard to underrepresented students from low-income backgrounds. These considerations include the timing of evaluations, the use of standardized testing, educator expectations and prejudices, and retention rates.

Previous research indicates that disparities across race and socioeconomic status grow as students progress through school (Kim, 2004; Olszewski-Kubilius & Steenbergen-Hu, 2017). A likely reason for this is that small differences in resources and opportunities lead to slight differences in academic ability that compound over time (Ceci & Papierno, 2005). For example, students from higher socioeconomic backgrounds are more likely to participate in academic summer programs (Redford et al., 2018). As a result, they generally enter the following school year with slightly more academic skills and less summer loss than their peers from lower socioeconomic backgrounds, putting them in position to better understand and master academic material in the school year ahead (Alexander et al., 2007; Rambo-Hernandez & McCoach, 2015; Redford et al., 2018). Over time this can lead to different learning trajectories and subsequently meaningful differences across important academic outcomes (Ceci & Papierno, 2005; Olszewski-Kubilius et al., 2017; Steenbergen-Hu et al., 2016). Thus, underrepresented students from low-income backgrounds are probably more likely to qualify for GATE programs the earlier in their schooling careers they are evaluated and served compared to later in their academic careers, which is fairly typical for gifted programming (Callahan et al., 2013; National Association for Gifted Children [NAGC] & Council of State Directors of Programs for the Gifted [CSDPG], 2015).

A second ramification of the intersection between poverty and race that GATE personnel should consider is standardized testing. A critical widespread assumption in GATE is that those who perform at certain levels on standardized tests (usually at the 90th percentile or above on cognitive and academic tests) are likely to benefit from and should receive GATE services (McClain & Pfeiffer, 2012). However, several studies not only call this assumption into question (e.g., Olszewski-Kubilius et al., 2017), but also argue that it ignores a key concept—opportunity to learn. Peters and Engerrand (2016) outlined that a major assumption of standardized tests is that examinees must have had similar academic experiences and exposure to academic material in order to be able to infer academic and intellectual ability at a given age based on performance.

Yet, several studies have found that students of underrepresented groups, including racial minorities and low-income families, generally do not have similar prior academic experiences and exposure as their racial majority and high-income counterparts. For instance, Hallinan (1996) found that eighth-grade European American students were about twice as likely to be placed in honors or advanced math (35.2% vs. 14.3%) and English (46.5% vs. 24.2%) classes compared to their African American student counterparts. Further, Gilkerson and colleagues (2017) found that children from high-socioeconomic backgrounds, compared to children from low-socioeconomic backgrounds, not only were generally exposed to 4 million more words within their homes by the age of 4 (Hedges's g = .83), but also made more vocalizations (g = .76) and engaged in more verbal exchanges with adults (g = .83). Therefore, despite the evidence that most standardized tests used within GATE are valid and reliable measures of ability (see Warne et al., 2014), using them to assess for academic talent later in the academic career of a minority student from a low-income background may not be the most appropriate, as that student may not have had all of the academic experiences that is inherently assumed with standardized testing.

A third ramification of the intersection between poverty and race that GATE personnel should consider is discrimination and low expectations. Minority students from low-income backgrounds generally encounter lower expectations and more frequent discrimination than their majority and high-socioeconomic counterparts. For example, teachers generally have lower academic expectations of minority students from low-income backgrounds compared to majority students from high-SES backgrounds (Gregory & Huang, 2013). Teachers also generally believe that European American students, Asian American students, and students from high-socioeconomic backgrounds are better suited to be in GATE programs compared to students who are African American, Hispanic, or from low-income backgrounds, subsequently recommending them at disproportionally higher rates (Elhoweris et al., 2005; Grissom & Redding, 2016; McBee, 2006). Further, African American (g = 1.44) and Hispanic students (g = 1.42) report encountering macroaggressions within school at a meaningfully higher rate than European Americans (Forrest-Bank & Jenson, 2015).

Low expectations and discrimination on the basis of being underrepresented students from low-income backgrounds make both the path into and time within GATE programs more difficult for these students. To get into GATE programs, underrepresented students from low-income backgrounds typically have to: (a) exhibit their academic potential early and often because they generally have fewer opportunities to demonstrate their academic potential than those from other backgrounds (Card & Giuliano, 2015; McBee, 2006); (b) demonstrate a high amount of academic talent (even relative to their European American and Asian American peers) to overcome academic stereotypes (e.g., stereotype threat; Steele, 2010) associated with being a minority or low income (Elhoweris et al., 2005; Gregory & Huang, 2013; Grissom & Redding, 2016); (c) score meaningfully higher on standardized tests than others from similar backgrounds (Giessman et al., 2013); (d) overcome the belonging uncertainty that accompanies low expectations in academic environments for minority, but not majority, students (Walton & Cohen, 2011); and (e) navigate the GATE identification process with few models to guide them (Office for Civil Rights, 2012).

A fourth ramification of the intersection between poverty and race that GATE personnel should consider is poor retention of underrepresented students from low-income backgrounds. The following scenario may shed light on why retaining these students is especially difficult. Imagine what it would be like to navigate the challenging GATE identification process and be admitted to a GATE program as a minority student from a low-income background. After entering the program, you, like many before you, realize that there are few others with a similar background as you (Evans, 2015; Francis & Darity, 2020), few role models that you can readily identify with to help you navigate issues like low expectations and discrimination (Gándara & Bial, 2001), few supports in place to help students like you transition to the rigors and expectations of a GATE program (Worrell & Dixson, 2018), and few others who look like you to visually confirm and reinforce to you and others (e.g., teachers, classmates, and administrators) that students like you belong in GATE program settings (Francis & Darity, 2020; Office for Civil Rights, 2012).

All of these are issues that are associated with poor retention of both students from ethnic/racial minority groups and students from low-income backgrounds. When a student is both a minority and from a low-income background, retention is likely even more difficult as the student is simultaneously combatting the issues and struggles associated with each. Thus, instead of just navigating adversities surrounding garnering resources to develop their academic talent (e.g., programs costs, class/talent material costs; Olszewski-Kubilius & Corwith, 2018), the student has to also navigate the perils of racism (Ford, 2014). This compounding of adversities on top of adversities can understandably lead many underrepresented students from low-income backgrounds to academically disengage or drop out of a GATE program altogether in favor of general education where they feel a higher sense of belonging and encounter fewer challenges with more support (Ford et al., 2008; Worrell & Dixson, 2018).

The intersection of race and poverty is multifaceted and complex, with multiple implications for serving underrepresented students with academic talent from low-income backgrounds. Within the context of GATE, these students face unique challenges that have to be addressed if they are to be well represented within and retained throughout GATE programs. Nonetheless, GATE programs that provide needed supports targeted specifically to this group can help these students live up to their full academic potential, a task that scholars have described as society's most important responsibility and greatest challenge (Subotnik et al., 2011).

English Proficiency

English language proficiency is another factor that is intertwined with poverty and has significant implications for developing the academic talent of students from low-income backgrounds. Although English language proficiency has only recently begun to receive considerable empirical attention relative to race within the context of GATE, many scholars have emphasized that English language learners (ELLs; those for whom English is not their native language) are just as underserved and overlooked as African American and Hispanic students (Harris et al., 2009). More specifically, some scholars have estimated, based on nationally representative data, that ELLs are 30% to 70% underrepresented in GATE programs (Harris et al., 2009; Plummer, 1995). Given this significant underrepresentation of ELLs, there are several ramifications of an ELL being from a low-income background that GATE personnel should consider. These considerations include the compounding of adversities, the appropriateness of standardized tests, negative expectations, and immigration challenges.

The intersection between English language proficiency and poverty within the context of GATE is similar in many ways to the intersection of race and poverty, with the primary similarity being a compounding of adversities. For instance, ELLs from low-income backgrounds have to navigate being identified as academically gifted in a system that is specifically tailored toward students with a different background (i.e., English native speakers) as well as contend with the multitude of challenges associated with trying to develop one's gifted academic potential with limited resources (Abedi, 2002; Lohman et al., 2008; Olszewski-Kubilius & Corwith, 2018). For example, only 21.6% of states include ELLs in their definition of giftedness (NAGC & CSDPG, 2015). Moreover, most teachers do not receive any training in identifying ELLs for GATE programs, and many schools miss ELLs as a result of not evaluating them at a rate consistent with their proportion of being academically gifted (Card & Giuliano, 2015; Cohen, 1998).

A second ramification of the intersection between poverty and language proficiency that GATE personnel should take into account is the inappropriateness of standardized testing. Like all other students, ELLs have to excel on standardized cognitive and/or academic tests in order to be considered academically gifted in most states (McClain & Pfeiffer, 2012). However, even if one were to put aside the multitude of studies that have criticized the issue of cultural content within these tests (e.g., Schon et al., 2008; Spinelli, 2008), the results of several other studies have called into question the appropriateness of these assessments for ELLs. One such study (Abedi, 2002), which consisted of a sample of more than 6 million students, found evidence that language may be a source of bias (i.e., construct-irrelevant variance) within standardized tests for ELLs and that the factor structure and reliability of these tests are not as sound or robust for ELLs as native English speakers. Moreover, several other studies indicate not only that ELLs consistently score at least a half standard deviation below their native English speaking counterparts on standardized tests, but also that the predictive validity of these tests (i.e., the ability of these tests to predict meaningful outcomes in the future) was meaningfully lower for ELLs (Lohman et al., 2008; Matthews & Kirsch, 2011). All of these psychometric issues cast doubt on whether these tests exhibit construct validity with ELLs and whether their use unfairly disadvantages ELLs.

A third ramification of the intersection between poverty and language proficiency that GATE personnel should take into account is negative perceptions. ELLs from low-income backgrounds encounter pervasive negative perceptions about their group that work against them being identified as academically gifted and subsequently receiving GATE services (see Pettit, 2011, for a review). For example, Walker et al. (2004) found that many school personnel hold academic-related perceptions of ELLs that likely result in them being less likely to refer these students for GATE services. In a sample of more than 400 teachers, they reported: (a) only 18% of teachers thought that ELLs exhibit high academic skills, (b) only 43% of teachers thought that ELLs came from countries with educational systems similar to or better than the U.S. educational system, and (c) only 30% of teachers were actively interested in having ELLs placed in their classrooms. These findings are mirrored by other studies, such as Hansen-Thomas and Cavagnetto (2010), who found that 70% of teachers make the assumption that ELLs should be mostly unaffected in math as "numbers are universal," despite ample evidence of the language-based skills needed to excel in math (p. 256). Further, Hansen-Thomas and Cavagnetto found that more than 80% (n = 118 teachers) of their sample believed that motivation was the sole key factor in whether ELLs were successful in school— not language background, English proficiency, or adoption of a new culture, which were rated much lower in importance. A majority, 53% of their sample, believed that socioeconomic status was not an important factor in whether ELLs were successful in the classroom. These are the type of perceptions that ELLs encounter before, during, and after the GATE identification process. Even if they were to be admitted to a GATE program, these would be very difficult perceptions to overcome in addition to the perceptions and challenges associated with being from a low-income background.

A fourth ramification of the intersection between poverty and language proficiency that GATE personnel should take into account is immigration and knowledge gap adversities that ELLs commonly encounter. ELLs from low-income backgrounds commonly have to navigate the multitude of issues centered around immigration and knowledge gaps (Harris et al., 2009). For example, in 2015, the Migration Policy Institute found that more than 85% of all school-age ELLs had at least one parent who was born in a different country and subsequently immigrated to the U.S. (Capps, 2015). Further, the Migration Policy Institute also found that 40% to 50% of ELLs ages 12–18 have only immigrant parents (Capps, 2015). These findings, along with the finding that about a third (32.2%) of families with at least one immigrant parent are low income (Sugarman & Geary, 2018), indicate that many ELLs are likely dealing with the multitude of GATE-related challenges associated with being from a low-income background outlined previously (e.g., lack of opportunity to learn, lack of assumed exposure to academic material, and lack of resources to aid in talent development outside of school) in addition to facing the GATE-related challenges of coming from an immigrant family.

Some immigrant-related GATE challenges include adapting to cultural differences within the schools (e.g., the individualist orientation of America), linguistic challenges (e.g., being able to effectively communicate with school personnel to both advocate for one's self and obtain needed assistance to develop academic potential), and a lack of knowledge surrounding the American school system, GATE in particular (including policies, regulations, and common practices; Abedi, 2002; Harris et al., 2009; Peters & Engerrand, 2016; Schon et al., 2008). Thus, even though challenges related to immigration and knowledge gaps vary widely and are multifaceted, in most cases they are significant headwinds to ELLs from low-income backgrounds being identified and receiving GATE services to develop their academic talent.

Overall, ELLs from low-income backgrounds commonly have lower systemic opportunities than students from other groups to demonstrate their academic talents (e.g., as a result of negative academic perceptions about their group or standardized tests that were developed primarily for native English speakers). In addition, ELLs from low-income backgrounds also have more overall challenges than students from many other groups that prevent them from either putting themselves in position to demonstrate their academic abilities (e.g., as a result of knowledge gaps about the GATE system) or advocating for themselves to be within GATE programs (e.g., as a result of communication and cultural differences). Thus, GATE personnel should consider these adversities for ELLs during the process of nominating students for GATE assessments, and school districts should provide school personnel with more training centered around identifying and serving ELLs, as well as engage in more proactive screening of ELLs with culturally neutral instruments for GATE services (Mun et al., 2016).

Geography

Geography is a third factor that is intertwined with poverty and has significant implications for students from low-income backgrounds receiving GATE services (Callahan et al., 2013). Although not the focus of as much research as race and English language proficiency, geography has been found to contribute to the likelihood that a student will be identified as academically gifted and subsequently receive GATE resources. For instance, the Colorado Department of Education (2018) found that the farther one got from the Denver metro area, the less likely students were to be identified as academically gifted. More specifically, they found the following gifted identification rates: Denver metro (9.2%), urban-suburban (6%; more than 30,000 residents outside metro area), outlying city (5%; 7,000 to 30,000 residents outside metro area), outlying town (3.3%; 1,000 to 7,000 outside metro area), and remote area (1.1%). In addition, a second takeaway from the same study was that students in remote and rural areas are generally underrepresented in GATE programs compared to their metro student counterparts.

Further complicating the relationship between geography, poverty, and talent development is the confounding factor of family resources—the farther one gets from major cities and metropolitan areas, the less resources are generally available to aid the talent development of school-age children in the home. For example, rural families generally have less financial resources to aid their child in developing their academic potential (average income: urban = $49,515; suburban = $46,081; and rural = $35,171) and are less optimistic that they will have adequate financial resources in the future as compared to suburban and urban families (urban = 46%, suburban = 49%, and rural = 36%; Parker et al., 2018). Thus, given the influence of geography on students' GATE status and academic talent development, there are ramifications of being a rural student from a low-income background that GATE personnel should consider. The two primary considerations are access to advanced educational resources and systemic financial resources.

The primary ramification of the intersection between poverty and geography that GATE personnel should take into account is access to advanced educational resources. This is an especially important GATE-related ramification for rural students from low-income backgrounds because students are unlikely to have their academic talents developed if they do not have access to resources, experiences, and models to aid/guide their academic development (Dixson et al., 2020). The farther students are from major cities and metropolitan areas, the less access they have to the knowledge, experiences, and people that can aid their talent development. For example, in a national study of elementary school gifted offerings, Callahan et al. (2013) found that rural school districts were significantly less likely to offer full-time GATE programing for their academically gifted students (13%) compared to urban (20.2%) and suburban (21.2%) school districts.

In a different study, Kettler et al. (2016) examined the academic offerings of more than 1,000 schools. They found that students schooled in rural contexts had less access to advanced academic programing than students being schooled in all other contexts ($p < .001$; $d = .30$), despite not exhibiting significantly lower performance on advanced academic outcomes ($p = .069$; $d = .11$). Similarly, Mann et al. (2017) found that rural students had less access to Advanced Placement (AP) courses overall (urban = 95%, suburban = 92%, and rural = 73%) and within STEM subjects (urban = 88%, suburban = 93%, and rural = 62%) compared to their urban and suburban counterparts. These studies indicate that rural students generally have less opportunity to develop their academic potential throughout their academic careers within the school context. If a rural student was also from a low-income background, they would also have little opportunity to pursue developing their academic potential outside of school, likely leading to them not living up to their academic potential (Olszewski-Kubilius & Corwith, 2018; Steenbergen-Hu et al., 2016).

A closely related second ramification of the intersection between poverty and geography that GATE personnel should take into account is systemic financial resources. Systemic financial resources also play a large role for rural students from low-income backgrounds, primarily through district monetary resources and personnel. For example, Kettler et al. (2015) examined the financial expenditure of 1,029 school districts in Texas. They found that rural districts, compared to both suburban and city districts, (a) spent about half as much money per student within GATE (rural = $32.33, suburban = $60.00, city = $69.50), (b) allocated about 60% less of their budget to GATE (rural = 0.41%, suburban = 1.00%, city = 0.96%), and (c) assigned about a sixth the percentage of faculty to GATE (rural = 0.28%, suburban = 1.81%, city = 1.63%). Moreover, these results were found despite all three variables only being moderately related to the total number of students (rs ranged from = .25 to .53), a potential confounding factor.

Relatedly, Jimerson (2003) found that for the year 2000, rural school teachers were paid less than teachers in other locales across the salary range, including beginning salaries ($24,170 vs. $26,895), average salaries ($29,828 vs. $33,838), and highest paid salary ($39,487 vs. $46,271). More recently, the National Center for Education Statistics (2017a) indicated that the same trend continues, as rural teachers ($47,790) still make meaningfully less than both suburban teachers ($59,790) and city teachers ($56,140). Teacher salaries are a powerful incentive to work for a school district (Jimerson, 2003). Given that rural school districts tend to pay less, many highly trained and experienced teachers tend to leave these districts in order to obtain higher pay, leaving rural school districts with higher percentages of inexperienced and less educated teachers who are not as competitive for the higher paying jobs (Monk, 2007). Altogether, these studies indicate that rural students are more likely than their city and suburban counterparts to be within an educational system that either has significantly fewer resources or exhibits less emphasis on developing advanced academic talent. Either way, for rural students from low-income backgrounds to develop their academic talent, they likely have to overcome the lack of systematic resources around them as well as the multitude of adversities related to being from a low-income background.

Overall, a lack of access to both advanced educational resources and systemic financial resources likely results in rural students being less likely to attend a school with the resources to properly identify them and develop their academic talent. Moreover, if a rural student was also from a low-income background, they not only would be faced with the low-income challenges outlined previously, but also would not have the resources to privately develop their academic talent, making it unlikely they will live up to their academic potential (Olszewski-Kubilius & Corwith, 2018). These adversities should be considered when GATE personnel are considering various students for nomination, as well as throughout the evaluation process, as rural students from low-income backgrounds in particular might not exhibit the same level of academic talent as their suburban and city counterparts. This is not because they do not possess it, but rather, they have not had the access to the people, places, and experiences that is inherently assumed throughout the GATE identification and programming process. Similar to the solutions outlined in the section on race, potential solutions to the issues facing rural students from low-income backgrounds include universal screening (i.e., assessing them all for GATE services) and front-loading rural students (i.e., providing them with advanced enrichment programing for a period of time before they are to be evaluated for GATE services) early in their educational careers so that they can be identified, and their talent developed, before their adversities start to compound.

How Race, English Proficiency, and Geography Affect Opportunities for Gifted Learners

As highlighted through this chapter, the context of poverty matters. The GATE experience of a European American native English speaker from a low-income family in the suburbs is likely much more positive than the GATE experience of an African American ELL from a low-income rural family. The biggest difference between the two is the amount of adversity that likely has to be overcome in order to get their academic talent discovered and nurtured. Put a different way, the more risk factors that students have within the context of GATE (i.e., race, English language proficiency, and urbanicity), the more their adversities compound, making the path to be identified as academically gifted and receive necessary services harder and more unlikely.

Important to note is that these students are not at fault for any of these risk factors. They did not choose to be African American or an ELL, or to live in a rural area. Instead, these risk factors and the challenges they create for students individually and collectively are products of circumstance, which, when interacting with poverty, can have even more pernicious effects than is recognized or completely understood (Olszewski-Kubilius & Corwith, 2018). Thus, in order to move toward equity, the field of GATE must make a concerted effort to address these major barriers to students from underrepresented groups being identified and getting their academic talent developed. These include: (a) changing prevailing negative thoughts and beliefs surrounding ethnic/racial minority groups, ELLs, and disadvantaged students; (b) providing all students with ample opportunities to display their academic talent at a young age before disparities compound; (c) leveraging standardized testing in a way that does not advantage some groups over others; (d) finding ways to provide schools, regardless of locale, with appropriate resources to identify and develop academic talent; and (e) providing students from underrepresented groups with the supports that they need to adapt to and succeed in GATE programs (Abedi, 2002; Card & Giuliano, 2015; Harris et al., 2009; Kettler et al., 2015; Peters & Engerrand, 2016; Worrell & Dixson, 2018). In short, the field of GATE needs to compassionately acknowledge the challenges of students from underrepresented backgrounds and take meaningful practical steps to lessen their burdens and move toward equity.

A final thought is that there are currently millions of students from low-income backgrounds whose talents were not developed or whose talents are not currently being developed as a result of faulty GATE identification and programing practices that put them at a disadvantage (Office for Civil Rights, 2012; Olszewski-Kubilius & Corwith, 2018; Olszewski-Kubilius & Steenbergen-Hu, 2017; Worrell & Dixson, 2018). According to several studies, this means that *a lot* of academic potential is being lost with each passing year (e.g., Steenbergen-Hu et al., 2016; Subotnik et al., 2011). Given that academically gifted individuals with fully developed talent have been found to make disproportional contributions to society (Wai et al., 2019), how much more advanced would society be if it made a more concerted effort to develop the academic talent of those without the resources and context to do it on their own?

References

Abedi, J. (2002). Standardized achievement tests and English language learners: Psychometrics issues. *Educational Assessment, 8*(3), 231–257. https://doi.org/10.1207/S15326977EA0803_02

Alexander, K. L., Entwisle, D. R., & Olson, L. S. (2007). Lasting consequences of the summer learning gap. *American Sociological Review, 72*(2), 167–180. https://doi.org/10.1177/000312240707200202

Callahan, C. M., Moon, T. R., & Oh, S. (2013). *Status of elementary gifted programs—2013.* University of Virginia, National Research Center on the Gifted and Talented. https://www.nagc.org/sites/default/files/key%20reports/ELEM%20school%20GT%20Survey%20Report.pdf

Capps, R. (2015). *Trends in immigration and migration of English and dual language learners* [Paper presentation]. National Research Council Committee on Fostering School Success for English Learners, Washington, DC, United States.

Card, D., & Giuliano, L. (2015). *Can universal screening increase the representation of low income and minority students in gifted education?* (No. 21519). https://www.nber.org/papers/w21519

Carman, C. A., & Taylor, D. K. (2010). Socioeconomic status effects on using the Naglieri Nonverbal Ability Test (NNAT) to identify the gifted/talented. *Gifted Child Quarterly, 54*(2), 75–84. https://doi.org/10.1177/0016986209355976

Ceci, S. J., & Papierno, P. B. (2005). The rhetoric and reality of gap closing: When the "have-nots" gain but the "haves" gain even more. *American Psychologist, 60*(2), 149–160. https://doi.org/10.1037/0003-066X.60.2.149

Cohen, L. (1998). *Meeting the needs of gifted and talented minority language students: Issues and practices.* Maryland National Clearinghouse for Bilingual Education.

Colorado Department of Education. (2018). *Chapter 7: Students identified as gifted and talented.* https://www.cde.state.co.us/fedprograms/2017-state-report-card-gifted-and-talented-chapter

Dixson, D. D., Olszewski-Kubilius, P., Subotnik, R. F., & Worrell, F. C. (2020). Developing academic talent as a practicing school psychologist: From potential to expertise. *Psychology in the Schools, 57*(10), 1582–1595. https://doi.org/10.1002/pits.22363

Elhoweris, H., Mutua, K., Alsheikh, N., & Holloway, P. (2005). Effect of children's ethnicity on teachers' referral and recommendation decisions in gifted and talented programs. *Remedial and Special Education, 26*(1), 25–31. https://doi.org/10.1177/07419325050260010401

Evans, E. (2015). Young, gifted, Black, and blocked: A critical inquiry of barriers that hinder Black students' participation in gifted and advanced placement programs [Doctoral dissertation, Georgia Southern University]. *Electronic Theses and Dissertations.* https://digitalcommons.georgiasouthern.edu/etd/1355

Fontenot, K., Semega, J., & Kollar, M. (2018). *Income and poverty in the United States: 2017* (Current Population Reports, P60-263). United State Census Bureau. https://www.census.gov/content/dam/Census/library/publications/2018/demo/p60-263.pdf

Ford, D. Y. (2014). Segregation and the underrepresentation of Blacks and Hispanics in gifted education: Social inequality and deficit paradigms. *Roeper Review, 36*(3), 143–154. https://doi.org/10.1080/02783193.2014.919563

Ford, D. Y., Grantham, T. C., & Whiting, G. W. (2008). Another look at the achievement gap: Learning from the experiences of gifted black students. *Urban Education, 43*(2), 216–239. https://doi.org/10.1177/0042085907312344

Forrest-Bank, S., & Jenson, J. M. (2015). Differences in experiences of racial and ethnic microaggression among Asian, Latino/Hispanic, Black, and White young adults. *Journal of Sociology and Social Welfare, 42*(1), 141–161.

Francis, D. V., & Darity, W. A., Jr. (2020). Isolation: an alternative to the "acting white" hypothesis in explaining Black under-enrollment in advanced courses. *Journal of Economics, Race, and Policy, 3,* 117–122. https://doi.org/10.1007/s41996-020-00051-4

Gándara, P., & Bial, D. (2001). *Paving the way to postsecondary education: K–12 intervention programs for underrepresented youth.* National Center for Education Statistics.

Giessman, J. A., Gambrell, J. L., & Stebbins, M. S. (2013). Minority performance on the Naglieri Nonverbal Ability Test, Second Edition, versus the Cognitive Abilities Test, Form 6: One gifted program's experience. *Gifted Child Quarterly, 57*(2), 101–109. https://doi.org/10.1177/0016986213477190

Gilkerson, J., Richards, J. A., Warren, S. F., Montgomery, J. K., Greenwood, C. R., Kimbrough Oller, D., Hansen, J. H. L., & Paul, T. D. (2017). Mapping the early language environment using all-day recordings and automated analysis. *American Journal of Speech-Language Pathology, 26*(2), 248–265. https://doi.org/10.1044/2016_AJSLP-15-0169

Gregory, A., & Huang, F. (2013). It takes a village: The effects of 10th grade college-going expectations of students, parents, and teachers four years later. *American Journal of Community Psychology, 52*(1–2), 41–55. https://doi.org/10.1007/s10464-013-9575-5

Grissom, J. A., & Redding, C. (2016). Discretion and disproportionality: Explaining the underrepresentation of high-achieving students of color in gifted programs. *AERA Open, 2*(1). https://doi.org/10.1177/2332858415622175

Hallinan, M. T. (1996). Race effects on students' track mobility in high school. *Social Psychology of Education, 1,* 1–24. https://doi.org/10.1007/BF02333403

Hansen-Thomas, H., & Cavagnetto, A. (2010). What do mainstream middle school teachers think about their English language learners? A tri-state case study. *Bilingual Research Journal, 33*(2), 249–266. https://doi.org/10.1080/15235882.2010.502803

Harris, B., Plucker, J. A., Rapp, K. E., & Martínez, R. S. (2009). Identifying gifted and talented English language learners: A case study. *Journal for the Education of the Gifted, 32*(3), 368–393. https://doi.org/10.4219/jeg-2009-858

Jimerson, L. (2003). *The competitive disadvantage: Teacher compensation in rural America* [Policy brief]. Rural School and Community Trust. https://www.ruraledu.org/user_uploads/file/Competitive_Disadvantage.pdf

Kettler, T., & Hurst, L. T. (2017). Advanced academic participation: A longitudinal analysis of ethnicity gaps in suburban schools. *Journal for the Education of the Gifted, 40*(1), 3–19. https://doi.org/10.1177/0162353216686217

Kettler, T., Puryear, J. S., & Mullet, D. R. (2016). Defining rural in gifted education research: Methodological challenges and paths forward. *Journal of Advanced Academics, 27*(4), 245–265. https://doi.org/10.1177/1932202X16656896

Kettler, T., Russell, J., & Puryear, J. S. (2015). Inequitable Access to gifted education: Variance in funding and staffing based on locale and contextual school variables. *Journal for the Education of the Gifted, 38*(2), 99–117. https://doi.org/10.11 77/0162353215578277

Kim, J. S. (2004). Summer reading and the ethnic achievement gap. *Journal of Education for Students Placed at Risk, 9*(2), 169–188.

Lohman, D. F., Korb, K. A., & Lakin, J. M. (2008). Identifying academically gifted English-Language Learners using nonverbal tests: A comparison of the Raven, NNAT, and CogAT. *Gifted Child Quarterly, 52*(4), 275–296. https://doi.org/10.11 77/0016986208321808

Mann, S., Sponsler, B., Welch, M., and Wyatt, J. (2017, August). *Advanced placement access and success: How do rural schools stack up?* Education Commission of the States. https://www.ecs.org/wp-content/uploads/Advanced-Placement-Access-and-Success-How-do-rural-schools-stack-up.pdf

Matthews, M. S., & Kirsch, L. (2011). Evaluating gifted identification practice: Aptitude testing and linguistically diverse learners. *Journal of Applied School Psychology, 27*(2), 155–180. https://doi.org/10.1080/15377903.2011.565281

McBee, M. T. (2006). A descriptive analysis of referral sources for gifted identification screening by race and socioeconomic status. *Journal of Secondary Gifted Education, 17*(2), 103–111. https://doi.org/10.4219/jsge-2006-686

McBee, M. (2010). Examining the probability of identification for gifted programs for students in Georgia elementary schools: A multilevel path analysis study. *Gifted Child Quarterly, 54*(4), 283–297. https://doi.org/10.1177/0016986210377927

McClain, M., & Pfeiffer, S. (2012). Identification of gifted students in the United States today: A look at state definitions, policies, and practices. *Journal of Applied School Psychology, 28*(1), 59–88. https://doi.org/10.1080/15377903.2012.643757

Monk, D. H. (2007). Recruiting and retaining high-quality teachers in rural areas. *The Future of Children, 17*(1), 155–174. https://doi.org/10.1353/foc.2007.0009

Mun, R. U., Langley, S. D., Ware, S., Gubbins, E. J., Siegle, D., Callahan, C. M., McCoach, D. B., & Hamilton, R. (2016). *Effective practices for identifying and serving English learners in gifted education: A systematic review of the literature.* National Center for Research on Gifted Education, University of Connecticut. https://ncrge.uconn. edu/wp-content/uploads/sites/982/2016/01/NCRGE_EL_Lit-Review.pdf

National Association for Gifted Children & Council of State Directors of Programs for the Gifted. (2015). *2014–2015 State of the states in gifted education: Policy and practice data.* https://www.nagc.org/sites/default/files/key%20reports/2014-2015%20 State%20of%20the%20States%20%28final%29.pdf

National Center for Education Statistics. (2017a). *Average salaries for full-time teachers in public and private elementary and secondary schools, by selected characteristics: 2011–12 and 2015–16.* https://nces.ed.gov/programs/digest/d18/tables/dt1 8_211.10.asp

National Center for Education Statistics. (2017b). *Number and percentage of related children under age 18 living in poverty, by family structure, race/ethnicity, and selected racial/ethnic subgroups: 2010 and 2016.* https://nces.ed.gov/programs/digest/d17/tables/dt17_102.60.asp

Nicholson-Crotty, S., Grissom, J. A., Nicholson-Crotty, J., & Redding, C. (2016). Disentangling the causal mechanisms of representative bureaucracy: Evidence from assignment of students to gifted programs. *Journal of Public Administration Research and Theory, 26*(4), 745–757. https://doi.org/10.1093/jopart/muw024

Office for Civil Rights. (2012). *The transformed Civil Rights Data Collection (CRDC).* https://www2.ed.gov/about/offices/list/ocr/docs/crdc-2012-data-summary.pdf

Olszewski-Kubilius, P., & Corwith, S. (2018). Poverty, academic achievement, and giftedness: A literature review. *Gifted Child Quarterly, 62*(1), 37–55. https://doi.org/10.1177/0016986217738015

Olszewski-Kubilius, P., & Steenbergen-Hu, S. (2017). Blending research-based practices and practice-embedded research: Project Excite closes achievement and excellence gaps for underrepresented gifted minority students. *Gifted Child Quarterly, 61*(3), 202–209. https://doi.org/10.1177/0016986217701836

Olszewski-Kubilius, P., Steenbergen-Hu, S., Thomson, D., & Rosen, R. (2017). Minority achievement gaps in STEM: Findings of a longitudinal study of Project Excite. *Gifted Child Quarterly, 61*(1), 20–39. https://doi.org/10.1177/0016986216673449

Parker, K., Horowitz, J., Brown, A., Fry, R., Cohn, D., & Igielnik, R. (2018). *What unites and divides urban, suburban and rural communities.* Pew Research Center. https://www.pewsocialtrends.org/2018/05/22/what-unites-and-divides-urban-suburban-and-rural-communities

Peters, S. J., & Engerrand, K. G. (2016). Equity and excellence: Proactive efforts in the identification of underrepresented students for gifted and talented services. *Gifted Child Quarterly, 60*(3), 159–171. https://doi.org/10.1177/0016986216643165

Pettit, S. K. (2011). Teachers' beliefs about English language learners in the mainstream classroom: A review of the literature. *International Multilingual Research Journal, 5*(2), 123–147. https://doi.org/10.1080/19313152.2011.594357

Plummer, D (1995). Serving the needs of gifted children from a multicultural perspective. In J. L. Genshaft, M. Birely, & C. L. Hollinger (Eds.), *Serving gifted and talented students: A resource for school personnel* (pp. 285–300). PRO-ED.

Rambo-Hernandez, K. E., & McCoach, D. B. (2015). High-achieving and average students' reading growth: Contrasting school and summer trajectories. *The Journal of Educational Research, 108*(2), 112–129. https://doi.org/10.1080/00220671.2013.850398

Redford, J., Burns, S., & Hall, L. (2018). *The summer after kindergarten: Children's experiences by socioeconomic characteristics.* U.S. Department of Education. https://nces.ed.gov/pubs2018/2018160.pdf

Reeves, R. V., & Halikias, D. (2017). *Race gaps in SAT scores highlight inequality and hinder upward mobility.* Brookings. https://www.brookings.edu/research/race-gaps-in-sat-scores-highlight-inequality-and-hinder-upward-mobility

Schmidt, W. H., Burroughs, N. A., Zoido, P., & Houang, R. T. (2015). The role of schooling in perpetuating educational inequality: an international perspective. *Educational Researcher, 44*(7), 371–386. https://doi.org/10.3102/0013189X15603982

Schon, J., Shaftel, J., & Markham, P. (2008). Contemporary issues in the assessment of culturally and linguistically diverse learners. *Journal of Applied School Psychology, 24*(2), 163–189. https://doi.org/10.1080/15377900802089395

Spinelli, C. G. (2008). Addressing the issue of cultural and linguistic diversity and assessment: Informal evaluation measures for English language learners. *Reading and Writing Quarterly, 24*(1), 101–118. https://doi.org/10.1080/10573560701753195

Steele, C. M. (2010). *Whistling Vivaldi: How stereotypes affect us and what we can do.* Norton.

Steenbergen-Hu, S., Makel, M. C., & Olszewski-Kubilius, P. (2016). What one hundred years of research says about the effects of ability grouping and acceleration on K–12 students' academic achievement: Findings of two second-order meta-analyses. *Review of Educational Research, 86*(4), 849–899. https://doi.org/10.3102/0034654316675417

Subotnik, R. F., Olszewski-Kubilius, P., & Worrell, F. C. (2011). Rethinking giftedness and gifted education: A proposed direction forward based on psychological science. *Psychological Science in the Public Interest, 12*(1), 3–54. https://doi.org/10.1177/1529100611418056

Sugarman, J., & Geary, C. (2018). *English learners in California: Demographics, outcomes, and state accountability policies.* Migration Policy Institute.

Wai, J., Makel, M. C., & Gambrell, J. (2019). The role of elite education and inferred cognitive ability in eminent creative expertise: An historical analysis of the TIME 100. *Journal of Expertise, 2*(2), 77–91.

Walker, A., Shafer, J., & Liam, M. (2004). "Not in my classroom": Teacher attitudes towards English language learners in the mainstream classroom. *National Association for Bilingual Education Journal of Research and Practice, 2*(1), 130–160.

Walton, G. M., & Cohen, G. L. (2011). A brief social-belonging intervention improves academic and health outcomes of minority students. *Science, 331*(6023), 1447–1451. https://doi.org/10.1126/science.1198364

Warne, R. T., Anderson, B., & Johnson, A. O. (2013). The impact of race and ethnicity on the identification process for giftedness in Utah. *Journal for the Education of the Gifted, 36*(4), 487–508. https://doi.org/10.1177/0162353213506065

Warne, R. T., Yoon, M., & Price, C. J. (2014). Exploring the various interpretations of "test bias." *Cultural Diversity and Ethnic Minority Psychology, 20*(4), 570–582. https://doi.org/10.1037/a0036503

Worrell, F. C. (2007). Ethnic identity, academic achievement, and global self-concept in four groups of academically talented adolescents. *Gifted Child Quarterly, 51*(1), 23–38. https://doi.org/10.1177/0016986206296655

Worrell, F. C., & Dixson, D. D. (2018). Retaining and recruiting underrepresented gifted students. In S. I. Pfeiffer (Ed.), *Handbook of giftedness in children: Psychoeducational theory, research, and best practices* (2nd ed., pp. 209–226). Springer.

Worrell, F. C., Subotnik, R. F., Olszewski-Kubilius, P., & Dixson, D. D. (2019). Gifted students. *Annual Review of Psychology, 70,* 551–576. https://doi.org/10.1146/annurev-psych-010418-102846

CHAPTER 3

Macro-Identification Approaches and Systems for Students From Low-Income Backgrounds

Frank C. Worrell, Isabella Ahrens,
Morgan Bessette, Maedeh Golshirazi,
Kevin H. Macpherson, Franklin B. Mejía,
Nicolas Saldivar, Jeremy Spence,
and Mercedes A. Zapata

From as early as the preschool years, children from lower income families report lower achievement outcomes than their more affluent peers (Snyder et al., 2018). This achievement gap is evident throughout the achievement distribution and has been referred to as an excellence or opportunity gap at the upper end of distribution of achievement outcomes (Carter & Welner, 2013; Plucker et al., 2010, 2013), resulting in disproportionately fewer students from lower income households being identified for gifted and talented education (GATE) programs (Wai & Worrell, 2016b; Worrell & Dixson, 2018). Research has indicated that the opportunity gap is associated with socioeconomic status (SES; Sirin, 2005), and Desimone and Long (2010) argued that educational inequality due to SES has been the focal point of research and policy at least since the war on poverty in 1965.

Some researchers have examined whether schools mitigate or exacerbate the achievement gap between students of different racial/ethnic backgrounds and SES levels. Borland and Wright (1994) found that lower achieving students tend to be assigned to teachers who emphasize basic instruction, and higher achieving students tend to be assigned to teachers who emphasize more advanced instruction. Other researchers have found that teachers often have lower expectations for students from low-income backgrounds (Rubie-Davies, 2015; Weinstein, 2002). Proposed solutions have included emphasizing site-appropriate methods and observations for identification and deemphasizing the use of standardized tests when identifying potentially gifted students from economically disadvantaged backgrounds. However, even nonverbal tests that are purported to be culturally fair result in children from low-SES families being identified at lower rates than their peers from high-SES families (see Carman & Taylor, 2010; Worrell, 2018). These findings should not be surprising, as the SES achievement gap is real (Michelmore & Dynarksi, 2017; Reardon, 2013).

However, more recent research has also indicated that the underidentification of students from low-income backgrounds for GATE programming is not only a function of the achievement or excellence gaps. Hamilton et al. (2018) found that (a) students from low-income backgrounds are "less likely to be identified for gifted services, even after controlling for prior math and reading achievement," and (b) "poor students in poor schools are even less likely to be identified as gifted" (p. 6). In other words, the level of school poverty is associated with the percentage of students that a school classifies as gifted (Hamilton et al., 2018). Thus, students living in poverty and students attending low-income schools are disadvantaged in the identification process not only by lower average achievement, but also by the context of poverty itself. Moreover, although the percentage of low-, middle-, and high-poverty schools that offer gifted programs is similar, the percentage of students in high-poverty schools who participate in gifted education programs is considerably lower (Yaluma & Tyner, 2018).

In this chapter, we discuss gifted education using what can be described as a macro-identification lens; we focus on large-scale social processes that are potentially associated with the underidentification of children from low-income backgrounds for GATE programming. We focus on societal level processes using two frameworks: stereotype threat and cultural ecological theory. Both of these frameworks have an impact on processes at the district and school levels, and are related to a third framework, teacher expectations. Societal beliefs about individuals from low-income backgrounds result in educators lowering their expectations for those students and for themselves as well. Much of the research on these frameworks has been conducted with a focus on ethnicity and race instead of socioeconomic status, as our review will show, but we argue that the frameworks are equally applicable to socioeconomic groups. We provide recommendations that districts and schools can use to increase the number of students from low-income backgrounds, and we highlight the connections between these macro-level processes and the micro-level processes that are discussed in Chapter 4. To set the context for this chapter, we begin with a brief review of the literature on income and achievement and our conceptualization of what it means to be gifted.

Before proceeding, an important observation must be made. That is, the underrepresentation of students from low-income and ethnic/racial minority backgrounds in gifted and talented education programs is not a merely a problem of identification, Hamilton et al.'s (2018) findings notwithstanding. Given current definitions of giftedness, underrepresentation in gifted education is primarily driven by the achievement gap (Worrell & Dixson, 2018). Achievement data for grades K–12 from the National Assessment of Educational Progress (e.g., Aud et al., 2010; de Brey et al., 2019; FairTest, 2019; Peters & Engerrand, 2016) and college enrollment rates (Ashkenas et al., 2017) reveal substantial achievement gaps, and academic performance is substantially lower in less advantaged schools (Gershenson, 2018). In the last High School Transcript Study conducted by the National Center for Education Statistics (Nord et al., 2011), the mean GPAs for graduating seniors in 2009 were as follows for the four major groups: African American (2.69), Latinx (2.84), European American (3.09), and Asian American (3.26). In short, the recommendations proposed in this chapter are not short term and will not "solve" the problem of underrepresentation.

Income and Achievement

The positive association between income levels and academic achievement is well established in the extant literature. Even before the start of formal schooling at the age of 5, children from households in the lowest income quintile have been found to have lower scores than their more affluent peers on a variety of academic indicators (e.g., vocabulary, reading, mathematics; Snyder et al., 2018). These achievement gaps extend from preschool into the adult years (Michelmore & Dynarksi, 2017), with students from lower income backgrounds (a) reporting lower scores on the National Assessment of Educational Progress, (b) graduating from high school and enrolling in college at lower rates than students from higher income backgrounds, and (c) obtaining lower paying jobs in adulthood (Aud et al., 2010; de Brey et al., 2019; Fry & Cilluffo, 2019; McFarland, Cui, et al., 2018), starting the cycle over again. Economic inequality has sharply increased since the 1970s, and recent data indicate that of people under the age of 18, 17.5% live in poverty (Fontenot et al., 2018). Moreover, there are substantial income disparities among ethnic and racial groups, with African American, American Indian, and some Latinx and Asian American subgroups earning substantially less than their peers (Fontenot et al., 2018), with concomitant overrepresentation at the lower end of the achievement and excellence gaps (McFarland, Hussar, et al., 2018). These educational gaps are manifest whether one focuses on absolute poverty, relative poverty, or economic poverty.

Recent research on the excellence gap has shown that students from low-income backgrounds continue to be underrepresented in GATE programs. For example, Yaluma and Tyner (2018) explored the extent to which students from low-income families participated in the GATE programs in their analysis of a nationally representative sample of high-poverty schools that offer GATE programs. In this sample, only 8.9% of the GATE-identified students were from low-income families, which was far below what was expected given the population of students from low-income backgrounds served. Adding to the literature on the poverty-based excellence gap, Callahan et al. (2014) surveyed 1,566 school districts surveyed across the United States and reported that the underrepresentation of students from low-income backgrounds in GATE programs was greater than the underrepresentation of students from ethnic/racial minority groups. Other research has indicated that poverty-based excellence gaps exist to a larger degree in the U.S. relative to most other developed countries (Finn & Wright, 2015).

Alongside the substantial body of research that has documented the wide-ranging effects of poverty and their negative impacts on academic achievement, researchers have also begun to investigate how experiencing poverty contributes to the excellence gap (Plucker & Peters, 2018). Poverty has been found to be "one of the most powerful determinants of whether and how children experience adversity" (Odgers & Jaffee, 2013, p. 33) and is known to have negative impacts on myriad outcomes, including academic functioning. Two commonly cited reasons for the negative relationship between poverty and achievement outcomes are (a) that poverty negatively impacts several aspects of children's health and development in ways detrimental to academic achievement (Duncan et al., 2013) and (b) that children's experience of poverty is often accompanied by substantial barriers to children's opportunities to learn (e.g., Olszewski-Kubilius & Corwith, 2018).

What Does It Mean to Be Gifted?

There are multiple models of giftedness in the literature (Sternberg & Davidson, 1986, 2005). Worrell et al. (2019) divided the major models into three broad categories: (a) ability-based models, (b) talent development models, and (c) integrative models. Ability-based models use cognitive ability as a marker of giftedness (e.g., Terman, 1922, 1925). Talent development models acknowledge the importance of ability but also highlight the importance of developmental processes and psychosocial constructs in the manifestation of giftedness (e.g., Bloom, 1985; Dai, 2010; Gagné, 1985; Renzulli, 1978; Renzulli & Reis, 2018; Tannenbaum, 1986). Integrative models are combinations or syntheses of several ability-based and talent development models (e.g., Subotnik & Jarvin, 2005; Subotnik et al., 2011). All of the models speak to outstanding performance in one or more areas, although this chapter focuses primarily on academic performance. As should be evident, the impacts of poverty described previously (e.g., negative impacts on health, barriers to learning) are in opposition to outstanding performance.

In his school-based conceptualization of giftedness, Marland (1972) defined gifted students as those with demonstrated achievement or potential ability in one or more of the following six areas: general intellectual ability, specific academic aptitude, creative or productive thinking, leadership ability, visual or performing arts, or psychomotor ability. At present, the federal government defines gifted students as those who demonstrate "evidence of high achievement capability in areas such as intellectual, creative, artistic, or leadership capacity, or in specific academic fields, and who need services or activities not ordinarily provided by the school in order to fully develop those capabilities" (No Child Left Behind Act, 2001). The notion of potential is no longer in the definition, although it is still in the definition put forward by the National Association for Gifted Children (NAGC, 2019), which acknowledges that gifted children need appropriate educational experiences to realize their potential.

Although the goals of gifted education have been subject to some debate in gifted education research circles, we argue that a central objective of gifted education is the identification of potential talent coupled with fostering and developing that talent (Subotnik et al., 2012). It is incumbent on educators to both identify students with potential to achieve at high levels and support the talent development of gifted students from *all* cultural and income groups (Peters & Engerrand, 2016). The notion of identifying potential talent and not just developed talent is central to identifying students from low-SES backgrounds for GATE programs.

Theoretical Frameworks That Address Academic Performance and Underperformance

There is a common assumption that ability is static and drives outstanding performance. However, ability's relationship with achievement is bidirectional, and potential will only result in outstanding performance if there are appropriate educational opportunities. The provision and acceptance of these opportunities depend on belief systems of individuals that are affected by the larger sociohistorical context. Cultural ecological theory (Ogbu, 1978, 1992, 2008) and stereotype threat (Steele, 1997, 2010; Steele & Aronson, 1995) are two models that speak to this broader context.

Cultural Ecological Theory

Grounded in Bronfenbrenner's (1977) notion that development involves the interaction between an individual and the ecological systems in which the individual exists (e.g., micro-, macro-, meso-, and exosystems), Ogbu's (1978, 1992, 2003) cultural ecological theory adds cultural context and cultural identity to the ecological systems that need to be considered. Based on data from several countries in which he identified successful and unsuccessful minority groups, Ogbu (1982, 1992; Ogbu & Simons, 1998) identified three groups of minorities. Group 1, labeled autonomous minorities, included groups who differ from the dominant group in the United States on the basis of language, religion, or some other cultural variable (e.g., Jews, Mormons, and the Amish). These autonomous minorities experience discrimination related to their cultural difference, but are not oppressed or marginalized in the way that some groups are, and they are not perceived to be academically or intellectually inferior; thus, students from autonomous minorities are not distinguished by poor performance in school (Ogbu, 1985).

Group 2 are voluntary or immigrant minorities. This group consists of individuals who have immigrated "more or less *voluntarily* to their host or new society for economic, social, or political reasons" (Ogbu & Matute-Bianchi, 1985, p. 87) and, in the United States, include immigrants from Africa, some Asian countries, and some West Indian nations. These immigrant minorities share several commonalities. First, they wanted to move to the United States. Second, they use their country of origin as a point of reference, which allows them to "put aside" discrimination from the dominant group and invest in the advantages of the United States. Third, they also believe that they can return home if they are not successful in the United States (Ogbu & Matute-Bianchi, 1985; Ogbu & Simons,

1998). Thus, immigrant minorities have a dual consciousness; that is, they participate selectively in American culture (Ogbu & Matute-Bianchi, 1985, p. 89) and never give up their original cultural frame of reference. Consequently, this group does not internalize the negative stereotypes about them and tends to be successful in school.

The third group are the involuntary minorities. Involuntary minorities have been incorporated into American society "through slavery, conquest, or colonization" (Ogbu, 1985, p. 863). Involuntary minorities in the United States include African Americans, Alaska Natives, American Indians, Native Hawaiians, and many Latinx groups (e.g., Puerto Ricans, Mexican Americans). Involuntary minorities experience substantial discrimination by the dominant group and, most importantly, are not allowed to become or perceived to be *equal* members of the society. Given their long history of discrimination in the United States, many involuntary group members develop a frame of reference in opposition to the dominant culture. They may not trust White-controlled institutions, including school (Fordham & Ogbu, 1986; Ogbu, 1992, 2004), and academic success is sometimes reframed as "acting White" and stigmatized. They also believe that effort is not sufficient to compensate for racism and discrimination. The end result is poor academic performance (Ogbu & Simons, 1998).

Cultural ecological theory is most frequently applied to ethnic/racial groups, and African Americans (e.g., Ogbu, 1989, 2003, 2004) in particular. For example, Ford et al. (2008) reported that African American students associated "acting White" with a strong achievement orientation and "acting Black" with underachievement and low academic skills. In another study, Ogbu (2003) examined the academic behaviors and attitudes of African American students living in an Ohio suburb called Shaker Heights. Ogbu (2003) reported that the African Americans from all socioeconomic levels (poor, middle-class, and wealthy) in this community were not doing as well as their majority and their immigrant minority peers. On the basis of interviews, Ogbu contended that the poorer academic performance was related to academic disengagement attitudinally and behaviorally. Although there are multiple critiques of cultural ecological theory in the literature (see Ogbu, 2008), the two studies that have focused on high-achieving populations (i.e., Ford et al., 2008; Ogbu, 2003) have provided support for cultural ecological theory's claims.

We contend that cultural ecological theory also applies to socioeconomic groups in several ways. First, it is no accident that substantial proportions of the groups most affected by cultural ecological theory—that is, African Americans, American Indians, and Latinx—live in poverty, and research studies frequently confound ethnicity/race with socioeconomic status by comparing minorities from low-income backgrounds with students from higher income backgrounds who are not minorities. Moreover, involuntary minorities were originally labeled "castelike minorities":

> Because in every case they were a subordinate group in a stratification system more rigid than social class stratification. In every case, the [castelike] minorities were historically denied *equal educational opportunities* in terms of access to educational resources, treatment in school, and rewards in employment and wages for educational accomplishments. (Ogbu & Simons, 1998, p. 157)

Consider the consequences of food and housing insecurity that affect individuals living in poverty, and it is not difficult to recognize that the cultural ecology of families in poverty is similar to that of other marginalized groups. In support of this thesis, Reardon et al. (2019) concluded that

> the association of racial segregation with achievement gaps is completely accounted for by differences in school poverty: racial segregation appears to be harmful because it concentrates minority students in high-poverty schools, which are, on average, less effective than lower-poverty schools. (p. 1)

In short, the cultural ecology of low-income families is similar regardless of ethnicity/race, with low-income minorities experiencing a doubly-negative environment.

Stereotype Threat

Steele's (1997) stereotype threat is another theoretical framework about the achievement of minority groups using a cultural identity framework. The underlying premise of stereotype threat is that there are negative stereotypes about most groups in society, and an individual may be judged on the basis of the negative stereotypes about one or more of the groups to which they belong (Steele, 2003). Stereotype threat is defined as "the threat of being viewed through the lens of a negative stereotype, or the fear of doing something that would inadvertently confirm that stereotype" (Steele, 2003, p. 111). The initial stereotype threat studies focused on the stereotype of African Americans being intellectually inferior to European Americans (e.g., Steele & Aronson, 1995), although subsequent studies have examined stereotypes for several other groups, including women being less capable in mathematics (e.g., Shih et al., 1999) and African Americans being more capable in sport (Stone et al.,

1999). Using a sample of Asian American females at Harvard, Shih et al. (1999) showed that participants whose gender was made salient performed less well on a mathematics task than participants who were not primed, demonstrating stereotype threat. Shih et al. also found that participants whose ethnicity (Asian American) was primed obtained higher scores on the mathematics task, demonstrating a stereotype facilitation effect. Finally, these authors showed that this pattern was disrupted in Canada, where they found only a threat effect but not a facilitation effect, with the hypothesis being that the ethnic stereotype was not salient in Canada.

Steele (1997) argued that for stereotype threat to occur, an individual must be invested in the domain. In other words, stereotype threat is more of an issue for stigmatized students who care about doing well in school (Steele, 2003). When individuals care about a domain in which their group is negatively stereotyped, stereotype threat is activated if they believe that their performance is being judged by others *with the stereotype in mind*. Activation of the stereotype results in an emotional reaction that interferes with performance and can lead to *disidentification* with the domain in the longer term (Steele & Aronson, 1995). This disidentification is akin to the decrease in effort predicted by cultural ecological theory (Ogbu & Simons, 1998) and results in protection of self-worth (Covington & Dray, 2002). By deidentifying with a domain and not working harder, success may decrease, but global self-concept is not affected.

Researchers have demonstrated stereotype threat effects in a large number of studies across a variety of ages (e.g., Harrison et al., 2006; McKown & Weinstein, 2003). Of specific relevance to this paper is the work extending stereotype threat to socioeconomic groups. In 1998, Croizet and Claire conducted a study with French undergraduates in which they primed SES. Their results indicated that students from low-SES backgrounds for whom SES was made salient performed less well than low-SES students for whom SES was not salient and high-SES students in both groups. Students in the primed group also completed fewer items and were less accurate on the items they did complete than their peers who were not primed. This finding has been replicated in several studies (e.g., John-Henderson et al., 2014; Spencer & Castrano, 2007).

Implications of Cultural Ecological Theory and Stereotype Threat for Achievement Gaps by Income

As we noted in the sections on cultural ecological theory and stereotype threat, low-socioeconomic status is a cultural variable that is associated with societal stigma, negative stereotypes, and concomitant lower achievement, especially in educational contexts where SES is salient. The impact of SES is evident in lower enrollment in gifted programs in K–12 schooling and continues into college. DeParle (2012) reported on three low-income Latinas who graduated from high school with the capacity to do college work based on their achievement records and enrolled in college. However, negotiating college on one's own with no family members with the experience or knowledge to assist is not easy: "Four years later, their story seems less like a tribute to upward mobility than a study of obstacles in an age of soaring economic inequality. Not one of them has a college degree . . . and two of them have crushing debts" (DeParle, 2012).

Moreover, although the percentage of students from low-income backgrounds attending college has continued to increase, these students are increasing in enrollment at the less selective or open-enrollment and for-profit institutions, which also have lower graduation rates (Fain, 2019; Fry & Cilluffo, 2019). Students' college completion rate 8 years after enrollment is 86% at institutions that accept 25% or less of applicants, and 31% at schools with open admissions. In other words, kids from high-income families who are more likely to attend selective institutions are more likely to graduate than kids from low-income families who are more likely to attend less selective institutions (Fain, 2019; Tough, 2014).

So far, we have focused on the impact of cultural ecological theory and stereotype threat on students themselves, but these frameworks also affect teachers' perceptions of students. In the only large-scale study of teacher referrals, McBee (2006) found that after controlling for automatic referrals of students with scores at the 90th percentile on a standardized test for gifted testing, teachers were more likely to refer students from high-income backgrounds than low-income backgrounds, generally (6.01 vs. 1.95, respectively) as well as for African American (2.60 vs. 1.69), American Indian (5.68 vs. 3.67), Asian American (11.90 vs. 5.01), European American (7.19 vs. 2.57), and Latinx (1.95 vs. 1.17) subgroups. Although it is likely that these differences in referral rates are associated with differences in academic functioning, it is also likely that some percentage of the variance in these differences is related to stereotypes related to income, gender, and ethnicity/race.

Thompson (2004) reported that teachers in an elementary school held low expectations for their Latinx students and did not challenge them academically, as they assumed most of the students would drop out before completing high school. Auwarter and Aruguete (2008) found that teachers had more negative attitudes toward boys from low-SES backgrounds than boys from high-SES backgrounds. Gregory and Huang (2013) found that student, parent, and teacher expectations contributed more variance to the prediction of college-going than students' race, gender, SES, and academic achievement, and concluded that "a 'village' of positive expectations can help set a student on a college-going trajectory" (p. 50). Finally, Pinchak (2018) found that teacher expectations had a greater impact on students from lower SES families.

These findings highlight the powerful influence of teachers' views on the performance of students from low-SES backgrounds. Work on teacher expectations indicates that they are cumulative (Weinstein, 2002), and Gregory and Huang (2013) noted that the expectations of students, their parents, and their teachers were also cumulative. Research has also indicated that negative and positive attitudes toward the future are predictive of educational and psychological outcomes (Worrell & Andretta, 2019), with positive attitudes leading to more adaptive outcomes. Andretta et al. (2013) found that adolescents from low-SES families reported higher past negative attitudes and lower past positive attitudes than peers from middle-SES and high-SES backgrounds. Prow et al. (2016) identified three attitude profiles in adolescents: Positives, Ambivalents, and Conflicted. Positives had the highest academic achievement, and Conflicted had the lowest achievement outcomes. Moreover, students from high-SES backgrounds were overrepresented in the Positives group and underrepresented in the Conflicted group, whereas students from low-SES backgrounds were underrepresented in the Positives group and overrepresented in the Conflicted group. Taken together, research suggests that a variety of societal factors combine to dampen the expectations, expenditures of effort, and achievement outcomes of students from lower SES backgrounds relative to their peers from higher SES backgrounds, and these factors also affect the expectations of students' parents and teachers.

Common Approaches to Identifying Gifted Students in Schools

Definitions of giftedness determine identification practices. Due to the absence of a federal mandate regarding special education, states determine their own definitions of giftedness (National Association for Gifted Children & Council of State Directors of Programs for the Gifted, 2015). Most states consider exhibited talents, called *manifest talents*, rather than gifted potential, called *latent talents*, in their definitions. Manifest talents are those that can be demonstrated because they have had the opportunity to become actualized. Latent talents reflect unactualized potential that can be masked by environmental or social factors. For example, a child who has potential to become an elite athlete but cannot afford to join an athletic league will not realize this potential; similarly, a child who may be musical prodigy but has no access to musical equipment or lessons may never recognize that they have potential to be developed. Definitions of giftedness as manifest talent are linked to use of ability and achievement testing.

The two most common approaches used to identify gifted students are ability or intellectual tests and standardized achievement tests. Gifted education originated in an effort to serve the needs of children with superior intelligence (Cross & Dockery, 2014). Thus, intelligence testing has been a dominant means of identifying children for gifted and talented services (Subotnik et al., 2011; Terman, 1925). However, children from households with less educational and social capital have fewer opportunities to turn latent talent or potential into manifest talent and, consequently, will obtain lower scores on intelligence tests on average (Nisbett et al., 2012). Standardized achievement tests are generally criterion-referenced measures, meaning that they compare a student's knowledge or skills against a predetermined standard or performance level. Achievement tests depend on the acquisition of formal learning in school or at home and measure what a student has learned over a set time period. Thus, achievement tests also measure manifest talent.

A third strategy for identifying gifted students, especially those from underrepresented groups, involves alternative assessments. In a recent study, Hodges et al. (2019) compared identification outcomes of traditional and alternative assessments. The premise for the study was that "underrepresentation of Black, Hispanic, and Native American students [in gifted education] is largely due to the use of traditional methods of identification (i.e., IQ and standardized achievement tests)" and that alternative methods of assessment, including "nonverbal tests, student portfolios, affective checklists" would resolve the underrepresentation issue (p. 147). The meta-analysis drew upon 54 studies with 85 effect sizes and more than 191 million students. Using the risk ratio as an indicator of effect size, with a value less than one indicating underrepresentation, Hodges et al. found that the risk ratio for the traditional measures of identification was 0.27, whereas the risk ratio for nontraditional methods was 0.34. Nontraditional measures had a very small effect. These authors concluded that "better identification methods are needed to address inequities in education" (Hodges et al., 2019, p. 147). In short, alternative assessments do not solve the problem, and Hodges et al.'s conclusion ignores the evidence that underrepresentation is not primarily due to type of identification procedure.

In many districts, teacher nominations are also used as a part of the identification process. In some cases, teacher nominations are required, whereas in others, teachers complete nominations for students who have not been automatically nominated on the basis of achievement test scores. In addition to concerns about the validity of scores on teacher rating scales (Callahan, 2005), as noted previously, students who are economically disadvantaged are less likely to be referred for a variety of reasons, including achievement gaps and teacher perceptions.

Two practices that are recommended to help in identifying students from low-SES backgrounds are universal screening and local norms. Both of these options are discussed in some detail in the Chapter 4, so our review here is brief. Universal screening bypasses the nomination phase, so that teacher, parent, and student perceptions do not have any impact on who is screened. Consequently, more students from underrepresented backgrounds are identified. Universal screening has two primary limitations. First, if traditional cut scores are used for placement decisions (e.g., 130 IQ or 95th percentile on an achievement test), universal screening will identify a very small percentage of additional students, as only students with high manifest abilities will be identified. Second, universal screening is expensive, as districts need to have the resources to assess all of their students.

Local norms are also potentially useful in identifying students who would not otherwise be identified. Local norms are based on using the normative data from the local school or district as the criteria against which students are identified. Thus, rather than having to score at the 95th percentile for the country, for example, a student only needs to obtain the 95th percentile relative to students in their school or district. Use of local norms at the school level is more useful than at the district level, as school-level norms guarantee that the students with the highest levels of performance will be identified and receive gifted services. Although district administrators are often reluctant to use local norms, their utility in some contexts is acknowledged in the *Standards for Educational and Psychological Testing* (American Educational Research Association [AERA] et al., 2014; see Standard 5.8, p. 104). In this case, gifted services are only limited by the budget that the district assigns to gifted education; these funds have to be provided by the state or district, as the federal government does not provide funding for gifted education. Note that local norms should be used primarily in the early grades, because as students transition through high school and enter college, their performance will increasingly be compared with that of individuals from other schools and states. At this level, meeting local norms is not sufficient.

Recommendations for Rethinking Gifted Identification

As we have argued, we view giftedness in terms of potential for outstanding achievements. If educators are to increase the number of gifted students from low-income backgrounds, they need to find the students with the most potential. We propose the following recommendations for increasing the numbers of students from low-income backgrounds in gifted and talented education programs. Our approach assumes that educators need to reach as many students as possible and work from potential. This approach does not mean getting rid of traditional identification practices and providing services to the students who qualify. Rather, it involves broadening the groups that services are provided to and the services provided to all youth.

Grow Your Own Gifted Students

As the data show, from as young as 2 years old, there are SES and ethnic/racial gaps in academic skills (e.g., expressive vocabulary, early reading and mathematics scores; Snyder et al., 2018). We recommend that schools and districts engage in the following activities:

> Partner with early childhood programs in their service areas so that these programs are aware of the skill deficits that students arriving in kindergarten are showing, with the goal of reducing or eliminating these achievement gaps at the beginning of formal schooling.

> Assess all students entering kindergarten for early numeracy and literacy skills and provide evidence-based interventions to students who are missing these skills. Reassess all students when they enter first grade to ascertain if there are still students who have skill deficits and need more intensive interventions.

> Have monthly enrichment afternoons in every classroom, from kindergarten to at least grade 5, in schools serving students from low-income backgrounds, with a wide variety of activities (academic, athletic, artistic) for students to choose from (see Renzulli & Reis, 2014). To ensure that groups are small enough to allow for meaningful interaction and individual attention, draw upon all adults who work in the schools (teachers, aides, administrators, cafeteria workers, etc.), as well as parents, community volunteers, and students from local high schools and colleges. The goal is to help students find something that they are passionate about and are able to pursue over time. Students' potential for giftedness may be in an extracurricular activity, and deep engagement in extracurricular participation facilitates academic engagement and persistence.

> Collect data on students' engagement and participation in these activities, and use these data to help steer students toward activities that reflect their interest. After students have found their areas of passion, be systematic in exposing them to increasingly more challenging curriculum in the domain.

> Use data from the enrichment afternoons to identify potentially gifted students for gifted education services.
> Have students share their accomplishments with their peers and parents at least once annually.

Identify Potentially Gifted Students

One of the premises of giftedness is that it is rare (McBee et al., 2012; Worrell et al., 2012, 2018). Although we agree with this premise, we would argue that giftedness is an adult characteristic that is at the end of a talent development process. Thus, although giftedness becomes increasingly rare as one moves from potential to expertise to eminence, potential is far less rare than expertise or eminence. In other words, gifted education is focusing on rareness far too early. We often use the 90th or the 95th percentile on achievement tests as screeners, or IQ scores of 130, which is at the 97.7th percentile. Given the shortage of STEM talents in the country and the projected shortage of medical and mental health professionals, it seems foolish to limit gifted education to a select few in the K–12 system instead of many more who have the potential to become experts in adulthood. Thus, *we recommend lowering the bar for gifted identification and programming to the 75th percentile on ability or achievement tests*. Although not every second or third grader who is at the 75th percentile will become an expert, considerably more students will get the chance to develop their potential, and this group will be considerably more diverse in socioeconomic status and ethnicity/race.

This recommendation is not as radical as it seems. Even with existing achievement gaps, there are students in schools who are performing considerably above the floor for their grade levels. Peters et al. (2017) reported that "among American elementary and middle school students 20% to 49% in English Language Arts and 14% to 37% in mathematics *scored 1 year or more above grade level* [emphasis added]" (p. 229). Thus, there is already a substantial group of students who can benefit from enrichment and acceleration activities. Moreover, two of the states included in Peters et al.'s analysis were California (with more than 70% non-White students and more than 40% students from economically disadvantaged backgrounds) and Texas (more than 70% non-White and more than 47% from economically disadvantaged backgrounds), which showcases what gifted programs could look like in those states. Project Excite (Olszewski-Kubilius & Steenbergen-Hu, 2017; Olszewski-Kubilius et al., 2017) provides an example of the benefits of this approach on a small scale. Finally, using a lower cut score will also bring gifted education more closely into alignment with sport, with more than 55% of middle and high school students participating in school athletic teams in 2017 (Child Trends, 2019). These are the programs that develop talent for the athletic programs in colleges and universities that are considerably more selective, as well as for the elite national athletic leagues.

Train Teachers to Hold High Expectations

Even though the substantial effect sizes in the Pygmalion in the Classroom (Rosenthal & Jacobson, 1968) study were never replicated, there is robust literature on teacher expectation effects on student performance and behavior (Weinstein et al., 2004). Research has indicated that from as early as grade 1, students are able to differentiate between high and low achievers in the classroom on the basis of differential behavior by teachers (Weinstein, 2002; Weinstein & Middlestadt, 1979; Weinstein et al., 1987). The nature and types of supports that teachers provide can hinder or enhance academic performance (Perry et al., 2007), and teacher expectation effects have also been shown to be additive (Rubie-Davies et al., 2014). Researchers have identified behaviors that are common among low- and high-expectation teachers (Rubie-Davies, 2007) and have demonstrated empirically that training teachers in the high-expectation practices results in increased student achievement and increased satisfaction by teachers (Rubie-Davies et al., 2015). Rubie-Davies et al. (2015) reported that high-expectation teachers engage in the following practices in their classrooms:

> ⟩ using grouping for instruction but not for other learning activities;
> ⟩ providing *all* students with challenging and exciting instructional activities;
> ⟩ building a warm, positive classroom climate and having warm, positive relationships with individual students;
> ⟩ setting mastery goals with students based on regular formative assessments;
> ⟩ providing students with clear feedback about progress toward their goals;
> ⟩ regularly reviewing and updating goals with students based on data; and
> ⟩ promoting student autonomy by allowing students to choose their goals using the data from the formative assessments.

Expanded descriptions of these recommendations can be found in Rubie-Davies (2015).

Invest in Social-Psychological Interventions in Schools

As we noted in the review of cultural ecological theory and stereotype threat, these phenomena contribute not only to teachers' perceptions of students but also to students' perceptions of themselves and their capabilities. Moreover, even in circumstances where students can succeed in gifted and talented education programs, they may opt not to do so to minimize conflicts between their cultural and academic identities. As Graham (2004) noted, these students' response is "I can, but do I want to?" (p. 125). In the past 3 decades, social-psychological interventions have resulted in increased academic performance in students from elementary schools to college (Yeager et al., 2019). The goal of social-psychological interventions is to change students' attitudes and cognitions about themselves and schooling "and thereby encourage students to take advantage of learning opportunities in school" (Yeager et al., 2019, p. 364). Although typically used with students who are not doing well in school, these interventions have been used with students in selective colleges as well, demonstrating their utility with high-achieving students. Interestingly, these interventions have increased achievement outcomes in underrepresented student groups while not affecting the achievement of other students, leading to a closing of the achievement gap.

Moreover, these interventions are designed to be cost-effective and scalable. Yeager and Walton (2011) described their efficacy in the following terms:

> Recent randomized experiments have found that seemingly "small" social-psychological interventions in education—that is, brief exercises that target students' thoughts, feelings, and beliefs in and about school—can lead to large gains in student achievement and sharply reduce achievement gaps even months and years later. (p. 267)

These interventions have been used primarily with ethnic/racial minorities, and effect sizes have been small. Given that some of them have been found to work after multiple years, it is probable that their effects are cumulative. Moreover, although the generalizability of some of these interventions is contested, they are based on solid theoretical foundations and have been found to work in some contexts. It is likely that some of them will be useful in increasing the achievement orientations of students from low-income backgrounds with academic potential.

A detailed description of these interventions is beyond the scope of this chapter. However, we highlight several of the interventions that have been recommended by Yeager and other colleagues (Cohen et al., 1999; Yeager & Walton, 2011; Yeager et al., 2014, 2019):

> teaching students to attribute negative academic outcomes to unstable factors,

> teaching students to adopt an incremental view of intelligence (i.e., growth mindset),

> having students affirm values that are important to them,

> helping students see that their academic future selves are consistent with their racial identity and within reach,

> making class material personally relevant to students, and

> using wise feedback in responding to students from underrepresented groups.

Provide Support After Identification

Risks After Identification

Identifying students from low-income backgrounds is the first step in the process; these students must be encouraged to participate and persist in gifted programs. Academically talented students from low-income backgrounds may experience unique stressors not experienced by their peers. For example, some gifted students experience isolation and alienation as a result of not feeling that they fit in well with their peers or their environment (Pfeiffer & Stocking, 2000; Seeley, 2004), and this is a stressor that may well be more prevalent in students from low-income backgrounds. As a result, these students may struggle to make friends (Pfeiffer & Stocking, 2000). Further, students of low-income status or ethnic/racial minority status may be less willing to remain in gifted programs because these programs are typically comprised of students who are ethnically different (Moore et al., 2005) and socioeconomically more well off.

Parents and teachers of academically talented students may hold unrealistic expectations for student progress and academic success (Freeman, 1995; Webb, 1993). Alternatively, they may not understand that enrichment or accelerated coursework may result in difficulties in keeping up for students who have substantial chores in the household. Related to unrealistic expectations, parents of some gifted youth have been characterized as overinvolved in their children's academic progress and "attempt to experience the rich rewards of life by living through their highly gifted children" (Pfeiffer & Stocking, 2000,

p. 68). Another potential risk experienced by academically gifted students is a mismatch between their academic capabilities and the academic support that they receive. These students may not receive the attention needed from their teachers due to the perception that they can succeed without support or opportunities (Pfeiffer & Stocking, 2000), and this factor may be exacerbated for students from homes with less fiscal resources and social capital. Finally, gifted students from ethnic/racial minority or disadvantaged backgrounds may endure a unique set of stressors due to having to integrate the beliefs and assumptions of the gifted program and their cultural background.

Protective Factors

The literature suggests that academically talented students possess protective factors that increase the likelihood of retention in gifted programs: level of intelligence, community ties, and identification. Level of intelligence has been shown to contribute to resilience (Doll & Lyon, 1998; Kitano & Lewis, 2005; Tiet et al., 1998; Werner, 2000). Further, Tiet et al. (1998) found that intelligence acts as a protective factor for youth of different ethnic/racial backgrounds, and students with higher IQ scores were found to be adept at coping with adverse life events. Community ties such as social relationships, belief systems, community supports, and connection to a community also increase resilience (Kitano & Lewis, 2005). Additionally, for students of African American, Native American, and Latinx backgrounds, having a dual identity—that is, a feeling of pride in one's ethnic/racial group as well as an awareness of connections to the larger society—makes them less vulnerable to stereotype threat (Oyserman et al., 2003). Identification as a strong student (i.e., a strong academic identity) also acts as a protective factor.

Using Response to Intervention to Support Gifted Students

The Council for Exceptional Children (2008) proposed the utilization of a Response to Intervention (RtI) model to establish programs that best support the unique needs of underrepresented gifted students. The RtI framework consists of collaborative, multitiered, evidence-based interventions that target the specific needs of all students in an educational setting (Bianco, 2010; McKevitt & Braaksma, 2014). This framework has the potential to promote the protective factors discussed in the previous section while simultaneously mitigating some of the detrimental effects of the risk factors that these students experience. Specifically, the RtI model in a gifted context would promote the utilization of culturally responsive, high-quality curriculum and intensive,

65

collaborative, evidence-based interventions by teachers, families, and schools (Bianco, 2010).

The RtI model is multitiered, with the first level supporting all students in the educational context. This foundation is built upon an emphasis on school curriculum, quality of instruction, and universal screening. Developing a high-quality curriculum with high-quality instruction increases the opportunities for students to cultivate and demonstrate their gifted potential (Gentry, 2009). Additionally, utilizing data from universal screening allows for a more consistent and effective way to identify students who may be performing above grade-level expectations and can benefit from more intensive interventions that continue to challenge and support their gifted learning (Bianco, 2010). Tier 1 practices promote protective factors, such as academic identification (Kitano & Lewis, 2005), by beginning to foster students' self-concept of their ability to achieve. Additionally, to help reduce feelings of social isolation and alienation, schools can enroll students in community service opportunities, sports teams, and clubs to increase their social engagement (Seeley, 2004). Using students as role models also provides gifted students with opportunities to interact with their peers and share their experiences (Worrell & Dixson, 2018).

Tier 2 targets identified students and provides increasingly more intensive interventions that best suit their needs. These interventions are collaborative, evidence-based, and expose the students to a more enriched curriculum. At Tier 2, interventions include differentiated instruction, curriculum compacting, and access to mentors and internship opportunities (Bianco, 2010). Tier 2 practices promote protective factors, such as community ties (Kitano & Lewis, 2005) through the connection to potential mentors in the community and internship opportunities that allow the student to be more involved with their community. Additionally, these students should be provided with skills-based supports related to studying, test taking, time management, and organizational skills, which are of particular importance for students living in poverty (Ford, 2011; Ford & Whiting, 2008). Students should receive explicit instruction in metacognition and active learning techniques to foster their academic achievement (Worrell & Young, 2011).

In order to provide such skills training, schools may decide to provide students with study labs staffed with tutors or role models of the same age and representatives of ethnic/racial minority communities to instruct students and help them adjust to their academic environment (Worrell & Dixson, 2018). These role models also serve as examples of individuals from ethnic, racial, and socioeconomic minorities who are academically successful graduates of gifted programs (Worrell & Dixson, 2018). Mentoring programs have been found to help students narrow their academic and career interests (Hébert, 2001). In sum, support for gifted students should emphasize academic resources that provide students with skills training and spaces to interact with and receive guidance from like-minded peers.

As identified students demonstrate a need for more intensive interventions (i.e., Tier 3), they may be placed in Advanced Placement classes, honors classes, or early college entrance (Bianco, 2010). Tier 3 practices provide opportunities for students to demonstrate their abilities in a more rigorous and intensive context. After identification, gifted students should be provided with not only academic supports to aid in their success in their academic endeavors, but also social-emotional supports (Weinstein & Bialis-White, 2016) and ample opportunities to engage with their peers.

Robertson and Pfeiffer (2016) published a procedural guide for implementing RtI with high-ability students. Their guide is meant to supplement the delivery of gifted education services to the students who meet the criteria and the students who are highly motivated but may not have formally qualified for gifted education. Their recommendations highlight the importance of promoting high-quality instruction in general education classrooms, as well as encouraging motivation and engagement among all students regardless of identification. Lastly, educators and administrators should consider their students' specific needs and support teacher training in effective high-quality and gifted education pedagogy before establishing and implementing an RtI framework in their schools (Bianco, 2010; Robertson & Pfeiffer, 2016).

Conclusion

There is no disputing the fact that students from low-income backgrounds—many of whom are also from ethnic and racial minorities—are underrepresented in gifted education (Ford & Whiting, 2008; Worrell & Dixson, 2018). There is also no doubt that disproportionality in the field of gifted education is viewed as a critical issue in urgent need of a remedy (Borland & Wright 1994; Cross & Dockery, 2014); indeed, this disproportionality is frequently framed as an educational equity issue (Kettler et al., 2015; Peters & Engerrand, 2016). It is the source of this inequity on which individuals differ, with some blaming schools and tests, and others putting the onus on the achievement gap. Although poverty plays a role in predicting gifted identification outcomes (Hamilton et al., 2018), especially for African Americans (Ricciardi et al., 2020), there is compelling evidence that achievement gaps are the largest source of variance in predicting identification (e.g., de Brey et al., 2019; Ricciardi et al., 2020).

Our point is simply this: Given that achievement gaps *exist* (Aud et al., 2010; de Brey et al., 2019), identification as it is currently conceived will not result in reducing the disproportionalities in gifted education, and everyone should question the scores on any test that does not reflect the reality of the existing achievement gaps. The important question, then, is how to move forward given the existing achievement and opportunity gaps. The most radical recommendations in this chapter are to take the notion of identifying potential seriously by (a) providing quality education and effective enrichment to all students in the United States and (b) identifying the top 25% of students for gifted and talented education. In other words, educators need to stop trying to identify "gifted learners" and identify learners with the potential for gifted contributions as adults. These strategies will also address, in the short term, the disproportionality issues, and in the long term, the achievement gaps. These strategies will expand the talent development pool and lead to more students from low-income and other underrepresented groups joining the ranks of gifted contributors in adulthood.

Of course, providing gifted education to a quarter of the students attending public schools will require substantial funding, but this country can afford to support its brightest students and should stop balking at doing so. As Wai and Worrell (2016a) noted, "of the $49.8 billion in the federal education budget in 2015, a total of 0.0002% [was] allocated to gifted and talented education" (p. 125). This level of funding for gifted education is criminally negligent given the contributions that outstanding contributors to society make, and it is time that the federal and state governments live up to the currently false claim that *all* students have a right to a free *and appropriate* public education. Smarick (2019) observed that "gifted education puts in tension two equally treasured American ideals: egalitarianism and individualism" (para. 5). This is a false choice, just as pitting remedial and special education against gifted education is a false choice. Consider the innovations that gifted individuals have made and continue to make in science, technology, music, art, athletics, and every other domain, and consider the many innovations and contributions that have been lost because students from low-income backgrounds did not have the opportunities required to develop their talents (Subotnik et al., 2011; Wai & Worrell, 2016a). According to Smarick (2019):

> Justice in education isn't realized through uniformity but by ensuring that *every* single child has the best shot at reaching their highest potential. Properly understood and executed, investing in kids with special talents serves both America's commitment to collective equality and individual excellence.

References

American Educational Research Association, American Psychological Association, & National Council on Measurement in Education. (2014). *Standards for educational and psychological testing*. American Educational Research Association.

Andretta, J. R., Worrell, F. C., Mello, Z. R., Dixson, D. D., & Baik, S. H. (2013). Demographic group differences in adolescents' time attitudes. *Journal of Adolescence, 36*(2), 289–301. https://doi.org/10.1016/j.adolescence.2012.11.005

Ashkenas, J., Park, H., & Pearce, A. (2017). *Even with affirmative action, Blacks and Hispanics are more underrepresented at top colleges than 35 years ago*. The New York Times. https://www.nytimes.com/interactive/2017/08/24/us/affirmative-action.html

Aud, S., Fox, M., & KewalRamani, A. (2010). *Status and trends in the education of racial and ethnic groups* (NCES 2010-015). National Center for Education Statistics.

Auwarter, A. E., & Aruguete, M. S. (2008). Effects of student gender and socioeconomic status on teacher perceptions. *The Journal of Educational Research, 101*(4), 243–246. https://doi.org/10.3200/JOER.101.4.243-246

Bianco, M. (2010). Strength-based RtI: Conceptualizing a multitiered system for developing gifted potential. *Theory Into Practice, 49*(4), 323–330. https://doi.org/10.1080/00405841.2010.510763

Bloom, B. S. (Ed.). (1985). *Developing talent in young people*. Ballantine Books.

Borland, J. H., & Wright, L. (1994). Identifying young, potentially gifted, economically disadvantaged students. *Gifted Child Quarterly, 38*(4), 164–171. https://doi.org/10.1177/001698629403800402

Bronfenbrenner, U. (1977). Toward an experimental ecology of human development. *American Psychologist, 32*(7), 513–531. https://doi.org/10.1037/0003-066x.32.7.513

Callahan, C. M. (2005). Identifying gifted students from underrepresented populations. *Theory Into Practice, 44*(2), 98–104. https://doi.org/10.1207/s15430421tip4402_4

Callahan, C. M., Moon, T. R., & Oh, S. (2014). *National surveys of gifted programs: Executive summary: 2014*. University of Virginia, National Research Center on the Gifted and Talented. https://www.nagc.org/sites/default/files/key%20reports/2014%20Survey%20of%20GT%20programs%20Exec%20Summ.pdf

Carman, C. A., & Taylor, D. K. (2010). Socioeconomic status effects on using the Naglieri Nonverbal Ability Test (NNAT) to identify the gifted/talented. *Gifted Child Quarterly, 54*(2), 75–84. https://doi.org/10.1177/0016986209355976

Carter, P. L., & Welner, K. G. (Eds.). (2013). *Closing the opportunity gap: What America must do to give every child an even chance*. Oxford University Press.

Child Trends. (2019). *Participation in school athletics*. https://www.childtrends.org/indicators/participation-in-school-athletics

Cohen, G. L., Steele, C. M., & Ross, L. D. (1999). The mentor's dilemma: Providing critical feedback across the racial divide. *Personality and Social Psychology Bulletin, 25*(10), 1302–1318. https://doi.org/10.1177/0146167299258011

Council for Exceptional Children. (2008). *CEC's position on response to intervention (RtI): The unique role of special education and special educators.*

Covington, M. V., & Dray, E. (2002). The developmental course of achievement motivation: A need-based approach. In A. Wigfield & J. S. Eccles (Eds.), *The development of achievement motivation* (pp. 33–56). Elsevier. https://doi.org/10.1016/b978-012750053-9/50004-8

Croizet, J.-C., & Claire, T. (1998). Extending the concept of stereotype threat to social class: The intellectual underperformance of students from low socioeconomic backgrounds. *Personality and Social Psychology Bulletin, 24*(6), 588–594. https://doi.org/10.1177/0146167298246003

Cross, J. R., & Dockery, D. D. (2014). *Identification of low-income gifted learners: A review of recent research.* Jack Kent Cooke Foundation.

Dai, D. Y. (2010). *The nature and nurture of giftedness: A new framework for understanding gifted education.* Teachers College Press.

de Brey, C., Musu, L., McFarland, J. Wilkinson-Flicker, S., Diliberti, M., Zhang, A., Branstetter, C., & Wang, X. (2019). *Status and trends in the education of racial and ethnic groups 2018* (NCES 2019-038). National Center for Education Statistics. https://nces.ed.gov/pubs2019/2019038.pdf

DeParle, J. (2012). *For poor, leap to college often ends in a hard fall.* The New York Times. https://www.nytimes.com/2012/12/23/education/poor-students-struggle-as-class-plays-a-greater-role-in-success.html

Desimone, L. M., & Long, D. (2010). Teacher effect and the achievement gap: Do teacher and teaching quality influence the achievement gap Between Black and White and high- and low-SES students in the early grade? *Teachers College Record, 12,* 3024–3073.

Doll, B., & Lyon, M. A. (1998). Risk and resilience: Implications for the delivery of educational and mental health services in school. *School Psychology Review, 27*(3), 348–363.

Duncan, G. J., Kalil, A., & Ziol-Guest, K. M. (2013). Early childhood poverty and adult achievement, employment and health. *Family Matters, 93,* 27–35.

Fain, P. (2019). *Wealth's influence on enrollment and completion.* Inside Higher Ed. https://www.insidehighered.com/news/2019/05/23/feds-release-broader-data-socioeconomic-status-and-college-enrollment-and-completion

FairTest. (2019). *2019 SAT scores: Gaps between demographic groups grows larger.* https://www.fairtest.org/2019-sat-scores-gaps-between-demographic-groups-gr

Finn, C. E., Jr., & Wright, B. L. (2015). *Failing our brightest kids: The global challenge of educating high-ability students.* Harvard Education Press.

Fontenot, K., Semega, J., & Kollar, M. (2018). *Income and poverty in the United States: 2017* (Current Population Reports, P60-263). United States Census Bureau. https://www.census.gov/content/dam/Census/library/publications/2018/demo/p60-263.pdf

Ford, D. Y. (2011). *Reversing underachievement among gifted Black students* (2nd ed.). Prufrock Press.

Ford, D. Y., Grantham, T. C., & Whiting, G. W. (2008). Another look at the achievement gap: Learning from the experiences of gifted Black students. *Urban Education, 43*(2), 216–239. https://doi.org/10.1177/0042085907312344

Ford, D. Y., & Whiting, G. W. (2008). Recruiting and retaining underrepresented gifted students. In S. I. Pfeiffer (Ed.), *Handbook of giftedness in children* (pp. 293–308). Springer. https://doi.org/10.1007/978-0-387-74401-8_15

Fordham, S., & Ogbu, J. U. (1986). Black students' school success: Coping with the "burden of 'acting White.'" *The Urban Review, 18,* 176–206. https://doi.org/10.1007/BF01112192

Freeman, J. (1995). Annotation: Recent studies in giftedness in children. *Journal of Child Psychology and Psychiatry, 36*(4), 531–547.

Fry, R., & Cilluffo, A. (2019). *A rising share of undergraduates are from poor families, especially at less selective colleges.* Pew Research Center. https://www.pewsocialtrends.org/2019/05/22/a-rising-share-of-undergraduates-are-from-poor-families-especially-at-less-selective-colleges

Gagné, F. (1985). Giftedness and talent: Reexamining a reexamination of the definitions. *Gifted Child Quarterly, 29*(3), 103–112. https://doi.org/10.1177/001698628502900302

Gentry, M. (2009). Myth 11: A comprehensive continuum of gifted education and talent development services: Discovering, developing, and enhancing young people's gifts and talents. *Gifted Child Quarterly, 53*(4), 262–265. https://doi.org/10.1177/0016986209346937

Gershenson, S. (2018, September). *Grade inflation in high schools (2005–2016).* Thomas B. Fordham Institute. https://fordhaminstitute.org/sites/default/files/20180919-grade-inflation-high-schools-2005-2016_0.pdf

Graham, S. (2004). "I can, but do I want to?" Achievement values in ethnic minority children and adolescents. In G. Philogène (Ed.), *Racial identity in context: The legacy of Kenneth B. Clark* (pp. 125–147). American Psychological Association.

Gregory, A., & Huang, F. (2013). It takes a village: The effects of 10th grade college-going expectations of students, parents, and teachers four years later. *American Jounal of Community Psychology, 52*(1–2), 41–55. https://doi.org/10.1007/s10464-013-9575-5

Hamilton, R., McCoach, D. B., Tutwiler, M. S., Siegle, D., Gubbins, E. J., Callahan, C. M., Brodersen, A. V., & Mun, R. U. (2018). Disentangling the roles of institutional and individual poverty in the identification of gifted students. *Gifted Child Quarterly, 62*(1), 6–24. https://doi.org/10.1177/0016986217738053

Harrison, L. A., Stevens, C. M., Monty, A. N., & Coakley, C. A. (2006). The consequences of stereotype threat on the academic performance of White and non-White lower income college students. *Social Psychology of Education, 9,* 341–357. https://doi.org/10.1007/s11218-005-5456-6

Hébert, T. P. (2001). Jermaine: A critical case study of a gifted Black child living in rural poverty. *Gifted Child Quarterly, 45*(2), 85–103. https://doi.org/10.1177/001698620104500203

Hodges, J., Tay, J., Maeda, Y., & Gentry, M. (2019). A meta-analysis of gifted and talented identification practices. *Gifted Child Quarterly, 62*(2), 147–174. https://doi.org/10.1177/0016986217752107

John-Henderson, N. A., Rheinschmidt, M. L., Mendoza-Denton, R., & Francis, D. D. (2014). Performance and inflammation outcomes are predicted by different facets of SES under stereotype threat. *Social Psychological and Personality Science, 5*(3), 301–309. https://doi.org/10.1177/1948550613494226

Kettler, T., Russell, J., & Puryear, J. S. (2015). Inequitable access to gifted education: Variance in funding and staffing based on locale and contextual school variables. *Journal for the Education of the Gifted, 38*(2), 99–117. https://doi.org/10.1177/0162353215578277

Kitano, M. K., & Lewis, R. B. (2005). Resilience and coping: Implications for gifted children and youth at risk. *Roeper Review, 27*(4), 200–205. https://doi.org/10.1080/02783190509554319

Marland, S. P., Jr. (1972). *Education of the gifted and talented: Report to the Congress of the United States by the U.S. Commissioner of Education and background papers submitted to the U.S. Office of Education,* 2 vols. U.S. Government Printing Office. (Government Documents, Y4.L 11/2: G36)

McBee, M. T. (2006). A descriptive analysis of referral sources for gifted identification screening by race and socioeconomic status. *Journal of Secondary Gifted Education, 17*(2), 103–111. https://doi.org/10.4219/jsge-2006-686

McBee, M. T., McCoach, D. B., Peters, S. J., & Matthews, M. S. (2012). The case for a schism: A commentary on Subotnik, Olszewski-Kubilius, and Worrell (2011). *Gifted Child Quarterly, 56*(4), 210–214. https://doi.org/10.1177/0016986212456075

McFarland, J., Cui, J., Rathbun, A., & Holmes, J. (2018). *Trends in high school dropout and completion rates in the United States: 2018* (NCES 2019-117). National Center for Education Statistics. https://nces.ed.gov/pubs2019/2019117.pdf

McFarland, J., Hussar, B., Wang, X., Zhang, J., Wang, K., Rathbun, A., Barmer, A., Forrest Cataldi, E., & Bullock Mann, F. (2018). *The condition of education 2018* (NCES 2018-144). National Center for Education Statistics. https://nces.ed.gov/pubs2018/2018144.pdf

McKevitt, B. C., & Braaksma, A. D. (2014). Best practices in developing a positive behavior support system at the school level. In P. L. Harrison & A. Thomas (Eds.), *Best practices in school psychology: Systems-level services* (pp. 165–180). National Association of School Psychologists.

McKown, C., & Weinstein, R. S. (2003). The development and consequences of stereotype consciousness in middle childhood. *Child Development, 74*(2), 498–515. https://doi.org/10.1111/1467-8624.7402012

Michelmore, K., & Dynarski, S. (2017). The gap within the gap: Using longitudinal data to understand income differences in educational outcomes. *AERA Open, 3*(1). https://doi.org/10.1177/2332858417692958

Moore, J. L., Ford, D. Y., & Milner, R. (2005). Recruitment is not enough: Retaining African American students in gifted education. *Gifted Child Quarterly, 49,* 51–67.

National Association for Gifted Children. (2019). *A definition of giftedness that drives best practice* [Position statement]. https://www.nagc.org/sites/default/files/Positi on%20Statement/Definition%20of%20Giftedness%20%282019%29.pdf

National Association for Gifted Children & Council of State Directors of Programs for the Gifted. (2015). *2014–2015 state of the states in gifted education: Policy and practice data.* https://www.nagc.org/sites/default/files/key%20reports/2014-20 15%20State%20of%20the%20States%20%28final%29.pdf

Nisbett, R. E., Aronson, J., Blair, C., Dickens, W., Flynn, J., Halpern, D. F., & Turkheimer, E. (2012). Intelligence: New findings and theoretical developments. *American Psychologist, 67*(2), 130–159. https://doi.org/10.1037/a0026699

No Child Left Behind Act, 20 U.S.C. §6301 (2001). https://www.congress.gov/107/plaws/publ110/PLAW-107publ110.pdf

Nord, C., Roey, S., Perkins, R. Lyons, M., Lemanski, N., Brown, J., & Schuknecht, J. (2011). *The nation's report card: America's high school graduates* (NCES 2011-462). National Center for Education Statistics. https://nces.ed.gov/nationsreportcard/pdf/studies/2011462.pdf

Odgers, C. L., & Jaffee, S. R. (2013). Routine versus catastrophic influences on the developing child. *Annual Review of Public Health, 34,* 29–48. https://doi.org/10.1146/annurev-publhealth-031912-114447

Ogbu, J. U. (1978). *Minority education and caste: The American education system in cross-cultural perspective.* Academic Press.

Ogbu, J. U. (1982). Cultural discontinuities and schooling. *Anthropology & Education Quarterly, 13*(4), 290–307. https://doi.org/10.1525/aeq.1982.13.4.05x1505w

Ogbu, J. U. (1985). Research currents: Cultural-ecological influences on minority school learning. *Language Arts, 62*(8), 860–869.

Ogbu, J. U. (1989). The individual in collective adaptation: A framework for focusing on academic underperformance and dropping out among involuntary minorities. In L. Weis, E. Farrar, & H. G. Petrie (Eds.), *Dropouts from school: Issues, dilemmas, and solutions* (pp. 181–204). SUNY Press.

Ogbu, J. U. (1992). Understanding cultural diversity and learning. *Educational Researcher, 21*(8), 5–14. https://doi.org/10.3102/0013189X021008005

Ogbu, J. U. (2003). *Black American students in an affluent suburb: A study of academic disengagement.* Erlbaum.

Ogbu, J. U. (2004). Collective identity and the burden of "acting White" in Black history, community, and education. *The Urban Review, 36,* 1–35. https://doi.org/10.1023/B:URRE.0000042734.83194.f6

Ogbu, J. U. (Ed.). (2008). *Minority status, oppositional culture, and schooling.* Routledge.

Ogbu, J. U., & Matute-Bianchi, M. E. (1985). Understanding sociocultural factors: Knowledge, identity, and school adjustment. In *Beyond language: Social and cultural factors in schooling language minority students* (pp. 73–142). California State University, Evaluation, Dissemination, and Assessment Center.

Ogbu, J. U., & Simons, H. D. (1998). Voluntary and involuntary minorities: A cultural-ecological theory of school performance with some implications for education.

Anthropology and Education Quarterly, 29(2), 155–188. https://doi.org/10.1525/aeq. 1998.29.2.155

Olszewski-Kubilius, P., & Corwith, S. (2018). Poverty, academic achievement, and giftedness: A literature review. *Gifted Child Quarterly, 62*(1), 37–55. https://doi. org/10.1177/0016986217738015

Olszewski-Kubilius, P., & Steenbergen-Hu, S. (2017). Blending research-based practices and practice-embedded research: Project Excite closes achievement and excellence gaps for underrepresented gifted minority students. *Gifted Child Quarterly, 61*(3), 202–209. https://doi.org/10.1177/0016986217701836

Olszewski-Kubilius, P., Steenbergen-Hu, S., Thomson, D., & Rosen, R. (2017). Minority achievement gaps in STEM: Findings of a longitudinal study of Project Excite. *Gifted Child Quarterly, 61*(1), 20–39. https://doi.org/10.1177/0016986216673449

Oyserman, D., Kemmelmeier, M., Fryberg, S., Brosh, H., & Hart-Johnson, T. (2003). Racial-ethnic self-schemas. *Social Psychology Quarterly, 66*(4), 333–347. https:// doi.org/10.2307/1519833

Perry, K. E., Donohue, K. M., & Weinstein, R. S. (2007). Teaching practices and the promotion of achievement and adjustment in first grade. *Journal of School Psychology, 45*(3), 269–292. https://doi.org/10.1016/j.jsp.2007.02.005

Peters, S. J., & Engerrand, K. G. (2016). Equity and excellence: Proactive efforts in the identification of underrepresented students for gifted and talented services. *Gifted Child Quarterly, 60*(3), 159–171. https://doi.org/10.1177/0016986216643165

Peters, S. J., Rambo-Hernandez, K., Makel, M. C., Matthews, M. S., & Plucker, J. A. (2017). Should millions of students take a gap year? Large numbers of students start the school year above grade level. *Gifted Child Quarterly, 61*(3), 229–238. https://doi.org/10.1177/0016986217701834

Pfeiffer, S. I., & Stocking, V. B. (2000). Vulnerabilities of academically gifted students. *Journal of Applied School Psychology, 16*(1–2), 83–93. https://doi.org/10.1300/J008v16n01_06

Pinchak, N. P. (2018). The relationship between teacher regard and college attendance expectations: Socioeconomic and racial-ethnic disparities. *Social Psychology of Education: An International Journal, 21*(1), 209–221. https://doi.org/10.1007/s11218-017-9396-8

Plucker, J. A., Burroughs, N., & Song, R. (2010). *Mind the (other) gap!: The growing excellence gap in K–12 education.* Center for Evaluation and Education Policy, Indiana University.

Plucker, J. A., Hardesty, J. & Burroughs, N. (2013). *Talent on the sidelines: Excellence gaps and America's persistent talent underclass.* Center for Education Policy Analysis, Neag School of Education, University of Connecticut.

Plucker, J. A., & Peters, S. J. (2018). Should millions of students take a gap year? Large numbers of students start the school year above grade level. *Gifted Child Quarterly, 62*(1), 56–67. https://doi.org/10.1177/0016986217738566

Prow, R. M., Worrell, F. C., Andretta, J. R., & Mello, Z. R. (2016). Demographic differences in adolescent time attitude profiles: A person-oriented analysis using model-

based clustering. *Berkeley Review of Education, 6*(1), 79–95. https://doi.org/10.50
70/B86110030_

Reardon, S. F. (2013). The widening income achievement gap. *Educational Leadership,
70*(8), 10–16.

Reardon, S. F., Weathers, E. S., Fahle, E. M., Jang, H., & Kalogrides, D. (2019). *Is separate still unequal? New evidence on school segregation and racial academic achievement
gaps* (CEPA Working Paper No. 19–06). Center for Education Policy Analysis, Stanford University. https://cepa.stanford.edu/content/separate-still-unequal-new-evid
ence-school-segregation-and-racial-academic-achievement-gaps

Renzulli, J. S. (1978). What makes giftedness? Reexamining a definition. *Phi Delta
Kappan, 60*(3), 180–184, 261.

Renzulli, J. S., & Reis, S. M. (2014). *The Schoolwide Enrichment Model: A how-to guide for
talent development* (3rd ed.). Prufrock Press.

Renzulli, J. S., & Reis, S. M. (2018). The three-ring conception of giftedness: A developmental approach for promoting creative productivity in young people. In S. I.
Pfeiffer, E. Shaunessy-Dedrick, & M. Foley-Nicpon (Eds.), *APA handbook of giftedness and talent* (pp. 185–199). American Psychological Association. https://doi.
org/10.1037/0000038-012

Ricciardi, C., Haag-Wolf, A., & Winsler, A. (2020). Factors associated with gifted identification for ethnically diverse children in poverty. *Gifted Child Quarterly.* Advance
online publication. https://doi.org/10.1177/0016986220937685

Robertson, S., & Pfeiffer, S. I. (2016). Development of a procedural guide to implement
response to intervention (RtI) with high ability learners. *Roeper Review, 38*(1),
9–23. https://doi.org/10.1080/02783193.2015.1112863

Rosenthal, R., & Jacobson, L. (1968). *Pygmalion in the classroom: Teacher expectation and
pupils' intellectual development.* Holt, Rinehart, and Winston.

Rubie-Davies, C. M. (2007). Classroom interactions: Exploring the practices of high-
and low-expectation teachers. *British Journal of Educational Psychology, 77*(2), 289–
306. https://doi.org/10.1348/000709906X101601

Rubie-Davies, C. M. (2015). *Becoming a high expectation teacher: Raising the bar.*
Routledge.

Rubie-Davies, C. M., Peterson, E. R., Sibley, C. G., & Rosenthal, R. (2015). A teacher
expectation intervention: Modeling the practices of high expectation teachers.
Contemporary Educational Psychology, 40(3), 72–85. https://doi.org/10.1016/j.
cedpsych.2014.03.003

Rubie-Davies, C. M., Weinstein, R. S., Huang, F. L., Gregory, A., Cowan, P. A., & Cowan,
C. P. (2014). Successive teacher expectation effects across the early school years.
Journal of Applied Developmental Psychology, 35(3), 181–191. https://doi.org/10.
1016/j.appdev.2014.03.006

Seeley, K. (2004). Gifted and talented students at risk. *Focus on Exceptional Children,
37*(4), 1–8.

Shih, M., Pittinsky, T. L., & Ambady, N. (1999). Stereotype susceptibility: Identity sali-
ence and shifts in quantitative performance. *Psychological Science, 10*(1), 80–83.
https://doi.org/10.1111/1467-9280.00111

Sirin, S. R. (2005). Socioeconomic status and academic achievement: A meta-analytic review of research. *Review of Educational Research, 75*(3), 417–453. https://doi.org/10.3102/00346543075003417

Smarick, A. (2019). *The contradiction at the heart of public education*. The Atlantic. https://www.theatlantic.com/ideas/archive/2019/10/gifted-and-talented-programs-arent-problem/599752

Snyder, T. D., de Brey, C., & Dillow, S. A. (2018). *Digest of education statistics 2016* (NCES 2017-094). National Center for Education Statistics. https://nces.ed.gov/pubs2017/2017094.pdf

Spencer, B., & Castrano, E. (2007). Social class is dead. Long live social class! Stereotype threat among low socioeconomic status individuals. *Social Justice Research, 20*(4), 418–432. https://doi.org/10.1007/s11211-007-0047-7

Steele, C. M. (1997). A threat in the air. How stereotypes shape intellectual identity and performance. *American Psychologist, 52*(6), 613–629. https://doi.org/10.1037/0003-066X.52.6.613

Steele, C. M. (2003). Stereotype threat and African-American student achievement. In T. Perry, C. Steele, & A. G. Hilliard, III (Eds.), *Young, gifted, and Black: Promoting high achievement among African-American students* (pp. 109–130). Beacon.

Steele, C. M. (2010). *Whistling Vivaldi and other clues to how stereotypes affect us*. Norton.

Steele, C. M., & Aronson, J. (1995). Stereotype threat and the intellectual test performance of African Americans. *Journal of Personality and Social Psychology, 69*(5), 797–811. https://doi.org/10.1037/0022-3514.69.5.797

Sternberg, R. J., & Davidson, J. E. (Eds.). (1986). *Conceptions of giftedness*. Cambridge University Press.

Sternberg, R. J., & Davidson, J. E. (Eds.). (2005). *Conceptions of giftedness* (2nd ed.). Cambridge University Press.

Stone, J., Lynch, C. I., Sjomeling, M., & Darley, J. M. (1999). Stereotype threat effects on Black and White athletic performance. *Journal of Personality and Social Psychology, 77*(6), 1213–1227. https://doi.org/10.1037/0022-3514.77.6.1213

Subotnik, R. F., & Jarvin, L. (2005). Beyond expertise: Conceptions of giftedness as great performance. In R. J. Sternberg & J. E. Davidson (Eds.), *Conceptions of giftedness* (2nd ed., pp. 343–357). Cambridge University Press.

Subotnik, R. F., Olszewski-Kubilius, P., & Worrell, F. C. (2011). Rethinking giftedness and gifted education: A proposed direction forward based on psychological science. *Psychological Science in the Public Interest, 12*(1), 3–54. https://doi.org/10.1177/1529100611418056

Subotnik, R. F., Olszewski-Kubilius, P., & Worrell, F. C. (2012). A proposed direction forward for gifted education based on psychological science. *Gifted Child Quarterly, 56*(4), 176–188. https://doi.org/10.1177/0016986212456079

Tannenbaum, A. J. (1986). Giftedness: A psychosocial approach. In R. J. Sternberg & J. E. Davidson (Eds.), *Conceptions of giftedness* (pp. 21–52). Cambridge University Press.

Terman, L. M. (1922). A new approach to the study of genius. *Psychological Review, 29*(4), 310–318. https://doi.org/10.1037/h0071072

Terman, L. M. (1925). *Mental and physical traits of a thousand gifted children. Genetic studies of genius* (Vol. 1). Stanford University Press.

Thompson, G. L. (2004). Playing God with other people's children. *The High School Journal, 87*(3), 1–4. https://doi.org/10.1353/hsj.2004.0004

Tiet, Q. Q., Bird, H. R., Davies, M., Hoven, C., Cohen, P., Jensen, P. S., & Goodman, S. (1998). Adverse life events and resilience. *Journal of the American Academy of Child and Adolescent Psychiatry, 37*(11), 1191–1200.

Tough, P. (2014, May 15). *Who gets to graduate?* The New York Times Magazine. https://www.nytimes.com/2014/05/18/magazine/who-gets-to-graduate.html

Wai, J., & Worrell, F. C. (2016a). Helping disadvantaged and spatially talented students fulfill their potential: Related and neglected national resources. *Policy Insights from the Behavioral and Brain Sciences, 3*(1), 122–128. https://doi.org/10.1177/2372732215621310

Wai, J., & Worrell, F. C. (2016b). *A nation at risk—how gifted low-income kids are left behind*. The Conversation. https://theconversation.com/a-nation-at-risk-how-gifted-low-income-kids-are-left-behind-56119

Webb, J. T. (1993). Nurturing social-emotional development of gifted children. In K. A. Heller, F. J. Monks, & A. H. Passow (Eds.), *International handbook of research and development of giftedness and talent* (pp. 525–538). Pergamon Press.

Weinstein, R. S. (2002). *Reaching higher: The power of expectations in schooling*. Harvard University Press.

Weinstein, R. S., & Bialis-White, L. H. (2016). A model for interweaving rigor and support. In R. S. Weinstein & F. C. Worrell (Eds.), *Achieving college dreams: How a university-charter district partnership created an early college high school* (pp. 289–315). Oxford University Press. https://doi.org/10.1093/acprof:oso/9780190260903.003.0014

Weinstein, R. S., Gregory, A., & Strambler, M. J. (2004). Intractable self-fulfilling prophecies: Fifty years after Brown v. Board of Education. *American Psychologist, 59*(6), 511–520. https://doi.org/10.1037/0003-066x.59.6.511

Weinstein, R. S., Marshall, H. H., Sharp, L., & Botkin, M. (1987). Pygmalion and the student: Age and classroom differences in children's awareness of teacher expectations. *Child Development, 58*(4), 1079–1093. https://doi.org/10.2307/1130548

Weinstein, R. S., & Middlestadt, S. E. (1979). Student perceptions of teacher interactions with male high and low achievers. *Journal of Educational Psychology, 71*(4), 421–431. https://doi.org/10.1037/0022-0663.71.4.421

Werner, E. E. (2000). Protective factors and individual resilience. In J. P. Shonokoff & S. J. Meisels (Eds.), *Handbook of early childhood intervention* (2nd ed., pp. 115–132). Cambridge University Press.

Worrell, F. C. (2018). Identifying gifted learners: Utilizing nonverbal assessment. In C. M. Callahan & H. L. Hertberg-Davis (Eds.), *Fundamentals of gifted education: Considering multiple perspectives* (2nd ed., 125–134). Routledge. https://doi.org/10.4324/9781315639987-12

Worrell, F. C., & Andretta, J. R. (2019). Time attitude profiles in American adolescents: Educational and psychological correlates. *Research in Human Development, 16*(2), 102–118. https://doi.org/10.1080/15427609.2019.1635860

Worrell, F. C., & Dixson, D. D. (2018). Retaining and recruiting underrepresented gifted students. In S. I. Pfeiffer (Ed.), *Handbook of giftedness in children: Psychoeducational theory, research, and best practices* (2nd ed., pp. 209–226). Springer.

Worrell, F. C., Olszewski-Kubilius, P., & Subotnik, R. F. (2012). Important issues, some rhetoric, and a few straw men: A response to comments on "Rethinking Giftedness and Gifted Education." *Gifted Child Quarterly, 56*(4), 224–231. https://doi.org/10.1177/0016986212456080

Worrell, F. C., Subotnik, R. F., & Olszewski-Kubilius, P. (2018). Talent development: A path toward eminence. In S. I. Pfeiffer, E. Shaunessy-Dedrick, & M. Foley-Nicpon (Eds.), *APA handbook of giftedness and talent* (pp. 247–258). American Psychological Association. https://doi.org/10.1037/0000038-016

Worrell, F. C., Subotnik, R. F., Olszewski-Kubilius, P., & Dixson, D. D. (2019). Gifted students. *Annual Review of Psychology, 70,* 551–576. https://doi.org/10.1146/annurev-psych-010418-102846

Worrell, F. C., & Young, A. E. (2011). Gifted children in urban settings. In T. L. Cross & J. R. Cross (Eds.), *Handbook for counselors serving students with gifts and talents: Development, relationships, school issues, and counseling needs/interventions* (pp. 137–151). Prufrock Press.

Yaluma, C. B., & Tyner, A. (2018). *Is there a gifted gap? Gifted education in high-poverty schools.* Thomas B. Fordham Institute. https://fordhaminstitute.org/national/research/there-gifted-gap-gifted-education-high-poverty-schools

Yeager, D. S., Hanselman, P., Walton, G. M., Murray, J. S., Crosnoe, R., Muller, C., Tipton, E., Schneider, B., Hulleman, C. S., Hinojosa, C. P., Paunesku, D., Romero, C., Flint, K., Roberts, A., Trott, J., Iachan, R., Buontempo, J., Yang, S. M., Carvalho, C. M., . . . Dweck, C. S. (2019). A national experiment reveals where a growth mindset improves achievement. *Nature, 573,* 364–369. https://doi.org/10.1038/s41586-019-1466-y

Yeager, D. S., Purdie-Vaughns, V., Garcia, J., Apfel, N., Brzustoski, P., Master, A., Hessert, W. T., Williams, M. E., & Cohen, G. L. (2014). Breaking the cycle of mistrust: Wise interventions to provide critical feedback across the racial divide. *Journal of Experimental Psychology: General, 143*(2), 804–824. https://doi.org/10.1037/a0033906

Yeager, D. S., & Walton, G. M. (2011). Social-psychological interventions in education: They're not magic. *Review of Educational Research, 81*(2), 267–301. https://doi.org/10.3102/0034654311405999

CHAPTER 4

Micro-Identification Processes

Joni Lakin

Students from low-income families are vastly underrepresented in gifted education (Plucker & Peters, 2018). A Fordham Institute study (Yaluma & Tyner, 2018) showed that although high- and low-poverty schools were equally likely to have gifted programs, the programs at high-poverty schools tended to have many fewer students involved. Further, the students that participated were often those few from a higher socioeconomic background. Estimates based on the National Education Longitudinal Study suggest that just 9% of students in gifted and talented programs came from the bottom quartile (25%) of socioeconomic status (SES; Callahan, 2005). Much of this mismatch in identification arises from inequity in society and educational opportunity; students from low-income backgrounds do not have access to the same challenges to develop their cognitive abilities. However, these inequities are clearly mirrored in the assessment tools educators use, and their misuse can perpetuate these early inequities throughout school. Some identification processes, such as teacher or parent referral, further disadvantage these students. Thus, it is vital to focus on identification processes as a tool for improving identification rates and providing access to appropriate services for students from low-income backgrounds.

Chapter 3 of this volume by Worrell et al. explored several approaches to identification that can help schools serve their students from low-SES backgrounds. Chief among these approaches is implementing a universal screening program so that nomination or referral is not an impediment to identification. In this chapter, I will explore some of the specific issues and challenges that must be addressed in creating a high-quality universal screening process. Many of these topics also apply to the use of assessments and rating scales for portfolios and other holistic reviews of student artifacts when assessment data are part of that process. Assessment data can also be essential in identifying students for any of the talent development approaches that Worrell et al. explored in depth, including providing talent development services to students from underrepresented groups who show potential. The sections that follow address identifying higher quality assessments, setting up universal screening processes, and using multiple normative reference points. The chapter concludes with suggestions on the effective use of multiple measures.

Selecting High-Quality Assessments

The empirical research is clear that academic talents appear in every subgroup of student that can be defined—including race, ethnicity, home language, and socioeconomic level. The research is equally clear that the predictors of academic and career success do not vary across these groups. The best predictors of a student's future performance in an academic domain are (1) their current performance in that domain, (2) their ability to reason in the symbol system of that domain, (3) their interest and motivation for that domain, and (4) the ability to persist in challenging learning environments (Lohman, 2005). In other words, academically successful students from any background tend to have high ability in verbal, quantitative, or general ability (particularly compared to students with similar opportunity to learn), and they leverage these and other skills in their success. Test developers who propose that different skills (e.g., nonverbal ability, practical intelligence, etc.) are vital for success for students from low-income backgrounds (or other underrepresented groups) have yet to show that these measures actually eliminate group differences while also showing similar predictive validity for educational outcomes. The literature on nonverbal assessments is reviewed in a later section.

The key to improving the identification of students from low-income backgrounds comes not from selecting all new assessments, but in making appropriate inferences about ability from high-quality data on student capacity. In this section, I will review how to identify high-quality assessments. A later section will address how to account for differences in opportunity to learn through subgroup and local norms.

Identifying High-Quality Ability Tests

The Cattell-Horn-Carroll (CHC) model of intelligence is by far the most widely accepted and empirically supported model of human ability. Other efforts to create "competing" types of broad intelligence, such as intuitively appealing models including creativity and "street smarts," have not stood up to empirical tests in the way that CHC has (Keith & Reynolds, 2010).

The CHC model is hierarchical, and at the apex of the model is general intelligence (g), which is defined not so much as a specific type of cognition but by averaging performance across a large number of diverse types of cognition (see Figure 4.1). Under g is a small set of broad abilities. The most important of these include crystallized intelligence (Gc) and fluid reasoning (Gf). Crystallized intelligence reflects acquired knowledge—what a person knows and can do based on formal or informal learning opportunities. In education, Gc is associated with achievement tests that are closely tied to curriculum and instruction. Fluid reasoning, on the other hand, is less tied to instruction and represents a more general ability to reason with ideas and acquire new knowledge. It is not innate—all abilities must be developed over time through experience—but it is less tied to formal education. Fluid reasoning is most associated with ability or aptitude tests. Below these broad abilities, there are a further array of specific or narrow abilities, which represent even narrower ranges of tasks and skills.

To measure Gc or Gf, like g, requires averaging across a number of these tests of specific abilities. Performance on one type of test question (e.g., verbal analogies) will reflect partly g, partly a broad ability (e.g., Gf), and partly a skill specific to that format. The implication is that achieving a good measure of one of the higher levels of the CHC model (g, broad abilities) requires averaging across multiple tasks that are related to the target construct to "average out" the specific skill and amass shared variance related to the broad ability. Test developers often find that they need at least three different types of questions or item formats to reduce the specific effects of individual tasks (Süß & Beauducel, 2005). For example, the Cognitive Abilities Test (CogAT) creates a composite measure of fluid reasoning by averaging across students' performance in verbal, quantitative, and figural content. Those three battery scores themselves are derived from an average of performance across three specific

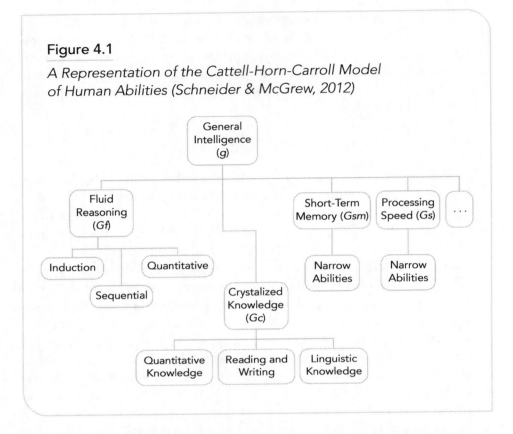

Figure 4.1

A Representation of the Cattell-Horn-Carroll Model of Human Abilities (Schneider & McGrew, 2012)

formats (e.g., verbal analogies, classification, and sentence completion comprise the verbal battery).

Which formats are best for a measure of ability? Looking at the narrow abilities aligned with the broad abilities suggests which types of narrow abilities should be included in a measure. For fluid reasoning, the most important domains to sample are inductive reasoning (figural matrices are a commonly used example), sequential reasoning (most closely related to verbal content), and quantitative reasoning (Carroll, 1993). Tests that sample broadly within the domain will be more effective measures of that ability than tests that use just one question format, such as only using sentence completion or figural analogies to measure reasoning skills.

What does all of this mean for the practitioner? Ultimately, it means that regardless of a student's socioeconomic status, scores based on a single-item format will not provide an adequate measure of a broad ability or *g*. Such a "unidimensional" measure is contaminated to some degree by the specific skills that the format requires. To adequately identify students with greater than typical reasoning ability, educators need multiple measures of a student's ability to reason that sample the most common domains of reasoning—in particular, verbal, quantitative, figural, and/or spatial reasoning. Tests with multiple formats (i.e., multidimensional tests) can provide not only better measures of the overall construct that educators seek to measure (by averaging out test-specific variance), but also potentially more nuanced evidence about students' reasoning abilities. A multidimensional ability test often provides battery-level scores so that students' specific abilities in verbal, quantitative, figural, or spatial domains can be contrasted. VanTassel-Baska et al. (2007) demonstrated the importance of battery scores for identifying students from low-income backgrounds. These researchers found that these students were much more likely to have a narrow area of cognitive strength (sometimes in figural domains) than to have uniformly high ability across all of the domains of the tests they studied. In a 3-year follow-up, these students' achievement scores were highest in their area of strength. Interpreting differences in battery performance is discussed in a later section on "uneven" ability profiles.

Nonverbal Tests and Students From Low-Income Backgrounds

One widespread misconception in the field of gifted identification is that nonverbal reasoning is its own form of cognitive ability and will increase the diversity of students identified, including those from low-income households. In fact, *nonverbal* describes the administration format, and most measures that are called "nonverbal reasoning" are better labeled "figural reasoning" with matrices (a single-question format). They are, in fact, measures of general or fluid reasoning ability that use figures and patterns to tap into those reasoning processes along with some portion of figure-specific reasoning ability. Likewise, verbal and quantitative formats measure general/fluid reasoning plus some proportion of task-specific reasoning skills. In the case of these formats, however, these specific skills, which are critical to education, are related to verbal and quantitative content. Figural reasoning formats measure a specific capacity to reason with figures and patterns that is not relevant to most forms of teaching and learning. Outside of geometry, the specific ability to reason with shapes is not relevant. In contrast, verbal and quantitative formats both measure the broad abstract ability plus an educationally relevant specific ability. This is what makes them better and more relevant measures of academic aptitude compared to "nonverbal" (really figural) tests.

Beyond this narrow definition of nonverbal testing, a wide spectrum of nonverbal question formats measure skills beyond figural reasoning. For example, CogAT Forms 7 and 8 include measures of verbal and quantitative reasoning that are "nonverbal" formats but do not measure figural reasoning skills.

Figure 4.2

Verbal Analogies Picture-Based Item Format

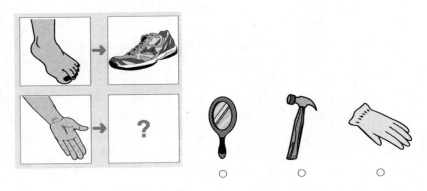

Note. This item format measures analogical reasoning with verbal concepts while not requiring the student to overtly use language (i.e., nonverbal). From *Cognitive Abilities Test* by D. F. Lohman and J. Lakin. Copyright© 2012 by Riverside Assessments, LLC. All rights reserved. Used by permission of the publisher.

Figure 4.2 shows an item format that measures analogical reasoning with verbal concepts while not requiring the student to overtly use language. Figure 4.3 shows an item format that measures the ability to recognize quantitative patterns in a nonverbal format.

However, even ignoring the practical issue of using figural reasoning to identify gifted students, nonverbal tests often do not yield substantially smaller differences in ability across socioeconomic groups when used in practice (Lohman, Korb, & Lakin, 2008). Unfortunately, there is more anecdotal than empirical evidence for this claim. Many research studies explore nonverbal measures in gifted identification but fail to provide comparison data for high-income students (e.g., Kaya et al., 2017), confound informal assessment approaches with their nonverbal measures (e.g., VanTassel-Baska et al., 2007), or do not contrast the differences found for nonverbal tests to differences for other measures of ability (e.g., Carman & Taylor, 2010). To show that nonverbal tests identify greater proportions of underrepresented groups requires researchers to show that they do not also identify vastly more students from well-represented groups, as Lohman, Korb, and Lakin (2008) found. The limited evidence available suggests that nonverbal tests will identify a larger num-

Figure 4.3

Number Series Picture-Based Item Format

ber of students from underrepresented groups, but also identify a larger number of overrepresented groups. Therefore, their percent representation will stay the same or even decrease because these tests tend to overidentify all students.

Spatial reasoning and noncognitive skills may be a more fruitful path to assessments that increase representation.[1] In a paper I wrote with a colleague (Wai & Lakin, 2018), we analyzed a large number of achievement and ability score gaps by socioeconomic status (among other demographic groups). Not surprisingly, we found that a measure of abstract reasoning (using figural matrices) yielded similar mean differences as measures of English and math achievement (differences around 0.5 SD). Intriguingly, differences in spatial reasoning were smaller (around 0.3 SD). Further, measures of leadership and artistic interest showed the smallest group differences (less than 0.1 SD). Although such noncognitive or personality measures would not be reliable to identify talents on their own, and their alignment to academic programming may be weak, this finding does suggest that ratings of student characteristics (from a teacher or the student themselves) may be valuable for identifying talents among students from low-income backgrounds. The next section addresses these types of measures.

---

1 Although figural reasoning and spatial reasoning are often confounded, they are distinct skills, and figural formats are often poor measures of spatial ability.

Measures of Interest and Persistence: Identifying High-Quality Rating Systems and Checklists

The 2019 Pre-K–Grade 12 Gifted Programming Standards (National Association for Gifted Children, 2019), particularly Standard 2, clearly state that multiple measures are needed to make decisions about the educational needs of students. Rating scales of academic ability and potential can be an important source of information alongside ability tests but can never replace the more objective information that an appropriately administered test can provide. More importantly, ratings can provide insight into other predictors of academic success, including interest, academic motivation, and persistence that are not easily assessed with traditional standardized tests. This section reviews some important features of effective rating scales.

The most important feature of a rating scale is the alignment between the constructs a scale measures and the characteristics that are of most interest to the school or program. Many teacher rating scales collect data on a large number of student characteristics. For example, the *Scales for Rating the Behavioral Characteristics of Superior Students* (SRBCSS; Renzulli et al., 2010) include separate scales for more than a dozen characteristics, including creativity, artistic skills, math skills, and expressive communication. Scores on these various characteristics should only be included in the decision process if these characteristics are relevant to success in the program.

Another important feature of a rating scale is the use of "behaviorally anchored" ratings rather than ratings of holistic, general, or vaguely defined characteristics. Holistic ratings directly ask the teacher or parent to rate the students in terms of abstract abilities that are complex in nature. Consider this example of a holistic item, similar to one on an available rating scale: "Student demonstrates high verbal ability." This rating item presumes that the rater holds an accurate, current, and unbiased understanding of high verbal ability and can weigh the relevant aspects appropriately. That's a serious challenge.

In contrast, behaviorally anchored ratings scales are designed to provide concrete examples of observable behaviors and characteristics that are indicative of an underlying and complex concept. These behaviors (when the instrument is well designed and based on current theory and research) reflect the complete construct of interest and reflect different levels of competency or skill (Klieger et al., 2018). Consider this example of a short rating scale of the same construct of verbal ability inspired by existing instruments:

1. Student learns new words quickly.
2. Student uses rich and inventive vocabulary.
3. Student can explain ideas in different ways to convey meaning to peers.
4. Student expresses ideas creatively and in a variety of registers and styles.

These varying examples of high verbal ability can be combined to give an overall rating of students' verbal ability that is much more reliable and accurate than the holistic rating in the previous example. When designed for the purpose of culturally relevant identification, the behaviorally anchored rating scale embeds accurate and culturally responsive definitions of verbal ability without expecting all students to demonstrate verbal strength in the same way.

Behaviorally anchored scales are usually much longer than holistic scales. The tradeoff in using longer scales is efficiency and time, but the benefits to equity and validity vastly outweigh that cost. That said, be sure that the raters completing the scale have enough experience with the student to reflect on the many specific behaviors and answer the questions accurately. Training on implicit bias and on culturally responsive education will also help teachers to provide accurate ratings and overcome internalized beliefs about students from low-income backgrounds.

Identification Strategies to Increase Representation

Choosing high-quality assessments is necessary but not sufficient to increase the representation of students from low-income backgrounds in gifted and talented programming. Universal screening is one strategy for identification that has consistently been shown to increase the representativeness of gifted and talented programs compared to referral-led screening. The specifics of this process and some suggestions for setting it up are presented in the section that follows. An additional, meaningful change schools can make to identify more students from low-income backgrounds is modifying how they use test results to make inferences about students' ability and potential for academic success. This involves creating multiple normative comparison groups to understand student performance, rather than just comparing a student score to a single, national normative sample. A later section will review the particular nuances of making these inferences for students from low-income backgrounds.

Figure 4.4

Contrasting Universal Screening and Referral Processes

Referral-led

Teacher or parent referral (including rating scales) initiates process

Universal Screening

Assessment process with all students initiates process

Holistic assessment and identification process

Universal Screening

Universal screening is an identification practice in which all students in a targeted grade are administered an initial screening instrument. Typically, scoring at or above a predetermined cut score on the screener leads to further consideration for placement and/or services in a gifted and talented program, usually involving at least one additional placement or confirmation assessment. See Figure 4.4. The alternative to universal screening is often a referral process in which parents or teachers recommend students for screening (or testing) for gifted services.

Research has suggested that teacher or parent referral creates more inequity in identification and provides an avenue for implicit bias and limiting beliefs about gifted children that influence the diversity of identified students (Olszewski-Kubilius & Corwith, 2018). In contrast, universal screening clearly improves the equitable representation of students in gifted programming, including students from low-income backgrounds (Card & Giuliano, 2015; Olszewski-Kubilius & Corwith, 2018; Plucker & Peters, 2018).

Because universal screening involves all students in a grade level, efficiency in administering an assessment and interpreting results is naturally a priority, which often means using a cut score on the screener to qualify for additional consideration. Based on what is known about measurement error and the cor-

Figure 4.5

Combination Scores Suggested in Lohman (2012)

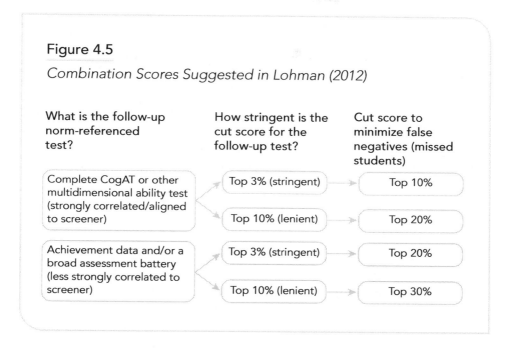

What is the follow-up norm-referenced test?	How stringent is the cut score for the follow-up test?	Cut score to minimize false negatives (missed students)
Complete CogAT or other multidimensional ability test (strongly correlated/aligned to screener)	Top 3% (stringent)	Top 10%
	Top 10% (lenient)	Top 20%
Achievement data and/or a broad assessment battery (less strongly correlated to screener)	Top 3% (stringent)	Top 20%
	Top 10% (lenient)	Top 30%

relation between two tests scores, the following are a few recommendations about selecting and using these screeners and cut scores.

First, schools should use screeners that measure abilities and traits that are related to the ultimate placement tests or portfolio, which in turn must align with the program goals (Lakin, in press). The more highly correlated the screener and placement assessments are, the more consistent the results in terms of not missing students who would do well on the placement test or overidentifying students who do not ultimately do well on the test. Empirical evidence indicates that as long as the screening tests are correlated to the placement measures, short and relatively less reliable screeners are adequate for this initial step.

Second, schools should be generous in their cut scores for the screening test. Because no two test scores (or any assessment process) are perfectly correlated, and because educators want to include every student who could be successful in the program, educators should "cast a wide net" with the screener and include more students in the placement process than they expect will actually qualify for a particular service. Figure 4.5 suggests that highly related screener plus placement assessments might require a ratio of two students who are identified by the screener compared to every three students who will be identified by the confirmation assessment. When quite different or less correlated measures are used (including teacher rating screeners used with ability placement tests), the ratio should be four students identified by the screener to every five students expected to actually be identified.

Third, in choosing assessments, it is important to consider the alignment of the measures to the programming options that are available (Lakin, in press). If students will be placed in an advanced math course, then it is vital to select students who have adequately high math achievement. Using a screener that measures creativity or figural reasoning will not be relevant. On the other hand, if the program offers compacted or accelerated instruction in math, *potential* for high achievement is more important to assess than actual high achievement. In this case, the program might administer a quantitative reasoning assessment or engage students in performance assessments around creativity with mathematical thinking. Students' current math achievement might not even be used in placing students.

What Role Should Achievement Play? Every definition of giftedness that I have seen includes identifying students with currently exceptional performance as well as those with *potential* for exceptional performance. Identifying current exceptional performance should include academic achievement, but identifying potential should downplay the importance of current academic achievement in identification. As a result, in identifying potential among students from low-income backgrounds, educators should focus on reasoning abilities in relevant symbol systems, interests and motivation, and persistence. Achievement scores should not be the only mechanism to refer students for gifted services based on potential.

Despite this distinction, because universal screening is an expensive and time-consuming effort, many specialists ask if they can use achievement scores as their universal screener and save their resources for those who pass an initial cut. The relative impact of using achievement as a screener has not been studied extensively. It seems likely that it would be more effective and equitable than a referral-led process (all else being equal) but will most probably *not* achieve the equity that would occur from using an ability test or performance assessment for universal screening. Research on achievement gaps for socioeconomic groups (Reardon, 2013), including those on excellence gaps (e.g., Plucker & Peters, 2018), demonstrated that socioeconomic status is associated with substantial gaps on achievement tests, starting at kindergarten and expanding overtime. Because ability tests are *less* tied to the curriculum, they tend to demonstrate smaller gaps and, therefore, would likely lead to smaller disparities in the number of underrepresented groups passing the screening phase (e.g., Wai & Lakin, 2018). More research is needed, but, based on the current evidence, it seems worth the cost of administering a universal screener or at least not *only* using achievement as a screening tool.

Interpreting Scores With Appropriate Norm Groups

A simple definition of high cognitive ability is that the student learns in a few trials what it takes other students many trials to learn. With ability tests, test users make inferences about this speed of learning or readiness to learn by comparing one student's performance to a large sample of other students. In testing speak, scores on ability tests are norm-referenced, meaning that educators can only decide if a score is high or low by comparing it to a reference group (a normative sample) of students who are similar to the student being assessed. Traditionally, educators make norm-referenced interpretations about ability by comparing a child's score to other children of the same age (down to the quarter-year or even month, depending on the test). The student who can demonstrate the most sophisticated or precise reasoning for their age is assumed to have the highest cognitive ability and readiness for academic challenge.

Comparisons based on age assume that society is homogeneous in terms of culture, opportunity, home language, and educational opportunity. In such a society, age would be a good proxy for exposure to culture information—also termed *opportunity to learn* (OTL)—and these inferences about efficiency of learning would be easily made. However, because the U.S. is heterogeneous with respect to these factors, age is not a good proxy for OTL for many students. A single set of national norms misleads those using test scores, as it sets the majority cultural and language backgrounds as the reference point for how growth in abilities should occur (Hessels & Hamers, 1993; Kvist & Gustafsson, 2008). Hessels and Hamers (1993) contended that:

> The acculturation patterns of minority group children and children from lower socioeconomic homes may be different from the patterns of children who are included in a test's standardization sample. The usefulness of a test decreases when a child's acculturation patterns differ significantly from the patterns that are normally provided for most other children. (p. 288)

The importance of OTL applies not only to the content, but also to ways of thinking and solution strategies that come from the culture through educational and child-rearing practices. To make inferences about ability, educators must compare a student to other students with similar opportunities to learn the reasoning skills tested. This allows educators to more accurately gauge whether the student can do more or learn faster than others. The implication is not that different tests are needed for different student populations, but that cultural background and OTL should be considered when trying to make inferences about individual scores on a test.

How do educators compare a student's score to an appropriate reference group? Several strategies have been offered, including subgroup norms and local norms.

Subgroup Norms. Subgroup norms are norm-referenced scale scores, such as percentile ranks (PR) that express relative rank, that are calculated for students based on demographic groupings. For example, the Wechsler Intelligence Scale for Children (WISC-IV and WISC-V) Spanish forms offer special norms based on variables such as parent education or years in U.S. schools (Braden & Iribarren, 2007). These special norms help contextualize test scores not only with the national standardization sample, but also with reference to samples of students who have roughly equal time in the U.S. or whose parents have similar educational levels. Students receive PRs based on the national norm as well as the special norm groups. Subgroup norms are useful because they help educators compare student performance to that of more similar students, making the inference about quickness of learning more valid and less biased by OTL.

Local Norms. Local norms are norm-referenced scale scores (again, PRs and similar scores) based on a small population of students. Local norms are most often seen at the school district or school building, where a student's scores are compared to those of other local students, yielding a local age-based PR. Unlike subgroup norms, there is no effort to identify students with different demographic backgrounds or types of experience. Only age and school district or building are taken into account in these norms.

Local norms can help identify students with the greatest instructional needs when school buildings tend to have average test scores that are much higher or lower than the national average (Lakin, in press). Using national norms, high-performing schools tend to have "too many gifted students" to reasonably serve. Low-performing schools often find they have "no gifted students" because their top performers do not have high scores compared to the national norms.

Many high-poverty schools fall into the misconception that they have "no gifted students" because the OTL of their students leads to underestimation of their ability based on national norms (e.g., their age PRs will be in the 80–90 PR range and not the top 95+). However, the standard curriculum in every school is targeted toward the average student in the classroom. For the student in a low-performing school with high ability relative to their peers, the standard curriculum in their school is inappropriate because it serves a population that is below average in achievement. These students will be bored in the regular classroom and have talents that can be developed better by accelerated instruction or instruction that is differentiated from the standard curriculum.

In these cases, local norms will better inform gifted education placement than national norms.

Occasionally educators and researchers will propose local norms as a strategy for increasing the diversity of students selected for gifted services. When school buildings or districts are relatively homogeneous in terms of poverty levels, this may be the case. However, in heterogeneous systems, group differences based on race or socioeconomic status in the national norms will be replicated between the same groups in the local norms. When this happens, gifted programs within the school will tend to segregate the students from high-income households from most of the students from low-income households, as Yaluma and Tyner (2018) observed.

Local norms only promote diversity when there is marked demographic differences across school buildings that lead to substantially different ability score distributions across schools. In many large cities, some school buildings have higher rates of poverty than others. In these contexts, estimating local norms within school buildings will allow each school to identify students most likely to benefit from specialized services within that student population. This will avoid the situation of some school buildings having "no gifted students" when in reality every school has students who require more challenge and accelerated learning than their peers. It will also avoid cases in which many students are identified for services in high-performing schools who would be adequately served in the regular classroom curriculum in their school.

Calculating Local or Subgroup Norms. Most test companies will provide local norms to a customer on request or through the standard reporting. Subgroup norms are not often available but easily calculated if an educator has a large database of student scores and basic familiarity with Excel. In either case, it is optimal to have multiple years of data to create a rich reference pool, but even relatively small samples of students (especially from universal screenings) can yield valuable information about the relative academic needs of specific students or a school building.

Figure 4.6 shows a simple analysis of a school's English language learner (ELL) population in which the educator used local rank order of scores to identify ELLs with strong verbal ability. Note that the verbal scores from CogAT were used. Assuming that the school used the primary levels of the test, which include picture-based items, or that the ELLs had some English proficiency, this is a valid test use (Lakin, 2012). The key is comparing ELLs to other students with similar OTL for English. Therefore, the scores reflect students' acquisition speed and ability to use language effectively. That is a very useful information to have for ELLs.

Figure 4.6

Contrasting Student Performance Using Subgroup Norms

These are the students who can reason best given the same opportunity to learn.

Student	Raw Score of 48	Agr PR	OTL Group PR
Caroline	42	84	100
Sofia	41	79	95
Camilla	41	79	95
Santiago	38	75	95
Sebastián	37	70	91
Sara	37	70	91
Matías	35	65	88
Nicolás	33	62	86
Daniel	31	50	84
Martina	29	45	80
Lucas	24	42	74
Samantha	17	40	72

Figure 4.6 shows the rank order of English language learners by their scores. Looking at the verbal scale score and thinking about the distribution of all students in the national normative sample (where the mean is 100 and the *SD* is 16), these are not very impressive national scores in and of themselves. However, the student scoring a 100 or 95 national PR is actually very impressive given that they have limited English exposure. If an educator were picking out students with the most potential for learning quickly and being academically advanced in the future, these students should be among those selected. The exact local PR estimate is not important.

If the school has a larger sample and wants to be more precise, Excel or other spreadsheet software can be used to calculate exact percentiles. A school that consistently administers the same test year after year can also build a longitudinal dataset so that local norms are consistent over time and not dependent on the students tested in any given year.

Conclusions About Subgroup and Local Norms. Subgroup and local norms offer advantages over national norms in making appropriate inferences about students' abilities. By comparing students to other students with similar backgrounds or opportunity to learn, educators are able to make more accurate interpretations about students' abilities. This increased usefulness does come at a cost. Creating a good normative sample is expensive and time-intensive, and the more subgroups that educators try to define, the larger the cost. Fortunately, it is not necessary to create finely grained norms to reap the benefits of multiple norm comparisons (Lohman, 2012).

The subgroup norms on the WISC-IV or WISC-V Spanish divide students into just 3–4 levels of each variable (parental education, years in the U.S.), and yet they go a long way toward contextualizing students' performance and helping test users evaluate the quality of students' cognitive skills by comparing them to those of students with similar backgrounds. Although locally developed norms will not have the same psychometric quality that national norms offer (such as consistency year to year), the norms are still valuable in understanding student performance and are useful in making low-stakes decisions. The primary advantage of subgroup or local norms is that they provide multiple normative perspectives on a child's performance on each of the test batteries. These can be used holistically to make decisions about instructional need.

Interpreting Full Scale Ability Scores Versus Uneven Subtest Performance

As discussed earlier, multidimensional measures of cognitive ability provide the best measures of general ability compared to single-format measures of ability. An additional benefit of measuring ability along multiple dimensions is that educators can use the relative performance of students across the dimensions to learn more about student potential for learning and how to differentiate instruction to their strengths and weaknesses.

Not all differences in performance across dimensions are meaningful. Measurement error (the random variations in test performance due to time, test content, and other impacts) alone will result in test scores that vary for an individual over administrations even when the exact same test is administered. Therefore, because of measurement error, not all differences in percentile rank or scale score are important differences.

Tests like CogAT use measurement error in calculating "profiles" that provide information about students' relative performance across the three CogAT batteries (verbal, quantitative, and figural). If profiles are not provided for a specific test program, educators can use the standard error of measurement

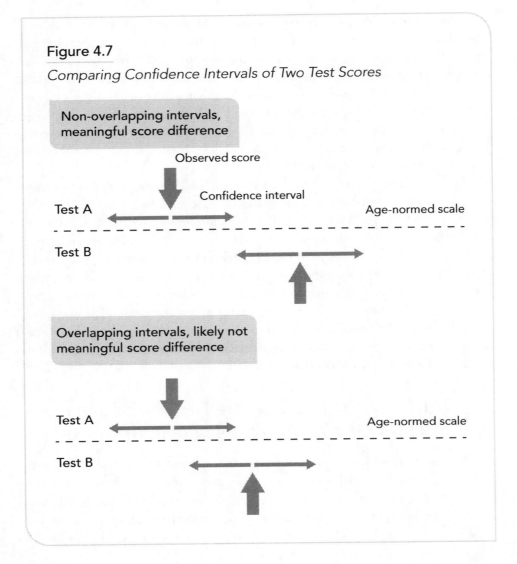

Figure 4.7

Comparing Confidence Intervals of Two Test Scores

Non-overlapping intervals, meaningful score difference

Observed score

Confidence interval

Test A   Age-normed scale

Test B

Overlapping intervals, likely not meaningful score difference

Test A   Age-normed scale

Test B

(SEM) provided by a test's technical manual to make interpretations about whether two scores are meaningfully different from each other. The SEM provides a range that tells educators what scores a student would likely receive if they took the test again under similar conditions. Educators can use the SEM to calculate the confidence interval of each score, which is the observed score plus or minus one SEM (a 68% confidence interval). These ranges of plausible scores can then be used to compare performance (see Figure 4.7). If a student's confidence intervals do *not* overlap, then one can assume the difference in scores is not due solely to measurement error and may be due to meaningful differences in performance, which warrants further exploration.

Using Profile Scores

With the profile scores, CogAT score reports include not only a general reasoning score (i.e., reasoning skills *across domains*), but also verbal, quantitative, and nonverbal battery reasoning scores. As a result, educators can use the contrasts between students' three battery scores to learn more about their current strengths and how to adapt instruction to improve areas of weakness.

Students with relatively even performance across batteries do not have particular strengths or weaknesses that need to be considered in the classroom. Their academic aptitude is captured well by their composite score (an average of the three battery scores). For these students, recommendations can be made based on overall ability. Table 4.1 provides example descriptions and instructional strategies for students with different levels of general reasoning abilities categorized by stanine scores. The need for autonomy versus scaffolding varies with the level of overall reasoning ability. Students with weaker reasoning skills will benefit from explicit coaching on learning strategies and how to tackle abstract problem solving. For students with stronger reasoning skills, autonomy and motivation to persist in the face of challenges are critical. Beyond the even profile of abilities, teachers may also notice other types of strengths that they can build on, including greater interest in reading, math, or science content or a student's creativity in a domain.

Other students will have relatively high or low performance in one or more domains when a multidimensional battery or multiple assessments are administered (Lohman, Gambrell, & Lakin, 2008). When considering why scores are quite different, first consider or investigate the testing conditions on each day. Was the student given their necessary accommodations on both testing occasions? Were both tests administered under standardized procedures? Were there any interruptions or issues for the student on one of the test days? Is there a known learning difference or English proficiency concern that may affect just one of the two tests? Basically, before reading anything into differences, rule out obvious causes that might suppress one or the other score. If there is no ready explanation for the difference, then consider that the difference is meaningful.

When students have meaningful differences in their scores, they will need some degree of differentiated instruction in various domains depending on their score pattern. When differences are extreme, students may require single-subject acceleration or may even need to be referred for testing for specific learning disabilities. There is limited research on what types of profiles might be expected for students from low-SES backgrounds. However, these students may especially benefit from differentiation. Differences in opportunity to learn may differentially affect some areas of performance, which would be reflected

Table 4.1

Differentiating Instruction to Overall Ability

Median Stanine	Example Characteristics	Example Scaffolding Strategies	Example Adaptations to Build on Strengths
Below-average reasoning abilities (Stanines 1–3)	› Difficulty learning abstract concepts. › Minimal or ineffective strategies for learning and remembering (tend to rely on trial and error).	› Require very specific directions for a new task. › Provide more structure, coaching, support.	Look for strengths in terms of specific interests and achievements. Even more than other students, those who are behind their peers in reasoning abilities often *learn more and sustain their efforts longer if the teacher discovers and builds on their interests.*
Average reasoning abilities (Stanines 4–6)	› Likely to use only previously learned methods when faced with new tasks. › Difficulty transferring knowledge/ skills.	› Require some structure, coaching, and support, but also benefit from some independence.	Help them develop the habit of analyzing new tasks to *detect relationships with previously learned tasks.* Do this by *modeling* the process for them.
Above-average reasoning abilities (Stanines 7–8)	› Ability to learn relatively quickly. › Good memory, effective learning strategies.	› Instruction that helps them plan the use of different strategies in different contexts. › Working with more-able peers, particularly on difficult problems or learning tasks.	Recognize that these students generally profit most when allowed to discover relationships themselves. Guided discovery methods work better than more structured teaching methods.

Table 4.1, continued

Median Stanine	Example Characteristics	Example Scaffolding Strategies	Example Adaptations to Build on Strengths
Very high reasoning abilities (Stanine 9)	› Preference for discovery learning rather than highly structured learning environments (not necessarily solitary environments).	› Learning to persist in the face of difficulty can also be an important affective or motivational issue for very able students. Working with an older and more experienced student (or adult) can be especially beneficial.	Carefully select *challenging instructional materials, special projects, or other enrichment activities.*

Note. Adapted from *CogAT: Forms 7 & 8: Teacher's Guide for Adapting Instruction* (pp. 22–27), by D. F. Lohman and J. M. Lakin, 2017, Riverside Insights. Copyright 2017 by Riverside Insights.

in uneven score profiles (VanTassel-Baska et al., 2007). Differentiation can be based on their strengths to help them build areas of weakness.

Table 4.2 shows some of the adaptations that could be made in the regular classroom to respond to students' relative strengths and weaknesses on the three CogAT batteries. These strategies may sound like they are based on learning style theory (Pashler et al., 2009). However, differentiating instruction based on ability profiles is focused on building student skills, not focusing instruction exclusively on certain modalities or allowing students to develop their strengths in one area to the exclusion of others. For example, a student with a strength in figural reasoning and a weakness in verbal reasoning should not be discouraged from writing an essay in social studies. Rather, they should be encouraged to use timelines to diagram historical events, which will then scaffold their writing. Concept maps may also be valuable learning supports for these students, not because they prefer visual learning, but because they have

Table 4.2
Build From Relative Strengths and Shore Up Weaknesses

	Building From a Relative Strength: Example Adaptations	**Shoring Up Relative Weakness: Example Adaptations**
Verbal	Avoid pitfalls in math: Students with relatively strong verbal abilities often *find it easier to memorize formulas than to build more abstract conceptual systems.* These abstract systems lead to the ability to transfer mathematical knowledge to unfamiliar domains.	Acquaint students with *unfamiliar ways of conversing and writing* by providing opportunities to imitate the speaking and writing styles of individuals they admire. Drama, poetry, and storytelling are particularly useful in this regard.
Quantitative	Provide opportunities for these students to *contribute at high levels to group projects* that require math skills. Group projects provide an avenue for building better verbal and spatial reasoning abilities.	If the difficulty is a lack of experience or the presence of *anxiety*, provide greater structure, reduce or *eliminate competition, reduce time pressures*, and *allow students greater choice* in the problems they solve. Experiencing success will gradually reduce anxiety; experiencing failure will cause it to spike.
General Ability	*Encourage students to create drawings when solving problems in mathematics*, concept maps when taking notes, or mental models of a scene when reading a text.	Provide *simple drawings* that encapsulate the essential features of the visual mental model required by the problem. Then, give students time to examine the drawing and to label it or coordinate it with the text.

Note. Adapted from *CogAT: Forms 7 & 8: Teacher's Guide for Adapting Instruction* (pp. 29–39), by D. F. Lohman and J. M. Lakin, 2017, Riverside Insights. Copyright 2017 by Riverside Insights.

developed visualization skills and can use these kinds of tools to build other skills.

In addition to content, areas of weakness may be built up by appealing to student interests, such as a writing project that can be tailored to a student's interest in space exploration or world travel. Whenever a relative weakness is apparent, it is essential to maintain student motivation and engagement.

Many of the suggestions made in Table 4.2 are strategies for differentiating instruction within the regular classroom. However, relative strengths can also be addressed by specific programming options. Schools with a single program or service option are assuming that all identified students have a flat profile relative to the demands of the program. However, when assessment data suggest that students have an uneven profile (which will happen quite often among gifted students; Lohman, Gambrell, & Lakin, 2008), there needs to be some opportunity to adapt programming or to provide different types of services. Depending on a student's profile of scores, single-subject acceleration may be more appropriate than whole-grade acceleration. Students may also need remediation if their relative weaknesses are marked.

Uneven Profiles Across Ability and Achievement

When both achievement and ability data are collected, this has its own implications for programming. Although concepts like underachievement are disputed in the research literature, differences in ability and achievement can have instructional implications. Figure 4.8 shows four possible outcomes to comparing one achievement to one ability score. Quadrants 1 and 4 correspond to even profiles, while Quadrants 2 and 3 are uneven.

Students in Quadrant 2 would have been called "underachievers" in past generations, but that term has some baggage attached to it (including blaming the student) that may not be appropriate. The most important implication of the score difference in this quadrant is that students may be ready for acceleration or extra challenge to raise their achievement level. Placement or gifted services should take into account the students' prior educational experiences in terms of content learning: Have they been exposed to high-quality instruction?[2] Have they been challenged enough or given the opportunity to learn the content? Students who have not been previously identified as high ability may not have received the attention and differentiation appropriate to their ability. If so, educators can expect that appropriate education, perhaps including curriculum compacting or remediation, will lead to rapid learning.

Another possible explanation for the score difference in Quadrant 2 is weak motivation for learning or a lack of confidence or interest. Perhaps building up students' motivation or interest in a topic will lead to greater learning. Getting to know the students and what motivates them will provide ideas for how to reignite their passion for learning. Another possibility: Have the students experienced learning difficulties that they were not prepared to overcome? These

2 ELLs also sometimes come to their U.S. school without continuous formal education. Consider whether they may have missed core content in previous grade levels, because that can also explain relatively low achievement scores.

101

Figure 4.8

Comparing Achievement Scores to Ability Scores

Ability Scores	Achievement Scores	
	Above Average	**Below Average**
Above Average	**1 (even profile)** Typically identified as gifted.	**2 (uneven profile)** May have behavioral issues, specific learning disabilities, low motivation, or otherwise undeveloped or unrecognized talent. *Students from low-income backgrounds are likely to appear here.*
Below Average	**3 (uneven profile)** Could be a "teacher pleaser," highly motivated in the classroom, or performing at their maximum already.	**4 (even profile)** May not require specialized services.

student may benefit from metacognitive strategies that help them monitor and improve their learning.

Quadrant 3 includes students who perform better on the achievement test than expected based on their ability. Because logically it is not possible to achieve above one's capability, it can be assumed that another factor influenced their ability score or the achievement score beyond what is typical for students of their age. There are many factors that can influence achievement scores. These students may be receiving extra support for their learning outside of the formal school experience. They may be exceptionally motivated or teacher-pleasing. Clearly, these students are using personal resources and skills (such as motivation or study strategies) to perform better than expected based only on information about their ability (certainly just one piece of what each learner brings to school). As long as the students really have mastered the skills and content, and did not achieve high scores simply due to narrow test prep, their performance is commendable, although they may not benefit from any additional challenge.

A factor that can affect ability tests more than achievement tests is the novelty of ability test questions. One factor I have heard from parents and teachers is that some students have a low tolerance for ambiguity or may be anxious around novel and creative problem solving. This can suppress ability scores. To overcome these challenges, students can work on managing test anxiety or be offered more practice opportunities to reduce the pressure on the testing event.

Making Sense of Scores: Talent Scout

All of the methods and topics in this chapter provide additional data or perspectives on student ability. They actually complicate identification procedures are require a level of comfort and flexibility with test data.

Highly effective directors of gifted and talented programs often say that their task and the task they give to teachers is that of a "talent scout" (a metaphor possibly originated by Renzulli, 1995). In athletic programs, talent scouts do a number of activities that help them to identify potential and match athletes to sports programs. First, they look for a variety of skill sets. No team sport requires all players to have the exact same skills. Scouts are looking for different types of potential. Second, scouts observe the players in authentic experiences and gather a variety of information to understand the strengths and weaknesses of a player. They do not rely exclusively on player statistics. Third, scouts may recognize when a player has potential that needs to be developed in specific ways. They may make recommendations to the future team of how to develop that player's strengths. All of these tasks translate to identifying and serving students from all backgrounds through gifted and talented services.

First, teachers must be empowered with a strong understanding of what it means to be gifted and to have exceptional academic needs (Horn, 2015). This often includes dispelling myths of precociousness that are overly focused on purely academic giftedness and middle-class conceptions of exceptional ability and how it should be expressed. Empowered teachers recognize how talents may manifest in different students and realize that all students have a range of strengths and weaknesses. Teachers should also be trained to have a better understanding of what potential looks like versus current high levels of achievement. With this training, teachers work in teams with the program director to scour the available data and compile profiles of each student and their academic potential and current instructional needs.

Second, teachers need to gather a range of valid information about student potential. This includes using multiple measures of potential, gathering authentic school products, and providing students with performance assessments as opportunities to demonstrate need for additional challenge.

Finally, schools must provide a range of services so that the variety of student needs are met by one or more services. Callahan (2005) noted that students should not be identified for "the" gifted program, but instead be identified for one of many services. This allows schools to serve students with different constellations of abilities and develop a wider range of talents, including those that are underdeveloped at present.

Teachers who are empowered as talent scouts create more development opportunities, even outside of the formal gifted programming. Equity is better addressed when educators dispel the notion that there is a set number of seats available for gifted programming and one type of academic need. This approach requires administrative support, but many schools are able to serve both a traditional gifted pool as well as a talent development pool of students who may show marked potential but need additional opportunities for academic enrichment and to learn higher order thinking skills before they are ready for more traditional gifted programs (Wells, 2020). Callahan (2005) suggested that programs be designed to appeal to student interest, provide challenging and engaging tasks, and allow students to develop and practice high-level critical thinking skills and exercise creativity. The regular classroom environment is vital to serving the talent pool. Renzulli (1995) defined the talent scout activities as including "a broad range of . . . enrichment experiences for all students" to observe "the many and varied ways that students respond to these experiences as stepping stones" (p. 76).

A particular challenge for many identification systems is recognizing nontraditional manifestations of traditional areas of talent. Partly this is reflected in the push toward nonverbal tests, assuming that students from low-SES backgrounds and other underidentified groups will not demonstrate traditional academic talent. In fact, there is a great deal of verbal and quantitative talent that is demonstrated by all student subgroups, but those talents may look different from those in middle-class, White students. For example, among ELLs, exceptional verbal ability will not sound like perfect English proficiency. Instead it may look like learning words quickly, being very adept at recognizing cognates with the home language, being flexible and creative with learning strategies, and making sense of incomplete verbal information (Gubbins et al., 2018). In some regions, students from low-income backgrounds may similarly show variations of language from their school peers, and their talents might be recognized by highly effective code switching and a fluency with using different types of language to accomplish various academic and social tasks. Teachers who act as talent scouts will learn to recognize these manifestations of academic need across many types of academic abilities (from verbal reasoning to artistic skills) with time and attention.

Conclusion

Students arrive at the first day of kindergarten with great variation in their preparation for school. Some of that variation is due to family income levels and the opportunities wealth can provide, including high-quality prekindergarten programs, or differences in home life, such as hearing more vocabulary words. This might suggest to some that equity could be achieved by moving gifted and talented identification later in the grades when schools have had a chance to equalize some of those gaps. However, those differences in achievement tend to grow over time (Reardon, 2013). Thus, paradoxically, earlier grades may be the most important opportunity to identify students who come from low-socioeconomic backgrounds.

The best strategy for equitably identifying students from various SES backgrounds is to use universal screening with multidimensional ability tests. If the required resources cannot be found, achievement scores can be used if special care is taken to identify students from low-income backgrounds who have potential. Teacher rating scales can also be used if teachers are trained in implicit bias and understanding academic talent. The scales themselves should be culturally responsive and behaviorally anchored measures.

Equity can also be supported in test interpretation when local or subgroup norms are used in addition to national norms to provide multiple vantage points in understanding how well a student performs relative to their opportunity to learn the content or cognitive strategy. When multiple indicators are available, consider profiles of performance and how those differences can inform instruction, from program placement to differentiation in every classroom.

Finally, teachers must be empowered to act as talent scouts for their students. Those involved in gifted and talented identification must be comfortable enough interpreting test results that they can use a wide range of information, including multiple norm reference points, to make holistic decisions about students' academic needs. Equity can be achieved through the expertise of the teacher and recognition of culturally diverse ways of manifesting talent. Flexibility with interpreting test scores, collecting diverse assessment information, and a broadened conception of potential are the keys to identification to promote the academic development of students from low-income backgrounds.

References

Braden, J. P., & Iribarren, J. A. (2007). Test Review: Wechsler, D. (2005). Wechsler Intelligence Scale for Children Spanish. San Antonio, TX: Harcourt Assessment. *Journal of Psychoeducational Assessment, 25*(3), 292–299. https://doi.org/10.1177/0734282907302955

Callahan, C. M. (2005). Identifying gifted students from underrepresented populations. *Theory Into Practice, 44*(2), 98–104. https://doi.org/10.1207/s15430421tip4402_4

Card, D., & Giuliano, L. (2015). *Can universal screening increase the representation of low income and minority students in gifted education?* (No. 21519). https://www.nber.org/papers/w21519

Carman, C. A., & Taylor, D. K. (2010). Socioeconomic status effects on using the Naglieri Nonverbal Ability Test (NNAT) to identify the gifted/talented. *Gifted Child Quarterly, 54*(2), 75–84. https://doi.org/10.1177/0016986209355976

Carroll, J. B. (1993). *Human cognitive abilities: A survey of factor-analytic studies.* Cambridge University Press.

Gubbins, E. J., Siegle, D., Hamilton, R., Peters, P., Carpenter, A. Y., O'Rourke, P., Puryear, J., McCoach, D. B., Long, D., Bloomfield, E., Cross, K., Mun, R. U., Amspaugh, C., Langley, S. D., Roberts, A., & Estepar-Garcia, W. (2018, June). *Exploratory study on the identification of English learners for gifted and talented programs.* University of Connecticut, National Center for Research on Gifted Education. https://ncrge.uconn.edu/wp-content/uploads/sites/982/2020/06/NCRGE-EL-Report-1.pdf

Hessels, M. G. P., & Hamers, J. H. M. (1993). The learning potential test for ethnic minorities. In J. H. M. Hamers, K. Sijtsma, & A. J. J. M. Ruijssenaars (Eds.), *Learning potential assessment: Theoretical, methodological and practical issues* (pp. 285–313). Swets & Zeitlinger.

Horn, C. V. (2015). Young Scholars: A talent development model for finding and nurturing potential in underserved populations. *Gifted Child Today, 38*(1), 19–31. https://doi.org/10.1177/1076217514556532

Kaya, F., Stough, L. M., & Juntune, J. (2017). Verbal and nonverbal intelligence scores within the context of poverty. *Gifted Education International, 33*(3), 257–272. https://doi.org/10.1177/0261429416640332

Keith, T. Z., & Reynolds, M. R. (2010). Cattell-Horn-Carroll abilities and cognitive tests: What we've learned from 20 years of research. *Psychology in the Schools, 47*(7), 635–650. https://doi.org/10.1002/pits.20496

Klieger, D. M., Kell, H. J., Rikoon, S., Burkander, K. N., Bochenek, J. L., & Shore, J. R. (2018). Development of the behaviorally anchored rating scales for the skills demonstration and progression guide. *ETS Research Report Series, 2018*(1), 1–36. https://doi.org/10.1002/ets2.12210

Kvist, A.V., & Gustafsson, J.-E. (2008). The relation between fluid intelligence and the general factor as a function of cultural background: A test of Cattell's investment theory. *Intelligence, 36*(5), 422–436. https://doi.org/10.1016/j.intell.2007.08.004

Lakin, J. M. (2012). Assessing the cognitive abilities of culturally and linguistically diverse students: Predictive validity of verbal, quantitative, and nonverbal batteries. *Psychology in the Schools, 49*(8), 756–768.

Lakin, J. M. (in press). Service-driven identification practices: Why the services you offer must drive identification decisions. *Teaching for High Potential.*

Lohman, D. F. (2005). The role of nonverbal ability tests in identifying academically gifted students: An aptitude perspective. *Gifted Child Quarterly, 49*(2), 111–138. https://doi.org/10.1177/001698620504900203

Lohman, D. F. (2012). Decision strategies. In S. L. Hunsaker (Ed.), *Identification: The theory and practice of identifying students for gifted and talented education services* (pp. 219–248). Prufrock Press.

Lohman, D. F., Gambrell, J., & Lakin, J. M. (2008). The commonality of extreme discrepancies in the ability profiles of academically gifted students. *Psychology Science, 50*(2), 269–282.

Lohman, D. F., Korb, K. A., & Lakin, J. M. (2008). Identifying academically gifted English-language learners using nonverbal tests: A comparison of the Raven, NNAT, and CogAT. *Gifted Child Quarterly, 52*(4), 275–296. https://doi.org/10.1177/0016 986208321808

Lohman, D. F., & Lakin, J. M. (2017). *CogAT: Forms 7 & 8: Teacher's guide for adapting instruction.* Houghton Mifflin Harcourt.

National Association for Gifted Children. (2019). *2019 Pre-K–Grade 12 Gifted Programming Standards.* https://www.nagc.org/sites/default/files/standards/Intro%2020 19%20Programming%20Standards.pdf

Olszewski-Kubilius, P., & Corwith, S. (2018). Poverty, academic achievement, and giftedness: A literature review. *Gifted Child Quarterly, 62*(1), 37–55. https://doi.org/ 10.1177/0016986217738015

Pashler, H., McDaniel, M., Rohrer, D., & Bjork, R. (2009). Learning styles: Concepts and evidence. *Psychological Science in the Public Interest, 9*(3), 105–119. https://doi. org/10.1111/j.1539-6053.2009.01038.x

Plucker, J. A., & Peters, S. J. (2018). Closing poverty-based excellence gaps: Conceptual, measurement, and educational issues. *Gifted Child Quarterly, 62*(1), 56–67. https:// doi.org/10.1177/0016986217738566

Reardon, S. F. (2013). The widening income achievement gap. *Educational Leadership, 70*(8), 10–16.

Renzulli, J. S. (1995). Teachers as talent scouts. *Educational Leadership, 52*(4), 75–81.

Renzulli, J. S., Smith, L. H., White, A. J., Callahan, C. M., Hartman, R. K., Westberg, K. W., Gavin, M. K., Reis, S. M., Siegle, D., & Sytsma Reed, R. E. (2010). *Scales for Rating the Behavioral Characteristics of Superior Students: Technical and administration manual* (3rd ed.). Prufrock Press.

Schneider, W. J., & McGrew, K. S. (2012). The Cattell-Horn-Carroll model of intelligence. In D. Flanagan & P. Harrison (Eds.), *Contemporary intellectual assessment: Theories, tests, and issues* (3rd ed., pp. 99–144). Guilford.

Süß, H.-M., & Beauducel, A. (2005). Faceted models of intelligence. In O. Wilhelm & R. W. Engle (Eds.), *Handbook of measuring and understanding intelligence* (pp. 313–332). SAGE.

VanTassel-Baska, J., Feng, A. X., & Evans, B. L. (2007). Patterns of identification and performance among gifted students identified through performance tasks: A three-year analysis. *Gifted Child Quarterly, 51*(3), 218–231. https://doi.org/10.1177/0016986207302717

Wai, J., & Lakin, J. M. (2018). *Finding the missing Einsteins: Expanding the breadth of cognitive and noncognitive measures used in academic services* [Manuscript in preparation].

Wells, A. (2020). *Achieving equity in gifted programming: Dismantling barriers and tapping potential.* Prufrock Press.

Yaluma, C. B., & Tyner, A. (2018). *Is there a gifted gap? Gifted education in high-poverty schools.* Thomas B. Fordham Institute. https://fordhaminstitute.org/national/research/there-gifted-gap-gifted-education-high-poverty-schools

A Curriculum Design Model for Students From Low-Income Households

Tamra Stambaugh

Access to high-quality and rigorous curriculum and instruction can be a great equalizer for students from low-income households. Yet not all students, especially those who attend high-poverty schools, have access to the same quality resources, instructors, and advanced curriculum opportunities as those from wealthier schools—especially in states where local funding formulas are the norm (Darling-Hammond, 2001). As a result, excellence gaps between students from lower and higher income households exist, and students from low-income households are less likely to score at the advanced level on national assessments (Plucker et al., 2015). In a review of excellence gaps by state, researchers compared the number of students from low- and non-low-income backgrounds who scored advanced on NEAP achievement tests. The excellence gaps between the two groups varied by state and differed from 5 to 24 percentage points in fourth-grade mathematics, suggesting that there is much to be done to support students from low-income households in accessing high-quality curriculum and instruction and closing existing excellence gaps.

This chapter reviews the features of evidence-supported curricula derived from research projects that showed significant achievement gains for students from low-income households. More specific information will be provided about curriculum and instruction in the humanities and STEM fields, respectively, in subsequent chapters. This chapter provides a frame for thinking about curriculum design at the macro level for this special population.

Why Is a Discussion About Curriculum for Students From Low-Income Households Important?

Students from low-income households require disproportionately more support in school to compete in future career endeavors, yet are among the least likely to receive advanced curriculum (Milner, 2014), which ultimately blocks their paths toward fulfilling their talents (Cawelti, 2006; Subotnik et al., 2011). A hallmark of effective curriculum is to respond to individual learner needs and capitalize on student strengths. Studies have shown that many students from low-income households have strengths in practical intelligence and real-world problem solving (VanTassel-Baska et al., 2007) and, as such, prefer and perform well doing authentic and pragmatic activities that allow for hands-on application and creativity as well as opportunities for oral discourse (VanTassel-Baska, 2018). Yet, in many instances, active learning and extended higher level thinking opportunities such as these are not part of the curriculum in low-income schools, as these activities have been replaced by rote and prescriptive curriculum in reading and math (Hirn et al., 2018; Milner, 2014).

Discrepant scores among verbal and nonverbal domains of reasoning can cause problems for students from low-income households in being recognized for gifted programs (Kaya et al., 2016) or accessing advanced opportunities for learning. This is especially true because success in school emphasizes verbal reasoning skills over other types such as spatial reasoning, and verbal reasoning has been shown to be a stronger predictor of ongoing achievement than nonverbal reasoning (Lakin & Lohman, 2011). Many gifted programs are built solely upon high verbal reasoning scores, thus missing many students with talent. In a study of spatial talent by Lakin and Wai (2019), spatial visualization skills were found to identify the largest number of students from low-socioeconomic backgrounds and a large number of rural students, and was the cognitive measure that most closely matched proportional representation for African American students. As Kaya et al. (2016) summarized, "nonverbal scores or fluid intelligence indicate the potential to learn, whereas verbal scores or crystallised intelligence indicate readiness to learn" (p. 9).

What are the implications of these findings when planning curriculum and instruction for the most able students from low-income households? Educators need to cultivate verbal skills as early as possible so that students are prepared for advanced coursework that relies heavily on verbal intelligence, while simultaneously capitalizing on and recognizing student strengths in authentic problem solving, spatial reasoning, creativity, practical application, and nonverbal skills. Many authors wisely caution against placing students from low-income households in verbally laden gifted programs based on nonverbal scores (Kaya et al., 2016; Lakin & Lohman, 2011) and emphasize that identification should match the nature of the services provided (Olszewski-Kubilius & Clarenbach, 2012; VanTassel-Baska & Stambaugh, 2007).

Therefore, curriculum for learners from low-income households, attuned to their strengths and needs, serves two purposes: (1) to develop skills necessary for continued success through targeted interventions that enhance higher level thinking skills prior to formal identification, as well as through bridging programs designed to fill in gaps and provide pathways to future achievement; and (2) to promote talent in areas of strength through access to targeted instruction and differentiated, accelerated curriculum and opportunities during and beyond the school day. Programs that support these approaches, such as Young Scholars, Project Excite, and STEM Starters+, among others, are explained in more detail in Chapters 7, 9, and 12 of this book and, as such, will not be included here. Still, it is important to note that all of the aforementioned specially designed programs committed to:

> preteaching with a focus on developing higher level thinking skills,
> filling in learning gaps attuned to students' testing profiles,
> utilizing hands-on activities tied to advanced curriculum, and
> providing access to higher level curriculum and instructional opportunities during and outside the school day combined with appropriate scaffolds.

These core elements result in increased achievement and engagement, a higher likelihood of gifted identification, and long-term talent development.

What Does Quality Curriculum for Gifted and Potentially Gifted Students From Low-Income Households Entail?

The Jacob K. Javits Gifted and Talented Students Act was first passed in 1988 and reauthorized through the Every Student Succeeds Act. The Act is the only federal program to provide funding for talent development through competitive research grants focused on closing the opportunity gap by identifying and serving students from historically underrepresented populations, including students of color, students who are twice-exceptional, and students from low-income, rural, or second-language households (National Association for Gifted Children, n.d.). Several Javits projects have resulted in packaged, evidence-supported curriculum resources found effective in promoting achievement gains in students from low-income households using quasi-experimental design research methods.

In a review of the curriculum available as of 2011, Stambaugh (2012) noted specific features consistent among all curriculum available at that time. The most effective curricula emphasized modeling, scaffolding, relevance, and conceptual and high-level approaches coupled with building-level accountability, ongoing performance-based assessments, professional development, and the use of consistent models over time. Since 2012, more projects and curricula have been piloted and are reviewed here with updates.

Table 5.1 provides an overview of curriculum resources that meet the following criteria for this review: (1) is a published or widely accessible packaged curriculum, (2) reported significant differences in achievement through quasi-experimental or experimental design, (3) included students from low-income households or students in Title I schools as the primary sample of inquiry, and (4) focused on high-level talent development or gifted education. (*Note.* Other curricula, such as those developed by Vanderbilt University's Programs for Talented Youth, Shelagh Gallagher's problem-based learning (PBL) units, the University of North Carolina's Project U-STARS, and the University of Virginia's CLEAR model, have shown positive effects for many gifted and talented students but were not included, as they did not meet all four of the criteria listed, although these curricula have many of the same features as outlined in this chapter.)

In an updated review, the following key features of an equitable curriculum model for academically advanced learners from low-income households included: conceptual and relevant learning, high-level curriculum with scaffolding as necessary, modeling of thinking within a specific domain (including language of the discipline and metacognitive approaches), and open-ended

Table 5.1
Published Curriculum Piloted With Students From Low-Income Households

Curriculum Model/Project	Content Area(s)	Grade Levels	Publisher	Developer	Evidence of Use With Talented Students From Comparative Field Studies in Low-Income Schools
Integrated Curriculum Model—Project Clarion	Science	K–3	Kendall Hunt (problem-based learning units) and Prufrock Press (Clarion units)	Center for Gifted Education, William & Mary	› Science process skills › Science content knowledge
Engineering is Elementary—STEM Starters+	Engineering	1–5	Engineering is Elementary (https://www.eie.org)	Museum of Science, Boston	› Science achievement › Engineering knowledge › Engagement › Increased nomination of children from low-income households for gifted education services
Schoolwide Enrichment Model—Project M³: Mentoring Mathematical Minds	Mathematics	3–5	Kendall Hunt	University of Connecticut	› Math concepts › Math achievement in numbers and operations, data analysis and probability, measurement and geometry, algebra

Table 5.1, continued

Curriculum Model/Project	Content Area(s)	Grade Levels	Publisher	Developer	Evidence of Use With Talented Students From Comparative Field Studies in Low-Income Schools
Integrated Curriculum Model—Language Arts Jacob's Ladder—Project Athena	English language arts	K–8	Prufrock Press	Center for Gifted Education, William & Mary	› Literacy analysis (ELA) › Persuasive writing (ELA) › Linguistic competency (ELA)
Integrated Curriculum Model—Project Athena	English language arts	K–9	Kendall Hunt	Center for Gifted Education, William & Mary	› Critical thinking › Reading comprehension
Blueprints for Biography—STEM Starters+	STEM/Social studies	1–8	https://ualr.edu/gifted	University of Arkansas, Little Rock, Jodie Mahony Center for Gifted Education	› Teachers report high engagement in students › Increases in student science achievement and engineering knowledge when linked with engineering curriculum
Project Civis	Social studies	6–8	Prufrock Press	Center for Gifted Education, William & Mary	› Social studies achievement using previous NAEP assessment

Note. Adapted from "Evidence-Based Curriculum Developed for or Field-Tested With Gifted Learners: A Deeper Dive Into Differentiated Curriculum That Works for Talented Students" [Panel discussion], by A. Robinson, C. Deitz, K. Kidd, and T. Stambaugh, 2016, The Arkansas Association of Gifted Education Administrators 24th Annual Fall Conference, Little Rock, AR, United States. Adapted with permission.

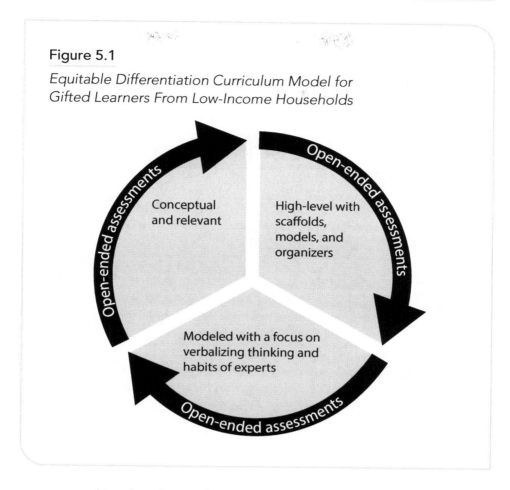

Figure 5.1

Equitable Differentiation Curriculum Model for Gifted Learners From Low-Income Households

assessment (Stambaugh, 2018). Each feature is discussed in more detail and represented as a model in Figure 5.1.

Conceptual and Relevant

Although the curricula reviewed varied in their approach, all units incorporated concepts and relevant problems or scenarios specific to the content domain. Relevance was infused into each unit in three different ways: real-world problem-based scenarios, embedded opportunities for students to gain hands-on or created/simulated experiences, and culturally relevant readings and examples. Bishop's (1990) concept of mirrors and windows was reflected in most units, although not explicitly mentioned. Bishop explained that students need mirrors to see themselves in the curriculum and windows to see diverse ideas, opinions, cultures, and people. Conceptual understanding was promoted in two different ways: emphasis on subject-specific concepts that are explicitly taught, practiced, and applied to real-world scenarios, and applications to universal generalizations and cross-disciplinary concepts, such as change, systems, or conflict. In the latter, students apply a real-world scenario just studied or learned to a generalization, such as how systems are interdependent or how change is linked to time.

The math and science units focused primarily on problem-based learning and domain-specific concepts, such as number sense, place value, engineering principles, or scientific concepts such as photosynthesis or evaporation and condensation. Students were asked to create or apply key principles and generalizations to real-world problems. For example, in one Project Clarion elementary science lesson (*What's the Matter?*; Center for Gifted Education, 2008), students examine the concept of evaporation and condensation by solving a mystery of the principal's missing water and then apply their solution to generalizations about natural and man-made changes and changes over time. In M³:Mentoring Mathematical Minds (MoLi Stone unit; Sheffield et al., 2015), after studying place value and number systems, students were asked to decipher a code on a stone, using what they had learned about number systems to justify their solution. In Engineering is Elementary's (n.d.) *Go Fish* unit, students apply principles of engineering to create a prosthetic fin for a dolphin that meets specific criteria after watching videos about a true story of Winter the dolphin. Opportunities were also provided for students to gain background knowledge. Students were instructed to watch videos, recreate or act out scenarios, or use math manipulatives to show ideas.

The English language arts and social studies curricula reviewed also incorporated relevance and conceptual understanding. In these units, students analyze the problems of characters in texts, read multicultural literature, and debate real-world problems through multiple stakeholder lenses and primary sources. Students apply their thinking to a universal theme or concept, such as changes over time in a character's actions. Students also have choices in some of their readings and may select a story with a character or theme relevant to their personal life. Unit subthemes include concepts such as social justice, racism, friendship, being different, success and failure, and the like. There are suggested readings that may be substituted to address the needs of different groups. Students may also engage in independent research on a specific topic or controversial, real-world issues as a way to apply their thinking, such as designing a debatable question and using a research and writing model to communicate their ideas. In the Project Civis unit on civil rights (*Engaging With History in the Classroom: The Civil Rights Movement*; Robins & Tieso, 2015), each lesson highlights a key question for students to engage with, such as "Was *Brown v. Board of Education* successful?" or "How can conflict be resolved without violence?" Key concepts relevant to social studies are emphasized, and primary sources and different perspectives are used to engage students in discussing real-world problems from historical and current perspectives. Blueprints for Biography curricula engage students in learning more about eminent individuals in a variety of fields, focusing on successful individuals from diverse racial and ethnic backgrounds, socioeconomic strata, and geographic regions—allowing students to connect with others similar to and different from them.

In each of these examples, regardless of the discipline, major concepts were emphasized and provided the lens with which students engaged in relevant and real-world issues, practiced creativity and problem-solving processes, and communicated their thinking, practicing verbal skills.

High Level With Scaffolds, Models, and Organizers

Another feature of most of the curricula reviewed that showed effectiveness with students from low-income households was the focus on higher level thinking skills with scaffolds or organizers designed to promote critical thinking in a content domain. Scaffolding for academically advanced students from low-income households assumes that higher level thinking skills and content can be attained with some targeted assistance. Rather than starting with lower level skills and building upward, educators start with higher level thinking skills and provide supports as needed to help students engage with those skills. Therefore, the units begin at a high level and provide supports and scaffolding as needed, such as graphic organizers and models. Just as relevance was not used in isolation but combined with conceptual understanding, scaffolding is integrated with higher level thinking. Scaffolding approaches that do not begin with higher level thinking and advanced instruction as the goal do not promote equity for students from low-income households or allow them the opportunities to engage in higher level curriculum. Too often, especially in Title I schools, students rarely get the opportunity to experience or engage in higher level thinking in the same ways as their colleagues from nonpoverty backgrounds. Scaffolding combined with higher level thinking goals allows students access with supports.

Scaffolding approaches in the M³ units focus on providing "hint" and "think deeply" cards as part of differentiation. Students who need more assistance or experience with a concept are given hint cards to help them figure out a problem, while those who have grasped a concept are provided a think deeply card to continue to engage at an in-depth level with the concept.

The Jacob's Ladder Reading Comprehension Program (e.g., Center for Gifted Education, 2017) was created solely as a supplemental scaffolding program to help students move from lower to higher level thinking skills in four key areas:

117

reasoning (Ladder A), conceptual understanding (Ladder B), content knowledge (Ladder C), and creative synthesis (Ladder D). Each student "climbs" the ladder, spending the most time on the top rung of the ladder, which is the most rigorous. Ladders are independent of each other and designed based on theoretical concepts and ideas in the field. Although most popularized in reading and language arts, the scaffolding approach can be applied to all subject areas. Table 5.2 provides an overview of the ladders with example question stems in a variety of content areas. For example, a scaffolded approach might work with Ladder B. If condensation is the concept of study, students may begin by listing examples of condensation, then move to organizing examples of condensation they have noticed through a variety of experiments conducted, and then finally write a true statement or generalization about condensation or the relationship among condensation and evaporation based on their learning. If they are studying social justice in reading or social studies and applying Ladder A (reasoning through issues and situations), students may begin at the bottom rung by creating a timeline for a specific event and then moving to the next rung, discuss the cause-and-effect relationships of the event on a particular group, and finally, at the top rung debate the implications and consequences of the event on current issues.

Language arts units from Project Athena provide scaffolding through graphic organizers such as the literature web, whereas science units from Project Clarion provide a science investigation wheel to help students think though and plan for scientific investigations. These curriculum models can be found at the Center for Gifted Education at William & Mary's website (https://educa tion.wm.edu/centers/cfge). For each of these organizers, students analyze the parts of a story (i.e., feelings, key words, ideas, structure, symbols) or an experiment (i.e., make observations, ask questions, learn more, design and conduct an experiment, create meaning, tell others what was found) respectively. The models serve as a scaffold to help them think like a scientist or literary analyst. Students are asked to combine the individual items into a cohesive explanation to show their understanding of scientific thinking, an experiment, or a text. Other curricula, such as Blueprints for Biographies and Project Civis units, scaffold instruction through Bloom's taxonomy and other leveled-questioning approaches.

Modeled With a Focus on Verbalizing Thinking and Engaging in Habits of a Scholar

Modeling, verbalizing thinking, and helping students engage in habits similar to that of an expert were central to all units. Regardless of the curriculum reviewed, students were held accountable for engaging in conver-

Table 5.2
Jacob's Ladder Questioning Stems

Ladder A: Implications and Consequences (Reasoning and connecting)	Ladder B: Concept Development (Abstract connections within and across disciplines)	Ladder C: Content Within a Discipline (Content understanding and inference-making)	Ladder D: Products or Discussions as a Synthesis of Learning and Creativity
Implications/Consequences	Generalizations/Concepts	Relationships Among Theories, Laws, Big Ideas	Creative Synthesis
> What are the short- and long-term effects of x on y? > What are the positive outcomes of x? Negative? > What might happen if x were changed? > What are the consequences of x on y? > What are the implications of . . .? > Should . . . ? Why?	> What does this passage say about changes over time . . . the use and abuse of power? > What are two true statements about ____ based on this passage/lecture/experiment/problem set? > What generalizations can you make about x from y? > What is the relationship between Concept A and Concept B in this problem/experiment/story/time period?	> Is ____ or ____ a better ____? > How do different perspectives support or deny the idea that . . .? > How does the author use tone and mood to support the idea that . . .? > How is the theme of x demonstrated/revealed through y?	> Create/design/write/develop a ____ that ____ and ____.

119

Table 5.2, continued

Ladder A: Implications and Consequences (Reasoning and connecting)	Ladder B: Concept Development (Abstract connections within and across disciplines)	Ladder C: Content Within a Discipline (Content understanding and inference-making)	Ladder D: Products or Discussions as a Synthesis of Learning and Creativity
Cause/Effect Relationships	Classifications	Inferences	Summarizing
➤ What caused x to ____? How do you know? ➤ What caused x, and how does x impact...? ➤ What effect does x have on y?	➤ How would you classify ...? How would you classify the problems into categories? ➤ Organize the ____ into a chart that shows.... ➤ Create a T-chart/Venn diagram that shows.... ➤ Examine multiple perspectives on the issue and....	➤ What is meant by ...? ➤ How do we know that.... ➤ What is the point of ...? ➤ What can you infer about x based on y? ➤ What evidence do you have to suggest that....	➤ What are the most important or key ideas that ____? ➤ This ____ was about ____ because.... ➤ Summarize the main idea of.... ➤ This is important because ....
Sequencing	Details	Facts/Elements/Factors	Paraphrasing
➤ Create a timeline of x that shows.... ➤ Sequence the events that led to.... ➤ Explain, step by step, how. ...	➤ What details in the passage/lecture/experiment/document support the idea that...? ➤ What do the details from x tell us about y? ➤ List examples that show different rules of....	➤ What is the ...? ➤ What elements support ...? ➤ What factors might we consider ...?	➤ Explain.... ➤ Retell.... ➤ What does ...? ➤ What is meant by ...? ➤ What are ____ facts that ...? ➤ Explain how you would solve....

sations using the language of the discipline and practicing habits of a professional. It is important in the talent development process for students to understand and engage in habits of scholars. Students who may not have as much access to this type of thinking on a regular basis need more explicit instruction and modeling of processes. Question such as "How does a _____ go about their job? (processes of the discipline), "How does a _____ talk?" (vocabulary of the discipline), and "How might a _____ think about _____?" (thinking and planning in the discipline) serve as a reminder to engage in these conversations on a regular basis. Reflecting upon progress and monitoring one's own thinking promotes student learning, goal setting, and independence. Stems such as the following may be used to support student reflection:

> › If I were going to approach this, I would. . . .
> › How did someone solve this a different way? How did that work?
> › What will you do first, second, third, etc.?
> › When discussing in your groups, try one of these stems:
>> › I agree/disagree with this statement because. . . .
>> › On page x it stated that. . . .
>> › As you read, think about. . . . (highlight, mark in text, annotate in the margin)
>> › What approach is best for . . . ?
>> › How can you say that like a _____? (scientist, historian, mathematician)

Most unit instructions encourage teachers to model thinking and engage students in reflecting on their own learning. M³ adopted accountable talk strategies as studied by Chapin et al. (2009). Throughout the unit, mathematical conversations focus on revoicing, repeating, reasoning, adding on, and waiting. These conversation strategies become part of a student's everyday mathematical vernacular. Similarly, in most of the language arts units, Socratic seminar approches are used to engage students in adding to the converation through questioning stems. In the teacher guides to *Jacob's Ladder Reading Comprehension Program* (e.g., Center for Gifted Education, 2017), question stems such as, "I agree with x because . . . ." "On page x it says that. . . ." "What does someone else think about . . . ." are provided to guide student conversation. In other curricula, written reflections such as science logs or math journals are regularly used to reflect on the processes of problem solving. Checklists of key criteria are also used to self-assess progress and assignment quality, and reflection sheets are used to examine personal learning processes and set a new goal for learning. These activities provide students with the skills necessary to continue reflecting on their own.

Open-Ended Assessments

Assessment is part of good instruction. The majority of units featured pre- and postassessments as a guide for monitoring progress and differentiating instruction. Ongoing assessment and reevaluation were an integral part of most lessons. Interestingly, assessments provided in the units were open-ended and allowed students to showcase their thinking and prior knowledge in a variety of ways as opposed to being limited to multiple-choice or closed-ended questions. In Project Clarion science units, students were asked to create concept maps of the topic of study, which was less intimidating than writing full sentences but still showcased knowledge of the discipline following Novak's model for concept attainment and assessment of thinking (Novak & Cañas, 2006). Most of the other unit assessments required students to explain or model their thinking through open-ended responses and emphasized explanation of the thinking process with evidence and rubric scoring.

Conclusion

Academically advanced students from low-income households may require more support than their more advantaged counterparts so that their abilities are identified and developed. It is inequitable to rob students of access to high-level curriculum because of their school's location and income status. Differentiating and planning curriculum and instruction for students from low-income households requires intentional planning. Educators must ensure that the curriculum offered is conceptual and relevant to students' needs, assumes high-level attainment with scaffolds built in, and promotes modeling and reflection of learning, such as ways to verbalize one's thinking and practice communicating within that discipline. Figure 5.2 provides a set of questions teachers may ask when planning instruction using this approach.

Each student and school has unique needs and a unique student population that ultimately impacts curriculum planning and design. The equitable differentiation curriculum model for gifted learners from low-income households (Figure 5.1) can be used as a guide for planning within each school's context. In addition to the application of this model, ongoing professional development with accountability and strength-based approaches will support curriculum differentiation and encourage teachers to become talent scouts and promote access and equity through curriculum design and delivery.

Figure 5.2

Questions to Ask When Planning Instruction for Students From Low-Income Households

Modeled	Relevant and Conceptual	High Level and Scaffolded
› How will I explicitly model the thinking processes and habits of the discipline? › Which models or graphic organizers will I use on a consistent basis to promote habits of the discipline? › How will I show my thinking and encourage students to show theirs?	› How will I make the curriculum relevant to my students' lives, experiences, and/or backgrounds? › What concepts will my students use to make meaning, based on their situation? › What real-world issues are relevant to the content and students' lives? › What resources are most appropriate to connect with my students? What other perspectives do I need to include? › How can I adapt the experience, build the experience, or provide access?	› What questions will I ask and what organizers will I use to build understanding of a model or concept? › What skills are necessary to teach in order for students to reach higher level questions? › How will I help students meet high-level expectations?

References

Bishop, R. S. (1990). Mirrors, windows, and sliding glass doors. *Perspectives: Choosing and using books for the classroom, 6*(3).

Cawelti, G. (2006). The side effects of NCLB. *Educational Leadership, 64*(3), 64–68.

Center for Gifted Education. (2017). *Jacob's Ladder Reading Comprehension Program: Grade 3* (2nd ed.). Prufrock Press.

Center for Gifted Education. (2008). *What's the matter?: A physical science unit for high-ability learners in grades 2–3*. Prufrock Press.

Chapin, S. H., O'Connor, C., & Anderson, N. C. (2009). *Classroom discussions: Using math talk to help students learn* (2nd ed.). Math Solutions.

Darling-Hammond, L. (2001). Inequality in teaching and schooling: How opportunity is rationed to students of color in America. In B. D. Smedley, A. Y. Stith, L. Colburn, & C. H. Evans (Eds.), *The right thing to do, the smart thing to do: Enhancing diversity in health professions* (pp. 208–233). The National Academies Press.

Engineering is Elementary. (n.d.). *Go fish: Engineering prosthetic tails*.

Hirn, R. G., Hollo, A., & Scott, T. M. (2018). Exploring instructional differences and school performance in high-poverty elementary schools. *Preventing School Failure: Alternative Education for Children and Youth, 62*(1), 37–48. https://doi.org/10.1080/1045988X.2017.1329197

Jacob K. Javits Gifted and Talented Students Education Program, 20 U.S.C. § 7294 (2015). https://congress.gov/114/plaws/publ95/PLAW-114publ95.pdf

Kaya, F., Stough, L. M., & Juntune, J. (2016). The effect of poverty on the verbal scores of gifted students. *Educational Studies, 42*(1), 85–97. https://doi.org/10.1080/03055698.2016.1148585

Lakin, J. M., & Lohman, D. F. (2011). The predictive accuracy of verbal, quantitative, and nonverbal reasoning tests: Consequences for talent identification and program diversity. *Journal for the Education of the Gifted, 34*(4), 595–623. https://doi.org/10.1177/016235321103400404

Lakin, J., & Wai, J. (2020). Spatially gifted, academically inconvenienced: Spatially talented students experience less academic engagement and more behavioural issues than other talented students. *British Journal of Educational Psychology*. Advance online publication. https://doi.org/10.1111/bjep.12343

Milner, H. R., IV (2014). Scripted and narrowed curriculum reform in urban schools. *Urban Education, 49*(7), 743–749. https://doi.org/10.1177/0042085914549685

National Association for Gifted Children. (n.d.). *Jacob Javits Gifted & Talented Students Education Act*. https://www.nagc.org/resources-publications/resources-university-professionals/jacob-javits-gifted-talented-students

Novak, J. D., & Cañas, A. J. (2006). The origins of the concept mapping tool and the continuing evolution of the tool. *Information Visualization, 5*(3), 175–184. https://doi.org/10.1057/palgrave.ivs.9500126

Olszewski-Kubilius, P. & Clarenbach, J. (2012). *Unlocking emergent talent: Supporting high achievement of low-income, high-ability students*. National Association for Gifted Children.

Plucker, J., Giancola, J., Healey, G., Arndt, D., & Wang, C. (2015). *Equal talents, unequal opportunities: A report card on state support for academically talented low-income students*. Jack Kent Cooke Foundation.

Robins, J. I., & Tieso, C. L. (2015). *Engaging with history in the classroom: The Civil Rights movement*. Prufrock Press.

Robinson, A., Deitz, C., Kidd, K., & Stambaugh, T. (2016). *Evidence-based curriculum developed for or field-tested with gifted learners: A deeper dive into differentiated curriculum that works for talented students* [Panel discussion]. The Arkansas Association of Gifted Education Administrators 24th Annual Fall Conference, Little Rock, AR, United States.

Sheffield, L. J., Chapin, S. H., Dailey, J., & Gavin, K. (2015). *Project M³: Level 3–4: Unraveling the mystery of the MoLi Stone: Exploring place value and numeration.* Kendall Hunt.

Stambaugh, T. (2012). *Patterns of curriculum effectiveness for students from low income backgrounds* [Paper presentation]. The National Association of Gifted Children Annual Conference, Denver, CO, United States.

Stambaugh, T. (2018). *Patterns of curriculum effectiveness for students from low income backgrounds, updated* [Paper presentation]. Texas Association for Gifted Children Annual Conference, Dallas, TX, United States.

Stambaugh, T., & Chandler, K. L. (2012). *Effective curriculum for underserved gifted students.* Prufrock Press.

Subotnik, R. F., Olszewski-Kubilius, P., & Worrell, F. C. (2011). Rethinking giftedness and gifted education: A proposed direction forward based on psychological science. *Psychological Science in the Public Interest, 12*(1), 3–54. https://doi.org/10.1177/1529100611418056

VanTassel-Baska, J. (2018). Achievement unlocked: Effective curriculum interventions with low-income students. *Gifted Child Quarterly, 62*(1), 68–82. https://doi.org/10.1177/0016986217738565

VanTassel-Baska, J., Feng, A. X., & de Brux, E. (2007). A study of identification and achievement profiles of performance task-identified gifted students over 6 years. *Journal for the Education of the Gifted, 31*(1), 7–34. https://doi.org/10.4219/jeg-2007-517

VanTassel-Baska, J., & Stambaugh, T. (Eds.). (2007). *Overlooked gems: A national perspective on low-income promising learners.* National Association for Gifted Children.

CHAPTER 6

Instructional Strategies to Support Learners From Low-Income Backgrounds: *The Humanities*

Catherine A. Little and Stacy M. Hayden

The classification of "the humanities" is a broad one, encompassing the arts, literature, languages, history, philosophy, classics, and a range of other disciplines. Stanford University's Stanford Humanities Center, a leading institution for scholarship in these areas, described the humanities as "the study of how people process and document the human experience" (Stanford Humanities Center, n.d.). Study of the humanities involves understanding how people have made sense of the world in the past across different times and places, how they envision the world today, and how past, present, and future intersect. Such study engages critical and creative thinking, questioning, and self-reflection. Further, work in the humanities involves creative productivity, as individuals work to develop new representations of how people make sense of their experiences.

Within the traditional K–12 school subjects, the term *the humanities* may capture reading/language arts, much of the work in social studies, world languages, and "specials" such as art and music. Across those subjects, some receive greater priority in schools than any other areas of study, with the primacy placed on reading instruction and the necessity of developing reading skills and vocabulary as the foundation for studying all other school subjects. At the same time, among the "big four" school subjects, the lowest allocation of time and resources often goes to social studies (see Bisland, 2015; National Center for Education Statistics, n.d.), and the arts are frequent casualties of budget cuts and reallocation of time (Americans for the Arts, 2019).

The wide range of subjects in the humanities also encompasses a wide range of relevant instructional approaches. These approaches include presenting different types of texts and other stimuli; responding to these texts with analysis and reflection; engaging in discussion and interaction; building connections across sources, perspectives, and experiences; and developing creative products. For gifted learners, each area of the humanities may provide scope for rigorous content study and intensive engagement in high-level thinking, as well as for exploration of deep interdisciplinary connections around the "big ideas" that underlie human experience and how we make meaning and communicate (VanTassel-Baska & Wood, 2010).

Gifted learners from backgrounds of poverty may face particular challenges in these rigorous learning experiences, related in part to their access to opportunities to learn and issues around finding connection and relevance (Gay, 2010; Gorski, 2018; Knapp & Woolverton, 2001; Mixon, 2005). Further, schools serving high-poverty populations tend to see fewer teachers who perform well on measures of teacher quality (Goldhaber et al., 2015). This chapter explores some of the challenges to learning in the humanities that gifted learners from low-income backgrounds may encounter, as well as some instructional approaches recommended for supporting them and encouraging their talent development.

Considerations and Challenges for Learning in the Humanities

Access, Opportunity to Learn, and Exposure

As illustrated throughout this text, opportunities to learn and access to particular kinds of experiences may be among the challenges for learning in the humanities facing gifted students from backgrounds of poverty. The humanities are grounded in studying how human beings have made sense of their experiences and documented or represented them across time and space; these content areas are, therefore, eminently *human* and accessible to all. However, history demonstrates that some perspectives have been prioritized over others. Thus, the humanities, in an academic sense, have become about exposure to *specific* avenues of documentation, representation, and sense-making that build on each other to form canons of culture.

In a discussion of the challenges faced by some students from backgrounds of poverty, it is critical first to acknowledge and address several prevalent assumptions about these students. Gorski (2018) outlined several critical understandings, including emphasizing that parents from low-income families *do* care about their children's education and *do* engage in literacy-relevant experiences with their children (see also Bhattacharya, 2010). Assumptions to the contrary contribute to a deficit-focused ideology that is counterproductive in promoting student growth, teacher responsiveness, and school-family connections. Sometimes students' background experiences may have been in a language other than English, and sometimes their experiences may be influenced by cost and time, but these differences should be valued for their own sake and also considered relative to student needs as they encounter the school curriculum.

Compared to students from more economically advantaged backgrounds, students from backgrounds of poverty may bring a different set of experiences that influence their readiness for learning in the humanities. All students come to school bringing potentially relevant background experiences—language, stories, and encounters with music, history, and art. However, the scope and specific detail of those experiences will vary widely, particularly in the degree to which they connect to the experiences of the humanities valued in the school curriculum. Further, student experience of school-relevant content may be limited for families in poverty by such issues as access to print, not only in the home, but also in the local community (e.g., public libraries) in high-poverty areas (Neuman & Celano, 2001, 2006).

Students from low-income backgrounds do not form a monolithic group. There is extensive variation in experiences among those from low-income backgrounds, linked to many other demographic factors. Students from backgrounds of poverty may have had limited access to the language and cultural references most likely to be referenced in schools. When a novel chosen for class reading and discussion carries allusions to stories from a particular cultural tradition, for example, students raised in a different culture may not have automatic knowledge of the same stories—suggesting a need for teachers to raise their own consciousness of such allusions, provide access to needed background information, and consider what other stories and perspectives should be represented during instruction (Gay, 2010; Ladson-Billings, 1995).

The challenges presented by limited exposure to traditional school-relevant content for some students from backgrounds of poverty may be compounded by further limits on exposure at school. This issue is particularly relevant with regard to access to the arts and other subjects that may be relegated to being "specials" in the school setting. Students from backgrounds of poverty may have less access to arts experiences in schools and extracurricular settings, in part because of family inability to afford the experiences (Snellman et al., 2015) and the frequent cuts to such experiences in school budgets (DeLuca et al., 2016). Once again, students from backgrounds of poverty do have experiences that they bring to school; however, they may have had less access than their peers to "cognitive enrichment opportunities that *mirror notions of intelligence most rewarded at school* [emphasis added]" (Gorski, 2018, p. 95).

Language and Vocabulary Experience

Many of the disciplines within the humanities are heavily grounded in language, including specific study of different languages, literature, and other heavily language-dependent subjects, such as history. Thus, attention to access and challenge in the humanities is highly linked to students' experiences with language and vocabulary.

The press has given extensive attention to claims regarding the language experiences of children from low-income backgrounds and the implications for their achievement. In one widely cited study, Hart and Risley (1995, 2003) found that children from low-income backgrounds were exposed to substantially less vocabulary in their early years—up to 30 million fewer words—than their peers from higher income backgrounds. In subsequent analyses, other researchers raised questions on the details and generalizability of the original study (e.g., Dudley-Marling & Lucas, 2009) and demonstrated that the "word gap" is substantially less than originally estimated (Sperry et al., 2019).

Nevertheless, vocabulary researchers have still acknowledged the challenges of access to school-related literacy experiences for many students from economically marginalized groups. Vocabulary researchers have consistently found poverty to be a significant risk factor affecting scores on vocabulary assessments, linked not only to baseline scores but also to gain scores over time (Marulis & Neuman, 2013). To some degree, the issue may not be so much overall quantity of words heard or vocabulary learned, but rather the degree of experience students may have had of the "language of schooling" (Dudley-Marling & Lucas, 2009), words necessary to the current school curriculum and their use across multiple academic contexts (Cummins, 2014; Schleppegrell, 2012).

Relevance and Representation

As noted, students from backgrounds of poverty may have had less exposure to the cultural references embedded throughout the arts, literature, language, and history covered in school than some of their peers. For some students, these differences in exposure may result from their families' limited time and funds for supporting experiences linked to school content. For other students, the differences may be linked to the cultural background students bring to school and the degree to which the perspectives of people in their communities are reflected in the school curriculum. This issue of limited exposure to school-relevant content suggests, in part, a need for educator attention to supporting students in building the background they will need for academic success as such content increases in volume over time. At the same time, educators must recognize that the content deemed "important" in the school curriculum represents a limited range of perspectives and experiences and that other content may be more deeply known and valued by students and their families (Gay, 2010). Students may feel alienated or disconnected from much of the content of schooling, both because of limited background experience and the lack of clear representation of their own lives in the materials they encounter (Gorski, 2018; Knapp & Woolverton, 2001).

All students must be able to see themselves and the experiences familiar to them reflected in the curriculum. This familiarity allows students to ask and answer questions and build understanding; at a deeper level, when students are able to make connections and feel emotional relevance, their understanding of content will likely be deeper. Gorski (2018) emphasized the importance of using examples and illustrations that are "relevant and compelling" to students from backgrounds of poverty (p. 139). This emphasis on *relevance* to students' own experiences must not be relegated just to particular times of year (e.g., holiday studies) or reactive situations, but should be proactively addressed throughout the curriculum (Henfield et al., 2014). The emphasis on *compelling* suggests the importance of helping students to see how what they learn will help them progress toward personal and social goals that they care about. For example, Cummins (2014) and Haneda (2014) illustrated that students from disadvantaged backgrounds developed their academic language with greater facility when engaged in exploring issues that were personally meaningful.

In the humanities, the increasing range of perspectives reflected in children's literature and increasing attention to diverse perspectives in historical study may help teachers to broaden the degree of representation in course materials. Efforts to increase relevance and representation in course materials include attention to the perspectives that are addressed and how individuals from different backgrounds are portrayed in classroom resources. However, there is still considerable room to grow in the range of perspectives reflected in common use in the classroom, as illustrated in these examples:

> A recent analysis from *The New York Times* highlighted startling differences in representation and description of historical content in textbooks used in different regions of the country (specifically Texas and California; Goldstein, 2020).

> Harris and Reynolds (2014) reviewed multiple studies exploring how much students felt they saw themselves in the history curriculum, emphasizing that students from minority ethnic groups and low-income backgrounds saw considerably less attention in course materials to people who looked like them than their White and more affluent peers.

> Sano (2009) examined children's books frequently used in classes with English language learners and found that there were clear reflections of stereotypes around the types of jobs held by members of various ethnic immigrant groups.

These findings suggest a need for broader attention to course materials. They also indicate opportunities to engage students in examining varied perspectives and questioning which perspectives are and are not included in their learning experience (Knapp & Woolverton, 2001).

Beyond the concrete course materials students see, a further key consideration is the attitude and perspective that teachers bring to their interactions with these students and their experiences. In developing relationships with students and families, teachers must recognize and respect that the experiences of all students and families have relevance to the learning environment. Deficit thinking from teachers is likely to lead to lowered expectations for students and dissatisfaction with the work for teachers (Gorski, 2013; J. G. Robinson, 2007). On the other hand, genuine respect for the experiences students bring, as well as consistent communication of belief in students' ability to succeed, can be significant in promoting a climate of respect and helping students feel connected to the learning experience (Cuthrell et al., 2009).

Instructional Approaches to Support Gifted Students From Backgrounds of Poverty

Despite the prevalent variations among gifted students from backgrounds of poverty and the combination of factors that may influence the challenges they face at school, there are still guidelines that are relevant for supporting rich and rigorous learning for these students in the subject areas that make up the humanities. Specifically, instructional approaches should emphasize providing exposure for all students to unfamiliar content and new perspectives, supporting students' ability to connect to and find relevance and meaning in their learning experiences, building skills and habits that students can rely on as they encounter new content, and promoting respect for the range of perspectives and experiences students bring. Further, instructional approaches should support challenge and growth for gifted learners through the level of rigor and complexity of the tasks and high expectations for student engagement and performance. The following sections address several instructional approaches that may support gifted students from backgrounds of poverty in developing their talents in the humanities and pursuing deeper understanding of these disciplines and students' own growth as learners.

Questioning and Discussion

Questioning and discussion are integral to all classroom activities and are critical tools for teachers as they engage gifted learners. Questioning is widely recognized as a central and important part of instruction (Cotton, 1989; Hattie, 2009), and recommendations for higher level questioning and discourse to promote deep learning and engagement are prevalent in the literature (e.g., Soter et al., 2008; Taylor et al., 2003; Walsh & Sattes, 2011). Nevertheless, most classroom talk continues to reflect lower level questioning and teacher-centric discussion (Smith et al., 2004; Taylor et al., 2003; Tienken et al., 2009; van der Veen et al., 2017).

This pattern is especially evident in schools with high populations of students from poverty (Knapp & Woolverton, 2001; Taylor et al., 2000). Even in high-poverty schools deemed to be "more effective" (usually based on state test scores), researchers have observed a strong focus on basic skills and limited attention to higher level questioning (Jesse et al., 2004; Taylor et al., 2000). When questioning focuses too narrowly on determining whether students can reproduce answers instead of how they think through problems and develop their own authentic questions, it is unlikely to promote engagement, thinking, and growth (Wolf et al., 2005, 2006).

Walsh and Sattes (2011) proposed that supporting a "culture for thinking" requires framing high-quality questions, building capacity for thinking, using feedback effectively, and promoting ownership and self-direction. Again, the humanities are about *how people make sense* of the world, and sense-making requires asking and exploring questions. Discussion of high-quality questions engages students in deep thinking about ideas and information. It also instills a habit of questioning to promote ongoing engagement with learning.

For example, in the Schoolwide Enrichment Model Reading Framework (SEM-R), an approach tested and found to be effective in a range of high-poverty schools at elementary and middle school levels (Little et al., 2014; Reis et al., 2011), teachers use bookmarks with high-level questions about themes, genres, or literary elements to prompt conversation and further questioning as students engage in independent reading in books of their choice. As illustrated in Figure 6.1, the bookmark questions are general enough to be applied to many different texts, and any given bookmark reflects a range of levels of complexity in the questions. These questions may be used with a group read-aloud lesson, in individualized conferences, or as writing prompts. The focus is on engaging students with thinking, not confirming a specific desired answer. Discussions of these questions should lead to further questions worth exploring.

Researchers have found connections between use of high-level questions and student achievement. For example, in observations in low-income schools, Taylor and colleagues (2000) found that more effective teachers asked more high-level questions in reading instruction than their less effective colleagues (with effectiveness defined by student achievement levels). Nevertheless, as previously noted, these researchers also found that the overall use of high-level questions in these schools was relatively low. Further, Zwiers (2007) found that teachers were less likely to pursue follow-up questioning or press for further response among certain learners perceived to be disadvantaged; in this study the focus was specifically on questions asked of English language learners, but it reflects an overall pattern related to teacher behaviors with students perceived to be at risk that may limit these students' experience of challenge.

Rich questions for discussion tend to be those that engage students in higher level cognitive processes, such as analysis, synthesis, and evaluation, and these types of questions are at the core of curriculum and instruction that support deep thinking (VanTassel-Baska, 2018). Further, when students are engaging in such higher level processes, their focus should be on content that is deep and relevant and that incorporates an emphasis on big ideas. Students may access this content in a variety of ways—reading, listening, visual or hands-on experiences—but exposure to rich content is an important starting place for promoting high-level discussion. Thus, instructional planning in the humanities requires giving students access to a wide range of stimuli, including literature, historical documents, art and music selections, and other resources representing varied perspectives and experiences—including those authentically relevant to students from backgrounds of poverty—and then using these pieces as the foundations of questioning and discussion.

Along with asking high-quality questions as prompts for thinking and models of questions, teachers must also guide students with specific instruction around *how to engage* with challenging questions. This includes scaffolding and support for how to approach questions, including ensuring broad-based and

Figure 6.1

Sample Bookmarks

Character	Plot	Theme: Courage
Think of two questions you have about the protagonist. Do you think the questions will be answered as you continue with the story? Why or why not?	Describe a scene that you would include in a movie preview for this book. Why would you choose that scene?	How do characters show courage in the book? In what ways do their acts of courage differ?
What is a question that one of the characters seems to be struggling with in the story? How does this character seek answers or advice to resolve the question?	Visualize a timeline for the events of the book. Should it be drawn in a straight line, or would another shape (circle, triangle, etc.) capture the sequence of events more effectively?	Mark Twain wrote that "Courage is resistance to fear . . . not absence of fear." In what ways does this book demonstrate that idea?
Identify a decision or choice made by a character. Do you agree with this decision? Why or why not?	Select a chapter of the book and give it a new title. Explain your rationale for your title.	Tell about a way that a character showed courage by not doing something. Do you agree with the character's decision? Why or why not?
Describe a character's action that surprised you. In what ways was the action consistent or inconsistent with what you know about the character?	Describe a point in the story at which you didn't want to put the book down or couldn't wait to find out what happened next. What made that moment in the plot so compelling?	What events earlier in the story helped a character show courage at a later point? How do you know?

Note. Samples drawn from materials developed for Project SEM-R: Schoolwide Enrichment Model—Reading Framework (https://gifted.uconn.edu/semr-re sources). Materials developed under funding from the Jacob K. Javits Gifted and Talented Students Education Program, U.S. Department of Education, PR/Award #S206A080001.

deliberate exposure to the types of academic vocabulary that appear in questions and tasks across content areas. Students from backgrounds of poverty may have had less practice with such vocabulary or with speaking and listening in academic registers than their peers (Schleppegrell, 2012). Consequently, they may be facing unfamiliar content and unfamiliar questioning words all at once in the classroom; instruction and practice are important for building facility with those academic registers.

Support for engaging with questions can include a lot of attention to question words and how they are used, with variation based on the developmental level of the students. In the sample activity in Figure 6.2, an elementary teacher can encourage students to develop questions using *who, what, when, where, why,* and *how,* focusing on interesting pictures as a precursor to developing questions about nonfiction texts they are reading. Both the specific pictures and specific texts may be selected based on teacher understanding of students' interests, as well as consideration of the varied levels of complexity that will provide appropriate challenge. For older students, similarly, activities might involve guiding students to recognize the distinctions between directions to "describe," "explain," "compare," and "evaluate"—again, first with application to high-interest topics or texts, and then with increasingly challenging and complex content. Note that these activities not only reinforce the meaning of question words, but also emphasize developing authentic questions about a text.

Modeling and practice with different types of questions promote students' facility with responding to them (Zwiers, 2007), and once again, the degree of challenge of the content is critical. Further, questions and activities for wrestling with questions should be purposeful. Walsh and Sattes (2011) encouraged planning the instructional purpose of core questions for a given lesson or discussion, emphasizing that questions may look and sound different depending on whether they are designed to hook students' attention, carry a diagnostic or specific assessment function, foster reflection, or address some other purpose. Teachers may also focus on asking questions in a deliberate sequence, to support such purposes as moving from specific to general points (or vice versa), increasing the depth of thinking, or building connections across perspectives or disciplines (Vogler, 2008).

For example, *Jacob's Ladder Reading Comprehension Program* (e.g., Stambaugh & VanTassel-Baska, 2017) was designed to build student capacity to wrestle with higher level questions through engagement with a set of questions in a sequence linked to a text. Each ladder incorporates three levels of related questions, with the lowest rung addressing comprehension-level strategies and the subsequent rungs building toward greater complexity. The ladder structure

Figure 6.2

Sample Activity: Question Words

Opening Activity: Lesson on Question Words

Materials:

> 4–5 high-color, high-interest photographs (https://unsplash.com is a useful source for free photographs)
> "Question cube": a small wooden block with one question word on each face—who, what, when, where, how, why.

Activity:

Start with one photograph likely to engage student interest. Ask students to talk to a partner to share one thing they observe and one thing they wonder about the picture. Roll the question cube, and invite students to ask a question about the picture that starts with the question word you rolled.

Post the additional photos on the board. Use the question cube, and after each roll, ask students to work with a partner to come up with a question starting with the rolled word about one of the photos. Record 2–3 questions for each photo, trying to represent a variety of question words.

Explain to students that in some ways, nonfiction texts are basically authors answering questions about the topic for readers. If we have questions about a topic, we can read a book on that topic, and find answers to some of our questions. We might also find that different books on the same topic might answer some of the same questions and some different questions.

Note. This is an "engage" or initiating activity for a grade 2 lesson focusing on nonfiction texts and questioning. The overall lesson builds toward the Common Core State Standard for English Language Arts and Literacy RI.2.9: Compare and contrast the most important points presented by two texts on the same topic. Adapted from *Project LIFT: Reading and Mathematics Lessons 2019–2020* (pp. 68–69), 2019, University of Connecticut. Materials developed under funding from the Jacob K. Javits Gifted and Talented Students Education Program, U.S. Department of Education, PR/Award # S206A170030.

is repeated with multiple texts, so that students have opportunities to practice the interrelated skills in varied contexts and encounter the language of the questions and skills repeatedly. For example, one ladder moves students from a sequencing question to a cause-and-effect question to a question on consequences and implications; another builds from specific literary elements to inferencing to a focus on theme. (See also Chapter 5 for more discussion of *Jacob's Ladder* as a resource.)

Just as important as structuring questions well and asking questions to encourage thinking is honoring students' answers by listening carefully to how they respond, fostering a culture of listening and discussion, and guiding the conversation based on students' questions and ideas. The ability to engage in discussion around a topic, reading, or idea is a learned behavior, and elements of discussion should be specifically taught, modeled, and supported with constructive feedback. Frameworks for accountable talk (Michaels et al., 2008; Wolf et al., 2006) and talk moves (Chapin et al., 2009) support building classroom conversations in which (a) all students understand and draw upon the ideas shared in discussion, (b) all participants use evidence to support their positions, and (c) participants explain their thinking.

Specific strategies or moves that teachers can model and reinforce include repeating, revoicing, or rephrasing what a student says, which emphasizes careful listening; articulating agreement or disagreement with a stated perspective, including explanation of reasons for agreeing/disagreeing; and demonstrating how a comment builds on what another person has already said. In the early grades, this modeling and reinforcement should be done to a degree that may seem excessive to an observer; for example, a teacher might ask, "Can someone repeat what so-and-so said?" multiple times within a short discussion, along with inviting, "Show thumbs up if you agree and thumbs down if you disagree" and so forth. This level of repetition, however, underscores for students the importance of listening to others speak in a discussion and thinking through their own responses. By fostering these kinds of specific elements in discussion, teachers help to provide structure for students to organize and communicate their ideas effectively. Clear expectations for discussion moves also provide a good context for supporting respectful dialogue and a classroom culture of valuing multiple perspectives.

As students work to develop their discussion skills, teachers may employ a variety of formats to deepen the conversation. For example, Socratic seminars and Socratic circles are approaches that engage students in high-level thinking and discussion (VanTassel-Baska, 2018). Socratic seminars or Socratic circles are deep discussions around a central piece of text that foster connections to other texts and experiences, teach students to respond to questions using evidence, and provide the opportunity for students to practice speaking and listening skills (Copeland, 2005; Hunsaker et al., 2018). Contrary to the bulk of conversation in the classroom, which tends to be very teacher-centric, Socratic circles are student-led and student-driven (Copeland, 2005). Students use discussion strategies they have learned and questions and observations they develop about the text as the organizers for discussion (Cuny, 2014; Paul & Elder, 2007). The teacher may support students by asking a few facilitating questions (Senn, 2018), but teacher participation should decrease as students gain more experience.

Socratic circles typically have students sitting in an inner circle and an outer circle. The inner circle is involved in discussing the text at hand, while the outer circle observes the discussion. After a period of time, students switch roles, and the inner circle becomes the outer circle and vice versa. The outer circle provides feedback about the discussion to the inner circle after the inner circle has finished (Copeland, 2005; Senn, 2018). Through participation in Socratic circles, students build a range of academic and social skills, including critical thinking, creativity, understanding of multiple perspectives, and conflict resolution (Beghetto & Kaufman, 2009; Copeland, 2005). The responsibility for engaging in the discussion and processing the ideas adds to students' readiness for more rigorous and demanding work (Jensen, 2009).

As students continue to progress, other types of conversations and interactions may be integrated as well, such as varied types of debate. Debate engages students with thinking about issues critically, finding and using resources effectively, and understanding how to use evidence to support or refute a point of view. These skills also need to be modeled, taught, and practiced, with a focus on not only the content but also the academic vocabulary that forms the framework of the debate process. For example, a teacher might first model and then guide students in a process of finding and preparing relevant evidence from sources, asking each student in a group to complete the following:

> Read to find at least two pieces of evidence that inform the point of view the team will argue in the debate.
> Document the source for each piece of evidence, including sufficient information so that the team (or teacher, or opposing team) can quickly access the source to evaluate the evidence in context.
> Paraphrase the main points of the passage that provide evidence.
> Explain how and why the evidence adds strength and validity to the team's position.

Working together through this process and other aspects of debate, students can collaboratively develop readiness to argue a point of view and provide rebuttal to a different position (Field, 2017). Throughout, students are engaging their thinking skills and discussion skills to clarify understanding and build effective communication.

Classroom dialogue is an important contributor to students' development of critical thinking skills, particularly when there are deliberate efforts to support dialogue in connection with authentic problems that matter to students (Abrami et al., 2015; Cummins, 2014). The strategies for discussion outlined in this section should be paired with efforts to support content relevance for students, with emphasis on connecting thinking and problem solving to the goals that matter in students' own lives and communities (Cummins, 2014; Haneda, 2014).

Focus on Concepts

A focus on concept learning is an important recommendation for curriculum and instruction for all learners (Haberman, 2010) and a useful mechanism for supporting rigor and relevance for advanced learners (VanTassel-Baska & Little, 2017). A conceptual focus guides students to make meaning; they are not just memorizing or focusing on "a parade of facts" (Brophy & Alleman, 2006, p. 449), but rather organizing ideas into categories connected with prior learning (Jeffrey, 2018). Teachers can use this focus to support students from diverse backgrounds in accessing content based on connections they can make to their own experiences. Conceptual thinking involves several elements reflecting the depth and complexity that infuse good curriculum and instruction for gifted learners, including an emphasis on seeing patterns and relationships, using evidence to support and evaluate claims, and transferring understanding to new contexts and problems (Erickson, 2007; Kaplan, 2009; Partington & Buckingham, 2012).

Some years ago, Knapp and colleagues (1995) examined practices in 140 classrooms in high-poverty elementary schools and demonstrated that in classrooms in which teachers took a "meaning-focused" approach to instruction as opposed to a basic skills approach, students demonstrated higher capacity for advanced skills by the end of the year and, in most cases, also higher performance with basic skills. Yet, only about one quarter to one third of the classrooms they examined demonstrated this meaning-focused approach. Subsequent research across school demographic groups has continued to demonstrate the benefits of a meaning-focused approach (e.g., Connor et al., 2014), particularly for supporting engagement, understanding, and language development in underserved populations (Cummins, 2014).

VanTassel-Baska (2018) emphasized the value of concept-based learning as a focus in curriculum and instruction field-tested with learners from low-income backgrounds, highlighting the value of deep connections between advanced content and big ideas that served as organizers for student thinking. Such a focus on big ideas includes not only the concepts themselves, but also a thorough exploration of concepts, principles, and generalizations (Rogers, 2007). Further, such big ideas promote increased potential for student engagement, particularly because of a strong focus on connections and patterns to a wide range of prior experiences. Students do not have to have the *same* experiences as their peers to begin to make conceptual connections. Rather, students enrich the classroom conversation by bringing different types of examples of concepts, thus demonstrating the universality of big ideas. In addition, a conceptual focus helps students explore both their similarities and differences in experience in ways that may be important for engagement with transformational learning and efforts toward social change (Ladson-Billings, 1995).

A conceptual focus during instruction also promotes opportunities for teachers to recognize and address misconceptions in student thinking, which may result from limits in students' background knowledge or misunderstandings from prior learning experiences. Through a conceptual focus, including such activities as concept mapping and related discussion, teachers invite students to articulate and elaborate on their understanding of content (Jonassen, 2006). This allows the teacher to conduct a much deeper assessment of student knowledge and help build schemas that are more thoroughly grounded in the disciplines. Once again, this kind of instruction and assessment requires that students have access to rich resources that will allow them to make connections and see concepts in multiple contexts.

An instructional focus on concepts involves actively engaging students in recognizing big ideas and applying key conceptual understandings. Teachers invite students to explore their own experiences with a particular concept and then refine that understanding through articulating the critical features that make something part of a conceptual category. This understanding may then be deepened through identification of essential generalizations about the concept, with follow-up opportunities to examine those generalizations with multiple examples (Little, 2017).

For example, recall that several of the SEM-R bookmark questions shown in Figure 6.1 focused on the theme of courage. A teacher might ask students to work in groups to engage in a concept development activity related to courage through the following steps:
> Generate examples of courage, including real and fictional situations in which individuals demonstrated courage.
> Classify the examples into groups based on shared features and assign category labels to the groups.

> › Classify the examples into groups in a different way, again with category labels.
> › Generate nonexamples of the concept of courage.
> › Develop generalizations about courage and explore how they connect back to the original examples.

An activity like this can precede or follow questions about courageous characters in a book and can deepen a novel or theme study overall with emphasis on connections to real-world contexts. Such a focus on the essential aspects of a concept and a wide range of examples can help to build relevance and connection for students. As students read, listen, or view works of literature and art or documents from history, including those that they choose for themselves and those that the teacher may provide, they can engage with guiding questions that support them in recognizing themes and key ideas that appear across sources and perspectives, including exploring the relevance of the concepts in their own lives.

Connecting to the previous section, Socratic seminar can be used to promote concept-based learning as well. For example, in a unit focusing on the concept of injustice, students may have a variety of novels to choose and read in literature circles. Teachers may choose to engage the whole class in a discussion on their novels and connect it with another key piece of text, such as Martin Luther King, Jr.'s "Letter From a Birmingham Jail." Students may read and prepare this shared text for discussion in a Socratic seminar. Students may discuss how the generalizations about injustice resonate in the text from the letter while also relating it to their selected literature circle books. Although students may have read different novels, they can come to a shared understanding about injustice through this strategy.

Habits of the Disciplines

Why does this matter? How will I ever use this? These types of questions frequently frame students' encounters with new content, particularly when students do not see themselves reflected in their learning materials. Linking learning experiences in school to the authentic work of the disciplines is another consideration in promoting relevance and supporting students in making meaning, particularly when some students may have less background than their peers in school-relevant content. In many cases, however, instruction in high-poverty schools may be characterized by a focus on basic skills more than application of these skills in real-world (or simulated) contexts. Taylor et al. (2000) found patterns in low-income schools that the more effective teachers were those who emphasized greater application of skills. Active engagement with the myriad ways people approach understanding of the world has long been highlighted as "good teaching" and the antithesis of a "pedagogy of poverty" that limits opportunity for learners from low-income backgrounds (Haberman, 2010).

Teachers may start in the earliest grades talking about "what mathematicians do" or "what historians do" as they engage students in learning activities, including providing access to books, media, and other resources that will help students envision and understand what habits of the disciplines look, sound, and feel like in practice. Building connections between classroom activity and real-world applications is a way of increasing relevance for students and deepening students' thinking through authentic engagement (Abrami et al., 2015).

As part of engaging learners with practices reflective of the habits of the disciplines, teachers may build direct connections for students with experts in relevant fields. One starting place for this, for all students and particularly for those who may have had limited past experience with a wide range of experts, is to expose students to some of the many possible career directions in their areas of interest. Students may be familiar with librarians, authors, and museum curators from their experiences in school. However, they may have had less exposure to anthropologists, archivists, journalists, editors, or public relations specialists, along with many other career directions that might engage students' interests but that are not ordinarily a focus of the regular curriculum (Renzulli & Reis, 2014). Exposing students to a wide range of careers in the humanities may help them to develop a path from an interest to a future goal. Learning experiences related to career interests and exposure may begin with presentations and demonstrations with discussion and follow up, and then lead to more intensive experiences, such as simulations, mentorships, and internships. In turn, these more intensive experiences not only promote connection and relevance, but also help demonstrate to students the degree of effort involved in high levels of talent development.

Experiences with disciplinary practice and habits of mind are not limited only to visiting speakers, field trips, and out-of-school activities. Technology access provides opportunities for students to engage virtually with innovative museum exhibits, connect with mentors, watch experts talk about their practices, and gain a greater overall sense of the opportunities and possibilities linked to what they are learning. The explosion in podcasts in recent years means that there are multiple audio resources for almost any topic, including explorations of what people do in different careers. For example, "Doing History" is a podcast in which historians talk about their work. For younger students, "Kids Ask Authors" includes short (5–10-minute) interviews with children's book authors about writing and illustrating books.

Such exposure experiences are an important starting place for students to build a sense of relevance that may increase their motivation to engage with the content. Further, through connections to possible career trajectories and exposure to the experiences of experts, students gain a sense of the value of investing effort and honing high-level skills in the talent development process.

Teachers may also use the instructional context to promote strong learning habits that are relevant across the many disciplines of the humanities students will encounter. For example, a strong emphasis on the value of reading for learning, enjoyment, and deepening understanding of varied disciplines and perspectives should be central to the study of the humanities disciplines (VanTassel-Baska, 2013). Through modeling of habits of reading and providing access to a wide range of reading material and time for reading, teachers can promote this foundational emphasis in student learning—including demonstrating for advanced learners the experiences and benefits of challenging oneself to tackle more difficult reading material (Reis, 2009). Further, the questioning and discussion habits described in this section provide a strong foundation for critical thinking across contexts and disciplines.

Language and Vocabulary Focus

As noted previously, poverty is a strong predictor of student performance on assessments of vocabulary (Marulis & Neuman, 2013; Townsend et al., 2012). Although other variables also influence patterns of performance related to vocabulary knowledge, the evidence about the influence of poverty suggests the need for specific attention to development of academic vocabulary in particular—across all content areas but most certainly in language-heavy content areas, such as many of the humanities (Cummins, 2014; Schleppegrell, 2012).

Researchers have highlighted the importance of supporting students in the development of general academic vocabulary, as well as discipline-specific new terms, particularly when students may come from backgrounds in which their families are not socialized to build experience with academic registers from an early age (Cummins, 2014; Townsend et al., 2012). Townsend et al. (2012) gave the example that a teacher may engage students in a discussion of the "benefits of capitalism" with plenty of focus on understanding *capitalism* as new vocabulary but not, perhaps, on *benefits* and its multiple meanings, because it is a more generalized, yet still academic, term (pp. 501–502). Coxhead (2000) developed a widely referenced list of more than 500 frequently used general academic vocabulary words, drawn from textbooks across multiple disciplines. As illustrated in a small sample of that list in Figure 6.3, these words are not necessarily specific to any one discipline yet may have different meanings in

Figure 6.3

Sample of Terms from the Academic Word List (Coxhead, 2000)

aspect	credit	justify	scheme
category	element	method	sequence
component	factor	potential	survey
conclude	function	project	transfer
context	invest	relevant	volume

different contexts, and they may show up in questions or directions across many subject areas.

Recommendations around specific instruction in vocabulary, particularly in the early grades, tend to include emphasis on exposure to vocabulary in context and direct instruction around word use and meaning (Beck & McKeown, 2007; Coyne et al., 2004). In other words, read-alouds of storybooks for young children may have many benefits but are unlikely to support high levels of vocabulary growth on their own; targeted instruction related to the vocabulary used in the stories is also necessary (Beck & McKeown, 2007; Biemiller, 2003). Of course, part of building such attention to vocabulary in context requires access to reading materials that incorporate rich vocabulary. Even very young children can engage with sophisticated words and learn to use them, provided they have opportunities to experience those words in context and learn their meanings thoroughly (Beck & McKeown, 2007).

A strong emphasis on discussion in the classroom, as described previously, also may connect to improved outcomes for vocabulary knowledge through linking specific vocabulary instruction to discussion-focused activities (Elleman et al., 2009; Lesaux et al., 2014). Students' vocabulary knowledge may also be enhanced through teacher efforts to use classroom talk purposefully beyond specific vocabulary instruction—for example, in the early grades, helping students build connections to words and reinforcing students' use of words (Neugebauer et al., 2017). Biemiller (2003) also highlighted the importance of modeling and encouraging behaviors of seeking understanding of new words— in other words, actively encouraging children to ask about words that they do not know. In addition, building students' word knowledge through a focus on morphological awareness and a deeper exploration of how words connect to one another carries important benefits for overall vocabulary knowledge and

Figure 6.4

Sample Words With Word Families

Autobiography	Malevolent
Stems: *auto-* (self) *bio-* (life) *-graph* (something written or drawn)	**Stems:** *mal-* (bad) *-volens* (from *velle*, to wish or want)
Sample words in the family: autograph, autoimmune, automatic, automobile, autopsy, biography, biology, biome, biosphere, graphic, graphite, photograph	**Sample words in the family:** benevolent, dismal, malady, malaria, malicious, malign, malignant, malfunction, volition, voluntary, volunteer, welcome

students' skills for encountering new words (Lesaux et al., 2014; Thompson, 1996).

For example, students might work in groups to understand the stems or "pieces" of some vocabulary words relevant to what they are reading or studying and use their findings to connect to a wider range of words. Figure 6.4 shows two examples of words with their stems identified and other words that fall into the same word family through use of one or more of the same stems. Thompson (2001) advocated the value of teaching Greek and Latin roots of English words to promote a robust vocabulary for students; approaching vocabulary through teaching the roots and studying larger words provides students with tools that support them in new learning contexts. Pursuit of vocabulary with a focus on the stems of words and how they connect also supports connections with other languages and allows students coming from diverse linguistic backgrounds to demonstrate the strengths that their multiple languages give them. Further, there are playful and engaging ways to encourage students to pursue the roots of words as part of developing their vocabulary; for example, most of the magical spells and many character names in the Harry Potter series derive from Greek and Latin roots, suggesting the opportunity for a group vocabulary exploration in a popular book series (see Renfro, 2016, for examples).

Students need ongoing opportunities to practice and make use of academic vocabulary in meaningful contexts. Researchers exploring academic vocabulary have highlighted the value of engaging students from underserved populations in activities that help them to activate language toward specific personal, intellectual, and social goals (Cummins, 2014; Haneda, 2014). For example, teachers might promote use of students' language in an academic register by guiding them to write letters expressing their point of view on a concern in the community. Engaging with real problems and real audiences helps students to recognize the value of using language for effective communication: to accomplish a goal they care about.

Some researchers examining effects of vocabulary instruction have emphasized that these instructional approaches tend to be most beneficial for students whose vocabulary knowledge is underdeveloped prior to intervention (Elleman et al., 2009; Lesaux et al., 2014), particularly when the outcome of focus is reading comprehension. However, specific gains on vocabulary measures have been demonstrated across student ability levels from the same sources (Elleman et al., 2009). With gifted students, particularly those whose prior exposure to extensive academic vocabulary may be limited, the approaches described here can support rapid growth and deep learning, especially through the combinations of vocabulary study with discussion and deeper analysis of the morphological basis of the words studied.

In addition to the importance of vocabulary study, facility with language should be recognized, reinforced, and supported as part of thinking about students' talent development. In particular, students who are learning English when they come to school and speak a different language at home are often less likely to be recognized and referred for gifted services because their facility with English may seem low compared to their peers who are native English speakers. However, rapid learning of English and skills such as strong facility with code-switching between languages may be indicators of high ability and a need for advanced instructional experiences (Mun et al., 2016).

Problem-Based Learning

Problem-based learning (PBL) is an approach that employs a rich, real-world problem as the stimulus for a learning experience. Students encounter a problem that reflects the real world in that (a) it is ill-structured or not clearly defined, (b) not all of the necessary information is immediately known, (c) the context of the problem changes over time, and (d) there are a variety of implications for any action taken in response to the problem. The approach was initially developed in graduate schools for medicine and business as a way of engaging developing professionals with the complexity of real-world problems, but for several decades there has been further development and implementation of PBL with students in K–12 education as well, with particular emphasis on its use in science and social studies education (Gallagher, 1997, 2015).

In a PBL scenario, students take on the role of stakeholders as they work to define and respond to the problem, and the teacher facilitates their exploration as a coach or guide. The problem provides a point of entry for students to important knowledge and understanding within the content area under study, and the teacher's facilitation of the problem exploration is grounded in attention to the intended learning goals (Gallagher, 2015). Within the humanities, PBL may be most relevant in the context of studying history and other aspects of the social studies, although multiple interdisciplinary connections are possible across many subjects. In some PBL contexts, students take on a stakeholder role in a simulation of a historical period; for example, one unit has students taking on the role of villagers in Europe during the Black Death (Gallagher & Gallagher, 2013), and another has students taking on the role of civil rights leaders immediately after the assassination of Martin Luther King, Jr. (Brush & Saye, 2008). In each case, students are presented with a situation carrying considerable uncertainty, and they must develop understanding of the historical context to fulfill their role.

Students might also work with a problem that is more current but connected with understanding the dynamics of government, economics, or other aspects of the community. For example, students might take the role of leaders developing a museum exhibit for the history of their town, or planning an event to commemorate the contributions of particular people or groups. Any of these types of problems may be addressed with varying levels of complexity depending on the age of the students, although at every level there should be careful planning to determine the key content learning outcomes to be addressed (Ertmer & Simons, 2006).

PBL is an approach that is engaging and accessible for all learners but also provides a useful context for supporting gifted learners because of the degree of flexibility and openness an ill-structured problem presents. Despite PBL being a natural fit for gifted students, Gallagher (2015) stressed the need to modify PBL to fit the needs of gifted learners in five ways: ensuring advanced content, providing interdisciplinary connections, attending to complexity of concept, providing opportunities to discuss ethical dilemmas, and supporting learners as they acquire and develop higher order thinking skills.

A PBL approach is most useful when applied to problems with which students feel an authentic connection and that they perceive as genuine problems. For students from low-income backgrounds—or truly from any background—educators must ensure that students are able to see the problem as meaningful and their own role as relevant and influential in addressing the real or simulated situation. The stakeholder role and some kind of authentic audience (not just the classroom teacher) are key elements to promoting engagement.

This strategy is also suggested as an ideal way to support students from poverty in developing attentional and sequencing skills, a vital piece of the puzzle for educators to consider as they work with this special population (Jensen, 2009). When students engage in PBL, they are asked to work with a real-life problem for an extended period of time. Teachers support students by helping learners divide the task into manageable steps, modeling metacognitive behaviors around understanding the problem and how it changes, and slowly releasing more responsibility to the students as they demonstrate readiness. In addition, students who come from backgrounds of poverty may bring special strengths to a PBL scenario, because of their own experiences with having to manage and navigate challenges within real-world problem situations.

PBL has been reported as a successful way to support gifted learners from poverty (Gallagher, 2000; Swanson, 2006). It has also been found to support identification of students with potential who are traditionally overlooked, including those from poverty (Gallagher & Gallagher, 2013). VanTassel-Baska (2018) analyzed a series of studies that used the Integrated Curriculum Model (ICM) with students from poverty to determine common characteristics and found that PBL and real-world problem solving were successful in supporting those learners.

Community Connections

Creating a culture that values all communities and families is vital for any school. Particularly when the students in a school reflect a population that is socioeconomically diverse (and diverse in other demographic variables as well), educators must examine their own assumptions, build connections, and demonstrate authentic valuing of the funds of knowledge within the community (Moll et al., 1992; Moll & Greenberg, 1992; Risko & Walker-Dalhouse, 2007). This includes making connections with students' families, participating in community events, and supporting professional learning around cultural responsiveness (Wright et al., 2017). It also includes incorporating community-based learning into instructional experiences. Such experiences can provide exposure, promote relevance and connection, and help students to understand and respect a range of perspectives.

Many arts organizations seek opportunities for active engagement with schools, particularly schools that serve students who may not otherwise be able to access museum exhibits or symphony performances. When schools build learning partnerships with community arts organizations, students have opportunities for access, finding relevance to their own experiences, and potentially exploring new talent areas to pursue. As previously noted, arts programs are frequently in budgetary jeopardy in schools, limiting students' school-based access to these important disciplines; therefore, building connections beyond the school can be an important approach. At the same time, especially in many rural communities affected by poverty, arts departments within the schools can be vital sources for community building, and the efforts of art and music teachers to work beyond the school are significant for student learning and community connections (Hunt, 2009; VanDeusen, 2016).

As described, PBL provides an engaging and multifaceted way for students to develop content learning through a real-world problem that is relevant to them because of their role as a stakeholder. Although sometimes these types of PBL contexts are conducted as simulations, there are also applications of the approach grounded in real problems in local communities. Identifying and engaging with a local issue in the community may be linked to students' study of civics, history, or nonfiction reading and potentially other areas of content as well. For example, in a community discussing where to locate a new school or community center, students can learn about land use, architecture, and local government from engaging with the emerging information about the problem. In addition, PBL reflects the emphasis on practices of the disciplines as well as opportunities for connecting actively with professionals in the community (Gallagher, 2015).

Active community connections are a key element in high-poverty schools that "beat the odds" in terms of student achievement and other success factors (Cunningham, 2006; Jesse et al., 2004). As outlined, engaging students in PBL experiences requires building their authentic connections to the problem—a goal that can be supported through focus on real problems in the local community. The authenticity of community connections helps to build a sense of purpose, promote leadership development, and support students' motivation to leverage their academic language and learning toward shared goals (Cummins, 2014; Little & Kearney, 2015).

Problem-based learning and other instructional experiences that are community-based require concentrated attention to and respect for the needs and values of the local community. The opportunities and challenges for students affected by poverty differ depending on many aspects of the local community. For example, in rural areas affected by issues of poverty, students' opportunities to advanced learning opportunities may be limited by geographic access to resources, and they may be wrestling with expectations around whether to leave their hometown for educational experiences that might be available to them elsewhere. High school or middle school students might engage in interviews with alumni who chose to leave the area and alumni who chose to stay to develop understanding of different perspectives on career pursuits and the influences on career decision making. In rural communities affected by issues of poverty, place-based education is one recommendation for framing students' educational experiences in ways that affirm the backgrounds students bring and encourage school-community connections (Azano, 2014). It places value on the rural setting as opposed to viewing rural as not valued in school.

Across these types of community-connected experiences, educators work to acknowledge and affirm the learning experiences that students have outside of the school building and to build authentic connections between these experiences and the school curriculum. These connections not only help to build relevance for students, but also strengthen educators' cultural responsiveness and understanding of the funds of knowledge that students and their families bring (Brayko, 2013; Moll et al., 1992). Gallego (2001) and Brayko (2013) demonstrated ways in which preservice teacher placements in community contexts outside of the school day supported these professionals in deepening their understanding of their students' lives, particularly the multiple literacies that shape students' experiences. Active efforts on the part of school leaders to build community connections are beneficial to the mutual understanding of teachers and the communities they serve.

Supporting Teachers in the Humanities

Throughout this discussion, key ideas for supporting gifted students from backgrounds of poverty in the humanities included (a) providing exposure to a wide range of resources, (b) promoting relevance and connection for students to their own experiences, (c) targeting development of particular skills while ensuring high levels of challenge and growth, and (d) working to build a classroom culture of respect for varied perspectives and backgrounds. These are no small goals, and they demonstrate the importance of support for professional learning, investment in curricular resources, and considerations for time, grouping, and planning. Some of these points are discussed in greater detail elsewhere in this book but are acknowledged here for their specific relevance in the context of humanities instruction.

Unfortunately, preservice teachers spend minimal time (if any) in their preparation programs learning about gifted students, which likely means that special populations of the gifted, including those from poverty, may never even be discussed (Callahan et al., 2014; Loveless et al., 2008). Practicing teachers may also have limited opportunity for professional learning in gifted education, and the focus of professional learning in high-poverty schools tends to be much more on bringing struggling students up to expected levels and not on supporting gifted learners. In addition, teachers may need opportunities to deepen their professional learning around the specific content of the humanities subjects they are expected to teach, particularly if they are trying to respond to students working above grade level or even just to keep up with what titles in children's literature may be engaging, challenging, and personally and culturally meaningful for their students. Further, approaches such as problem-based learning require support for professional learning to ensure the kind of facilitation likely to promote student growth from these experiences (Ertmer & Simons, 2006). Thus, opportunities for professional learning to address these issues are an important investment for schools (Gubbins, 2014; Wycoff et al., 2003).

To support teachers in implementing the strategies discussed throughout this chapter, and to give them guidance for some of the books, artworks, documents, and other resources for instruction, schools can invest in high-quality, evidence-based resources that are effective for a wide range of students and incorporate specific emphasis on differentiation for advanced learners. Curriculum-based support can be a critical element of talent spotting (A. Robinson et al., 2018) and preparing students for more advanced coursework later (Horn, 2015). However, a change in curriculum does not always yield a change in pedagogy (Trujillo & Woulfin, 2014), and teachers with shallower knowledge of what they are teaching may affect student learning negatively with weak efforts to implement rich resources (Piasta et al., 2009). Thus, consistent and high-quality support for teachers in their efforts to implement high-level curriculum is necessary to ensure fidelity and the intended outcomes of such curriculum.

The instructional approaches reflected in this chapter rely on learning contexts in which teachers and students have the time and flexibility to engage in rich discussion, pursue depth in understanding, and explore new questions that emerge. Time and flexibility are critical resources for teachers to be able to make appropriate and informed instructional choices and to promote gifted students' experiences of depth in learning. Further, promoting a schoolwide emphasis on talent development and responding to strengths must include flexibility in scheduling and grouping that would allow students to access different types of experiences as they are needed (Horn, 2015; Renzulli, 1999; Renzulli & Brandon, 2017).

Roland Greene, director of the Stanford Humanities Center, said of the humanities, "Some other disciplines solve problems. We return to the problems that can never be solved but must be addressed again by each intellectual generation in its own ways" (Jabbar, 2019). Educational experiences in the humanities can support gifted students from backgrounds of poverty as they take a role in addressing these eternal problems and questions, even while they are seeking their interests and talents, honing their thinking and skills, and building deep connections within their own communities and with the broader scope of human experience.

References

Abrami, P. C., Bernard, R. M., Borokhovski, E., Waddington, D. I., Wade, C. A., & Persson, T. (2015). Strategies for teaching students to think critically: A meta-analysis. *Review of Educational Research, 85*(2), 275–314. https://doi.org/10.3102/003465 4314551063

Americans for the Arts. (2019). *Arts advocacy day: 2019 congressional arts handbook.* https://www.americansforthearts.org/sites/default/files/Handbook%202019-- %20All.pdf

Azano, A. P. (2014). Gifted rural students. In J. A. Plucker & C. M. Callahan (Eds.), *Critical issues and practices in gifted education: What the research says* (2nd ed., pp. 297–304). Prufrock Press.

Beck, I. L., & McKeown, M. G. (2007). Increasing young low-income children's oral vocabulary repertoires through rich and focused instruction. *The Elementary School Journal, 107*(3), 251–271. https://doi.org/10.1086/511706

Beghetto, R. A., & Kaufman, J. C. (2009). Intellectual estuaries: Connecting learning and creativity in programs of advanced academics. *Journal of Advanced Academics, 20*(2), 296–324. https://doi.org/10.1177/1932202X0902000205

Bhattacharya, A. (2010). Children and adolescents from poverty and reading development: A research review. *Reading and Writing Quarterly, 26*(2), 115–139. https:// doi.org/10.1080/10573560903547445

Biemiller, A. (2003). Vocabulary: Needed if more children are to read well. *Reading Psychology, 24*(3–4), 323–335. https://doi.org/10.1080/02702710390227297

Bisland, B. M. (2015). An exploration of the impact of accountability testing on teaching in urban elementary classrooms. *The Urban Review, 47*, 433–465. https://doi. org/10.1007/s11256-014-0296-3

Brayko, K. (2013). Community-based placements as contexts for disciplinary learning: A study of literacy teacher education outside of school. *Journal of Teacher Education, 64*(1), 47–59. https://doi.org/10.1177/0022487112458800

Brophy, J., & Alleman, J. (2006). A reconceptualized rationale for elementary social studies. *Theory and Research in Social Education, 34*(4), 428–454. https://doi.org/10 .1080/00933104.2006.10473317

Brush, T., & Saye, J. (2008). The effects of multimedia-supported problem-based inquiry on student engagement, empathy, and assumptions about history. *Interdisciplinary Journal of Problem-Based Learning, 2*(1), 21–56. https://doi.org/10.77 71/1541-5015.1052

Callahan, C. M., Moon, T. R., & Oh, S. (2014). *National surveys of gifted programs: Executive summary: 2014.* University of Virginia, National Research Center on the Gifted and Talented https://www.nagc.org/sites/default/files/key%20reports/20 14%20Survey%20of%20GT%20programs%20Exec%20Summ.pdf

Chapin, S. H., O'Connor, C., & Anderson, N. C. (2009). Classroom discussions: Using math talk to help students learn, grades K–6. Math Solutions.

Connor, C. M., Spencer, M., Day, S. L., Giuliani, S., Ingebrand, S. W., McLean, L., & Morrison, F. J. (2014). Capturing the complexity: Content, type, and amount of instruction and quality of the classroom learning environment synergistically predict third graders' vocabulary and reading comprehension outcomes. *Journal of Educational Psychology, 106*(3), 762–778. https://doi.org/10.1037/a0035921

Copeland, M. (2005). *Socratic circles: Fostering critical and creative thinking in middle and high school*. Stenhouse.

Cotton, K. (1989). *Classroom questioning (Close-up #5)*. Northwest Regional Educational Laboratory. https://educationnorthwest.org/sites/default/files/resources/classro om-questioning-508.pdf

Coxhead, A. (2000). A new academic word list. *TESOL Quarterly, 34*(2), 213–238. https://doi.org/10.2307/3587951

Coyne, M. D., Simmons, D. C., Kame'enui, E. J., & Stoolmiller, M. (2004). Teaching vocabulary during shared storybook readings: An examination of differential effects. *Exceptionality, 12*(3), 145–162. https://doi.org/10.1207/s15327035ex1203_3

Cummins, J. (2014). Beyond language: Academic communication and student success. *Linguistics and Education, 26*(1), 145–154. https://doi.org/10.1016/j.linged.2014.01.006

Cunningham, P. M. (2006). High-poverty schools that beat the odds. *The Reading Teacher, 60*(4), 382–385. https://doi.org/10.1598/RT.60.4.9

Cuny, C. (2014). What is the value of life? and other Socratic questions. *Educational Leadership, 72*(3), 54–58.

Cuthrell, K., Stapleton, J., & Ledford, C. (2009). Examining the culture of poverty: Promising practices. *Preventing School Failure: Alternative Education for Children and Youth, 54*(2), 104-110. https://doi.org/10.1080/10459880903217689

DeLuca, S., Clampet-Lundquist, S., & Edin, K. (2016). *Coming of age in the other America*. SAGE.

Dudley-Marling, C., & Lucas, K. (2009). Pathologizing the language and culture of poor children. *Language Arts, 86*(5), 362–370. https://www.jstor.org/stable/41483561

Elleman, A. M., Lindo, E. J., Morphy, P., & Compton, D. L. (2009). The impact of vocabulary instruction on passage-level comprehension of school-age children: A meta-analysis. *Journal of Research on Educational Effectiveness, 2*(1), 1–44. https://doi.org/10.1080/19345740802539200

Erickson, H. L. (2007). *Concept-based curriculum and instruction for the thinking classroom*. Corwin.

Ertmer, P. A., & Simons, K. D. (2006). Jumping the PBL implementation hurdle: Supporting the efforts of K–12 teachers. *Interdisciplinary Journal of Problem-Based Learning, 1*(1), 40–54. https://doi.org/10.7771/1541-5015.1005

Field, K. (2017). Debating our way toward stronger thinking. *Gifted Child Today, 40*(3), 144–153. https://doi.org/10.1177/1076217517707235

Gallagher, S. A. (1997). Problem-based learning: Where did it come from, what does it do, and where is it going? *Journal for the Education of the Gifted, 20*(4), 332–362. https://doi.org/10.1177/016235329702000402

Gallagher, S. A. (2000). Project P-BLISS: An experiment in curriculum for gifted disadvantaged high school students. *NASSP Bulletin, 84*(615), 47–57. https://doi.org/10.1177/019263650008461506

Gallagher, S. A. (2015). Adapting problem-based learning for gifted students. In F. A. Karnes & S. M. Bean (Eds.), *Methods and materials for teaching the gifted* (4th ed., pp. 413–444). Prufrock Press.

Gallagher, S. A., & Gallagher, J. J. (2013). Using problem-based learning to explore unseen academic potential. *Interdisciplinary Journal of Problem-based Learning, 7*(1), 111–131. https://doi.org/10.7771/1541-5015.1322

Gallego, M. A. (2001). Is experience the best teacher? The potential of coupling classroom and community-based field experiences. *Journal of Teacher Education, 52*(4), 312–325. https://doi.org/10.1177/0022487101052004005

Gay, G. (2010). *Culturally responsive teaching: Theory, research, and practice* (2nd ed.). Teachers College Press.

Goldhaber, D., Lavery, L., & Theobald, R. (2015). Uneven playing field? Assessing the teacher quality gap between advantaged and disadvantaged students. *Educational Researcher, 44*(5), 293–307. https://doi.org/10.3102/0013189X15592622

Goldstein, D. (2020). Two states. Eight textbooks. Two American stories. *The New York Times.* https://www.nytimes.com/interactive/2020/01/12/us/texas-vs-california-history-textbooks.html

Gorski, P. C. (2013). Building a pedagogy of engagement for students in poverty. *Phi Delta Kappan, 95*(1), 48–52. https://doi.org/10.1177/003172171309500109

Gorski, P. C. (2018). *Reaching and teaching students in poverty: Strategies for erasing the opportunity gap* (2nd ed.). Teachers College Press.

Gubbins, E. J. (2014). Professional development. In J. Plucker & C. M. Callahan (Eds.), *Critical issues and practices in gifted education: What the research says* (2nd ed., pp. 505–517). Prufrock Press.

Haberman, M. (2010). The pedagogy of poverty versus good teaching. *Phi Delta Kappan, 92*(2), 81–87. https://doi.org/10.1177/003172171009200223

Haneda, M. (2014). From academic language to academic communication: Building on English learners' resources. *Linguistics and Education, 26*(1), 126–135. https://doi.org/10.1016/j.linged.2014.01.004

Harris, O., & Reynolds, R. (2014). The history curriculum and its personal connection to students from minority ethnic backgrounds. *Journal of Curriculum Studies, 46*(4), 464–486. https://doi.org/10.1080/00220272.2014.881925

Hart, B., & Risley, T. R. (1995). *Meaningful differences in the everyday experiences of young American children.* Brookes.

Hart, B., & Risley, T. R. (2003). The early catastrophe: The 30 million word gap by age 3. *American Educator, 27*(1), 4–9.

Hattie, J. (2009). *Visible learning: A synthesis of over 800 meta-analyses relating to achievement.* Routledge.

Henfield, M. S., Washington, A. R., & Byrd, J. A. (2014). Addressing academic and opportunity gaps impacting gifted Black males: Implications for school counselors. *Gifted Child Today, 37*(3), 147–154. https://doi.org/10.1177/1076217514530118

Horn, C. V. (2015). Young scholars: A talent development model for finding and nurturing potential in underserved populations. *Gifted Child Today, 38*(1), 19–31. https://doi.org/10.1177/1076217514556532

Hunsaker, S. L., Rose, C. C., & Nedreberg, E. R. (2018). Principles and practices of Socratic circles in middle level classrooms. In J. Danielian, C. M. Fugate, & E. Fogarty (Eds.), *Teaching gifted children: Success strategies for teaching high-ability learners* (pp. 41–50). Prufrock Press.

Hunt, C. (2009). Perspectives on rural and urban music teaching: Developing contextual awareness in music education. *Journal of Music Teacher Education, 18*(2), 34–47. https://doi.org/10.1177/1057083708327613

Jabbar, N. (2019). Greene, a scholar of early modern literature, will lead the Stanford Humanities Center starting this fall. *Stanford News.* https://news.stanford.edu/2019/07/29/literature-professor-roland-greene-named-director-stanford-humanities-center

Jeffrey, T. (2018). Differentiating content using a conceptual lens. In J. Danielian, C. M. Fugate, & E. Fogarty (Eds.), *Teaching gifted children: Success strategies for teaching high-ability learners* (pp. 117–122). Prufrock Press.

Jensen, E. (2009). *Teaching with poverty in mind: What being poor does to kids' brains and what schools can do about it.* ASCD.

Jesse, D., Davis, A., & Pokorny, N. (2004). High-achieving middle schools for Latino students in poverty. *Journal of Education for Students Placed at Risk, 9*(1), 23–45. https://doi.org/10.1207/S15327671ESPR0901_2

Jonassen, D. H. (2006). On the role of concepts in learning and instructional design. *Educational Technology Research and Development, 54,* 177–196. https://doi.org/10.1007/s11423-006-8253-9

Kaplan, S. N. (2009). The grid: A model to construct differentiated curriculum for the gifted. In J. S. Renzulli, E. J. Gubbins, K. S. McMillen, R. D. Eckert, & C. A. Little (Eds.), *Systems and models for developing programs for the gifted and talented* (2nd ed., pp. 235–252). Prufrock Press.

Knapp, M. S., Shields, P. M., & Turnbull, B. J. (1995). Academic challenge in high-poverty classrooms. *Phi Delta Kappan, 76*(10), 770–776. https://www.jstor.org/stable/20405455

Knapp, M. S., & Woolverton, S. (2001). Social class and schooling. In J. A. Banks & C. A. McGee Banks (Eds.), *Handbook of research on multicultural education* (2nd ed., pp. 548–569). Jossey-Bass.

Ladson-Billings, G. (1995). Toward a theory of culturally-relevant pedagogy. *American Educational Research Journal, 32*(3), 465–491. https://doi.org/10.3102/00028312032003465

Lesaux, N. K., Kieffer, M. J., Kelley, J. G., & Harris, J. R. (2014). Effects of academic vocabulary instruction for linguistically diverse adolescents: Evidence from a randomized field trial. *American Educational Research Journal, 51*(6), 1159–1194. https://doi.org/10.3102/0002831214532165

Little, C. A. (2017). The use of overarching concepts in the Integrated Curriculum Model. In J. VanTassel-Baska & C. A. Little (Eds.), *Content-based curriculum for high-ability learners* (3rd ed., pp. 169–194). Prufrock Press.

Little, C. A., & Kearney, K. L. (2015). Leadership development for high-ability secondary students. In F. A. Dixon & S. M. Moon (Eds.), *Handbook of secondary gifted education* (2nd ed., pp. 483–508). Prufrock Press.

Little, C. A., McCoach, D. B., & Reis, S. M. (2014). Effects of differentiated reading instruction on student achievement in middle school. *Journal of Advanced Academics, 25*(4), 384–402. https://doi.org/10.1177/1932202X14549250

Loveless, T., Farkas, S., & Duffett, A. (2008). *High-achieving students in the era of NCLB.* Thomas B. Fordham Institute.

Marulis, L. M., & Neuman, S. B. (2013). How vocabulary interventions affect young children at risk: A meta-analytic review. *Journal of Research on Educational Effectiveness, 6*(3), 223–262. https://doi.org/10.1080/19345747.2012.755591

Michaels, S., O'Connor, C., & Resnick, L. B. (2008). Deliberative discourse idealized and realized: Accountable talk in the classroom and in civic life. *Studies in Philosophy and Education, 27,* 283–297. https://doi.org/10.1007/s11217-007-9071-1

Mixon, K. (2005). Building your instrumental music program in an urban school. *Music Educators Journal, 91*(3), 15–23. https://doi.org/10.2307/3400071

Moll, L. C., Amanti, C., Neff, D., & Gonzalez, N. (1992). Funds of knowledge for teaching: Using a qualitative approach to connect homes and classrooms. *Theory Into Practice, 31*(2), 132–141. https://doi.org/10.1080/00405849209543534

Moll, L. C., & Greenberg, J. B. (1992). Creating zones of possibilities: Combining social contexts for instruction. In L. C. Moll (Ed.), *Vygotsky and education: Instructional implications and applications of sociohistorical psychology* (pp. 319–348). Cambridge University Press.

Mun, R. U., Langley, S. D., Ware, S., Gubbins, E. J., Siegle, D., Callahan, C. M., McCoach, D. B., & Hamilton, R. (2016). *Effective practices for identifying and serving English learners in gifted education: A systematic review of the literature.* University of Connecticut, National Center for Research on Gifted Education. https://ncrge.uconn.edu/wp-content/uploads/sites/982/2016/01/NCRGE_EL_Lit-Review.pdf

National Center for Education Statistics. (n.d.). *Schools and staffing survey (SASS).* https://nces.ed.gov/surveys/sass

Neugebauer, S. R., Gámez, P. B., Coyne, M. D., McCoach, D. B., Cólon, I. T., & Ware, S. (2017). Promoting word consciousness to close the vocabulary gap in young word learners. *The Elementary School Journal, 118*(1), 28–54. https://doi.org/10.1086/692986

Neuman, S. B., & Celano, D. (2001). Access to print in low-income and middle-income communities: An ecological study of four neighborhoods. *Reading Research Quarterly, 36*(1), 8–26. https://doi.org/10.1598/RRQ.36.1.1

Neuman, S. B., & Celano, D. (2006). The knowledge gap: Implications of leveling the playing field for low-income and middle-income children. *Reading Research Quarterly, 41*(2), 176–201. https://doi.org/10.1598/RRQ.41.2.2

Partington, A., & Buckingham, D. (2012). Challenging theories: Conceptual learning in the media studies classroom. *International Journal of Learning and Media, 3*(4), 7–22. https://doi.org/10.1162/IJLM_a_00079

Paul, R., & Elder, L. (2007). Critical thinking: The art of Socratic questioning. *Journal of Developmental Education, 31*(1), 36–37.

Piasta, S. B., Connor, C. M., Fishman, B. J., & Morrison, F. J. (2009). Teachers' knowledge of literacy concepts, classroom practices, and student reading growth. *Scientific Studies of Reading, 13*(3), 224–248. https://doi.org/10.1080/10888430902851364

Reis, S. M. (2009). *Joyful reading: Differentiation and enrichment for successful literacy learning, grades K–8.* Jossey-Bass.

Reis, S. M., McCoach, D. B., Little, C. A., Muller, L. M., & Kaniskan, B. (2011). The effects of differentiated instruction and enrichment pedagogy on reading achievement in five elementary schools. *American Educational Research Journal, 48*(2), 462–501. https://doi.org/10.3102/0002831210382891

Renfro, K. (2016, January 12). *The real linguistic inspiration behind 13 "Harry Potter" spells.* Business Insider. https://www.businessinsider.com/harry-potter-spells-latin-orig in-2016-1

Renzulli, J. S. (1999). What is this thing called giftedness, and how do we develop it? A twenty-five year perspective. *Journal for the Education of the Gifted, 23*(1), 3–54. https://doi.org/10.1177/016235329902300102

Renzulli, J. S., & Brandon, L. E. (2017). Common sense about the under-representation issue: A school-wide approach to increase participation of diverse students in programs that develop talents and gifted behaviours in young people. *International Journal for Talent Development and Creativity, 5*(2), 71–94.

Renzulli, J. S., & Reis, S. M. (2014). *The Schoolwide Enrichment Model: A how-to guide for talent development* (3rd ed.). Prufrock Press.

Risko, V. J., & Walker-Dalhouse, D. (2007). Tapping students' cultural funds of knowledge to address the achievement gap. *The Reading Teacher, 61*(1), 98–100. https://doi.org/10.1598/RT.61.1.12

Robinson, A., Adelson, J. L., Kidd, K. A., & Cunningham, C. M. (2018). A talent for tinkering: Developing talents in children from low-income households through engineering curriculum. *Gifted Child Quarterly, 62*(1), 130–144. https://doi.org/10.1177/0016986217738049

Robinson, J. G. (2007). Presence and persistence: Poverty ideology and inner-city teaching. *The Urban Review, 39,* 541–565. https://doi.org/10.1007/s11256-007-0072-8

Rogers, K. B. (2007). Lessons learned about educating the gifted and talented: A synthesis of the research on educational practice. *Gifted Child Quarterly, 51*(4), 382–396. https://doi.org/10.1177/0016986207306324

Sano, J. (2009). Farmhands and factory workers, honesty and humility: The portrayal of social class and morals in English language learner children's books. *Teachers College Record, 111*(11), 2560–2588.

Schleppegrell, M. J. (2012). Academic language in teaching and learning: Introduction to the special issue. *The Elementary School Journal, 112*(3), 409–418. https://doi.org/10.1086/663297

Senn, L. (2018). Socratic circles: Round and round the wheels of thought. In J. Danielian, C. M. Fugate, & E. Fogarty (Eds.), *Teaching gifted children: Success strategies for teaching high-ability learners* (pp. 51–57). Prufrock Press.

Smith, F., Hardman, F., Wall, K., & Mroz, M. (2004). Interactive whole class teaching in the National Literacy and Numeracy Strategies. *British Educational Research Journal, 30*(3), 395–411. https://doi.org/10.1080/01411920410001689706

Snellman, K., Silva, J. M., Frederick, C. B., & Putnam, R. D. (2015). The engagement gap: Social mobility and extracurricular participation among American youth. *Annals of the American Academy of Political and Social Science, 657*(1), 194–207. https://doi.org/10.1177/0002716214548398

Soter, A. O., Wilkinson, I. A., Murphy, P. K., Rudge, L., Reninger, K., & Edwards, M. (2008). What the discourse tells us: Talk and indicators of high-level comprehension. *International Journal of Educational Research, 47*(6), 372–391. https://doi.org/10.1016/j.ijer.2009.01.001

Sperry, D. E., Sperry, L. L., & Miller, P. J. (2019). Reexamining the verbal environments of children from different socioeconomic backgrounds. *Child Development, 90*(4), 1303–1318. https://doi.org/10.1111/cdev.13072

Stambaugh, T., & VanTassel-Baska, J. (2017). *Jacob's ladder reading comprehension program: Grades 6–7* (2nd ed.). Prufrock Press.

Stanford Humanities Center. (n.d.). *What are the humanities?* https://shc.stanford.edu/what-are-the-humanities

Swanson, J. D. (2006). Breaking through assumptions about low-income, minority gifted students. *Gifted Child Quarterly, 50*(1), 11–25. https://doi.org/10.1177/001698620605000103

Taylor, B. M., Pearson, P. D., Clark, K., & Walpole, S. (2000). Effective schools and accomplished teachers: Lessons about primary-grade reading instruction in low-income schools. *The Elementary School Journal, 101*(2), 121–165. https://doi.org/10.1086/499662

Taylor, B. M., Pearson, P. D., Peterson, D. S., & Rodriguez, M. C. (2003). Reading growth in high-poverty classrooms: The influence of teacher practices that encourage cognitive engagement in literacy learning. *The Elementary School Journal, 104*(1), 3–28. https://doi.org/10.1086/499740

Thompson, M. C. (1996). Formal language study for gifted students. In J. VanTassel-Baska, D. T. Johnson, & L. N. Boyce (Eds.), *Developing verbal talent: Ideas and strategies for teachers of elementary and middle school students* (pp. 149–173). Allyn & Bacon.

Thompson, M. C. (2001). Vocabulary and grammar: Critical content for critical thinking. *Journal of Secondary Gifted Education, 13*(2), 60–66. https://doi.org/10.4219/jsge-2002-367

Tienken, C. H., Goldberg, S., & DiRocco, D. (2009). Questioning the questions. *Kappa Delta Pi Record, 46*(1), 39–43. https://doi.org/10.1080/00228958.2009.10516690

Townsend, D., Filippini, A., Collins, P., & Biancarosa, G. (2012). Evidence for the importance of academic word knowledge for the academic achievement of diverse middle school students. *The Elementary School Journal, 112*(3), 497–518. https://doi.org/10.1086/663301

Trujillo, T. M., & Woulfin, S. L. (2014). Equity-oriented reform amid standards-based accountability: A qualitative comparative analysis of an intermediary's instructional practices. *American Educational Research Journal, 51*(2), 253–293. https://doi.org/10.3102/0002831214527335

van der Veen, C., de Mey, L., van Kruistum, C., & van Oers, B. (2017). The effect of productive classroom talk and metacommunication on young children's oral communicative competence and subject matter knowledge: An intervention study in early childhood education. *Learning and Instruction, 48,* 14–22. https://doi.org/10.1016/j.learninstruc.2016.06.001

VanDeusen, A. (2016). "It really comes down to the community": A case study of a rural school music program. *Action for Change in Music Education, 15*(4), 56–75. https://doi.org/10.22176/act15.4.56

VanTassel-Baska, J. (Ed.). (2013). *Using the Common Core State Standards for English language arts with gifted and advanced learners.* Prufrock Press.

VanTassel-Baska, J. (2018). Achievement unlocked: Effective curriculum interventions with low-income students. *Gifted Child Quarterly, 62*(1), 68–82. https://doi.org/10.1177/0016986217738565

VanTassel-Baska, J., & Little, C. A. (Eds.). (2017). *Content-based curriculum for high-ability learners* (3rd ed.). Prufrock Press.

VanTassel-Baska, J., & Wood, S. (2010). The Integrated Curriculum Model (ICM). *Learning and Individual Differences, 20*(4), 345–357. https://doi.org/10.1016/j.lindif.2009.12.006

Vogler, K. E. (2008). Asking good questions. *Educational Leadership, 65*(9). https://www.ascd.org/publications/educational-leadership/summer08/vol65/num09/Asking-Good-Questions.aspx

Walsh, J. A., & Sattes, B. D. (2011). *Thinking through quality questioning: Deepening student engagement.* Corwin.

Wolf, M. K., Crosson, A. C., & Resnick, L. B. (2005). Classroom talk for rigorous reading comprehension instruction. *Reading Psychology, 26*(1), 27–53. https://doi.org/10.1080/02702710490897518

Wolf, M. K., Crosson, A. C., & Resnick, L. B. (2006). *Accountable talk in reading comprehension instruction* (CSE Technical Report 670).

Wright, B. L., Ford, D. Y., & Young, J. L. (2017). Ignorance or indifference? Seeking excellence and equity for under-represented students of color in gifted education. *Global Education Review, 4*(1), 45–60.

Wycoff, M., Nash, W. R., Juntune, J. E., & Mackay, L. (2003). Purposeful professional development: Planning positive experiences for teachers of the gifted and talented. *Gifted Child Today, 26*(4), 34–64. https://doi.org/10.4219/gct-2003-116

Zwiers, J. (2007). Teacher practices and perspectives for developing academic language. *International Journal of Applied Linguistics, 17*(1), 93–116. https://doi.org/10.1111/j.1473-4192.2007.00135.x

CHAPTER 7

Instructional Strategies to Support Talented Students From Low-Income Households: *The STEM Fields*

Ann Robinson and Monica C. Meadows

The science, technology, engineering, and mathematics (STEM) fields present a pathway out of poverty for children and adolescents from low-income households. Two reasons make these content domains an effective match. First, STEM fields are in high demand and therefore offer individuals from low-income households career and professional attainment with adequate financial rewards. Second, science, technology, and engineering are inherently hands-on domains and therefore engage children and adolescents in active learning immediately.

In terms of demand, STEM education serves as a gateway to higher paying jobs and is an important linchpin to a growing economy. According to the U.S. Bureau of Labor and Statistics, STEM jobs are projected to increase 13% between 2017 and 2027, as compared to 9% for non-STEM jobs, with positions in computing, engineering, and advanced manufacturing leading the way (Fayer et al., 2017). In addition, STEM-related jobs pay well. Out of 100 STEM occupations, 93% had wages above the national average. In 2015, the national average for STEM annual salaries was $87,570, whereas the national average for non-STEM occupations sat at roughly half, $45,700 (Fayer et al., 2017).

With respect to diversity, the STEM workforce ranges widely within and across STEM occupations. According to the Pew Research Center, even though women have made gains in representation in the STEM workforce over the past 25 years, particularly in life and physical science jobs, they remain strongly underrepresented in some STEM job clusters, notably computer science and engineering (Funk & Parker, 2018). Racial and ethnic diversity in STEM is also varied. Black and Hispanic workers remain underrepresented overall; these groups are also underrepresented among those in STEM occupations with professional or doctoral degrees. Asian American individuals are overrepresented across all STEM occupational clusters and have an especially large presence in the college-educated STEM workforce, particularly in computer science occupations, relative to their share among employed college graduates overall (Funk & Parker, 2018). These economic and workforce trends provide context for developing STEM talents in K–12 settings, including low average-income schools.

Second, with respect to hands-on engagement, talent development in the STEM fields, particularly with children and adolescents from low-income households, is developmental. The challenge and engagement must begin early and continue through a trajectory into early career and must be persistent to make a difference in the lives of individuals in poverty. Several models of talent, which tend to be attentive to domain-specific differences, address lifespan development (Dai, 2017; Dai & Li, in press; Feldhusen, 1998; Subotnik et al., 2011). However, they do not necessarily address the unique challenges of children and adolescents from low-income households in accessing affordances in STEM domains. We adopt the perspective that developmental models are a good match for talented children living in poverty, but linkages to the STEM fields need to be explicit. Specifically, STEM affordances can be costly for both home and school.

Learners from low-income households routinely "make do" as part of economic constraints at home and at school. Instructional experiences in domains like science and engineering that emphasize hands-on investigation and creativity are critical components for the development of STEM talents (Robinson, Adelson, Kidd, & Cunningham, 2018). How to leverage the costly STEM affordances remains a challenge.

All students with STEM potential, including students from low-income households, should be provided powerful and rigorous STEM experiences and held to the highest standards. Students need access to a systematic, timely, continuous progression through a challenging and creative curriculum. All students should take appropriate, rigorous mathematics and science classes every year from elementary through high school. Recent trends indicate that students enroll in general (not advanced) science courses at comparable rates, regardless of sex, race, and ethnicity (National Girls Collaborative Project, 2018). Unfortunately, students whose parents are of lower socioeconomic status (SES) are less likely to take science courses (National Girls Collaborative Project, 2018).

Finally, in addition to science and mathematics courses, technology and engineering curricula should be an integral part of the K–12 continuum. Students of all ages should progress freely to greater rigor and complexity or higher level classes as they demonstrate their mastery of content across any or all of the STEM fields. Conceptual models of integrating STEM disciplines instructionally have been proposed (Kelley & Knowles, 2016) and explored by the National Research Council (NRC, 2011). The integrated STEM approach addresses the need for talented children and youth from low-income homes to be engaged in real-world problem solving, as most complex issues require a cross-disciplinary approach that includes science, technology, engineering, and mathematics.

Early Intervention in STEM for Children From Low-Income Households

Policy researchers and makers have produced a series of reports documenting the STEM pipeline problem, sounding a call to action, and offering recommendations to schools, foundations, and employers. One such report from the National Science Board (2010), *Preparing the Next Generation of STEM Innovators*, focused on the development of children and youth with interests and skills most likely to accelerate them into advanced STEM professions. Of the 18 recommendations, three were focused on early intervention for primary and elementary students and the preparation of their teachers in STEM content knowledge and pedagogical skills.

But what does early intervention look like in practice? We focus on three evidence-supported programs that emphasize talent identification for students from low-income households. These exemplars have similar features that include student identification, curricular affordances, and teacher professional development to identify and nurture STEM talents. In addition, they incorporate high-end instruction and curriculum as the primary platform for talent development. The interventions are: (1) STEM Starters and STEM Starters+, focused on science and science through engineering respectively; (2) U-STARS and U-STARS~PLUS, focused on science through in-school services and parental involvement in science and literacy at home; and (3) Project M³: Mentoring Mathematical Minds and Project M²: Mentoring Young Mathematicians, focused on accelerated curriculum units used within school and in out-of-school settings.

STEM Starters and STEM Starters+

The STEM Starters and STEM Starters+ interventions were developed through Jacob K. Javits funding to address the need for improved STEM services and teacher preparation in low-income elementary schools. STEM Starters and STEM Starters+ are a combination of two different curricula: Engineering is Elementary (EiE) from the Boston Museum of Science and *Blueprints for Biography* from the Jodie Mahony Center for Gifted at the University of Arkansas, Little Rock.

The instructional structure of the program includes two main components: challenging science or engineering curriculum (approximately 1–2 units per year) and a children's trade biography of a scientist, engineer, or inventor with an accompanying curriculum guide (approximately two biographies per year). For example, in grade 1, students complete a unit on acoustical engineering, which includes four lessons with enrichment extensions, *Sounds Like Fun* (EiE, 2011), and a biography of Jane Goodall, the scientist who investigated chimp vocalizations. In *Blueprints for Biography*, students engage in a science experiment or an engineering design challenge; a series of high-level questions drawing on the textual, illustrative, and graphic information in the trade biography; and extension strategies based on portrait analysis, persuasive writing prompts, primary source analysis, and point of view analysis as instructional strategies. For example, in the point of view analysis in the *Blueprints for Biography* curriculum guide for a trade biography of George Ferris, engineer and inventor of the observation wheel, students are asked to consider the information in Figure 7.1, craft responses to the engineering problem and to be aware of the important habits of mind needed by engineers to overcome problems and work within constraints.

The STEM Starters and STEM Starters+ interventions are evidence-based and have been used in high-poverty schools in both urban and rural settings. Field studies have demonstrated that the program increased science content knowledge, science concepts, and process skills for identified gifted students in grades 2–5 (Robinson, Dailey, Hughes, & Cotabish, 2014); science content and engineering knowledge for students in grade 1 (Robinson, Adelson, Kidd, & Cunningham, 2018); science achievement on an above-level test for identified

Figure 7.1

Point of View Analysis

Can you imagine Ferris's wheel? Imagine the sturdy steel compression spokes supporting and connecting the gigantic wheels and people-carrying cars. George used his understanding of a bicycle wheel to inspire his design. An engineer is responsible for the precise mechanical workings, overall safety, and function of a structure. George Ferris and his talented assistant, William Gronau, worked together to solve problems. Like other engineers, they created technical drawings, blueprints, and sketches that helped others "see" their ideas.

Sometimes William would become discouraged when tough problems occurred. But, George was determined to build an observation wheel that would never be forgotten!

First, imagine you are William. Write George a letter explaining your concerns about erecting the wheel once quicksand has been discovered at the building site.

Then, as George, write a reply to William with your solutions. You may want to include a sketch that will help communicate your idea. William would very much appreciate your words of encouragement.

Be sure to share your determination with William.

Note. From *Blueprints for Biography: Mr. Ferris and His Wheel* (p. 26), by M. C. Deitz, K. A. Kidd, & A. Robinson, 2017, Jodie Mahony Center for Gifted Education. Copyright 2017 by the Jodie Mahony Center for Gifted Education. Reprinted with permission.

gifted students in grades 2–3 (Robinson, Adelson, Kidd, Cash, Navarrete, & Cunningham, 2018); and engineering knowledge for identified gifted students in grades 2–3 (Robinson, Adelson, Navarrete, Kidd, Cash, & Cunningham, 2019). Differences in student engagement can also be attributed to the program (Robinson, Adelson, Kidd, & Cunningham, 2018).

In terms of teacher outcomes, STEM Starters and STEM Starters+ have resulted in increased nominations of children from low-income households for gifted and talented series (Robinson, Adelson, Kidd, & Cunningham, 2018), moderating teacher concerns about implementing STEM instruction following a year of the withdrawal of coaching services (Dailey & Robinson, 2016), and increasing teacher science content knowledge (Robinson, Dailey, Cotabish,

Hughes, & Hall, 2014). The instructional supports provided to teachers in the STEM Starters and STEM Starters+ interventions include instructional strategies in science content and processes, the engineering design process, and how to implement biography in the classroom to maximize the benefits of a role-model-in-a-book strategy for children from low-income households (Deitz, 2012; Deitz & Robinson, 2016; Robinson, 2017).

U-STARS and U-STARS~PLUS

Although Using Science, Talents, and Abilities to Recognize Students (U-STARS) and Using Science, Talents, and Abilities to Recognize Students~Promoting Learning for Underrepresented Students (U-STARS~PLUS) focus on identification practices, the intervention also provides curricular and instructional opportunities for children and guidance for teachers and parents (Coleman, 2016; Coleman et al., 2007; Coleman & Job, 2014). For example, instructional components of the intervention are high-end learning opportunities defined as curriculum differentiation in the classroom through curriculum compacting, tiered activities, learning centers, or stations and classroom support materials. The classroom support materials in U-STARS focus on integrating science and literature connections; in U-STARS~PLUS, they focus on integrating science and nonfiction texts. A comparison of integrating science and story with science and nonfiction is evident in the choice of two texts related to the same topic—rain forest ecosystems. *The Great Kapok Tree: A Tale of the Amazon Rain Forest* by Lynne Cherry includes a dramatic narrative as well as factual science information, while *Rainforest* by Elinor Greenwood includes graphs, charts, and science illustrations. Both types of reading—narrative and nonfiction—support science instruction but with different approaches.

Outreach to families to support STEM instruction is a key feature of U-STARS and U-STARS~PLUS. The family involvement science packets are described by the developers as "science-in-a-bag" and include instructions for completing an at-home science activity, questions for family discussion, and an observation sheet that prompts families to make predictions, collect data, and draw conclusions together. Excerpts from a family packet are included in Figure 7.2. Materials are sent home in a resealable bag. Information and resources are accessible through an online publication with supplementary files of instructional materials (Coleman, 2016). Providing inexpensive science materials for young children and families in low-income households removes barriers and increases the likelihood that STEM talents will be nurtured.

Although the programs include curricular interventions to support STEM learning for children, the research evidence reported for U-STARS and U-STARS~PLUS focuses on teacher recognition of gifts and talents in children

Figure 7.2

Evolving Ecospheres—Family Science Activity

This activity involves . . . collecting data, communicating, experimenting, formulating hypotheses, inferring, interpreting data, observing, and predicting.

Activity Duration: Allow 5 days to complete this activity.

What are we doing? Living things, such as plants, are called organisms. Organisms are able to survive in an environment where their basic needs are met. In this activity, your scientist is going to see if plants can grow in a sealed environment that he or she makes.

How are we going to do this? In this activity, you will make an *ecosphere*, a contained environment. You will make an ecosphere by adding several things to a cup and then sealing it. Once your ecosphere is made, you will observe it daily for changes and see if the seed sprout in the sealed cup.

Instructional Example:

Day 1: 1. On your Observation Record, predict what you think will happen inside your cup once you make your ecosphere. Your ecosphere will include soil, plant seeds, rocks, and water. Nothing will be added to the cup once it is sealed.

Family Time Question Examples:

> Did anything grow in your ecosystem? Why or Why not?
> Did your predictions match with your observations? Why/why not?
> What helped the seeds sprout in your ecosphere? How does your ecosphere relate to earth's ecosystems?

Family Notes Examples:

> The ecosphere will grow best in a sunny place. Windows with good sunlight and porches/decks are good places as well. Artificial sunlight (lamps) can also be used.
> Encourage your scientist to record what she or he observes and thinks about the activity. Words or drawings may be used to record the observations.
> Your scientist may need help to complete the activity and fill out the Observation Record. Please partner with your child on this.

Note. Reprinted with permission from the Council for Exceptional Children U-STARS Family Science Packet. Copyright 2010 by Council for Exceptional Children.

from underrepresented racial groups and low-income households and family responses to the intervention (Coleman, 2016; Harradine et al., 2014). In a survey of 230 teachers in 25 U-STARS~PLUS schools, approximately two-thirds of the teachers report they are recognizing more students who have potential and are doing more hands-on, inquiry-based science in their classrooms. They also report "doing more science with their classes" (58.9%). In addition to teacher self-reported outcomes, families served through the U-STARS~PLUS intervention report very positive interactions with teachers, schools, and their children. Notable are the family involvement data, which indicate that 90% of the 1,619 families surveyed reported helping their children with homework, nearly 80% of them reported they attend school conferences, and more than 50% reported that they participated in school activities.

Project M[3]: Mentoring Mathematical Minds and Project M[2]: Mentoring Young Mathematicians

Curriculum to foster mathematical talent has been developed, field-tested, and adopted in multiple projects and programs for children from low-income homes. These interventions are anchored by the development of mathematics curriculum for students in grades 3–4 and scaled up through grades 4–6, and down to grades K–2. The curricula have produced gains in mathematics achievement measured by open-ended items (Gavin, Casa, Firmender, & Carroll, 2013). The Project M[3] curriculum was developed to incorporate elements of both enrichment and acceleration to serve the learning needs of advanced learners (Gavin et al., 2007; Gavin & Casa, 2012). Acceleration was accomplished by incorporating mathematics content two to three grade levels above its placement in the National Council of Teachers of Mathematics (NCTM, 2000) Content Standards. Content standards included in Project M[3] were number and operation, geometry and measurement, data analysis and probability, and algebra. Enrichment was generally accomplished by focusing on the NCTM process standard for communication. By incorporating talk moves as defined by Chapin et al. (2003), the developers prepared teachers to encourage their young students to talk like mathematicians. They also developed the *Student Mathematicians' Journal* to support written mathematical communication.

Project M[2], developed through funding from the National Science Foundation, includes eight mathematics curriculum units on number, geometry, and measurement. An example activity, which addresses the need talented learners have for depth, is illustrated by the Think Beyond Cards incorporated into Project M[2] and Project M[3] units (see Figure 7.3).

Project M[2] has demonstrated effects on mathematics achievement in kindergarten children in low-income schools (Casa et al., 2017) and in grades 1

Figure 7.3

Think Beyond Card: The Name Game

1. Sarah's best friend is Christobol. Christobol says that it is easy for him to figure out what letter he would be on for any number when he writes his own name many times, even for the 2,287th letter.
2. Can you think of a pattern that Christobol might be using that would help him figure this out?
3. What would the 2,287th letter be that Christobol would write when he writes his name over and over? Explain your thinking.
4. Sarah said that it would also be easy for her to figure out the 2,287th letter if she continued to write her own name over and over.
5. Why would this also be easy for Sarah? What other names might this be easy for? Explain.
6. What would be the 2,287th letter that Sarah would write? Explain.

Note. From *Awesome Algebra: Looking for Patterns and Generalizations* by M. K. Gavin, J. Dailey, S. H. Chapin, & L. J. Sheffield, 2015, Kendall Hunt. Copyright 2015 by Kendall Hunt Publishing Company. Reprinted by permission.

and 2 respectively (Gavin, Casa, Adelson, & Firmender, 2013; Gavin, Casa, Firmender, & Carroll, 2013). Both Project M^3 and Project M^2 curriculum units have been implemented in other interventions focused on gifted children from low-income households. Specifically, Project Spark incorporated the Project M^2 mathematics units into a summer enrichment program with evidence that it boosted mathematics achievement for students who attended when compared with students who did not (Little et al., 2018).

The three evidence-based STEM examples for young children included in this section vary by grade level and disciplinary focus, yet key patterns emerge. Their key features, rationale, and sources are summarized in Figure 7.4, and patterns are discussed in the next section.

Patterns of Instructional and Curriculum Interventions for Young Children

Across the evidence-based STEM instructional interventions described previously, which address poverty, underrepresentation, and talent develop-

Figure 7.4

Summary of Effective Elementary Instructional Interventions

Project/Program/ Curriculum	Key Features	Rationale for Students From Low-Income Households
STEM Starters and STEM Starters+ Engineering is Elementary (EiE), Museum of Science, Boston https://www.eie.org	› Teachers guide with detailed lesson plans and background content in engineering, science, and social studies. › Storybook about a child who solves a real-world problem through engineering. › Low-cost materials. › Grades 1–5.	› Stories featuring children from world cultures. › Real-world problems. › Hands-on learning. › Low-cost, everyday materials.
STEM Starters and STEM Starters+ *Blueprints for Biography,* University of Arkansas at Little Rock, Jodie Mahony Center for Gifted Education https://ualr.edu/gifted	› Trade biography. › Teachers guide with a science experiment or an engineering design challenge, discussion questions, and extension strategies. › Low-cost materials. › Grades 1–8.	› Trade biographies provide students with role models. › Real-world problems. › Hands-on learning. › Low-cost, everyday materials.
U-STARS and U-STARS~PLUS Council for Exceptional Children https://exceptional children.org	› Classroom materials for connecting science and literature through questioning strategies. › Fiction and nonfiction books. › Family science take-home packets. › Low-cost materials. › Grades K–3.	› Family engagement through at-home science activities. › Real-world problems. › Hands-on learning. › Low-cost, everyday materials.

Figure 7.4, continued

Project/Program/Curriculum	Key Features	Rationale for Students From Low-Income Households
Project M2 and Project M3 Kendall Hunt https://k12.kendallhunt.com	› Teacher guide with information on mathematics, learning environment, mathematical communication, and differentiation. › Real-world problems. › Think, write, and read like a mathematician activities. › Grades K–2 (M^2). › Grades 3–6 (M^3).	› Real-world problems. › Hands-on learning.

ment, a pattern of three shared instructional features emerges for young children, as follows.

Design-Based or Problem-Based Focus. First, STEM instruction focuses on design-based or problem-based curricula that incorporate complexity in terms of real-world scenarios (Robinson et al., 2007). The scenarios, problem statements, and solutions cannot be undertaken without hands-on involvement of the young learners. In addition, the materials often include language to encourage children to develop habits of mind indicative of adult engineers and scientists. Teacher use phrases such as "Let's think like an engineer or a mathematician," or "What would a scientist observe?" These habits of a scholar are specific to the particular STEM area and are also noted in Chapter 5.

Out-of-School Experiences With Sufficient Dosage. A second pattern that emerged was the use of out-of-school STEM experiences either as a bridge to more advanced achievement or to engage children and families in activities at home (Robinson & Stanley, 1989). In terms of afterschool or summer programs broadly available in many communities, the key feature was sufficient dosage (Robinson & Stanley, 1989). Short-term programs may engage students, but children from low-income households require more than a 2-week exposure to boost achievement in core STEM areas like mathematics (Little et al., 2018).

At the elementary level, the STEM interventions also used a parental app-roach to out-of-school instruction by providing STEM activities in family pack-ets. In some cases, the family packets in science and literacy were commercially available (Coleman & Job, 2014) or could be accessed at a curricular website, such as Engineering is Elementary (Robinson, 2017).

STEM Interventions for Young Children That Integrate Literacy. The example interventions in this chapter also share an instructional pat-tern of integrating literacy into STEM experiences. STEM Starters and STEM Starters+ feature biography, and U-STARS and U-STARS~PLUS include fiction and nonfiction books as part of their instructional framework. Project M³ sets the expectation that students will learn to talk about and write about their mathematical thinking. Given the importance placed on literacy in the early grades and the concerns that children from low-income households may not have the affordances of homes filled with books, the integration of literacy at this developmental level is not surprising. Provided that the literacy materials are of high quality and children are asked to interact with them in a complex and hands-on manner, the integration of literacy is one avenue for children in high-poverty schools to have access to STEM content. Each intervention incorporated literacy through high-end instructional activities at the book rather than the story or short passage level, or included multiple opportunities to write nonfiction prose, such as think-alouds for solving math problems or expository writing and argumentation in science and engineering. Integrating literacy and STEM addresses the pressing problem of limited time in the school day for instructional enrichment, an affordance particularly important for chil-dren who have had few opportunities to learn.

STEM in the Middle Grades

Most available STEM programs offered at the middle level are enrichment-based experiences offered outside the regular school day. According to Mun and Hertzog (2018), STEM enrichment programs designed to support and enhance the talents of students from ethnic/racial minority groups and low-income backgrounds incorporated components of open-ended questioning and discov-ery through play. These features help to create a positive learning environment, which is a predictor of STEM sense of belonging (Meadows, 2018). Developing a sense of belonging to a STEM community is critical at the middle school years (Meadows, 2018). Effective instructional interventions that develop the sense of belonging while building STEM knowledge, skills, and interests include sev-eral key features for building STEM talent pathways. Students who participate in STEM enrichment programs report being better prepared for advanced coursework (Olszewski-Kubilius et al., 2017).

Middle-level features are family involvement, low-cost or free out-of-school options, and role modeling or mentoring components. Three examples of middle grade instructional interventions aimed at developing STEM talents in preadolescents from low-income homes are summarized in the following section: the STEM Excellence and Leadership Project, Project BEAM, and Girls of Promise (a program embedded in the National Girls Collaborative).

STEM Excellence and Leadership

STEM Excellence and Leadership encourages gifted students from low-income households to take extra classes in science and mathematics outside their regular school day (Assouline & Ihrig, 2019). Students in grades 5–8 spend 2 hours after school, twice a week for 24 weeks, for a total of 96 hours each school year taking additional classes (Assouline, 2019) designed to enhance students' engagement and understanding of STEM-related topics (Ihrig et al., 2017). According to Assouline and Ihrig (2019), "students are divided into small teams and asked to conduct investigations that incorporate advanced engineering and science concepts" (p. 2). Additionally, as part of the STEM Excellence and Leadership program, the middle school students visit universities where they have the opportunity to work with university instructors on science and engineering investigations. For example, one group of students "built robots and researched recycling with the end result of making biodegradable water bottles" (Goodell, 2017, para. 7). The short-term laboratory experiences expose students to STEM professionals in a hands-on, real-world context.

Teachers at participating schools receive extra funding to purchase STEM-related equipment, such as resources for experiments or classroom projects (Assouline et al., 2017). Currently funded by the National Science Foundation, the STEM Excellence and Leadership program yields promising results. Feedback from participating students and teachers has been positive. During the pilot project, sixth-grade students demonstrated a statistically significant increase in academic growth when compared to the typical growth observed in talented students (Assouline et al., 2017). In addition, teachers at participating schools collected and examined their students' test scores, and many of them noted observable improvement in their students' standardized assessment scores (Assouline & Ihrig, 2019). According to a participating teacher, "the extra classes provided to participating students are a chance for them to build relationships that they would not develop in ordinary classrooms" (Assouline & Ihrig, 2019, p. 4). Key features of the intervention include increased exposure to STEM through out-of-school classes and university laboratory visits.

Project BEAM

Project BEAM, a Jacob K. Javits project, focuses on increasing the number of mathematically promising Native Hawaiian, Native American, Pacific Island, and Hispanic students in high school STEM courses through instructional interventions at the middle school level. The program uses the BEAM model, which is described as a "culturally responsive, accelerated and enriched algebra intervention using multiple evidence-based strategies" (Jacob K. Javits Gifted and Talented Students Education Program, 2017, p. 1). Project BEAM provides afterschool and weekend support and online supplemental instruction. Participants engage in hands-on, real-world algebra lessons that integrate STEM problem solving and projects (Takahashi & Park, 2019). One such instructional example is using schematic diagrams to build model race cars. Once constructed, students collect data on the distance and time their model cars travel. Subsequently, they use the data to investigate the concepts of speed and acceleration and to learn about algebraic functions and graphing.

The BEAM model provides academic acceleration and enrichment and 50 hours of mentoring in mathematics, problem-based hands-on learning, and blended learning opportunities that combine computer-based and hands-on learning (Takahashi & Park, 2019). Although data on curricular outcomes are not yet available, Project BEAM aims to improve middle school students' mathematics achievement and better prepare students for advanced and honors courses in STEM once they enter high school. Project BEAM will investigate the following student outcomes: attitude toward mathematics, cultural competence, mathematics achievement, and STEM identity development (Takahashi & Park, 2019). Key features of this intervention include exposure to STEM through out-of-school classes, problem-based hands-on learning, and mentoring.

The National Girls Collaborative Project and Girls of Promise

The middle school years are important in the development of STEM interest and identities—two variables that affect persistence in STEM pathways (Barton & Tan, 2010; Tai et al., 2006). Programs that target underrepresented STEM-talented youth, such as adolescent girls from low-income households, can address interest, identity, and achievement. A positive trend is that female students' achievement in mathematics and science is on par with male peers and that female students participate in high-level mathematics and science courses at similar rates as their male peers, with the exception of computer science and engineering (National Science Board, 2018). Nevertheless, gaps exist between students from different socioeconomic backgrounds, with the gaps increasing over time (see Figure 7.5).

Programs like the National Girls Collaborative Project (NGCP) and Girls of Promise encourage girls to pursue higher level STEM courses beyond eighth grade, with goals toward careers in these fields. Programs sponsored by the NGCP give priority to and actively recruit students from low-income backgrounds (regardless of gender or race). The purpose of the NGCP is to bring together organizations throughout the United States committed to informing girls about careers in STEM. Currently, 33 collaboratives, serving 41 states, facilitate collaboration between 36,400 organizations that serve 20.15 million girls and 9.5 million boys (NGCP, n.d.-a). Through professional development webinars and face-to-face training, the NGCP prepares and mentors project organizers to create partnerships at the state and local level. Most states have a local collaborative branch that works with organizations throughout their state to provide students with opportunities for programs to increase their ability to maintain interest and participation in STEM (NGCP, n.d.-b).

One such project, Girls of Promise, is a 2-day STEM conference for high-achieving eighth-grade girls. First priority for the conference is given to students from ethnic/racial minority groups and students from low-income schools. The program focuses on the importance of higher education and the payoff of effort in a fun environment (Kanadlt, 2019). Girls are introduced to and learn from women with careers in STEM fields, participate in hands-on learning activities, and meet other girls passionate about learning through their attendance at Girls of Promise conferences. For example, at the 2018 Girls of Promise conference, participants worked with: a university science professor to dissect a cow heart, a food scientist to learn about the chemistry behind cooking, an engineer to build electrical circuits, a veterinarian to check a dog's heart rate, and much more (Girls of Promise, 2018). Data from the first 10 years of conferences and from alumnae of the program indicate that Girls of Promise does encourage young women to remain in high school and to further their studies of STEM fields through postsecondary education (NGCP, n.d.-b). In order to keep students moving along the STEM pathway, it is important that students stay interested and engaged in STEM throughout their school trajectory (Meadows, 2016). Programs like Girls of Promise are designed to foster that interest and engagement. Key features of this intervention include exposure to STEM through out-of-school conference settings, problem-based hands-on learning, building a STEM community, and mentoring. These instructional experiences at no cost to students are one pathway to cultivating STEM talents in adolescents from low-income households.

Figure 7.5

Average Scores of Students in Grades 4, 8, and 12 on the Main NAEP Mathematics Assessment by Socioeconomic Status: 2015

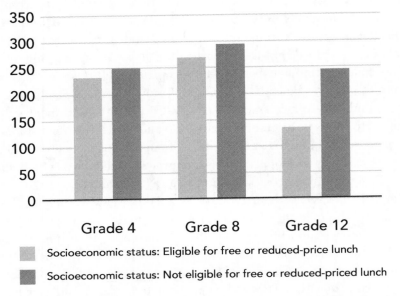

Grade 4   Grade 8   Grade 12

Socioeconomic status: Eligible for free or reduced-price lunch

Socioeconomic status: Not eligible for free or reduced-priced lunch

Note. Data gathered from National Science Board (2018). Main NAEP mathematics assessment scores range from 0 to 500 for grades 4 and 8. Main NAEP mathematics assessment scores range from 0 to 300 for grade 12.

Patterns of STEM Interventions for Middle-Level Students

Like the interventions for young children, middle school interventions display a pattern of hands-on, real-world design or a problem-based focus, features of the integrated STEM approach to curriculum and instruction. Across the three example interventions, patterns unique to middle school emerged. In addition to the patterns shared with elementary interventions, two additional middle-level patterns emerge.

Access to Adult STEM Professionals as Role Models. First, STEM interventions that focus on talented middle school students from low-income households are rich in access to adult STEM professionals. In some cases, the access is on a university campus with individuals who guide experiences in research groups or laboratories. In other cases, the access is short-term exposure to inspirational STEM professionals as is the case in conference attendance and participation.

Out-of-School Opportunities. All three exemplar interventions provide instruction in informal, out-of-school settings. In some cases (i.e., conferences), the out-of-school experiences are accessed during the school day but in settings physically located away from the school campus. More frequently, the opportunities, particularly short-term experiences, are after school, on Saturdays, or during the summer. Perhaps reflecting the greater autonomy of middle school students, out-of-school STEM experiences appear to increase across the grade level trajectory.

High School Opportunities for Adolescents From Low-Income Households

As talented children and adolescents from low-income households move through the K–12 trajectory, their instructional options are more aggregated by specific program model. In other words, instruction is less likely to focus on the activity or unit level and more likely to be at the course or syllabus level.

Advanced Placement and International Baccalaureate

In many high schools, Advanced Placement (AP) or International Baccalaureate (IB) are the only within-school, credit-bearing STEM curricular options for talented students. With respect to the STEM fields, there are 12 College Board AP courses: Calculus AB, Calculus BC, Computer Science A, Computer Science Principles, Statistics, Biology, Chemistry, Environmental Science, Physics 1: Algebra-Based, Physics 2: Algebra-Based, Physics C: Electricity and Magnetism, and Physics C: Mechanics.

In terms of instruction, for example, the AP Chemistry course content includes atomic structure, intermolecular forces and bonding, chemical reactions, kinetics, thermodynamics, and equilibrium, which emphasize big ideas and cross-cutting concepts. The science practices central to the AP approach to STEM focus on inquiry-based investigation (College Board, 2020).

In contrast, the International Baccalaureate Diploma Programme for high schools is interdisciplinary, with STEM opportunities embedded within the curriculum. Science courses include: Biology, Chemistry, Computer Science, Design Technology, Environmental Systems and Societies, Physics, and Sports, Exercise and Health Science. As an example of how STEM integration may be organized at the course level, the IB chemistry course allows students to develop a wide range of practical skills and to increase facility in the use of mathematics. It also allows students to develop interpersonal and information technology skills essential to life in the 21st century (International Baccalaureate, n.d.). Students can earn a certificate for passing the IB exam in a single subject (as with AP), or they can earn a full IB diploma if they pass six subjects, pass a course in Theory of Knowledge, write an extended essay, and complete creativity, action, and service hours outside of class.

According to Theokas and Saaris (2013), students from low-income households tend to have the lowest enrollment in AP and IB courses. Thus, those students with the greatest need for access to accelerated courses tend to have the least access. Therefore, booster or bridge programs, such as those described in the section on middle school STEM programs, are one means of engaging and retaining talented high schoolers in advanced STEM courses.

Specialized STEM High Schools

A growing number of states and districts have specialized STEM high schools and secondary programs that provide opportunities for talent development (Forman et al., 2015). Many states have initiatives to create STEM-focused high schools, and thus the number of inclusive STEM high schools around the country has increased. Inclusive STEM high schools have no admissions criteria for students and, as such, serve a broader and often more diverse group of students than selective schools and exam schools. Therefore, an inclusive STEM high school can be seen both as an educational opportunity structure in itself, and as the means to develop and extend students' other opportunity structures (Lynch et al., 2017). According to Lynch and her colleagues (2017), some of the opportunities that inclusive STEM high schools provide students from low-income households include networking with STEM professionals, interacting with peers who have similar interests, and acquiring skills that aid in college admissions and success.

Both inclusive and selective STEM high schools provide access not only to high-quality STEM curriculum and instruction or "opportunity to learn," but also to learning environments where students build STEM social capital and develop the knowledge, skills, and networks to be successful in STEM college majors and careers (Finn & Hockett, 2012). Inclusive and selective STEM high schools tend to have programs in place to support students; for example, the Gatton Academy of Mathematics and Science in Kentucky offers summer internship and research programs that can bridge economic need (Roberts et al., 2016), and the Arkansas School for Mathematics, Sciences, and the Arts

(ASMA, n.d.) provides students with a faculty mentor to ease the transition to a public residential high school.

In summary, STEM high schools can be viewed as opportunity structures for students from low-income households. One of the benefits of the specialty high schools is that they ensure that students have access to an array of STEM courses and experiences. Such schools typically offer more rigorous curricula, in-depth STEM-focused curriculum, qualified teachers, instructional time, and resources than traditional high schools (NRC, 2011). Additionally, STEM high schools that are residential and non-fee-paying offer an affordable option for students from low-income households. Effective practices in specialized STEM schools include grounding STEM education in real-world practical problems, student participation in original research projects, and student internships and mentorships with STEM professionals.

STEM Laboratory Experiences

One way of providing students from low-income backgrounds with hands-on, real-world STEM experiences is through research apprenticeships. Mentoring high school students in university or independent research laboratories encourages students to pursue higher level STEM courses and STEM careers (Budassi & Rafailovich, 2018). Participants in high school research apprenticeships were more likely to major in STEM fields in college and to pursue careers in STEM disciplines. Additionally, Tai et al. (2017) found that participants in high school summer laboratory research apprenticeships were more than 4 times more likely to matriculate into STEM programs than their peers who did not have these experiences. These findings were even more pronounced among the racial/ethnic minority and low-SES groups.

An example collegiate laboratory experience was the High School Summer Research Program (HSSRP) at the University of California, Los Angeles (UCLA) Henry Samueli School of Engineering and Applied Sciences (HSSEAS), an 8-week summer research-intensive program geared toward actively immersing high-achieving high school seniors in engineering research laboratories. HSSRP selected students largely on merit, with most students being motivated and academically high-performing. In order to increase diversity, HSSRP actively recruited low-income, first-generation, and underrepresented students (Kittur et al., 2017). The program emphasized collaborative learning; students worked together with experienced research professionals. Specific research projects were selected by each host laboratory to make specialized research foci available to student participants. By providing practice and feedback, the laboratory staff set the tone for a collaborative learning environment to build interpersonal skills and interdependence within groups of diverse students: "The intervention fosters a strong social aspect to unite students and staff from various backgrounds (including those from low-income, first-generation, and underrepresented minority) and interests to achieve a common goal—increased exposure to and excitement for STEM education" (Kittur et al., 2017, p. 31).

Patterns of Effective High School STEM Interventions and Contexts

Like the elementary interventions and middle school interventions, high school interventions display a pattern of real-world design or a problem-based focus. High school interventions also share out-of-school laboratory experiences and access to STEM professionals with the middle school STEM programs. High school programs, however, increase the length and nature of exposure to STEM professionals in the workplace. The following three patterns emerge and highlight the need for ongoing and increasingly complex levels of access for high school students, especially—but not limited to—those from low-income households.

Access to Advanced-Level STEM Coursework. At the high school level, STEM courses are not as integrated as they are at the lower grade levels. However, one of the most common high school interventions is to provide students with rigorous, challenging courses, such as AP, IB, or other college-level courses. Many of these STEM courses provide hands-on opportunities for students to explore real-world problems and scenarios embedded in the curriculum.

Sustained Laboratory Mentorship. A key feature of successful high school STEM interventions for adolescents from low-income households is out-of-school experiences in real-world laboratories or research groups. These opportunities provide students with authentic experiences in scientific research, with the culture of collaborative lab context, and with presentation experiences to real-world audiences.

Building a STEM Community. Another key feature is deliberately constructing a community of students attracted to STEM disciplines and careers by providing students with access to adult STEM professionals and peers with similar STEM interests. In some cases, the access is on a university campus with individuals who guide experiences in research groups or laboratories. In other cases, the access is through specialized high schools and enriched or accelerated STEM coursework.

Conclusion: Pathways, not Pipelines

The STEM fields provide opportunities for children and adolescents from low-income households through multiple pathways. Changing the metaphor of the STEM pipeline to the model of pathways acknowledges that multiple patterns of STEM talent development are possible (Cannady et al., 2014). A pipeline is confined by volume and is relatively linear. A pathway can be more circuitous to find a way around barriers; in fact, by definition that is what pathways do—find an accessible route. The barriers of poverty, racism, and sexism are addressed by instructional opportunities, high expectations, and dedication to building diverse, communal, and developmental STEM pathways.

Viewed from above, instructional experiences across elementary, middle, and high school display both shared and unique affordances. Their common patterns are summarized in Figure 7.6.

STEM integration refers to the confluence of the STEM disciplines in instructional experiences and curricular organization. The integration may be across two disciplines (for example, science and mathematics, or engineering and technology) or more broadly integrative across the four key STEM disciplines.

The patterns of exemplary instructional and curricular interventions explored in this chapter indicate that integration is more easily accomplished in the earlier grades than in the later. For example, all three elementary exemplars integrated across science and literacy, engineering and literacy, or mathematics and literacy. In terms of curricular offerings, high school appeared to be the least amenable to STEM integration in formal settings. In contrast, the real-world settings of laboratories and research groups provided opportunities for students to experience multidisciplinary and integrated informal instruction. At these developmental levels, real-world exposure to complex problems is foregrounded and therefore more revealing to emerging adolescents and adolescents who are exploring their career aspirations and possible pathways to bring their aspirations to fruition. Students from low-income households live every day with the challenges of constraints and scarce resources. The ability to define and solve problems that require an integrated STEM approach; to offer the hope of innovation; and to assess career possibilities, financial security, and life satisfaction makes these disciplines a powerhouse of affordances for children and adolescents from low-income households.

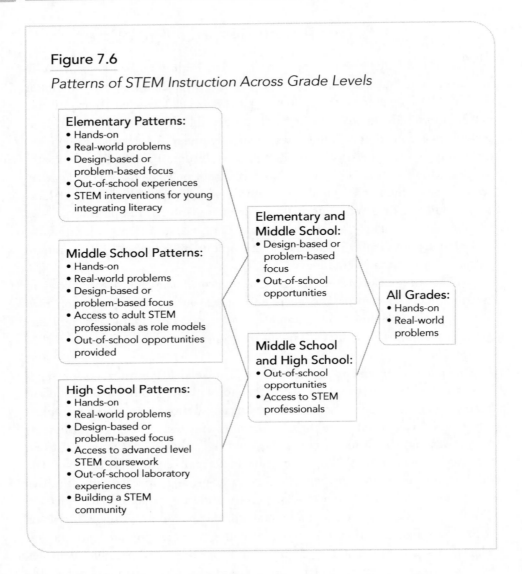

Figure 7.6

Patterns of STEM Instruction Across Grade Levels

Elementary Patterns:
- Hands-on
- Real-world problems
- Design-based or problem-based focus
- Out-of-school experiences
- STEM interventions for young integrating literacy

Middle School Patterns:
- Hands-on
- Real-world problems
- Design-based or problem-based focus
- Access to adult STEM professionals as role models
- Out-of-school opportunities provided

High School Patterns:
- Hands-on
- Real-world problems
- Design-based or problem-based focus
- Access to advanced level STEM coursework
- Out-of-school laboratory experiences
- Building a STEM community

Elementary and Middle School:
- Design-based or problem-based focus
- Out-of-school opportunities

Middle School and High School:
- Out-of-school opportunities
- Access to STEM professionals

All Grades:
- Hands-on
- Real-world problems

References

Arkansas School for Mathematics, Sciences, and the Arts. (n.d.). *Igniting Arkansas' potential*. https://www.asmsa.org

Assouline, S. (2019). *STEM excellence: A model for equalizing opportunities for STEM*. https://www.openaccessgovernment.org/opportunities-for-stem/74466

Assouline, S., & Ihrig, L. (2019). *The STEM Excellence and Leadership Program*. Scientia. https://doi.org/10.33548/scientia350

Assouline, S. G., Ihrig, L. M., & Mahatmya, D. (2017). Closing the excellence gap: Investigation of an expanded talent search model for student selection into an extracurricular STEM program in rural middle schools. *Gifted Child Quarterly, 61*(3), 250–261. https://doi.org/10.1177/0016986217701833

Barton, A. C., & Tan, E. (2010). We be burnin'! Agency, identity, and science learning. *Journal of the Learning Sciences, 19*(2), 187–229. https://doi.org/10.1080/1050840 0903530044

Budassi, J., & Rafailovich, M. (2018). The effect of university research apprenticeships for high school students on science, math, engineering, and technology learning and the pursuit of science, math, engineering, and technology degrees and careers. *MRS Communications, 8*(2), 387–397. https://doi.org/10.1557/mrc.2018.92

Cannady, M. A., Greenwald, E., & Harris, K. N. (2014). Problematizing the STEM pipeline metaphor: Is the STEM pipeline metaphor serving our students and the STEM workforce? *Science Education, 98*(3), 443–460. https://doi.org/10.1002/sce.21108

Casa, T. M., Firmender, J. M., Gavin, M. K., & Carroll, S. R. (2017). Kindergarteners' achievement on geometry and measurement units that incorporate a gifted education approach. *Gifted Child Quarterly, 61*(1), 52–72. https://doi.org/10.1177/00 16986216671806

Chapin, S. H., O'Connor, C., & Anderson, N. C. (2003). *Classroom discussions: Using math talk to help students learn*. Math Solutions.

Coleman, M. R. (2016). Recognizing young children with high potential; U-STARS Plus. *Annals of the New York Academy of Sciences, 1377*(1), 32–43. https://doi.org/ 10.1111/nyas.13161

Coleman, M. R., & Job, J. (2014). *U-STARS~PLUS Science & Nonfiction Connections*. Council for Exceptional Children.

Coleman, M. R., Shah-Coltrane, S., Harradine, C., & Timmons, L. (2007). Impact of poverty on promising learners, their teachers, and their schools. In J. VanTassel-Baska & T. Stambaugh (Eds.), *Overlooked gems: A national perspective on low-income promising learners* (pp. 59–61). National Association for Gifted Children.

College Board. (2020). *AP Chemistry course and exam description*. https://apcentral.col legeboard.org/pdf/ap-chemistry-course-and-exam-description.pdf

Dai, D. Y. (2017). Envisioning a new foundation for gifted education: Evolving Complexity Theory (ECT) of talent development. *Gifted Child Quarterly, 6*(3), 172–182. https://doi.org/10.1177/0016986217701837

Dai, D. Y., & Li, X. S. (in press). *Behind an accelerated scientific research career: Dynamic interplay of endogenous and exogenous forces in talent development*.

Dailey, D., & Robinson, A. (2016). Elementary teachers: Concerns about implementing a science program. *School Science and Mathematics, 116*(3), 139–147. https://doi. org/10.1111/ssm.12162

Deitz, M. C. (2012). *Gifted education teachers' perceptions on implementation of Blueprints for Biography: STEM Starters* [Unpublished doctoral dissertation]. University of Arkansas at Little Rock.

Deitz, M. C., Kidd, K. A., & Robinson, A. (2017). *Blueprints for biography: Mr. Ferris and his wheel*. Jodie Mahony Center for Gifted Education.

Deitz, M. C., & Robinson, A. (2016, April). *Using biography and biographical methods in the classroom: Lives that teach* [Paper presentation]. The Annual Meeting of the American Educational Research Association, Washington, DC, United States.

Engineering is Elementary. (2011). *Sounds like fun: Seeing animal sounds.* Museum of Science, Boston.

Fayer, S., Lacey, A., & Watson, A. (2017, January). *STEM occupations: Past, present, and future.* U.S. Bureau of Labor Statistics.

Feldhusen, J. F. (1998). A conception of talent and talent development. In R. C. Friedman & K. B. Rogers (Eds.), *Talent in context: Historical and social perspectives on giftedness* (pp. 193–209). American Psychological Association. https://doi.org/10.1037/10297-010

Finn, C. E., Jr., & Hockett, J. A. (2012). *Exam schools: Inside America's most selective public high schools.* Princeton University Press.

Forman, J., Gubbins, E., Villanueva, M., Massicotte, C., Callahan, C., & Tofel-Grehl, C. (2015). National survey of STEM high schools' curricular and instructional strategies and practices. *NCSSS Journal, 20*(1), 8–19.

Funk, C., & Parker, K. (2018). *Women and men in STEM often at odds over workplace equity.* Pew Research Center. https://www.pewsocialtrends.org/2018/01/09/women-and-men-in-stem-often-at-odds-over-workplace-equity

Gavin, M. K., & Casa, T. M. (2012). Nurturing young student mathematicians. *Gifted Education International, 29*(2), 140–153. https://doi.org/10.1177/0261429412447711

Gavin, M. K., Casa, T. M., Adelson, J. L., Carroll, S. R., Sheffield, L. J., & Spinelli, A. M. (2007). Project M³: Mentoring Mathematical Minds: A research-based curriculum for talented elementary students. *Journal of Advanced Academics, 18*(4), 566–585. https://doi.org/10.4219/jaa-2007-552

Gavin, M. K., Casa, T. M., Adelson, J. L., & Firmender, J. M. (2013). The impact of advanced geometry and measurement units on the achievement of grade 2 students. *Journal for Research in Mathematics Education, 44*(3), 478–510.

Gavin, M. K., Casa, T. M., Firmender, J. M., & Carroll, S. R. (2013). The impact of advanced geometry and measurement curriculum units on the mathematics achievement of first-grade students. *Gifted Child Quarterly, 57*(2), 71–84. https://doi.org/10.1177/0016986213479564

Gavin, M. K., Dailey, J., Chapin, S. H., & Sheffield, L. J. (2015). *Project M³: Level 3: Awesome algebra: Looking for patterns and generalizations.* Kendall Hunt.

Girls of Promise. (2018). *Girls of Promise 2018: What's your STEM power* [Conference program].

Goodell, A. (2017, April). STEM Excellence and Leadership invigorates learning for high-ability students in rural Iowa. *The University of Iowa College of Education Alumni Magazine.* https://education.uiowa.edu/news/stem-excellence-and-leadership-invigorates-learning-high-ability-students-rural-iowa

Harradine, C. C., Coleman, M. R. B., & Winn, D.-M. C. (2014). Recognizing academic potential in students of color: Findings of U-STARS~PLUS. *Gifted Child Quarterly, 58*(1), 24–34. https://doi.org/10.1177/0016986213506040

Ihrig, L. M., Lane, E., Mahatmya, D., & Assouline, S. G. (2017). STEM Excellence and Leadership Program: Increasing the level of STEM challenge and engagement for high-achieving students in economically disadvantaged rural communities. *Journal for the Education of the Gifted, 41*(1), 24–42. https://doi.org/10.1177/016235 3217745158

Jacob K. Javits Gifted and Talented Students Education Program. (2017). *Awards.* U.S. Department of Education. https://www2.ed.gov/programs/javits/awards.html

Kanadlt, S. (2019). A meta-summary of qualitative findings about STEM education. *International Journal Instruction, 12*(1), 959–976. https://doi.org/10.29333/iji.20 19.12162a

Kelley, T. R., & Knowles, J. G. (2016). A conceptual framework for integrated STEM education. *International Journal of STEM Education, 3,* Article 11. https://doi.org/ 10.1186/s40594-016-0046-z

Kittur, H., Shaw, L., & Herrera, W. (2017). A new model for a multi-disciplinary engi-neering summer research program for high school seniors: Program overview, effectiveness, and outcomes. *Journal of STEM Education, 18*(4), 25–31.

International Baccalaureate. (n.d.). *Diploma Programme.* https://www.ibo.org/program mes/diploma-programme

Little, C. A., Adelson, J. L., Kearney, K. L., Cash, K., & O'Brien, R. (2018). Early opportuni-ties to strengthen academic readiness: Effects of summer learning on mathematics achievement. *Gifted Child Quarterly, 6*(1), 83–95. https://doi.org/10.1177/00169 86217738052

Lynch, S. J., Burton, E. P., Behrend, T., House, A., Ford, M., Spillane, N., Matray, S., Han, E., & Means, B. (2017). Understanding inclusive STEM high schools as opportunity structures for underrepresented students: Critical components. *Journal of Research in Science Teaching, 55*(5), 712–748. https://doi.org/10.1002/tea.21437

Meadows, M. (2016). Where are all the talented girls? How can we help them achieve in science technology engineering and mathematics? *Journal for the Education of the Young Scientist & Giftedness, 4*(2), 29–42.

Meadows, M. C. (2018). *Gender differences in STEM sense of belonging for academically advanced middle school students* [Unpublished doctoral dissertation]. University of Arkansas at Little Rock.

Mun, R. U., & Hertzog, N. B. (2018). Teaching and learning in STEM enrichment spaces: From doing math to thinking mathematically. *Roeper Review, 40*(2), 121–129. https://doi.org/10.1080/02783193.2018.1434713

National Girls Collaborative Project. (n.d.-a). *About NCGP.* https://ngcproject.org/abo ut-ngcp

National Council of Teachers of Mathematics. (2000). *Principles and standards for school mathematics.* https://www.nctm.org/standards

National Girls Collaborative Project. (n.d.-b). *Arkansas Girls STEM Collaborative.* https:// ngcproject.org/collaborative/arkansas-girls-stem-collaborative

National Girls Collaborative Project. (2018). *The state of girls and women in STEM.* https://ngcproject.org/sites/default/files/ngcp_the_state_of_girls_and_women_ in_stem_2018a.pdf

National Research Council. (2011). *Successful K–12 STEM education: Identifying effective approaches in science, technology, engineering, and mathematics.* The National Academies Press. https://doi.org/https://doi.org/10.17226/13158

National Science Board. (2010). *Preparing the next generation of STEM innovators: Identifying and development our nation's human capital* (NSB-10-33). National Science Foundation. https://www.nsf.gov/nsb/publications/2010/nsb1033.pdf

National Science Board. (2018). *Science and engineering indicators 2018* (NSB-2018-1). National Science Foundation. https://www.nsf.gov/statistics/indicators

Olszewski-Kubilius, P., Steenbergen-Hu, S., Thomson, D., & Rosen, R. (2017). Minority achievement gaps in STEM: Findings of a longitudinal study of Project Excite. *Gifted Child Quarterly, 61*(1), 20–39. https://doi.org/10.1177/0016986216673449

Roberts, J. L., Breedlove, L., & Strode, D. B. (2016). Experiential learning at the Gatton Academy of Mathematics and Science in Kentucky. *Gifted Child Today, 39*(4), 228–235. https://doi.org/10.1177/1076217516662097

Robinson, A. (2017). Developing STEM talent in the early school years: STEM Starters and its next generation scale up. In K. S. Taber, M. Sumida, & L. McClure (Eds.), *Teaching gifted learners in STEM subjects: Developing talent in science, technology, engineering and mathematics* (pp. 21–30). Routledge.

Robinson, A., Adelson, J. L., Kidd, K. A., Cash, K. M., Navarrete, K. M., & Cunningham, C. M. (2018). *Effects of an engineering and science intervention on the science achievement of talented elementary students* [Paper presentation]. The Annual Meeting of the American Educational Research Association, New York, NY, United States.

Robinson, A., Adelson, J. L., Kidd, K. A., & Cunningham, C. M. (2018). A talent for tinkering: Developing talents in children from low-income households through engineering curriculum. *Gifted Child Quarterly, 62*(1), 130–144. https://doi.org/10.1177/0016986217738049

Robinson, A., Dailey, D., Cotabish, A., Hughes, G., & Hall, T. (2014). STEM Starters: An effective model for elementary teachers and students. In R. E. Yager & H. Brunkhorst (Eds.), *Exemplary STEM programs: Designs for success* (pp. 1–18). NSTA.

Robinson, A., Dailey, D., Hughes, G., & Cotabish, A. (2014). The effects of a science-focused STEM intervention on gifted elementary students' science knowledge and skills. *Journal of Advanced Academics, 25*(3), 189–213. https://doi.org/10.1177/1932202X14533799

Robinson, A., Shore, B. M., & Enersen, D. L. (2007). *Best practices in gifted education: An evidence-based guide.* Prufrock Press.

Robinson, A., & Stanley, T. D. (1989). Teaching to talent: Evaluating an enriched accelerated mathematics program. *Journal of Gifted Education, 12*(4), 253–267. https://doi.org/10.1177/016235328901200402

Robinson, A. E., Adelson, J. L., Navarrete, K. M., Kidd, K., Cash, K., & Cunningham, C. M. (2019, April). *Engineering practices and talented students: Investigating design under constraints* [Paper presentation]. The Annual Meeting of the American Educational Research Association, Toronto, Canada.

Subotnik, R. F., Olszewski-Kubilius, P., & Worrell, F. C. (2011). Rethinking giftedness and gifted education: A proposed direction forward based on psychological science.

Psychological Science in the Public Interest, 12(1), 3–54. https://doi.org/10.1177/1529100611418056

Tai, R. T., Kong, X., Mitchell, C. E., Dabney, K. P., Read, D. M., Jeffe, D. B., Andriole, D. A., & Wathington, H. D. (2017). Examining summer laboratory research apprenticeships for high school students as a factor in entry to MD/PhD programs at matriculation. *CBE Life Sciences Education, 16*(2), Article 37. https://doi.org/10.1187/cbe.15-07-0161

Tai, R. T., Liu, C. Q., Maltese, A. V., & Fan, X. T. (2006). Planning early for careers in science. *Science, 312*(5777), 1143–1144.

Takahashi, K., & Park, H. (2019). *About Project BEAM.* Center on Disability Studies, University of Hawaii at Manoa.

Theokas, C., & Saaris, R. (2013). *Finding America's missing AP and IB students.* The Education Trust. https://edtrust.org/resource/finding-americas-missing-ap-and-ib-students

CHAPTER 8

Effective Intervention Models to Support the Talent Development of Students From Low-Income Households Beyond the School Day

Eric Fecht and Tamra Stambaugh

The development of expertise requires students to access and take advantage of relevant opportunities that enhance their strengths (Subotnik et al., 2011). Many of these opportunities for gifted students occur beyond the school day. Gifted students spend the majority of their time in general education settings with minimal options for differentiation of instruction (National Association for Gifted Children & Council of State Directors of Programs for the Gifted, 2015). Even when gifted students are provided differentiated instruction in school, students who have a demonstrated ability in a certain area, or have individually advanced beyond the content taught at their school, may not have access to content experts, materials, or resources during the school day in ways that are necessary to develop expertise and gain a higher level of understanding. Many families of gifted students, especially wealthier households, supplement their child's in-school experience with opportunities outside of the school day so they can expose their students to a variety of academic options, enable them to develop and pursue their interests, and enhance their abilities through these guided experiences within an area of strength.

When these opportunities are not provided, potential and talent may remain dormant, leading students to fall into a category that Bell et al. (2019) would describe as "lost Einsteins" (p. 648). This lack of access is a contributing factor to the excellence gap, which consists of the disparity in representation of students from low-income backgrounds at advanced academic levels when compared to their wealthier counterparts (Jack Kent Cooke Foundation [JKCF], n.d.; Plucker & Peters, 2016). Additionally, time on task, meaningful practice, and the productive use of leisure time are essential components for accessing advanced content and being exposed to areas of inquiry that allow student strengths to shine. Leisure time with higher degrees of challenge and a greater degree of concentration, including extracurricular academics, has a lasting impact on mastery or acquisition of content and skills (Csikszentmihalyi et al., 1993; Kleiber et al., 1986). When students from low-income households are unable to participate in academically engaging activities outside of their regular school day, they are more likely than their affluent peers to participate in nonacademic activities, such as watching television, often out of boredom (Dearing et al., 2009; Posner & Vandell, 1999). Without the productive use of leisure time, students from low-income households are missing opportunities to explore advanced content, access mentors and content experts, develop strategies for resiliency in the face of challenge, and build an understanding of what it takes to be a scholar. Therefore, it is recommended that families, schools, and communities work together to promote enrichment programs outside of the school day as means to support talent development (Plucker et al., 2015).

Access to opportunities for talent development is crucial as students move from being interested in a content area to developing efficacy and expertise. Not surprisingly, students who access accelerated opportunities beyond the school day show statistically significant and important gains in academics as well as social and emotional growth (Kim, 2016). When students from low-income households do participate in afterschool, Saturday, and summer programs, positive benefits are noted, including a greater likelihood of taking more advanced high school courses and successful matriculation to more academically selective colleges (Clasen, 2006; Kaul, 2014; Kaul et al., 2016; Olszewski-Kubilius et al., 2017).

Unfortunately, the ability to access such experiences is not met with equity (Corwith, 2018). Afterschool, Saturday, and summer accelerated programming generally require additional resources and supports. Paying tuition (if required), negotiating transportation, and acquiring necessary materials or special equipment for the area of talent make these crucial opportunities less attainable for many students from low-income households. Other barriers may also prohibit access, such as disparities associated with underidentification, not being nominated or recommended for programs, information gaps about existing programs, competing commitments such as second jobs or sibling responsibilities, and a lack of trust in the system causing hesitation to enroll. Yet, given the benefits and importance of access to and participation in out-of-school programming for developing talent, educators must find ways to make it happen and learn from those who have had success in this area. This chapter highlights ways out-of-school programs can successfully support academically gifted students from low-income backgrounds, and reviews patterns and lessons learned from successful out-of-school programs that focus on supporting students with high potential from low-income households.

Types of Programming Models Utilized Beyond the School Day

For gifted students from low-income backgrounds, there is a need for challenging experiences so they can practice overcoming adversity, finding success, and developing strategies for coping (Kitano & Lewis, 2005). A number of programming models exist outside of the school day to benefit students academically and socially; most notable are afterschool programs, Saturday programs, and summer enrichment and accelerated academic experiences. These opportunities increase learning time and provide access to more challenging content, like-ability peers, and content experts (Corwith, 2018; Horn, 2018). It can be argued that afterschool enrichment programs, which are often based out of a school or community center, are the easiest to access for families as students can transition into them from their regular instructional day. They also provide a productive way for students to engage if parents are working well after the school day ends and not home to meet their students. Afterschool programs can focus on enrichment or extensions beyond what is covered during the regular school day or acceleration, such as advanced academics in a given area that is matched to a student's individual learning needs. High school or college credit may accompany accelerated out-of-school programs.

Saturday experiences can happen anywhere but more typically have a presence in university settings, which allow gifted students to access more advanced learning spaces (e.g., labs), resources, and content experts. Wood and Feldhusen (1996), in their review of Purdue's Super Saturday programs

(Feldhusen & Wyman, 1980), emphasized the value of providing professional development to instructors, reviewing and supporting curriculum and lesson plans, and keeping Saturday enrichment courses smaller than general education classrooms, enrolling 12–16 students per class depending on the age of students. Elementary programs that follow a similar Saturday model tend to serve students for a portion of the day (2–4 hours of instruction), for a range of consecutive Saturdays, with courses offered both in fall and spring sessions. In a study of students in grades K–5 from low-income backgrounds participating in Super Saturday experiences falling on six consecutive Saturdays, students learned above-grade-level content, experienced positive social support, engaged in interactive learning, and self-reported positive learning experiences (Miller & Gentry, 2010). Saturday programming for students from low-income backgrounds can provide not only academic and social emotional growth, but also exposure to new fields of study and career exploration through instruction that is supported by content experts. Students who attend gifted programming outside of the school day experience a rise in social self-concept (Rinn, 2006).

Summer programming can provide enrichment or acceleration depending on the scope and approach of the program, as well as the needs of the group, and may be developmental, focusing on different skills and aptitudes as students age. With day programs, often developed with elementary students in mind, programming is similarly structured to courses covered over a series of Saturdays during the school year with a focus on enrichment. Middle and high school students may have additional opportunities to participate in residential programming, where a course or topic is studied in-depth and with more intensity and complexity over the course of one or multiple weeks, combined with time outside of class devoted to affective growth and opportunities for socialization with like-minded peers (Rinn, 2006). Like day programs, residential experiences provide access to accelerated or enriched material and content experts, and also foster a stronger sense of belonging, as community is developed during nonacademic hours through activities and social time, with many students "finding their people" in ways they could not during the school day.

Some intervention models utilize multiple enrichment opportunities in order to provide an all-encompassing, seemingly year-round approach to supporting students with the goal of closing the excellence gap. For example, the Center for Talent Development's Project Excite, which focused on students from low-income and underrepresented backgrounds, combined afterschool enrichment, classes through a university-based weekend enrichment program, and summer programming to provide a significant level of additional academic opportunity for those students (Olszewski-Kubilius et al., 2004). These opportunities combined advanced content with scaffolding to fill in gaps that might have been missed earlier due to competing priorities of lack of an academic focus in the regular school.

Determining what type of out-of-school program is best is dependent upon what the student needs and when. Some students from low-income households need scaffolding and opportunities to fill in learning gaps or develop habits of scholars, while others need access to accelerated and high-level material or opportunities to be more productive in their use of leisure time. Students from low-income households vary in a number of ways, and their unique backgrounds and academic positioning should be considered as out-of-school program options and support systems are developed or explored. Olszewski-Kubilius (2007), in reflecting on decades of working with students and families from low-income backgrounds, wrote:

> There is a great variation among poor families in terms of the reasons that they are poor. Some families are low income because, while parents are educated, they are new immigrants and cannot work in their professions in this country. Some parents simply work in low-income jobs such as church ministry. In other families, parents are not well-educated, work at minimum wage jobs, and both employment and living arrangements are very unstable. These variations have tremendous implications for what kinds of assistance and interventions are needed to ensure talent development for a child. (p. 43)

Therefore, educators and parents need to consider what types of out-of-school programs are necessary and when for their particular students. It is not enough to offer a program beyond the school day and just see who shows up. Instead educators must clearly determine the purpose of the program, intended outcomes, and audience, based on student needs. Parents must be assisted and guided to seek programs that are a match for their student. Students from low-income households who have potential but have not yet demonstrated that potential will require a different type of afterschool or Saturday experience than students from low-income households who are performing above grade level and just lack the extra support necessary to move to the next level of expertise.

Program Examples and Patterns

Given the positive short- and long-term implications that programs beyond the school day can have in the lives of students from low-income households, a closer look at successfully executed programming and models is necessary. The programs selected for review in this chapter met the following criteria. Each program:

> was held over multiple days,
> had an afterschool or beyond-the-school-day (Saturday or summer) component as a central tenant,
> focused primarily on students from low-income households or other underrepresented populations, and
> produced data to show the effectiveness of programs for academically advanced students from low-income households.

The majority of programs focused on students in late elementary school through high school. Few programs as discussed in the literature focused specifically on preschool through fourth grade. We also acknowledge that it is likely that we have missed many great programs, as this is not an inclusive listing. The following projects were selected based on the criteria listed: Project Excite, Project LIVE, Project STREAM, RAV, Project HOPE, Project Promise, Project Launch, Young Scholars, and SPARK.

> Project Excite provided Saturday and summer programming in math and science enrichment to students in grades 3–8 (Olszewski-Kubilius & Steenbergen-Hu, 2017).
> Modeled in part after Project Excite, Project LIVE (Launch Into Verbal Excellence) supported language arts enrichment to students in grades 6–8 (Lee et al., 2010; Olszewski-Kubilius & Thompson, 2010).
> Project STREAM (Support, Training, and Resources for Educating Able Minorities) serves students in middle and high school through Saturday and summer programming (Clasen, 2006).
> A humanities-based enrichment and acceleration program, the Reading Academy at Vanderbilt (RAV; T. Stambaugh, 2018) focused on students in grades 5–8 by providing access to Saturday and summer programs, as well as in-school academically advanced work.
> Project HOPE (Having Opportunities Promotes Excellence) served students in grades K–5 through Super Saturday experiences (Miller & Gentry, 2010).
> Project Launch from Duke Talent Identification Program (TIP) focuses on providing out-of-school problem-based education and academic guidance to students in grades 5–6.
> Fairfax County, VA's Young Scholars Program provides summer enrichment in a variety of subject areas (Horn, 2015, 2016) in addition to in-school opportunities and support.

> Project Promise provided summer enrichment, which included cohorts and mentors, for students in grades 4–12 who resided in low-income households (Kaul et al., 2016).

> Project SPARK, inspired by the Young Scholars model, worked with K–2 students in math as they attended summer programs (Little et al., 2018).

Several of these programs continue to operate and provide programming for students from low-income backgrounds throughout the school year and summer. For additional information on each program, including organization and student outcomes, see Table 8.1.

Patterns of Successful Programs

As we reviewed each program design, we found seven key features used by most programs. These key features are included here as a pattern if at least 50% of the programs utilized this feature. Each feature is discussed in more detail and include the following:

1. Programs recognized student potential over performance. Students were not required to have high scores to participate in the out-of-school experience, and many programs even focused their efforts on developing potential through scaffolding and filling achievement gaps so that more accelerated content could be accessed.

2. Many programs had alternative funding sources available to ease the financial burden of programs through grant- or community-funded cost reductions and other supports, or the provision of transportation and necessary resources.

3. Program directors recognized that a one-size-fits-all program could not be provided, and specialized interventions needed to be designed.

4. An emphasis on relationship building and the creation of support structures was a guiding premise for many programs. The focus of the relationship varied based on program goals. Some programs emphasized building relationships with families; others provided academic and social mentors to develop relationships with students. Still others emphasized peer-to-peer relationships with other gifted students as part of a cohort model.

5. Communication and education for students and their families was a priority. Both educational approaches and communication systems were adjusted from typical programs to better meet student needs.

Table 8.1
Out-of-School Program Overview

Program	Description	Results
Project Excite Northwestern University's Center for Talent Development and Evanston/Skokie School District 65, and Evanston Township High School District 202	Serving students in grades 3–12, Project Excite addresses the opportunity gap in math and science through participation in afterschool enrichment classes, as well as the Center for Talent Development's Saturday Enrichment Program and summer program. Beyond academic opportunities provided to students in grades 3–8, high school students are provided with academic tutoring, standardized testing, and college counseling.	› 70% of Excite students complete 1–2 years of high school math while still in middle school. › 10-year longitudinal data revealed that participants (Black and Hispanic students from low-income backgrounds) increased scores in reaching (+60) and math (+72) points in math on ISAT, meeting or exceeding scores of White peers. › Scores on ninth-grade course placement exam (EXPLORE) revealed that Excite students outperformed Latino and African American district averages in math, reading, and science.
Project HOPE Having Opportunities Promotes Excellence Purdue University and the Gifted Education Research and Resource Institute	For a period of 3 years, students in grades K–5 participated in a Super Saturday enrichment course for 6 consecutive weeks, selecting courses based on interest in fields within STEM, as well as humanities and the arts.	› Based on interviews, students self-reported: positive experiences, learned new things, engaged in interactive learning, and experienced social support.

Table 8.1, continued

Program	Description	Results
Project Launch Duke TIP	Through Project Launch, students in grades 5 and 6 are provided with access to technology, weeklong summer programming designed around tackling a problem within their community, above-grade-level testing, email "nudging" for academic guidance and mentoring, and a book club.	> Positive social effects for students who participated; study still in progress.
Project LIVE Launch Into Verbal Excellence Northwestern University's Center for Talent Development and Evanston/Skokie School District 65	Designed to provide outside-of-school enrichment for middle school students who were reading 2 or more years above grade level, LIVE provided students with weekly reading/discussion clubs after school, two 3-week writing workshops during the summer, and Saturday enrichment activities (field trips or workshops by published authors).	> 97.5% of LIVE students met or exceeded standards on the Illinois Standard Achievement Test (compared to 84% within the district and 81.4% across the state). > Based on the EXPLORE placement exam, 70% of the students in Project LIVE were placed in honors English their freshman year of high school (compared to a 47% placement districtwide). 77% voluntarily elected to attend additional Saturday courses.

Table 8.1, continued

Program	Description	Results
Project Promise Baylor University's University for Young People	Developed as a part of the summer program University for Young People, Project Promise students, ranging from grades 4–12, attend 3–4 weeks each year. During their summer courses, which are self-selected and range from STEM to liberal arts, students are organized into small groups of 10 or 11 and assigned a mentor. Mentors engage and encourage students at the beginning of the day and during a prolonged lunch where they reflect through journal writing and engage in discussion.	› Of the 89 students who completed a survey (out of 128 total), 100% completed high school. Their experience prompted them to select more challenging middle and high school courses, prepared them for higher education, and influenced their decision to attend college. › Students self-reported a better understanding of their strengths and abilities to succeed academically, and parents reported higher expectations.
RAV Reading Academy at Vanderbilt Vanderbilt University Programs for Talented Youth and Metro Nashville Schools	Using local norms, the top 20% of middle school students (grades 5–8) were grouped in an English language arts classroom. Teachers were provided with additional professional development and support in planning and instruction. Student were provided with access to Saturday programs during the academic year and summer (day or residential) programs depending on the age.	› More frequent participation in out-of-school programming during the academic year or summer led to statistically significant gains on pre-post reading scores (comparing spring to fall). › Students self-reported stronger interest in college attendance, openness to academic experiences, and changes in personal identity. › Positive shift in culture schoolwide with regard to reading.

Table 8.1, continued

Program	Description	Results
Project SPARK Supporting and Promoting Advanced Readiness in Kids University of Connecticut	Serving students in grades K–2 across 10 schools, SPARK served students through teacher professional development and access for students to summer programs lasting 3 or 4 weeks. Coursework centered around Project M² math units, which included important mathematical ideas, verbal discourse, and culminating activities.	› Early access to engaging math programming, inside and outside of the school day lead to a more diverse pool of later identified gifted students. › Statistically significant growth for students who attended summer programs.
Project STREAM Support, Training, and Resources for Educating Able Minorities University of Wisconsin–Whitewater	Along with in-school accommodations through instructional differentiation in honors classes, STREAM students were provided with the opportunity to attend Saturday classes at local universities, participation in residential programs for gifted students, and biannual visits to college/university campuses.	› A 13-year follow-up showed a strong relationship between academic achievement and participation in the program. › More frequent participation in STREAM courses and activities corresponded to a greater likelihood of college attendance or completion.
Young Scholars Fairfax Public Schools	Beyond schoolwide services, identified Young Scholars have access to additional extension and enrichment through summer school programs. The problem-based 3-week courses that Young Scholars participate in are concept-based and center around STEM content.	› Increase in access to advanced academic services to historically underrepresented populations.

6. Affective and psychosocial skill development were part of the overall programmatic approach. It has been well documented that academic and job success are due in part to ability, access, opportunities taken, and the development and use of affective and psychosocial skills, such as perseverance, motivation, and growth mindset (Subotnik et al., 2011). Out-of-school programs designed for students from low-income backgrounds recognized this and provided guidance and informational sessions to students on everything from college life and applications to building growth mindset and perseverance.

7. School and university partnerships were formed to garner ongoing support for students and encourage access to advanced resources and content experts. These partnerships typically involved external funding to support the project.

Recognition of Potential Over Performance

As previously discussed, there is a wide gap in achievement between students from low-income households and their wealthier counterparts. As such, many students who have potential do not have the access to develop that potential without experience. Therefore, many students from low-income households who are gifted may go unrecognized, which could limit access to specialized programs beyond the school day. However, most of the programs reviewed considered student potential over performance or test scores, using a variety of methods for selection. Students from low-income households can benefit from programming that utilizes flexible identification approaches, including the use of local norms or lower thresholds for screening and access to programs that bridge and fill gaps in learning. Research tends to focus on local norms for identification in schools (Jordan et al., 2012; McBee, 2006; Peters & Engerrand, 2016; Plucker & Peters, 2018), but this method can carry over into students served through outside-of-school programming. Use of local norms, where students are compared with other students within their environment/community rather than to national norms, is one of the more supported methods of finding and supporting students from low-socioeconomic households (McBee, 2006; Plucker & Peters, 2018). The argument for the use of local norms for outside-of-school programming is based on the assumption that if only those who qualify for gifted services within a school or district are granted entry into programming outside of the school day, unidentified students, including students from low-income households, would continue to be underrepresented (Olszewski-Kubilius & Clarenbach, 2012). Although identifying or admitting students into outside-of-school programming using local norms can help close the income-based achievement gap, considerations for curriculum and what students will experience once there should also be a top priority.

Programs such as Young Scholars (Horn, 2016) and RAV (T. Stambaugh, 2018) supported students who were not identified as gifted but showed potential through district benchmarking, school achievement tests, or local norms. Project HOPE (Miller & Gentry, 2010) screened for students in the 70th percentile and above in order to include students who may not have had the previous academic advantages that their more affluent peers had. Project Excite looked for students performing at the 75th percentile or above on either ability or achievement tests for participation in the program. With Project STREAM (Clasen, 2006), a wide variety of criteria, including seven categories that were a mix of nonacademic and academic, was included in the identification process. As part of the process, teachers were asked to identify students who were underachieving but showed high potential. Research has shown that the earlier a student started an enrichment program, the greater the likelihood that they would remain engaged in school endeavors (Woods, 2005). This is a crucial consideration to keep in mind, as early recognition of talent and participation in extracurricular academic programming can lead to positive habit formation, sense of belonging, and building of content-based efficacy. Most of the programs included in the review—such as STREAM, which identified in sixth grade, and RAV, in fifth grade—began serving students during their middle school years, with many continuing support/programming through high school.

Access by Easing the Financial Burden

Most summer and out-of-school programs are fee-based, which tends to exacerbate the academic access gap that exists between low-socioeconomic and affluent students (Burney & Beilke, 2008). Clearing the financial path for participation in a program for talent development, or often any experience that happens outside of the school day, opens doors to access and allows families to feel as though an additional experience does not mean an additional expense. Making sure that families do not shoulder the financial burden is an important feature in providing equitable access. Almost all of the programs that were reviewed covered a majority of the tuition and programming costs, with many covering all fees when possible (Munger, 2018, 2019). Other programs, such as RAV, asked families to pay a small percentage, less than 5% of tuition, under the notion that having a small financial stake ultimately helps with buy-in and self-sufficiency. With day programs, such as Saturday or daily programming in the summer, transportation was also provided, as was the case with Project Promise, which ultimately ensured attendance (Fogleman, 2017).

Providing Student-Focused Educational Interventions

In their review of poverty, giftedness, and achievement, Olszewski and Corwith (2018) noted the existence of a persistent opportunity gap that followed students as they moved from elementary school into middle school and high school. Despite their capacity, by the time high-achieving students from low-income households reach high school they are less likely than their more affluent peers to take the SAT and ACT or enroll in advanced coursework, such as Advanced Placement or International Baccalaureate programs (Bromberg & Theokas, 2014), thereby contributing to the excellence gap (Plucker & Peters, 2016). Therefore, just as the identification procedures were student-centered in these out-of-school programs, the educational interventions and programs for students were adjusted as well, recognizing that the opportunity gap has to be acknowledged so that potential can be realized. Even if preexisting out-of-school programs were in place, specialized educational opportunities were provided for students from low-income households selected to participate. Some programs provided students with scaffolding to fill in gaps prior to participating in out-of-school programs, while other programs organized their entire out-of-school service around preparing students for advanced courses or the next level of education so that they were on equal footing with others who previously had access. For example, students participating in RAV were supported by classroom teachers and university staff who used scaffolded questioning strategies with accelerated texts and relevant themes and concepts to help prepare students for engaging in more academically rigorous out-of-school programs. Similarly, Project LIVE and Project Excite did not immediately usher students into accelerated out-of-school course work, but offered cohort-specific preparation through tutoring and classes, intentionally "designed to intensely build the skills of students so that they could enter and be successful in traditional advanced coursework" (Olszewski-Kubilius & Thomson, 2010, p. 62). The focus for each program was to set students up for success in the more academically rigorous experiences. Students were provided with the academic and social supports necessary to access and succeed in accelerated programming for which they were capable, once opportunities were provided and physical needs were met.

Establishing Trust and Building Relationships With Students and Families

Asking parents and families to entrust their children into the hands of individuals and instructors operating nonschool-based programming and activities can be a big step, especially when those individuals or institutions do not already have an existing or positive relationship with their school or community. Low-income families are more likely to prioritize relationships when compared to their more affluent peers (Payne, 2019), which speaks to the need for individuals coordinating programs to connect with school leaders, teachers, families, and students. Building trust with students and families in a school-based setting/partnership is key (T. Stambaugh & T. W. Stambaugh, 2020). Meeting with students and families before programming begins provides comfort to families and enables program personnel to build relationships. When meeting with families, it is recommended that program directors provide a space that is easily accessible within the community, provide babysitting, and make food available (Parrett & Budge, 2012).

Many programs also provided mentoring opportunities. Mentors and individuals taking an interest in the lives of students from low-income households play an important role in students' ability to continue pursuing their dreams (Olszewski-Kubilius et al., 2017). These individuals, often serving in an instructor or chaperone/camp counselor capacity in outside-of-school programming, can play an important role in the lives of students from low-income households, modeling and encouraging resiliency in the face of adversity. Although there are generalized benefits of mentoring for all gifted students, there are more significant benefits for students from low-income households (Moon & Callahan, 2001), including representation in gifted programming (Grantham, 2004), college and career guidance (Olszewski-Kubilius et al., 2017) and higher academic self-concept (Rinn, 2006). In a longitudinal study of students from low-income households who participated in Project Promise, researchers found that mentors had positive impacts on students socially, emotionally, and academically. The mentors had high academic expectations for students, and 78% of students expressed a desire to have an ongoing relationship with their mentor (Kaul et al., 2016).

Although mentors serve as an additional benefit from participation in outside-of-school programming, peer support for this programming also plays an important role. Almost all of the programs referenced in this chapter worked with individual schools or districts, and as students participated together in outside-of-school programs, strong networks and bonds were built between students and families, and with program providers. This cohort model is beneficial, as it provides positive peer pressure and a safety zone when it comes to enrolling in the programs, especially Saturday or summer programs that typically take place at a location other than a student's school, providing students with a sense of familiarity. The shared experiences have somewhat of a ripple effect when students transition back to their schools, as students now have peers who can continue to influence and encourage them, building lasting friendships with like-ability peers.

When specifically looking at students from low-income households at summer programs (Project Promise), peers were reported to be a positive influence, and students made close friends who positively influenced them socially, emotionally, and academically (Kaul, 2014; Kaul et al., 2016). This is in line with research that suggests that when students are with like-minded peers and feel a sense of belonging, they report lower levels of stress, anxiety, depression, and disruptive behavior (T. W. Stambaugh, 2017). Participants from low-income households also note the importance of peer support networks and the carry-over into the school day (Olszewski-Kubilius et al., 1994). In another study, Native American students from low-income backgrounds reported that they were motivated by their experience and excited for future challenging opportunities, driven by positive social interactions with peers from diverse backgrounds (Wu & Gentry, 2014). In a different follow-up study of students who had participated in Project Launch (Munger, 2018, 2019), 82% reported they had stayed in contact with one or more of their fellow campers, with relationships serving as a factor for future enrollment in upcoming programs.

Communication and Education of Student and Families

Due to the required investments of time by the student and family, most impactful programs clearly outlined the benefits of the program right from the start. The clear outlining of expectations, benefits, and support structures continued to build a strong foundation of trust between program coordinators and families/communities. For some families, this was their first time participating in a nonschool academic program. Providing information about how programs served students in a different way than the regular school day was often a catalyst for engagement. Young Scholars, which provides both gifted and high-potential students with a continuum of services during both the school year and summer programming, outlined benefits for students during initial conversations with parents, which ultimately lead to additional support and buy-in from families (Horn, 2016). Project Launch utilized email reminders with academic guidance (Munger, 2018). Outlining program benefits and engaging parents and families not only support student participation, but also encourage parental advocacy for more rigorous experiences during the school day (Olszewski-Kubilius & Lee, 2004). RAV employed multiple communication methods, including in-school meetings with students and solicitation of individuals in the school who knew and had relationships with individual families to provide introductions to program staff. In all instances, students and families were seen as partners and treated as such, with staff outlining educational objectives, program purpose and outcome, and expectations while also listening to what students and families needed and wanted out of the project. The programs were intended to walk alongside families in support of their child's endeavors as equal partners with similar goals to help the child succeed.

Attention to Affective and Psychosocial Needs

When participating in programs beyond the school day, students from low-income households gain more than just academic experiences. They strengthen affective muscles as well. A focus on teaching skills such as resilience, college planning and survival, perseverance, and social skills was an important component of many programs. With HOPE scholars, program leaders were provided professional development and feedback on curriculum and instruction so teachers could better meet the specific affective needs of students from low-income households as they pursued more academically rigorous experiences (Miller & Gentry, 2010). Other programs like RAV provided students who were participating in residential programs with psychosocial support. In the safety of their school library, students talked through concerns about participating in residential programs, such as being away from home, what to do in class when they did not know the answer, and how to self-regulate in academically and socially new experiences with staff members who would further support them during their immersive summer experience. In terms of college planning and survival, Project Promise helped develop affective development through the use of mentors who regularly engaged in reflection with students (Kaul, 2014; Kaul et al., 2016). Almost all of the projects discussed here also held career and college planning conversations when age appropriate.

Collaboration With University Partners

Developing and implementing programming outside of the school day requires not only financial support, but also administrative and logistical support, including professional development for instructors, curriculum implementation training, and ongoing communication with a variety of stakeholders. As noted by Clasen (2006) in her longitudinal evaluation of STREAM, "forces working in collaboration are more likely to effect change than forces operating independently" (p. 57). Many of the successful models and programs reviewed for this chapter utilized connections between a local school and a university that offered existing gifted programming on Saturdays or during the summer (e.g., Project Excite and Northwestern University, Project Launch and Duke University, RAV and Vanderbilt University, Project Promise and Baylor

University, HOPE and Purdue University, Project SPARK and the University of Connecticut). These university-driven projects were beneficial in that they provided students with access to content experts, scholarly resources, and exposure to higher education. University settings can also prove to be both motivating and inspiring. For example, when middle school students who were part of the RAV program first arrived to campus, both parents and students noted that for the first time they could "see themselves" belonging to a university community.

Although the examples provided here are only a snapshot of the many programs available for students from low-income programs, the patterns are clear. Most of the programs started with specific outcomes and goals in mind. Each emphasized enriched or accelerated academics in tandem with social and emotional skill development. Even with different approaches, the outcomes were similar, producing positive academic and social-emotional gains and positively impacting students' views of themselves and their ongoing educational and learning endeavors. Program participation also gave them more equal footing to showcase their potential.

Conclusion

When striving to close the excellence gap, parents, educators, and advocates for gifted students from low-income households need to look beyond the school day for opportunities to explore, nurture, and develop talent; these opportunities offer more freedom for creating enrichment and fostering relationships between families, universities, content experts, and like-ability peers. Talent development requires enrichment, acceleration, and the guidance of mentors and content experts that can only be obtained through ongoing practice, access, and productive use of leisure time. To clear that path and provide equitable access, those working with students or developing such programs must expend effort in building relationships, teaching psychosocial or affective skills, removing obstacles to access (such as identification or admissions thresholds, tuition, gaps in education, and transportation), integrating appropriate curriculum and instructional approaches with scaffolds that are slowly removed, and providing mechanisms for sustained support.

References

Bell, A., Chetty, R., Jaravel, N., Petkova, N., & Van Reenen, J. (2019). Who becomes an inventor in America? The importance of exposure to innovation. *The Quarterly Journal of Economics, 134*(2), 647–713. https://doi.org/10.1093/qje/qjy028

Bromberg, M., & Theokas, C. (2014). *Falling out of the lead: Following high achievers through high school and beyond.* The Education Trust.

Burney, V. H., & Beilke, J. R. (2008). The constraints of poverty on high achievement. *Journal for the Education of the Gifted, 31*(3), 171–197. https://doi.org/10.4219/jeg-2008-771

Clasen, D. (2006). Project STREAM: A 13-year follow-up of a pre-college program for middle- and high-school underrepresented gifted. *Roeper Review, 29*(1), 55–63. https://doi.org/10.1080/02783190609554385

Corwith, S. (2018). Programming for talent development outside of school. In P. Olszewski-Kubilius, R. F. Subotnik, & F. C. Worrell (Eds.), *Talent development as a framework for gifted education: Implications for best practices and applications in schools* (pp. 63–94). Prufrock Press.

Csikszentmihalyi, M., Rathunde, K., & Whalen, S. (1993). *Talented teenagers: The roots of success and failure.* Cambridge University Press.

Dearing, E., Wimer, C., Simpkins, S. D., Lund, T., Bouffard, S. M., Caronongan, P., Krieder, H., & Weiss, H. (2009). Do neighborhood and home contexts help explain why low-income children miss opportunities to participate in activities outside of school? *Developmental Psychology, 45*(6), 1545–1562. https://doi.org/10.1037/a0017359

Feldhusen, J. F., & Wyman, A. R. (1980). Super Saturday: Design and implementation of Purdue's special program for gifted children. *Gifted Child Quarterly, 24*(1), 15–21. https://doi.org/10.1177/001698628002400104

Fogleman, L. (2017). *Project Promise to continue through Baylor community outreach grant.* https://www.baylor.edu/mediacommunications/news.php?action=story&story=183732

Grantham, T. (2004). Multicultural mentoring to increase Black male representation in gifted programs. *Gifted Child Quarterly, 48*(3), 232–245. https://doi.org/10.1177/001698620404800307

Horn, C. V. (2015). Young Scholars: A talent development model for finding and nurturing potential in underserved populations. *Gifted Child Today, 38*(1), 19–31. https://doi.org/10.1177/1076217514556532

Horn, C. V. (2016). *Putting it all together: A continuum of K–12 services for gifted learners* [Paper presentation]. Vanderbilt Gifted Education Institute Strategies That Work: Developing Talent in Low-Income Gifted Learners, Nashville, TN, United States.

Horn, C. V. (2018). Serving low-income and underrepresented students in a talent development framework. In P. Olszewski-Kubilius, R. F. Subotnik, & F. C. Worrell (Eds.), *Talent development as a framework for gifted education: Implications for best practices and applications in schools* (pp. 129–152). Prufrock Press.

Jack Kent Cooke Foundation (n.d.). *What is the excellence gap?* https://www.jkcf.org/our-research/what-is-the-excellence-gap

Jordan, K., Bain, S., McCallum, R, & Mee Bell, S. (2012). Comparing gifted and non-gifted African American and Euro-American students on cognitive and academic variables using local norms. *Journal for the Education of the Gifted, 35*(3), 241–258. https://doi.org/10.1177/0162353212451701

Kaul, C. R. (2014). *Long-term effects of a summer enrichment program on low-income gifted students* (UMI No. 1566278) [Master's thesis, Baylor University]. ProQuest Dissertations and Theses Global.

Kaul, C. R., Johnsen, S. K., Saxon, T. F., & Witte, M. W. (2016). Project Promise: A long-term follow-up of low-income gifted students who participated in a summer enrichment program. *Journal for the Education of the Gifted, 39*(2), 83–102. https://doi.org/10.1177/0162353216640938

Kim, M. (2016). A meta-analysis of the effects of enrichment programs on gifted students. *Gifted Child Quarterly, 60*(2), 102–116. https://doi.org/10.1177/0016986216630607

Kitano, M. K., & Lewis, R. B. (2005). Resilience and coping: Implications for gifted children and youth at risk. *Roeper Review, 27*(4), 200–205. https://doi.org/10.1080/02783190509554319

Kleiber, D., Larson, R., & Csikszentmihalyi, M. (1986). The experience of leisure in adolescence. *Journal of Leisure Research, 18*(3), 169–176. https://doi.org/10.1080/00222216.1986.11969655

Lee, S.-Y., Olszewski-Kubilius, P., & Peternel, G. (2010). Achievement after participation in a preparatory program for verbally talented students. *Roeper Review, 32*(3), 150–163. https://doi.org/10.1080/02783193.2010.485301

Little, C. A., Adelson, J. L., Kearney, K. L., Cash, K., & O'Brien, R. (2018). Early opportunities to strengthen academic readiness: Effects of summer learning on mathematics achievement. *Gifted Child Quarterly, 62*(1), 83–95. https://doi.org/10.1177/0016986217738052

McBee, M. T. (2006). A descriptive analysis of referral sources for gifted identification screening by race and socioeconomic status. *Journal of Secondary Gifted Education, 17*(2), 103–111. https://doi.org/10.4219/jsge-2006-686

Miller, R., & Gentry, M. (2010). Developing talents among high-potential students from low-income families in an out-of-school enrichment program. *Journal of Advanced Academics, 21*(4), 594–627. https://doi.org/10.1177/1932202X1002100403

Moon, T. R., & Callahan, C. M. (2001). Curricular modifications, family outreach, and a mentoring program: Impacts on achievement and gifted identification in high-risk primary students. *Journal for the Education of the Gifted, 24*(4), 305–321. https://doi.org/10.1177/016235320102400402

Munger, K. (2018). *Project Launch continues for fifth year*. Duke TIP. https://tip.duke.edu/about/news/project-launch-continues-fifth-year

Munger, K. (2019). *Major grant from Jack Kent Cooke Foundation to help Duke TIP serve even more gifted students with financial needs*. Duke TIP. https://tip.duke.edu/about/news/major-grant-jack-kent-cooke-foundation-help-duke-tip-serve-even-more-gifted-students

National Association for Gifted Children & Council of State Directors of Programs for the Gifted. (2015). *2014–2015 state of the states in gifted education: Policy and practice data*. https://www.nagc.org/sites/default/files/key%20reports/2014-2015%20State%20of%20the%20States%20%28final%29.pdf

Olszewski-Kubilius, P. (2007). Working with promising learners from poverty: Lessons learned. In J. VanTassel-Baska & T. Stambaugh (Eds.), *Overlooked gems: A national perspective on low-income promising learners* (pp. 43–46). National Association for Gifted Children.

Olszewski-Kubilius, P., & Clarenbach, J. (2012). *Unlocking emergent talent. Supporting high achievement of low-income, high-ability students*. National Association for Gifted Children.

Olszewski-Kubilius, P., & Corwith, S. (2018). Poverty, academic achievement, and giftedness: A literature review. *Gifted Child Quarterly, 62*(1), 37–55. https://doi.org/10.1177/0016986217738015

Olszewski-Kubilius, P., Grant, B., & Seibert, C. (1994). Social support systems and the disadvantaged gifted: A framework for developing programs and services. *Roeper Review, 17*(1), 20–25. https://doi.org/10.1080/02783199409553612

Olszewski-Kubilius, P., & Lee, S.-Y. (2004). Parent perceptions of the effects of the Saturday enrichment program on gifted students' talent development. *Roeper Review, 26*(3), 156–165. https://doi.org/10.1080/02783190409554261

Olszewski-Kubilius, P., Lee, S.-Y., Ngoi, M., & Ngoi, D. (2004). Addressing the achievement gap between minority and nonminority children by increasing access to gifted programs. *Journal for the Education of the Gifted, 28*(2), 127–158. https://doi.org/10.1177/016235320402800202

Olszewski-Kubilius, P., & Steenbergen-Hu, S. (2017). Blending research-based practices and practice-embedded research: Project Excite closes achievement and excellence gaps for underrepresented gifted minority students. *Gifted Child Quarterly, 61*(3), 202–209. https://doi.org/10.1177/0016986217701836

Olszewski-Kubilius, P., Steenbergen-Hu, S., Thomson, D., & Rosen, R. (2017). Minority achievement gaps in STEM: Findings of a longitudinal study of Project Excite. *Gifted Child Quarterly, 61*(1), 20–39. https://doi.org/10.1177/0016986216673449

Olszewski-Kubilius, P., & Thomson, D. L. (2010). Gifted programming for poor or minority urban students: Issues and lessons learned. *Gifted Child Today, 33*(4), 58–64. https://doi.org/10.1177/107621751003300413

Payne, R. K. (2019). *A framework for understanding poverty: A cognitive approach* (5th ed.). aha! Process.

Parrett, W., & Budge, K. (2012). *Turning high poverty schools into high performing schools*. ASCD.

Peters, S. J., & Engerrand, K. G. (2016). Equity and excellence: Proactive efforts in the identification of underrepresented students for gifted and talented services. *Gifted Child Quarterly, 60*(3), 159–171. https://doi.org/10.1177/0016986216643165

Plucker, J., Giancola, J., Healey, G., Arndt, D., & Wang, C. (2015). *Equal talents, unequal opportunities: A report card on state support for academically talented low-income students*. Jack Kent Cooke Foundation.

Plucker, J. A., & Peters, S. J. (2016). *Excellence gaps in education: Expanding opportunities for talented students*. Harvard Education Press.

Plucker, J. A., & Peters, S. J. (2018). Closing poverty-based excellence gaps: Conceptual, measurement, and educational issues. *Gifted Child Quarterly, 62*(1), 56–67. https://doi.org/10.1177/0016986217738566

Posner J. K., & Vandell, D. L. (1999). After-school activities and the development of low-income urban children: A longitudinal study. *Developmental Psychology, 35*(3), 868–879. https://doi.org/10.1037//0012-1649.35.3.868

Rinn, A. N. (2006). Effects of a summer program on the social self-concepts of gifted adolescents. *Journal of Secondary Gifted Education, 17*(2), 65–75. https://doi.org/10.4219/jsge-2006-682

Stambaugh, T. (2018). *Report on the effects of the Reading Academy at Vanderbilt (RAV)*. Vanderbilt University.

Stambaugh, T., & Stambaugh, T. W. (2020). Advocating for gifted students in low-income households. In J. Davis & D. Douglas (Eds.), *No more dreams deferred: Breaking the barriers to self advocacy for underserved gifted learners*. Free Spirit.

Stambaugh, T. W. (2017). *Gifted students and mental health: The role of boredom, belonging, friendship, service delivery, and academic challenge* [Unpublished doctoral dissertation]. Trevecca Nazarene University.

Subotnik, R. F., Olszewski-Kubilius, P., & Worrell, F. C. (2011). Rethinking giftedness and gifted education: A proposed direction forward based on psychological science. *Psychological Science in the Public Interest, 12*(1), 3–54. https://doi.org/10.1177/1529100611418056

Wood, B., & Feldhusen, J. F. (1996). Creating special interest programs for gifted youth: Purdue's Super Saturday serves as successful model. *Gifted Child Today, 19*(4), 22–42. https://doi.org/10.1177/107621759601900411

Woods, M. B. (2005). *Factors affecting the degree of participation among enrichment program attendees* (Publication No. 3198885) [Doctoral dissertation, Baylor University]. ProQuest Dissertations and Theses Global.

Wu, J., & Gentry, M. (2014). Summer residential program experiences as perceived by gifted Diné youth. *Journal of American Indian Education, 53*(2), 66–84.

CHAPTER 9

Effective Strategies for Career Counseling of Gifted Learners From Low-Income Backgrounds

Susannah M. Wood
and Carol Klose Smith

Career counseling and vocational guidance continue to be necessary and desired services, specifically for gifted and talented learners (Greene, 2003; Moon et al., 1997; Smith & Wood, 2018; Wood, 2010; Yoo & Moon, 2006). Vocational researchers and practitioners have clearly recognized the role that demographic and contextual variables play within career development (e.g., Lent et al., 2000; Lui et al., 2004). The role of ethnicity and race upon career development of gifted and talented students has received some attention in the past 2 decades (Flowers & Banda, 2018). However, the role of social class has received minimal attention (Jung & Young, 2019). For gifted learners from low-income backgrounds, career counseling is even more vital, as these students lack access, information, or the resource capital to navigate an "efficient pathway" to the world of work or postsecondary education (VanTassel-Baska, 2010, p. 269).

Social Class, Control, Community, Constraints, and Chance

Gifted adolescents from economically disadvantaged backgrounds are more likely to experience career decision making differently as compared to the general gifted population (Jung & Young, 2019) and other adolescents (Muratori & Smith, 2015). Jung and Young (2019) noted that intellectually gifted students from economically disadvantaged backgrounds are likely to approach career decision making with a more complex set of interrelated factors regarding their future career choice. These students face specific challenges that influence their life design, including lack of access to quality education and health care, limited financial support and increased financial stress, and few career role models (Eshelman & Rottinghaus, 2015; Hsieh & Huang, 2014). Although these students place importance upon the economic security of their future occupation (Gore et al., 2015), they are also more likely to be more strongly influenced by their family's opinions (Jung & Young, 2019) and values (Blustein et al., 2002) when compared to perceived interest/enjoyment, prestige, and/or satisfaction (Blustein et al., 2002; Gore et al., 2015). Recent research conducted with adolescents indicated that an individual's social status is linked to career aspirations, interests, perceptions of career barriers, and access to positive role models. This negative relationship can result in lower career self-efficacy or hope for one's future and reduced access to career development resources (Aries & Seider, 2007; Jung & Young, 2019). Notably, all of these factors are all influenced by the gifted student's perceptions in an environment that is more likely to have limited opportunities for role modeling. Students' perceptions of their career opportunities, vocational future, jobs, and/or working are influenced by their observations of their family and the community in which they live. In short, context matters.

Social Class

The effects of social class on occupational aspirations and attainment are complex (Brown et al., 1996). Social scientists have examined how social mores and norms have influenced vocational behavior (Blustein et al., 2002). There are two main ways in which this is examined. First is the belief that social class plays a strong structural component to career behavior, such as determining access to resources and opportunities that allow for a broader range of choices (Ali, 2013). Second is the idea that social class plays a role in creating cultural mores and norms about the world of work (Blustein et al., 2002; Milner, 2013). Hypothetically, this internalization of cultural norms encourages individuals to embrace working class or lower socioeconomic work values and reject middle-class work mores and norms, which include higher education aspirations and occupational goals. The family context may be of paramount importance because this is where perceptions and beliefs about education and careers are transmitted (from family members to adolescents) and is the primary context in which students develop their identity (Blustein et al., 2002). Research suggests that parents and family members are highly influential to the budding career development of adolescents from low-income backgrounds (Ali & Saunders, 2009; Peterson et al., 1986), as well as future job outcomes (Caspi et al., 1998).

In a qualitative study, Thompson and colleagues (2018) examined the explicit and implicit transmission of the concept of social class and work in parent-adolescent dyads. Thompson et al. (2018) suggested that "social class is a complicated topic and yet is intricately connected to hopes and concerns about the future world of work" (p. 705). On the one hand, parents in the study worried about their students' future with regard to the current economic realities, and on the other hand they wanted their students to "dream big" about their future. Teens felt their parents withheld information about family finances and perceptions of class, so these adolescents found ways to inform themselves with regard to social class and work. The biggest divide in perception between the parent and child unit was their beliefs about higher education:

> While all parents expressed their desire for them to pursue advanced degrees, most adolescents were skeptical of the promise of higher education. They noted challenges to this line of thinking, referencing warnings that an advanced degree does not guarantee a high paying job and that individuals should not expect too much from a college degree. (Thompson et al., 2018, p. 710)

Social class also plays a major role within the career decision-making process, the career pathways of students, and how students connect academic work to the world of work. From an educator's perspective, education is often seen as a way to rise above humble beginnings. Middle-class values and ideas are ingrained within the educational system. Through the lens of these values, if a student does not reach their full potential something has gone wrong. However, achievement motivation and a sense of being able to control one's

Table 9.1
Middle-Class and Lower Socioeconomic Work Values of Youth

Middle Class	Working Class
⟩ Talk about the value of work being more intrinsic	⟩ Talk about the value of work as being more extrinsic
⟩ View work as a definition of self: "what you do"	⟩ View work as a way to meet external demands: economic survival
⟩ Families support and encourage career exploration	⟩ More likely to take jobs that are available rather than "finding a good fit"
⟩ Exposure to a wide variety of role models from a variety of occupations	⟩ Career exploration is not encouraged nor practical
⟩ Have resources to explore career options	⟩ Role models are often limited to who the parents know
⟩ Value autonomy, self-direction, and independence	⟩ More likely to find fulfillment in activities outside of work
⟩ Are time-orientated at work; punctual and purposeful	⟩ May value community and working together
⟩ May delay gratification for long periods of time	⟩ May see manual labor as honorable and honest work
⟩ High task persistence regardless of monotony	
⟩ May have difficulty relaxing and enjoying leisure (Type A behavior is rewarded)	
⟩ Upward mobility is highly regarded	

Note. This is a summary of work values found among those living in a middle class and working-class backgrounds and represents an etic view. Individual within-group differences are very likely to exist.

future are middle-class values and are often not embraced by students who are growing up in poverty. By the time students from economically disadvantaged backgrounds begin high school, they are already engaged in understanding that not all opportunities and resources are available to them and are simply out of reach. Table 9.1 describes the differences in work value systems between individuals from working-class backgrounds versus middle-class backgrounds.

Control

Individuals who grow up in economically disadvantaged homes often view work differently than their middle-class counterparts. For this population, work is seen as necessary to meet the basic needs to survive (e.g., food, shelter, clothing, etc.). Therefore, career exploration is not seen as important nor practical because many students will seek jobs that are available rather than finding a career that is a good fit between personality and skills. Individuals from poverty are more likely to have an external locus of control, meaning that they believe they have only little control over the outcome of events in their lives or that their efforts have no relationship to their success (Turner & Conkel Ziebell, 2011). They are also more likely to find fulfillment in activities outside of work.

When answering the question, "Do you work to live or live to work?", the individuals with a working-class framework are more likely to work to meet basic needs. Work is seen as a job to pay bills, not as a path to personal expression or fulfillment. Individuals from middle-class backgrounds are more likely to identify self through their work. At the same time, those who are economically disadvantaged often take pride in the work that they do and see an honest day's work and productivity as important to them. The idea of upward mobility may not be congruent with a working-class perspective, as mobility can require distancing individuals from their families and communities.

Community

Geography, poverty and unemployment rates, and participation in school-sponsored breakfast and lunch programs act as both supports and barriers to career planning (Thompson et al., 2017). In their study of high school sophomores enrolled in gifted programs at Northwestern University, Olszewski-Kubilius and Scott (1992) found that academically advanced students from poverty demonstrated a greater desire to stay close to their families and placed more importance on family, community responsibilities, and involvement. Eshelman and Rottinghaus (2015) found that adolescents' perceived social class and status within their communities were significant predictors of *educational* aspirations and expectations, but not *occupational* aspirations and expectations. These authors suggested that:

> practically speaking, to be inspired to devote the necessary energy into school and the career development process, youth need to believe that their efforts pursuing careers will matter. It may be the case that SES-related factors (e.g., lack of finances for tuition, books) negatively affect students' outcome expectations and, in turn, their career goals. (p. 330)

Based on the findings from a study on rural Appalachian high school students' career aspirations, Ali and Saunders (2009) suggested that career interventions should integrate a community component, as a community focus helps students to discuss how their individual careers could contribute to their immediate context.

Constraints

Students who are economically disadvantaged often have the same type of career aspirations as other students in middle school. However, these aspirations are not aligned to grades or matched to high school academic planning. By the time they reach high school, students from disadvantaged backgrounds are twice as likely to have reduced their career aspirations from highly skilled professional positions to low-skill jobs (Sikora & Saha, 2011). In addition, these students often lack basic knowledge of the educational requirements of college but are very aware of the barriers to achievement (economic resources, family beliefs, etc.). In a study utilizing focus groups of high-ability students from low-income backgrounds, Cross et al. (2017) found that these students experienced several different types of barriers. For some students, parents and siblings were sources of support, resource, and modeling. However, in some cases, family members did not support student's career aspirations, or students were constrained by family responsibility, such as housekeeping and taking care of siblings while parents worked more than one job. When a student from a low-income background does attend college, they are often a first-generation college student.

First-generation college students are often not adequately prepared for college, not only academically but also emotionally, particularly if they are coming from a working-class or low-income background. When exposed to the middle- and upper-class values and aspirations of the typical college campus, students question whether they belong (Collier & Morgan, 2007; DeRosa & Dolby, 2014). They may struggle with issues of identity, social acceptance, and self-esteem as they aspire to integrate values identified with the white-collar world versus the traditional blue-collar values and occupations of their parents (Aspelmeier et al., 2012).

First-generation college students are also frequently faced with the difficulty of trying to adapt to the college environment while having limited time to devote to campus activities or studies (Gibbons et al., 2016). Financial constraints and financial dependents often dictate that these students live at home and/or work part-time (Gibbons et al., 2016; Pascarella et al., 2004). In addition, they are more likely to attend school part-time and take longer to reach their academic goals (Blustein et al., 2002). Thus, first-generation students face challenges that can at times seem insurmountable. Although first-generation students often see college as a way to get a better paying job, their orientation may be about checking off classes on a list rather than taking advantage of internships or extracurricular activities that may be important professional networking tools (Gibbons et al., 2016). This outlook may leave students unprepared for the norms and mores of professional work role expectations.

Chance

Another factor to consider is what Greene Burton (2016) called "global megatrends" (p. 264). The state of the economy in the United States is entangled in changing technology, globalization and outsourcing of jobs, and rapid shifts in types (e.g., green collar) and rates of employment. Gifted students, and students in general, live in a time in which ambiguity and change is the new norm in the job market: "If people change their jobs almost every two years on average, the unique choice of a single occupation for life becomes more of a myth than a reality" (Savickas et al., 2009, p. 242). In some ways, students are walking into an anxiety-provoking future riddled with a lack of certainty. Yet, uncertainty and change also mean opportunity and openness to possibilities. Watts (1996) wrote that "careers are forged, not foretold" (p. 46). This adage reflects the current reality of employment and serves as a reminder that gifted students are likely to want to forge their own career and are capable of doing so. Gifted and talented students in the 21st century need to be prepared to create careers that do not currently exist by focusing upon skills and talents that can be applied in multiple settings. This means counselors and educators need to focus on skills like problem solving, innovation, and collaboration, which are skills for any workplace.

For gifted students from economically disadvantaged backgrounds, workplace skills are frequently practiced in the home and in their communities. Problem solving can mean balancing caregiving of younger siblings with school requirements and part-time jobs after school hours. When academic assignments require supplies that students may not be able to afford, they are resourceful in finding ways to negotiate or bargain for supplies or repurpose old materials. These examples might not necessarily come to mind when educators think of problem solving, but time management, negotiating skills, and creative approaches are all desirable skills that can appeal to employers and are useful in navigating college life.

Career and Vocational Theories

Literature on career counseling for gifted students from low-income backgrounds is sparse given that it is directed toward a very specific subpopulation. However, suggested career counseling interventions for these students can be generated based on research from multiple fields, including gifted education (Chen & Wong, 2013; Jung, 2014; Smith & Wood, 2018), school counseling (American School Counselor Association, 2014; Couture et al., 2018; Deslonde et al., 2018; Gilfillan, 2018; McMahon et al., 2017; Villares & Brigman, 2019), and vocational psychology and career counseling (Ali, 2013; Fouad & Fitzpatrick, 2009; Hsieh & Huang, 2014; Thompson et al., 2018). Interestingly these fields have similar historical roots.

Vocational psychology has long been associated with facilitating ways out of poverty. Frank Parsons in the early 20th century was designated the father of the vocational guidance movement (Baker, 2009; Wilson, 2013). His work and writing focused on helping youths from immigrant families find work by finding a fit between the youth (characteristics, talents, abilities, interests) and an occupation's requirements. Ali (2013) wrote that "Parson's work was built upon the premise of creating a more efficient society by assisting youth in becoming and *staying* employed in occupations that would provide them with life's necessities and ultimately transcend poverty" (p. 130). Parsons wanted to see vocational guidance as a part of American schools, a vision that Jesse B. Davis later helped bring into reality through his book *Vocational and Moral Guidance* in 1914. Leta Hollingworth (1926) has been credited as one of the major historical contributors to gifted education. However, she was also a proponent of women's vocational psychology and contributed a chapter to *Vocational Psychology: Its Problems and Methods* on women's aptitudes for work (Baker, 2009; Hollingworth, 1916). History plays a role in understanding how current career theories, and the interventions derived from them, have been developed and utilized.

Numerous career development theories attempt to capture and explain the complicated process of career decision making in the general population. Traditionally these theories have focused on matching people to jobs with the examination of person and work environment fit (Holland, 1997), exploring working and life roles over one's lifespan (Gottfredson, 2005), and career development through a social cognitive lens (Lent, 2013). Recently there have been criticisms of traditional career theories, which have been largely based on college-going educated White men and/or are biased toward a middle-class orientation while "ignoring those living in poverty and non-college bound individuals" and the very real barriers that exist for those individuals (Ali, 2013,

p. 131; Duffy et al., 2016). Career development theories have emphasized stability of individual traits, a broad market with secure jobs, and careers as fixed sequence of stages (Savickas et al., 2009), which may not apply to the current context.

Researchers in the field have called for a return to the original social justice roots of vocational psychology and the development of theories, frameworks, and approaches that attend to systemic barriers such as poverty, unequal educational opportunities, lack of choice, and social stratification in relation to people's work lives (Ali, 2013; Blustein et al., 2005). Blustein (2006) suggested a change in terminology from *career counseling* to *vocational counseling*, with a focus on "various stages of the processes of preparing for, finding, and maintaining meaningful work . . . [that] would encompass the full spectrum of developmental interventions" (Ali, 2013, p. 133). One theory that shows promise in working with economically disadvantaged gifted youth is Savickas's (n.d.) career construction theory.

Career Construction Theory

Career construction theory (CCT; Savickas, n.d.) is a flexible framework that views a person's career and vocational behavior (including their abilities, values, interests, language, culture, and meaning making) as "storied" and contextualized (Del Corso & Rehfuss, 2011, p. 334). The strength of this theory is its emphasis on how one interprets and imposes meaning upon their own vocational choices. Rooted in a postmodernist philosophy and using a narrative approach, this theory is known for its flexibility in allowing for adaptation in today's ever-changing work environment (Duffy et al., 2016; Hartung & Santilli, 2017). CCT assists in helping an individual find personal meaning from work in their lives (Hartung & Santilli, 2017). Several researchers in gifted education have also suggested that a constructivist theory may be an effective guide for choosing and implementing career interventions (Chen & Wong, 2013; Maxwell, 2007).

CCT has three areas of focus that lend themselves to application to gifted students from low-income backgrounds. These focus areas are life themes, vocational personality, and career adaptability. *Life themes* focus on the career stories people use and tell to describe their vocational choices over time and, more importantly, what matters to the individual. Life themes are derived from an individual's work life and explore the "why" of vocational behavior (Savickas, 2005). The goal is to examine the essential meaning of work in one's life through the stories an individual relates about tasks, transitions, and trauma. The process involves asking individuals about their career story in order to reveal how they made meaningful choices. Classic examples of a life theme would be the stories of the individual who rises out of poverty to be wealthy, the shy child who becomes an actor, or the sickly child who becomes a world-class athlete. Career stories explain why individuals make choices that they do and the private meaning that guides these choices. Within the field of gifted education, Silverman (1993) also suggested the use of life themes as a focus of career counseling for gifted students.

According to CCT, *vocational personality* is an individual's values, interests, needs and abilities (Savickas, 2008). Before these characteristics are expressed in occupations, they are expressed in school, home, hobbies, and games (Savickas, 2005). Vocational personality uses Holland's (1997) nomenclature and framework RAISEC (Realistic, Artistic, Investigative, Social, Enterprising, and Conventional) in order to examine an individual's adaptation to their environment. Using this nomenclature allows for a common language while moving toward an understanding of an individual's socially constructed meaning of time, environment, and culture. Within this framework, CCT does assess interests and abilities, which is a traditional approach in career counseling among gifted and talented students, but it also includes and places a greater focus on assessing individual values. Kerr and Sodano (2003) wrote that "values-based decisions are important for people in general, wherever possible. For gifted students, values-based decisions can prevent students from feeling obligated to develop abilities for which they have little interest and career paths that have little meaning for them" (pp. 175–176).

Last, *career adaptability* refers to an individual's readiness, self-regulation, and/or capabilities to change and cope with current and future vocational development (Savickas, 2005). Basically, career adaptability is one's ability to navigate and connect with society and regulate one's own vocational choices, thus creating a work life and building a career. This process includes career developmental tasks, occupational transitions, and personal traumas. Specifically, Savickas (2005) articulated four dimensions of career adaptability: *concern* (about one's vocational future), *control* (personal choice over preparation of vocational future), *curiosity* (exploration of self and possible career paths), and *confidence* (determination to pursue personal aspirations and anticipation of success). In theory, adolescents should approach these tasks with concern for the future, a sense of control over it, the curiosity to experiment with possible choices, and the confidence to plan and attain their vocational goals. In reality, gifted individuals from economically disadvantaged backgrounds may experience many challenges and delays in these four dimensions of career adaptability as compared to their middle-class counterparts (Blustein et al., 2002). Accordingly, comparing development among the four dimensions is a useful way to assess career adaptability and to understand barriers. More importantly, comparing development in these areas is a way for those working with gifted students from lower income backgrounds to provide interventions that foster goals, increase competencies, and enhance career preparation.

Interventions

The barriers and challenges are very real for gifted students from economically disadvantaged backgrounds; hence they need solid comprehensive academic and career planning. Both schools and communities benefit from promoting alignment between the academic mission and the career development of students. Utilizing CCT, educators can design interventions that can be implemented in classrooms, small groups, and one-on-one conversations. Educators who may feel uncomfortable with some of these interventions might consider collaborating with a helping professional in the school, such as the school counselor. Career interventions benefit all students if they occur early in their educational career. Thus, interventions can be thought of in four major areas: (a) exposure to careers, (b) career exploration, (c) early opportunities to practice with career paths, and (d) enhancing family and student connections to postsecondary options.

Exposure to Careers

Per CCT, the stories that students tell and construct about themselves and their careers are bounded by their exposure to and knowledge about careers. One of the biggest challenges gifted students from poverty face is the lack of exposure to careers if the community in which they live presents only limited role models or if there is a high rate of unemployment (Chen & Wong, 2013). A second challenge is the desire students may have to pursue careers that are perceived as prestigious (or have higher perceived social standing) or are aligned to specific gender norms. In order to provide a broader array of options, educators could consider a schoolwide career fair that may bring in local families, community members, and businesses.

Career Fairs. Career fairs allow students to rotate through stations, booths, or tables with business and community members, or even alumni, who can knowledgeably address (a) what the particular job entails, (b) the educational or training required for the job, and (c) how the business contributes to the local community. Fairs can be bracketed by activities such as a prefair KWL chart that is career focused and illustrates what the student already knows about the career, what they want to know, and what they have learned as a result of the fair. Students can also create a preliminary resume that they can revisit as they learn more about skills and credentials that future employers may want to see. Educators can create their own activities that address what was learned about the jobs and careers present at the fair using the higher levels of Bloom's (1956) taxonomy. Borrowing from CCT, students can interview community members or business representatives about their career stories, including why/how the career they represent brings meaning to them and/or helps the local community. For example, one Rhode Island middle school put on a "Real-Life Fair" (Bafile, 2010). Prior to the fair, teachers from different core areas facilitated several different activities, including self-assessments. Students chose a particular career of interest based on the assessments, and then teachers led them through questions that focused on future income and earnings, starting salaries, postsecondary training, and exploration of cost of living and transportation. Other activities included the use of a mock checking account and trial and error with spending and saving.

Research suggests that students are exposed to careers via watching and communicating with caregivers and their siblings (Keller & Whiston, 2008; Thompson et al., 2017). Because families and siblings will play an important role in career development, building relationships with the whole family is essential (Jung & McCormick, 2011). One way to support and explore these relationships is through career genealogies, which educators can utilize as a class assignment. Career genealogies deepen students' knowledge about family members. Interviewing family members brings out discussions about values, hobbies, education, and vocation. Johnson (2010) wrote that career genealogies can bring new family information to light and help educators and counselors identify patterns and themes in family members' career development, which is consistent with CCT. Some of these patterns might be: (a) identifying students who may be the first in their families to attend college, (b) traditional gendered careers, and (c) periods of unemployment. Students can designate who they wish to incorporate into the genealogies, allowing for extended family members or individuals who are not related by blood or marriage.

Social Network Mapping. Social network mapping can complement genealogies. In fact, Jones (n.d.) wrote that social network mapping can help individuals identify their social capital. Social network mapping is both a process and a product. Students map out relationships between people or groups of people in their lives. A mapped social network is the visual representation of those relationships. Network maps can be hand drawn or computer generated and typically include circular nodes (representing people or entities) and lines that can be directional or bidirectional (representing connections between and among the people or entities in students' lives). The analysis of social network maps includes examining who in the nodes are influential to the person constructing the map or who may influence other people in the map. Students may also determine the strength and type of the relationship (family member, acquaintance, employer).

Adding a focus on careers in the process of mapping can help students identify the vocational personality of the people in their lives regardless of depth or "nearness" of the relationship. Students who live in smaller communities may see significant overlap of relationships among the people in their network. An adult could be family friend for whom the student babysits who is also their past third-grade teacher and the director of the local church choir. A classmate could be a student leader in 4H or ROTC who also works part time at a local grocery store. In these examples, a student's network map may show a close relationship to the adult and a more distant connection to the peer. However, the student has already uncovered the adult's vocation and hobbies. This adult who was the student's former teacher may be able to give the student feedback on babysitting skills, information on why they became a teacher and the educational path they took, and what they love about directing a choir. The peer could be interviewed about leadership skills that they use in their 4H position and the skills they need to work at the grocery store. If a job, hobby, or business is of interest to the student, they could then investigate their Holland's (1997) code (RAISEC) and how that code is expressed within their jobs, hobbies, and even postsecondary education. Social network mapping can provide the starting point for the next activity, such as linking students with mentors or vising local businesses.

Mentors. Mentors may be the most important component in a gifted student's career development. The concept of mentorship has been explored in the gifted education literature (Berger, 1990; Bisland, 2001; Silverman, 1993) and highlighted within career counseling with students from economically disadvantaged backgrounds (Ortega, 2018; Tate et al., 2015). Schools frequently utilize mentorship programs by harnessing local resources, such as local colleges, the YMCA, or the Big Brothers Big Sisters program. However, many mentorship programs focus on academic skills. Typically, mentoring programs entail screening of both potential mentees and mentors, organization of structured time, and training of mentors. Finding appropriate mentors can be a challenge. Students need to connect with role models who are like themselves; students of color need mentors of color, and young women need professional women as models and mentors (Berger, 1990). VanTassel-Baska (2018) noted that mentorship matches for students from poverty may be limited, although they are much needed in order to "teach them informally what they need to know to be successful" (p. 70).

When considering the needs of gifted students, Berger (1990) proposed factors to consider when helping to screen and select mentors, including the mentor's understanding of gifted and talented students, teaching style versus student learning style, ability to share the excitement of learning, and optimism. Bisland (2001) suggested that mentors for gifted students possess (a) expertise in a specific field of interest that matches one of the gifted mentees; (b) willingness to share professional knowledge; (c) patience; (d) sensitivity to the uniqueness of gifted students; (e) ability to wear multiple "hats," including teacher, advisor, and model; (f) ability to show support; and (g) commitment to the process, including time and effort. Likewise, the individual student needs to be considered, as not all students will be a good fit for the program.

Borden (n.d.) cautioned that mentoring programs are not a panacea for all needs or all students. Bisland (2001) recommended that educators examine background information, interest inventories or interviews, as mentees "should be students who have exhausted the educational resources within the school and need to go to members of the community for further growth and development" (p. 23). Educators should consider obstacles that can result in lack of quality or even potential damage to students, including lack of support or resources, limited knowledge of the best practices surrounding mentorship programs, and unrealistic expectations (Borden, n.d.). Lack of resources may be the biggest obstacles that schools in low-income communities face. Educators may wish to investigate iCouldBe (https://icouldbe.org), an online mentoring program for at-risk students, or iMentor (https://imentor.org), which connects students interested in postsecondary education with a college-educated mentor.

Exploration of Careers

This process of understanding one's individual vocational personality needs to begin early in the educational life of a student. Many gifted students begin contemplating their future careers in elementary school. Often this process is interwoven with the emergence of a child's passion for a singular topic (Matthews & Foster, 2005). Delaying career exploration until secondary school does a disservice to gifted students, and it is recommended that career exploration interventions begin in elementary school (Muratori & Smith, 2015).

Elementary school students need time to develop and explore various career opportunities as well as develop important social skills. Emotional regulation, executive skills, problem solving, creativity, and teamwork will all contribute to a child's work and academic future (Kim, 2012). Early vocational exploration involves learning about work: the types of work available in the community, the role of work in people's lives, as well as a basic understanding that passion areas can be developed into the career path. For example, a child who likes to study bugs may learn that they could become an entomologist, or a child who enjoys learning about dinosaurs may wish to explore the idea of becoming a paleontologist. This is a time to expand awareness of all of the possibilities their future can hold.

By late elementary or middle school, academic preparation becomes more of a focus in student's career construction. Academic plans and future career plans ideally serve as a blueprint for preparing a student for their postsecondary training or college aspirations. Unfortunately, students "may be poorly prepared for college because their schools often fail to recognize their abilities, or schools may place them in programs that do not develop their higher-level skills" (VanTassel-Baska, 2018, p. 77). Students from low-income backgrounds need to understand the critical link between high school courses and their preparation for future education or career opportunities. During middle school a child may begin to question the relevance of some of their academic course work to their work future. Creating academic assignments relevant to today's needed skills and knowledge is important. Enrollment in challenging coursework can help students prepare for the academic rigor of college as well as help them connect with like-minded, high-achieving peers (Hébert, 2018). The development of an academic plan is an ideal time for teachers, parents, and students to engage in discussions about future career aspirations and pathways to achieve students' hopes and dreams (Smith & Wood, 2018). In addition, including lists of hobbies and extracurricular activities can provide important clues in how a student chooses to spend their time, their talent areas, and what they may enjoy doing in the future (Smith & Wood, 2018).

Educators can facilitate career exposure and connect relevant content to careers through online tools. Many schools today used web-based career interest inventories, ability measurements, and job exploration software. These tools are an excellent way to explore what types of activities a student enjoys and create a list of potential careers that match those activities (Smith & Wood, 2018). One free tool developed by the federal government is O*NET OnLine (https://www.onetonline.org), which houses a database of occupation-specific descriptors. The U.S. Bureau of Labor Statistics offers resources for students who are interested in career exploration (https://www.bls.gov/k12/students.htm). Other web resources include Mapping Your Future (https://mappingyourfuture.org/PlanYourCareer) and myFuture (https://www.myfuture.com). For younger elementary students, Paws in Jobland (https://www.xap.com/paws) may be more appropriate. Many of these websites have opportunities and activities for students to connect with educators and include their family members when discussing careers, postsecondary education paths, or military or trade schools. Educators should check to see if sites are free to use or consider if their budget could facilitate buying some of the available tools.

Assessing Interests, Values, and Abilities. In addition to O*NET, many schools will have interest inventories that they use with their students. However, these tools need to be carefully selected when used with the gifted population. Ability and interest inventories that are normed with above-level or adult scales should be chosen in order to avoid a high flat profile that does not differentiate enough to be of any value. In addition, ability and interest inventories do not take into consideration all of the important information. Interest inventories can only capture a portion of the puzzle at one point in time—interests change over time. Thus, at every educational level, educators and counselors need to provide time for gifted students to reflect and engage in a dialog about their future career path and work life. The use of individual conversations and small-group discussions allows for the necessary reflection for students to make an informed choice (Muratori & Smith, 2015; Smith & Wood, 2018). Educators can also facilitate values exploration in large class settings through the Career Values Action Activity and the Career Values Four Corner Activity.

Career Values Action Activity. The purpose of this activity is for the student to determine the career values that matter the most to them and differentiate and prioritize their most important career values. For this activity, the teacher will need to display a list of approximately 15 to 25 career values. Each student is given an imaginary $500 to spend and instructed to purchase as many of their career values as possible. The teacher is the auctioneer and sells the career values to the highest bidder. Each value is held on the auction block and awarded to the student who outbids the competition. At the end of the auction, the process is debriefed and discussed: What did the students learn about what they chose to bid on? What values did they get? What did they choose not to bid on, and why? Do the values they won reflect them accurately or not? What did they learn about their classmates that surprised them?

Career Values Four Corner Activity. The purpose of this activity is to assist students in learning about which values are most important to them. For this activity, the educator shares a list of 20 career values. Students are instructed to label the values from 1 to 20, with 1 being the most important to them and 20 the least important. In each corner of the room, there are four labels: 1–4, 5–9, 10–14, and 15–20. When the students have completed ordering their list of career values, the teacher will state one value. Students will then walk to the corner of the room that represents the number they placed on that value. Then, students are asked why they placed that value in that spot: Why is this value important to them? How do they see this value within their future lives and their career? Sharing their own thoughts and hearing the thoughts of their peers through the process of reflection provide opportunities for personal growth and increased vocational personality awareness.

Early Opportunities to Practice With Career Paths

Part of building efficacy is practice. For gifted students, early practice with skills and roles in their career interest areas is needed in order to solidify career decision making or eliminate potential dead ends. Engaging in job shadowing, internships, and apprenticeships may open gifted students' eyes to future roles and skills. Work experience and exposure *to different types of work* facilitates career adaptability and adds more experience to students' life themes. Some real-world work experience can be of a short-term duration, while other types can last a summer or a semester.

Job shadowing consists of daylong opportunities in which students observe an individual engaging in their typical job duties. Worksites can vary, from manufacturing plants, to local businesses, to medical facilities. Students ask questions of the person they are shadowing, and educators can work together with students to create their interviews. On occasion, the student may be asked to perform a typical task required by that job. Students can investigate the site prior to the visit and are encouraged to dress professionally and even practice professional emails or write thank-you notes—specific steps toward real-world experience. Afterward students can reflect on what they learned from the experience. This process allows students to examine their preconceived perceptions of a career path and compare it to the reality. Reese (2005) provided the example of a student who wanted to be a veterinarian but realized they hated the sight of blood. Other students may find that tasks or jobs they may have written off as unappealing could hold the potential to be meaningful as well as lucrative. Trying out new skills in a limited time frame with little pressure can help students decide if they want to do these skills as a daily exercise and can give them a better idea of how long it will take to master a skill (especially if students assume all job skills will come as easily to them as academic skills may have). Job shadowing is one way of answering a student's question of "Why do I have to learn this?" with regard to academic content (Reese, 2005).

Internships and apprenticeships are opportunities for school-to-work transitions that are of longer duration, from a month to a semester. Internships programs are as varied as the schools that host them. Levine (2010) cautioned that, like mentorship programs, internships need to be carefully structured and supported. He suggested that internship programs do the following: (a) provide opportunities for students to explore their interests via assessments, biographies, and learning about other students' internships; (b) connect students to worksites in which they can pursue their interests; (c) ensure there are appropriate mentors on the site; (d) cultivate sites and mentors via networking with local community members and students' families; (e) vet sites and mentors, including using background checks; and (f) connect students with mentors by having students practice making cold calls and navigating worksite structures and hierarchies. For an internship program to work, curriculum modifications may need to happen. Schedules may need to be adjusted in order to visit worksites or facilitate end-of-experience reports or presentations. Transportation, credit options, scheduling, staffing, liability coverage, and specific requirements that need to be fulfilled prior to the internship also must be considered. Levine (2010) wrote:

> Simply spending time in a professional setting is valuable for teenagers, but interns also routinely take on active and valued roles such as repairing bicycles, leading math groups, or reconciling accounts payable records. Students complete internship projects and research papers that demand both academic and professional skills, and for their exhibitions they teach their classmates about topics ranging from Alzheimer's therapy to environmental policing to making neon signs. (p. 46)

Facilitating Family and Student Connections to Postsecondary Options

First-generation college-going students encounter unique challenges when it comes to their preparation for and transition to college life. One of the most important things educators and helping professionals can do is to help both the student and their family connect with postsecondary options. Long-term planning, which is necessary for college entrance and postsecondary planning, may be difficult for gifted students from poverty "given the immediate and often overwhelming demands of everyday life in the family" (VanTassel-Baska, 2018). For those students who plan on attending trade school, the website Trade Schools, Colleges and Universities (https://www.trade-schools.net/pro grams.asp) allows students to search for local and well as national programs in a wide variety of trades and vocations.

Although early entrance programs may be appropriate for some students, being aware of other options is important. Taking college or community college courses during high school (e.g., dual enrollment) is one such option, as well as taking Advanced Placement (AP) courses. Dual enrollment courses and programs vary across the United States, as they are contingent upon the relationship between the high school and the postsecondary institutions in the immediate locale. AP courses are college-level courses taught in the high school that prepare students for college-level academic expectations. One challenge for taking advantage of either dual enrollment or AP courses is that there are often prerequisites that exist within the high school. Again, creating a plan early allows for the completion of any prerequisites prior to the start of the dual enrollment or AP courses.

Any postsecondary planning must include discussions about financial aid. Hosting financial aid evenings to assist families with the completion of the Free Application for Federal Student Aid (FAFSA) and college/postsecondary training can assist with this process. Completing the FAFSA is an important step in understanding what financial aid a student will qualify for at a particular higher education institution. FAFSA is used in determining eligibility for need-based postsecondary options that may be available, such as Pell Grants, Work-Study, and student loan programs. In addition to FAFSA, students should be encouraged to seek out scholarship award programs. These are generally merit-based scholarships and are available at or through the institutions of higher education as well as community-based programs. Often these scholarship programs are based upon specific criteria set by the organization offering the scholarship (e.g., GPA, SAT/ACT scores, athletic achievement, etc.). Asking about scholarships during campus visits and looking online can yield valuable information.

Last, students need to know what university assistance programs exist. Many colleges and universities provide programs for students that are designed to assist in reducing many barriers that could impede academic success of students from lower income homes. One such program is Upward Bound, a program that is under the umbrella of TRIO and funded by the federal government. The purpose of this program is to prepare students from economically disadvantaged backgrounds for college, with a focus on academic and social-emotional preparation. The program works through individual grants and is often administered through a local college or university. The high school student participates in a yearlong program with a 6-week summer program as well. For more information about TRIO Upward Bound programs, please see https://www2.ed.gov/programs/trioupbound/index.html. Another TRIO program is the McNair Scholars Program, which provides valuable mentoring programs designed to prepare first-generation students from economically disadvantaged backgrounds for doctoral studies. For more information, please see https://mcnairscholars.com. In addition to federally funded programs, there may be university-funded programs.

A summary of the challenges and interventions discussed in this section can be found in Table 9.2.

Table 9.2
Challenges and Interventions

Challenges	Possible Interventions
School Culture and Climate	⟩ Creating strong connections with families ⟩ Creating a supportive and encouraging message that all students can succeed ⟩ Providing clear and consistent messaging about the link between academic achievement and future postsecondary options ⟩ Designing a challenging and culturally responsive curriculum
Increasing Exposure to Careers	⟩ Mentorship programs ⟩ Career fairs ⟩ Role models for classroom presentations ⟩ Using class materials that highlight gender nonconforming role models ⟩ Family career genealogies ⟩ Career social network mapping
Increasing Career Knowledge and Information	⟩ Linking ability assessment to future career areas that are communicated with child and parents ⟩ Providing/discussing career interest inventories with students and families ⟩ Clearly linking academic preparation for future postsecondary options early and consistently throughout K–12 education ⟩ Encouraging challenging coursework ⟩ Encouraging students to take AP and postsecondary courses in high school
Increasing Knowledge of Career Values	⟩ Work values inventories ⟩ Exploring work values with activities like the values auction and career values four-corner activity
Creating Early Opportunities for Career Exposure	⟩ Mentorships ⟩ Job shadowing ⟩ Internships and apprenticeships ⟩ Exploring academic summer and weekend programs
Supporting Postsecondary Planning	⟩ Invitation and inclusion of family within the process ⟩ Creating academic plans linked to postsecondary goals starting early ⟩ Financial aid information about financing postsecondary options and assistance with the FAFSA application ⟩ Assisting in the exploration of scholarship opportunities from community organizations and postsecondary schools ⟩ Exploration of available university programs for lower income families ⟩ Exploring the option of Upward Bound

Guidelines for Educators and Helping Professionals

Supportive educators and helping professionals can make the difference between lack of guidance in career construction and successful career planning for gifted students from low-income backgrounds. Hébert (2018) wrote that "young people benefit from educators who deliver messages that they are talented and their self-identities are valued" (p. 107). However, educator preparation programs may not address ways to facilitate relationships with students or fully address biases toward specific populations, like gifted students from low-income backgrounds. In order to provide effective and supportive interventions to gifted students from poverty, educators need to understand the effects of classicism and poverty on academic achievement. Amatea and West-Olatunji (2007) suggested several ways school counselors could take the lead in supporting students from poverty in their schools. Current authors expand on these to create guidelines for school counselors, school-based career counselors, gifted educators, and administrators to utilize while implementing the interventions suggested previously.

1. Evaluate personal attitudes, beliefs, and biases regarding gifted students from economically disadvantaged situations. The words *gifted*, *talented*, and *high ability* bring their own connotations, which can evoke resentment, confusion, or negativity (Colangelo & Wood, 2015). Similarly, there is a definitive stigma attached to poverty (e.g., lazy, inferior, uninterested in education). Educators may see students and their families through a deficit lens or with a middle-class bias (Tomlinson & Jarvis, 2014). According to Wood and Peterson (2014), "Some cultures do not value placing anyone above others or displaying what one knows, instead valuing such elements as quietly serving one's community, being able to inspire others, listening, teaching, overcoming adversity, and having wisdom (rather than "book" knowledge)" (p. 646). Educators may wish to consult reflective questions posed by Wood and Peterson (2014) and Wood and Lane (2015) in order to explore these concepts. Not addressing biases and preconceptions can result in microaggressions against these students, especially gifted students from low-income backgrounds who are also students of color (Ford et al., 2013).

2. Consider new roles in the school to increase sensitivity and service to gifted students from low-income backgrounds. Counselors, teachers, and administrators all play important roles in making their schools welcoming to all students and their families. Amatea and West-Olatunji (2007) suggested that these roles include being a cultural broker or

cultural bridge by focusing on strengths of students and families, and "blocking blame" that can occur in school-family interactions (p. 83). Acting as a cultural bridge may also mean identifying negative climate issues that can make parents and families reluctant to work with school personnel. Parents and family members may have had negative interactions with schools when they themselves were students, and educators can misconstrue this as lack of interest or concern in their student's academic life (Amatea & West-Olatunji, 2007). In addition, when meeting about academic planning and thus career construction, educators need to focus on students' strengths, encourage parent/family perceptions about areas of strengths and weaknesses, and "block blame from undermining the collaborative process" (p. 84). Last, educators should consider learning more about their students' family and community contexts, including language, household configuration, bus routes, and extracurricular activities (Amatea & West-Olatunji, 2007).

3. Design and implement a challenging and culturally responsive curriculum that can integrate aspects of career construction and life designing. Olszewski-Kubilius and Corwith (2018) reviewed supplemental school programming that was designed to combat "opportunity gaps by providing access to enriching academic summer and weekend programs and exposure to higher education, like-ability, peers, mentors, and professionals" (p. 49). These programs include Young Scholars, Project Promise, Project STREAM, and Project Excite. Flexible curriculum may identify and adapt to students' "funds of knowledge" or "the various social and linguistic practices and the historically accumulated bodies of knowledge that are essential to students' homes and communities" (Amatea & West-Olatunji, 2007, p. 84). Funds of knowledge can be very different for students from poverty than their middle-class counterparts, especially if their "ways of knowing are not culturally compatible with the schooling environment" (p. 84). Programming should integrate career construction. Challenging curriculum that is constructivist and developmental in nature should allow for activities that facilitate life themes, career personality, and career adaptability, and emphasize the relevance of knowledge and skills students need in their future world of work.

Conclusion

The limited research on gifted students from low-income backgrounds suggests barriers and hurdles that may confront them. The career future of these students relies not only on the promise of their abilities, but also upon the relationships forged that can assist student success in navigating those barriers. Relationships can provide hope and promote resilience among gifted students with big dreams for their future. Educators who utilize CCT in their approach to working with gifted learners may see students reauthor or re-story their potential career planning narrative. Implementing interventions via programming, curricula, independent projects, class assignments, and changes in school cultures can assist gifted students in gaining access to educational opportunities, forging community relationships, and receiving early exposure to careers. Ultimately, interventions based in CCT are designed to help gifted students become aware of the values they associate with the world of work and how those values, along with their unique abilities and interests, connect with both their current academic situation and life after high school. Gifted students from poverty have the ability to explore their career construction deeply, but must be given the structured opportunities to do so as early as possible with the help of supportive educators. As VanTassel-Baska (2018) wrote:

> Promising learners from poverty then must understand that they are in charge of their lives and must chart the course, whatever it may be. Ironically, the road out of poverty may be better defined if one has an impossible dream, an area of defined talent or ability, and a desire to work hard to achieve a modicum of success. Seeing oneself as an artist in life's creation is the mind-set that may make the vital difference to these individuals over time, as it frees them from a faulty belief system based on a predestined fixed sense of fate control or blind faith that can easily dissipate the drive needed to excel in an area. (p. 78)

References

Ali, S. R. (2013). Poverty, social class, and working. In D. L. Blustein (Ed.), *The Oxford handbook of the psychology of working* (pp. 127–140). Oxford University Press.

Ali, S. R., & Saunders, J. L. (2009). The career aspirations of rural Appalachian high school students. *Journal of Career Assessment, 17*(2), 172–188. https://doi.org/10.1177/1069072708328897

Amatea, E. S., & West-Olatunji, C. A. (2007). Joining the conversation about educating our poorest children: Emerging leadership roles for school counselors in high-poverty schools. *Professional School Counseling, 11*(2), 81–89. https://doi.org/10.1177/2156759X0701100202

American School Counselor Association. (2014). *ASCA mindsets and behaviors for student success: K–12 college- and career-readiness standards for every student.*

Aries, E., & Seider, M. (2007). The role of social class in the formation of identity: A study of public and elite private college students. *The Journal of Social Psychology, 147*(2), 137–157. https://doi.org/10.3200/SOCP.147.2.137-157

Aspelmeier, J. E., Love, M. M., McGill, L. A., Elliott, A. N., & Pierce, T. W. (2012). Self-esteem, locus of control, college adjustment, and GPA among first- and continuing generation students: A moderator model of generational status. *Research in Higher Education, 53,* 755–781. https://doi.org/10.1007/s11162-011-9252-1

Bafile, C. (2010). *A "real-life fair" shows kids the real deal about careers.* Education World. https://www.educationworld.com/a_curr/curr196.shtml

Baker, D. B. (2009). Time, context, and change: Vocational guidance at 100. *Career Development Quarterly, 4,* 31–39.

Berger, S. L. (1990). *Mentor relationships and gifted learners* (#E486). ERIC. https://eric.ed.gov/?id=ED321491

Bisland, A. (2001). Mentoring: An educational alternative for gifted students. *Gifted Child Today, 24*(4), 22–25, 64. https://doi.org/10.4219/gct-2001-550

Bloom, B. (Ed.). (1956). *Taxonomy of educational objectives: The classification of educational goals. Handbook I: Cognitive domain.* Longmans Green.

Blustein, D. L. (2006). *The psychology of working: A new perspective for career development, counseling, and public policy.* Erlbaum.

Blustein, D. L., Chaves, A. P., Diemer, M. A., Gallagher, L. A., Marshall, K. G., Sirin, S., & Bhati, K. S. (2002). Voices of the forgotten half: The role of social class in the school-to-work transition. *Journal of Counseling Psychology, 49*(3), 311–323. https://doi.org/10.1037//0022-0167.49.3.311

Blustein, D. L., McWhirter, E. H., & Perry, J. C. (2005). An emancipatory communitarian approach to vocational development theory, research, and practice. *The Counseling Psychologist, 33*(2), 141–179. https://doi.org/10.1177/0011000004272268

Borden, C. S. (n.d.). *Implementing effective youth mentoring relationships for high school students.* https://www2.ed.gov/programs/slcp/finalimplem.pdf

Brown, M. T., Fukunaga, C., Unemoto, D., & Wicker, L. (1996). Annual review, 1990–1996: Social class, work, and retirement behavior. *Journal of Vocational Behavior, 49*(2), 159–189. https://doi.org/10.1006/jvbe.1996.0039

Caspi, A., Wright, B. R. E., Moffit, T. E., & Silva, P. A. (1998). Early failure in the labor market: Childhood and adolescent predictors of unemployment in the transition to adulthood. *American Sociological Review, 63*(3), 424–451. https://doi.org/10.2307/2657557

Chen, C. P., & Wong, J. (2013). Career counseling for gifted students. *Australian Journal of Career Development, 22*(3), 121–129. https://doi.org/10.1177/1038416213507909

Colangelo, N., & Wood, S. M. (2015). Counseling the gifted: Past, present, and future directions. *Journal of Counseling and Development, 93*(2), 133–142. https://doi.org/10.1002/j.1556-6676.2015.00189.x

Collier, P. J., & Morgan, D. L. (2007). 'Is that paper really due today?' Differences in first-generation and traditional college students' understandings of faculty expectations. *Journal of Higher Education, 55,* 425–446. https://doi.org/10.1007/s10 734-007-9065-5

Couture, V., Bang, N., & McCoy Harless, A. (2018). *Successful career counseling interventions used with students in poverty: A preliminary report.* National Career Development Association. https://www.ncda.org/aws/NCDA/pt/sd/news_article/18 1017/_PARENT/CC_layout_details/false

Cross, J. R., Frazier, A. D., Kim, M., & Cross, T. L. (2017). A comparison of perceptions of barriers to academic success among high-ability students from high- and low-income groups: Exposing poverty of a different kind. *Gifted Child Quarterly, 62*(1), 111–129. https://doi.org/10.1177/0016986217738050

Del Corso, J., & Rehfuss, M. C. (2011). The role of narrative in career construction theory. *Journal of Vocational Behavior, 79*(2), 334–339. https://doi.org/10.1016/j. jvb.2011.04.003

DeRosa, E., & Dolby, N. (2014). 'I don't think the university knows me': Institutional culture and lower-income, first-generation college students. *InterActions, 10*(2).

Deslonde, V. L., & Becerra, M. D. (2018). High school counselors' influence on low socio-economic students' college enrollment. *Journal of School Counseling, 16,* Article 24.

Duffy, R. D., Blustein, D. L., Diemer, M. A., & Autin, K. L. (2016). The psychology of work theory. *Journal of Counseling Psychology, 63*(2), 127–148. https://doi.org/10. 1037/cou0000140

Eshelman, A. J., & Rottinghaus, P. J. (2015). Viewing adolescents' career futures through the lenses of socioeconomic status and social class. *The Career Development Quarterly, 63*(4), 320–332. https://doi.org/10.1002/cdq.12031

Flowers, A. M., & Banda, R. M. (2018). When giftedness and poverty collide and why it Matters: Gifted, poor, black males majoring in engineering. *Journal of African American Males in Education, 9,* 71–93.

Ford, D. Y., Trotman Scott, M., Moore, J. L., III, & Amos., S. O. (2013). Gifted education and culturally different student: Examining prejudice and discrimination via microaggressions. *Gifted Child Today, 36*(3), 205–208. https://doi.org/10.1177/1 076217513487069

Fouad, N. A., & Fitzpatrick, M. E. (2009). Social class and work-related decisions: Measurement, theory and social mobility. *Journal of Career Assessment, 17*(3), 266–270. https://doi.org/10.1177/1069072708330677

Gibbons, M. M., Rhinehart, A., & Hardin, E. (2016). How first-generation college students adjust to college. *Journal of College Student Retention: Research, Theory & Practice, 20*(4), 488–510. https://doi.org/10.1177/1521025116682035

Gilfillan, B. H. (2018). School counselors and college readiness counseling. *Professional School Counseling, 21*(1), 1–10. https://doi.org/10.1177/2156759X18784297

Gore, J., Holmes, K., Smith, M., Southgate, E., & Albright, J. (2015). Socioeconomic status and career aspirations of Australian school students: Testing enduring assumptions. *Australian Educational Researcher, 42,* 155–177. https://doi.org/10.1007/s1 3384-015-0172-5

Gottfredson, L. S. (2005). Applying Gottfredson's theory of circumscription and com-promise in career guidance and counseling. In D. Brown & R. Lent (Eds.), *Career development and counseling: Putting theory and research to work* (pp. 71–100). Wiley.

Greene, M. J. (2003). Gifted adrift? Career counseling of the gifted and talented. *Roeper Review, 25*(2), 66–72. https://doi.org/10.1080/02783190309554201

Greene Burton, M. J. (2016). Career and life planning for gifted adolescents. In M. Neihart, S. I. Pfeiffer, & T. L. Cross (Eds.), *The social and emotional development of gifted children: What do we know?* (2nd ed., pp. 259–268). Prufrock Press.

Hartung, P. J., & Santilli, S. (2017). My career story: Description and initial validity evidence. *Journal of Career Assessment, 26*(2), 308–321. https://doi.org/10.1177/1069072717692980

Hébert, T. P. (2018). An examination of high-achieving first-generation college students from low-income backgrounds. *Gifted Child Quarterly, 62*(1), 96–110. https://doi.org/10.1177/0016986217738051

Holland, J. L. (1997). *Making vocational choices: A theory of vocational personalities and work environments* (3rd ed.). Psychological Assessment Resources.

Hollingworth, L. S. (1916). The vocational attitudes of women. In H. L. Hollingworth (Ed.), *Vocational psychology: Its problems and methods* (pp. 222–244). Appleton and Company. https://doi.org/10.1037/10729-000

Hollingworth, L. S. (1926). *Gifted children: Their nature and nurture*. Macmillan. https://doi.org/10.1037/10599-000

Hsieh, H., & Huang, J. (2014). The effects of socio-economic status and proactive per-sonality on career decision self-efficacy. *The Career Development Quarterly, 62*(1), 29–267. https://doi.org/10.1002/j.2161-0045.2014.00068.x

Johnson, C. (2010). *Using the family tree of careers: Branching out with others!* National Career Development Association. https://www.ncda.org/aws/NCDA/pt/sd/news_article/37317/_PARENT/CC_layout_details/false

Jones, L. K. (n.d.). *Using a social network map to build social capital.* https://www.lynnkjones.com/appreciative-coaching-blog/social-network-map

Jung, J. Y. (2014). Modeling the occupational/career decision-making processes of intel-lectually gifted adolescents: A competing models strategy. *Journal for the Education of the Gifted, 37*(2), 128–152. https://doi.org/10.1177/0162353214529045

Jung, J. Y., & McCormick, J. (2011). The occupational decision: A cultural and motiva-tional perspective. *Journal of Career Assessment, 19*(1), 75–91. https://doi.org/10.1177/1069072710382616

Jung, J. Y., & Young, M. (2019). The occupational/career decision-making processes of intellectually gifted adolescents from economically disadvantaged backgrounds: A mixed methods perspective. *Gifted Child Quarterly, 63*(1), 36–57. https://doi.org/10.1177/0016986218804575

Keller, B. K., & Whiston, S. C. (2008). The role of parental influences on young adoles-cents' career development. *Journal of Career Assessment, 16*(2), 198–217. https://doi.org/10.1177/1069072707313206

Kerr, B., & Sodano, S. (2003). Career assessment with intellectually gifted students. *Journal of Career Assessment, 11*(2), 168–186. https://doi.org/10.1177/1069072 703011002004

Kim, M. (2012). Career planning. In T. L. Cross & J. R. Cross (Eds.), *Handbook for counselors serving students with gifts and talents: Development, relationships, school issues and counseling needs/interventions* (pp. 529–541). Prufrock Press.

Lent, R. W. (2013). Social cognitive career theory. In D. Brown & R. Lent (Eds.), *Career development and counseling: Putting theory and research to work* (pp. 115–146). Wiley.

Lent, R. W., Brown, S. D., & Hackett, G. (2000). Contextual supports and barriers to career choice: A social cognitive analysis. *Journal of Counseling Psychology, 47*(1), 36–49. https://doi.org/10.1037/0022-0167.47.1.36

Levine, E. (2010). The rigors and rewards of internships. *Educational Leadership, 68*(1), 44–88. https://www.ascd.org/publications/educational-leadership/sept10/vol68/num01/The-Rigors-and-Rewards-of-Internships.aspx

Lui, W. M., Ali, S. R., Soleck, G., Hopps, J., Dunston, K., & Pickett, T. R. (2004). Using social class in counseling psychology research. *Journal of Counseling Psychology, 51*(1), 3–18. https://doi.org/10.1037/0022-0167.51.1.3

Matthews, D. J., & Foster, J. F. (2005). A dynamic scaffolding model of teacher development: The gifted education consultant as a catalyst for change. *Gifted Child Quarterly, 49*(3), 222–230. https://doi.org/10.1177/001698620504900304

Maxwell, M. (2007). Career counseling is personal counseling: A constructivist approach to nurturing the development of gifted female adolescents. *Career Development Quarterly, 55*(3), 206–224. https://doi.org/10.1002/j.2161-0045.2007.tb00078.x

McMahon, G., Griffith, C., Mariani, M., & Zyromski, B. (2017). School counseling intervention research on college readiness, college access, and postsecondary success: A 10-year content analysis of peer-reviewed research. *Journal of College Access, 3*(2), 8–27.

Milner, H. R. (2013). Analyzing poverty, learning, and teaching through a critical race theory lens. *Review of Research in Education, 37*(1), 1–53. https://doi.org/10.3102/0091732X12459720

Moon, S., Kelly, K. R., & Feldhusen, J. F. (1997). Specialized counseling services for gifted youth and their families: A needs assessment. *Gifted Child Quarterly, 41*(1), 16–25. https://doi.org/10.1177/001698629704100103

Muratori, M. C., & Smith, C. K. (2015). Guiding the talent and career development of the gifted individual. *Journal of Counseling and Development, 93*(2), 173–182. https://doi.org/10.1002/j.1556-6676.2015.00193.x

Olszewski-Kubilius, P., & Corwith, S. (2018). Poverty, academic achievement, and giftedness: A literature review. *Gifted Child Quarterly, 62*(1), 37–55. https://doi.org/10.1177/0016986217738015

Olszewski-Kubilius, P. M., & Scott, J. M. (1992). An investigation of the college and career counseling needs of economically disadvantaged, minority gifted students. *Roeper Review, 4*(3), 141–148. https://doi.org/10.1080/02783199209553409

Ortega, K. E. (2018). Perspectives from a first-generation college student: Reflections on the value of mentoring relationships. *Health Promotion Practice, 19*(4), 492–494. https://doi.org/10.1177/1524839918780685

Pascarella, E. T., Pierson, C. T., Wolniak, G. C., & Terenzini, P. T. (2004). First-generation college students: Additional evidence on college experiences and outcomes. *Journal of Higher Education, 75*(3), 249–284. https://doi.org/10.1353/jhe.2004.0016

Peterson, G. W., Stivers, M. E., & Peters, D. F. (1986). Family versus nonfamily significant others of low-income youth: A longitudinal study with intervention implications. *Family Relations, 35*(3), 417–424.

Reese, S. (2005). Exploring the world of work through job shadowing. *Techniques: Connecting Education and Careers, 80*(2), 18–23

Savickas, M. L. (n.d.). *Career construction theory.* https://www.people.ku.edu/~tkrieshok/epsy846/lectures/career_construction.htm

Savickas, M. L. (2005). The theory and practice of career construction. In D. Brown & R. Lent (Eds.), *Career development and counseling: Putting theory and research to work* (pp. 42–70). Wiley.

Savickas, M. L. (2008). Career construction theory. In F. T. L. Leong (Ed.), *Encyclopedia of counseling* (pp. 1348–1349). SAGE. https://doi.org/10.4135/9781412963978.n483

Savickas, M. L., Nota, L., Rossier, J., Dauwalder, J., Duarte, M. E., Guichard, J., Soresi, S., Van Esbroek, R., & van Vianen, A. E. M. (2009). Life designing: A paradigm for career construction in the 21st century. *Journal of Vocational Behavior, 75*(3), 239–250. https://doi.org/10.1016/j.jvb.2009.04.004

Sikora, J., & Saha, L. (2011). *Lost talent? The occupational ambitions and attainments of young Australians.* National Centre for Vocational Education Research. http://www.lsay.edu.au/publications/2313.html

Silverman, L. (1993). Career counseling. In L. Silverman (Ed.), *Counseling the gifted and talented* (pp. 215–238). Love.

Smith, C. K., & Wood, S. M. (2018). Career counseling for the gifted and talented: A lifespan development approach. In S. I. Pfeiffer (Ed.), *Handbook of giftedness in children: Psychoeducational theory, research, and best practices* (2nd ed., pp. 315–334). Springer.

Tate, K. A., Caperton, W., Kaiser, D., Pruitt, N. T., White, H., & Hall, E. (2015). An exploration of first-generation college students' career development beliefs and experiences. *Journal of Career Development, 42*(4), 294–310. https://doi.org/10.1177/0894845314565025

Thompson, M. N., Her, P., Nitzariim, M. S., & Diestelmann, J. (2018). The transmission of social class and world of work information in parent-adolescent dyads. *Journal of Career Assessment, 26*(4), 697–716. https://doi.org/10.1177/1069072717727453

Thompson, M. N., Nitzarim, R. S., Her, P., Sampe, M., & Diestelmann, J. (2017). Financial stress and work hope beliefs among adolescents. *Journal of Career Assessment, 25*(2), 254–267. https://doi.org/10.1177/1069072715621517

Tomlinson, C. A., & Jarvis, J. M. (2014). Case studies of success: Supporting academic success for students with high potential from ethnic and economically disadvantaged backgrounds. *Journal for the Education of the Gifted, 37*(3), 191–219. https://doi.org/10.1177/0162353214540826

Turner, S. L., & Conkel Ziebell, J. L. (2011). The career beliefs of inner-city adolescents. *Professional School Counseling, 15*(1), 1–14. https://doi.org/10.5330/psc.n.2011-15.1

VanTassel-Baska, J. (2010). Curriculum development for low-income and minority gifted learners. In J. VanTassel-Baska (Ed.), *Patterns and profiles of promising learners from poverty* (pp. 193–218). Prufrock Press.

VanTassel-Baska, J. (2018). Achievement unlocked: Effective curriculum interventions with low-income students. *Gifted Child Quarterly, 62*(1), 68–82. https://doi.org/10.1177/0016986217738565

Villares, E., & Brigman, G. (2019). College/career success skills: Helping students experience postsecondary success. *Professional School Counseling, 22*(1b), 1–8. https://doi.org/10.1177/2156759X19834444

Watts, A. G. (1996). Toward a policy for lifelong career development: A transatlantic perspective. *Career Development Quarterly, 45*(1), 41–53. https://doi.org/10.1002/j.2161-0045.1996.tb00460.x

Wilson, F. (2013). *The creation of the National Vocational Guidance Association.* https://www.ncda.org/aws/NCDA/pt/sd/news_article/74076/_PARENT/CC_layout_details/false

Wood, S. M. (2010). Best practices in counseling the gifted in schools: What's really happening? *Gifted Child Quarterly, 54*(1), 42–58. https://doi.org/10.1177/0016986209352681

Wood, S. M., & Lane, E. (2015). Counseling and the rural gifted student. In T. Stambaugh & S. M. Wood (Eds.), *Serving gifted students in rural settings* (pp. 263–288). Prufrock Press.

Wood, S. M., & Peterson, J., & (2014). Superintendents, principals, and counselors: Facilitating secondary gifted education. In S. M. Moon & F. A. Dixon (Eds.), *The handbook of secondary gifted education* (2nd ed., pp. 627–649). Prufrock Press.

Yoo, J. E., & Moon, S. M. (2006). Counseling needs of gifted students: An analysis of intake forms at a university-based counseling center. *Gifted Child Quarterly, 50*(1), 52–61. https://doi.org/10.1177/001698620605000106

Teaching Psychosocial Skills and Modeling Habits of Achievement

Emily Mofield

What Are Psychosocial Skills, and Why Are They Needed?

Psychosocial skills are the personal and social skills that can help an individual achieve set goals. This includes developing goal-setting strategies, emotional regulation, motivation, and positive achievement attitudes, such as coachability and receptiveness to feedback (Olszewski-Kubilius & Calvert, 2016; Subotnik et al., 2017). In the context of talent development, they are catalysts that can transform talent to the next level, moving potential to ability, ability to competence, and competence to expertise (Subotnik et al., 2011). In terms of working with students from low-income families, these skills are especially important because they can equip students with coping and management skills needed to navigate the challenges and opportunities within their environment, which might include dealing with setbacks and persevering through difficulty.

In order to unlock the potential of gifted students, including those from low-income families, educators can deliberately model and teach these psychosocial skills to support high achievement. This includes promoting a resilient psychological identity through developing personal self-agency, self-efficacy, and the belief that effort matters in the development of talent. Building resilience through supportive networks is critical to success for students responding to the adversities of poverty. Further, skills such as mental toughness and coachability (the skill of being open to instruction, feedback, and guidance) are especially important for students from low-income families, as these skills can lead to increased self-efficacy and confidence, factors that can ignite motivation for tackling challenging tasks that grow talent. As students progress in their talent domains to increasingly demanding levels of performance or productive contribution, they must learn to manage and regulate emotions that may paralyze progress toward personal goals. Overcoming obstacles, facing failure, and dealing with self-doubt can involve unpleasant emotions related to fear and anxiety. For students from low-income families, such obstacles might be exacerbated by stereotype threats, the belief that negative perceptions about a group's ability to be "as smart" are true (Croizet et al., 2004). Students can be taught to process and self-regulate emotions related to fear, doubt, and anxiety so that they do not interfere with their achievement pursuits. As such, the focus on these socioaffective factors can arguably be just as important to the development of talent and long-term success as ability, and teaching students these important skills should not be left to chance (Subotnik, 2015; Subotnik et al., 2011).

Fostering Resilience

Resilience refers to "the positive adaptation in the context of risk or adversity" (Masten, 2014, p. 9), and so, students who are well-adjusted and successful are not necessarily "resilient" by definition unless there is a threat or adversity involved. Resilience includes coping with challenges and achieving positive outcomes even in the face of obstacles. Certainly, for students in poverty, cultivating resilience is important in the face of destabilizing threats, especially because "risk predicts risk" (p. 14). For example, inadequate nutrition negatively impacts brain development, which can impair executive functioning skills, which can impact grades and long-term academic success, which affect long-term pursuits of achievement. Masten (2014), a renowned researcher of resilience, described resilience through the concept of *developmental cascading*, the positive or negative effects in a child's life that "cascade" over time from one domain to another. To promote resilience, educators can seek to build opportunities to promote long-term positive cascading effects in a student's life that facilitate the development of talent.

What is known about resilient students, particularly those from low-socioeconomic backgrounds? Based on decades of research, Masten (2014) composed a short list of resilience factors in young people. These factors include effective caregiving and parenting; close relationships with other capable adults; close friends; intelligence and problem-solving skills; self-control, emotional regulation, and planfulness; motivation to succeed; self-efficacy; faith, hope, and belief that life has meaning; effective schools; effective neighborhoods; and collective efficacy (p. 148). Note that resilience involves both internal protective factors (e.g., emotional regulation, self-efficacy) as well as external systems of support from families, schools, and communities. Effective interventions for building resilience in marginalized youth include supporting them in building social capital and connectedness within their communities (LeMoine & Labelle, 2014). This social capital includes the networks among groups and individuals with shared values and norms. For students from low-income backgrounds, this can translate into accessing resources including assistance and support from others and outside educational opportunities (Davies et al., 2011).

Psychosocial skills related to resilience, mental toughness, persistence, and grit are quite popular in today's educational climate, especially in the context of promoting achievement. In recent years, these ideas have been popularized as a quality to be instilled in students for long-term success. Although these skills have positive implications for achievement motivation, the focus on boosting grit and related skills has received criticism because not all students have access to opportunities to actually pursue and develop their passions with long-term endurance, especially if they have other competing priorities (Mehta, 2015). Can students really be blamed for not having "grit" when they do not have the supports to develop it? In a similar vein, resilience cannot be viewed as an individual "trait" or attribute that a person has or does not have. Rather, resilience involves processes outside the individual, including supportive relationships and connections to external resources (Masten, 2014). It is a misconception to assume that a person experiencing adversity, such as poverty, is not resilient because they just do not have the inner drive to overcome such obstacles. Resilience is not an "inner strength" per se, but the embodiment of multiple systems of supports interacting to promote an adaptive response to adversity. As described by LeMoine and Labelle (2014), "current theoretical views on resilience point toward the adaptation of the environment and sys-

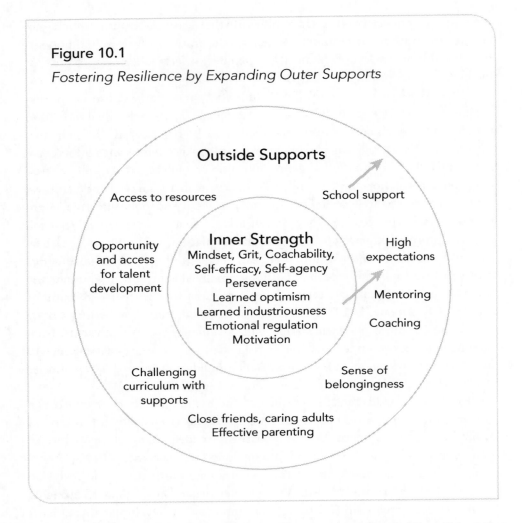

Figure 10.1

Fostering Resilience by Expanding Outer Supports

Outside Supports

Access to resources

School support

Opportunity and access for talent development

Inner Strength
Mindset, Grit, Coachability,
Self-efficacy, Self-agency
Perseverance
Learned optimism
Learned industriousness
Emotional regulation
Motivation

High expectations

Mentoring

Coaching

Challenging curriculum with supports

Sense of belongingness

Close friends, caring adults
Effective parenting

tems surrounding youth, as opposed to changes at the individual level" (p. 20). Figure 10.1 illustrates how capacity for inner strength is expanded when outer supports are also enlarged. As the outer circle grows, the inner circle of an individual's "inner strengths" has more space and potential to expand, as these are indeed considered malleable qualities.

Psychological Identity

A number of psychological factors are important to developing positive achievement motivation for marginalized gifted students, including stereotype threats and affiliation versus achievement (Olszewski-Kubilius & Clarenbach, 2012). Stereotype threat involves the awareness of negative perceptions of ability, particularly that being affiliated with a stereotyped group means being less competent or intelligent (Steele & Aronson, 1995). This awareness can affect how students achieve and pursue challenges, affecting their long-term academic outcomes. Regarding students from low-income families, stereotype threats have been shown to negatively affect the performance of students from low-socioeconomic backgrounds compared to students from high-socioeconomic backgrounds (Croizet et al., 2004; Harrison et al., 2006). The effects of stereotype threats can lead to disengagement or self-handicapping behaviors (not putting forth effort in a task to blame poor performance on lack of effort rather than intelligence). Combatting the effects of stereotype threats involves promoting high expectations of all students, talking openly with marginalized students about stereotype threats and their effects, and promoting growth mindsets (Good, 2012; mindsets will be discussed further in this chapter). Another psychological factor, the need for affiliation versus achievement, can also affect how students pursue academic endeavors. Sometimes high achievement comes at a social cost, such as experiencing ridicule or rejection from peers (Olszewski-Kubilius & Clarenbach, 2012). Students from low-income families may come from environments that do not value taking challenging classes or studying hard, so these students may be reluctant to participate in opportunities for talent development, such as advanced classes or special precollege programs that might negatively affect their peer relationships. However, this can be mitigated when these students can find a small group of like-minded peers who provide support through challenging academic endeavors. Further, a sense of belonging is a critical factor for persisting within a domain. A sense of belonging is fostered in environments that value effort and dedication to learning rather than environments with less emphasis on effort and more on innate talent (Good, 2012).

Schools, parents, mentors, and extracurricular programs can help provide the supports for resilience and foster the internal drive and agency among students from low-income families. First, this chapter will address what can be done in the context of schools.

The Role of Schools

Psychosocial skills do not develop in a vacuum but through the opportunity to interact with challenging academics through supportive environments. Students will never have opportunities to develop growth mindsets, grit, and the like in the absence of rigorous curriculum, specifically in a student's strength domain. Relevant to students from low-income families, this means that schools must adopt high expectations for *all* students, provide access to such rigorous curriculum through equitable identification and access, and ensure students have appropriate supports for learning advanced content. Through interacting with and learning advanced content, students can encounter opportunities to work through academic challenges that allow them to develop a sense accomplishment and self-efficacy for doing something hard. Within the context of the school environment, administrators and teachers can create climates of support and also explicitly teach or embed psychosocial skills within classroom instruction.

In order to develop and support resilience within the context of schools, the beliefs, relationships, and practices within a school climate should also include cultivating relationships and belongingness and fostering positive attitudes toward achievement. The development of psychosocial skills happens in such contexts that can ignite and maintain the motivation for students to pursue their self-set goals.

Establishing high expectations does not mean watering down advanced content but instead providing support to the child in making progress on a challenging endeavor. Educators should bear in mind the difference between providing adequate scaffolding and overly modifying curriculum. The former maintains high expectations because educators provide structures to help the student move toward mastery, but watering down curriculum assumes the student cannot learn the content. Watering down curriculum over time leads to less exposure to high-quality learning experiences, which can have lasting repercussions on a child's talent trajectory. When educators lower expectations for students, they are taking away opportunities for students to not only learn the content, but also develop self-regulation skills, self-efficacy, and self-agency that can result from applying effort in learning. High expectations pave the pathway for students to see the link between effort and success.

A sense of belonging within a community is a protective factor in resilience (Masten, 2014). As mentioned previously, it is also an important factor in combatting stereotype threats and strengthening an achievement-oriented identity. Schools can foster this sense of belonging in the classroom context by making efforts for high-ability students from low-income families to feel valued and know that they belong in advanced courses. Educators should be aware that some students from low-income backgrounds may be dealing with stereotypes related to their economic situation; they may not feel they fit in or see potential for themselves to be successful in a given domain (e.g., science, math, etc.). Good (2012) noted that the use of "belonging" words, such as *member* and *accepted*, embedded within tasks and used repeatedly in a classroom environment can improve a sense of belonging within a domain. Belongingness is also cultivated through building a sense of classroom community and culture, asking about students' interests, and allowing students to share about their lives. The recent popularity of the use of restorative circles (e.g., open time to share personal experiences and develop classroom trust) can be an avenue for fostering a sense of classroom belongingness (Clifford, 2019) even within the context of advanced classes. Classroom teachers can learn about students' personal stories, life experiences, obstacles, values, and fears while cultivating a sense of trust in the classroom during a small segment of reserved class time interspersed within the week.

Developing a sense of self-agency, the capacity to take action and shape future outcomes, is especially important for students from low-income backgrounds, as it can provide a sense of control and empowerment in the learning process and development of talent. Self-agency is affected by a person's social network, including peers, family, and the school. When students feel emotionally safe within relationships, they feel more confident in taking risks in learning because they do not feel the threat of being exposed when making mistakes (Frey et al., 2019). Thus, safe and supportive environments are a foundation for self-agency. Agency is also developed by providing feedback that acknowledges how student choices affected outcomes. Educators can provide causal process praise to help students see the value of their applied effort and the outcome, using structures such as "When you ___, I noticed that___" or "When you___, I could see___" (Johnston, 2012). For example, "When you added an explanation for your reasoning here, I could really see how your thesis statement is supported." Notice that the praise does not necessarily stop at noticing the process. Instead, it is a causal process statement that shows how effort led to a positive consequence—feedback that helps students see themselves as individuals with agency and potential.

Self-agency is also promoted when students are involved in community problem solving or engaged in community service learning. When students are provided opportunities to advocate for change within their school or community, they are empowered to see themselves as part of solutions (Davies et al., 2011). When schools promote high expectations, connectedness, agency, and student empowerment, they provide supports and contexts for building resilience in students' lives. To reiterate what has been stated earlier, students can only develop inner strength within contexts of such outside supportive systems.

Deliberate Teaching of Psychosocial Skills

There are a number of important skills that educators (as well as mentors) can teach students that facilitate developing an internal drive for achievement. This includes nurturing a growth mindset, preparing for obstacles, developing emotional regulation, teaching positive explanatory styles, and developing healthy habits of achievement.

Mindset. Dweck's (2006/2016) work on implicit theories of intelligence has certainly offered promise for developing positive habits toward achievement. Adopting a growth mindset (the belief that intelligence is malleable) includes the attitude of seeing mistakes as opportunities to grow and the view that effort and hard work are pathways to success. Those with fixed mindsets view talents and abilities as static, unchangeable traits. When abilities and talents are seen as unchanging, one views challenges and effort as threats rather than opportunities to grow. Although some studies show an association between achievement and growth mindsets (e.g., Blackwell et al., 2007; Paunesku et al., 2015), more current meta-analyses reveal that growth mindset interventions may not be as promising as one would hope (Sisk et al., 2018). The effects of mindset interventions on student achievement depend on how and with whom they are implemented. For example, in one study by Paunesku et al. (2015), mindset interventions were not necessarily effective for honors students, but were effective for underachieving students. However, relevant to the present chapter, Sisk et al.'s (2018) meta-analysis shows that students from low-SES backgrounds do show positive benefits from growth mindset interventions more so than students from other backgrounds.

The popularity of Dweck's (2006/2016) work has also spurred discussion on how to praise students for their success. If adults focus praise on a child's performance outcome ("Wow, this product looks amazing!") or a personal quality ("You are brilliant!") rather than the process of achieving the outcome ("I notice all of the work and effort you put into this."), the child may be more likely to assume that their abilities alone, not necessarily hard work, lead to success. This, in turn, reinforces the fixed mindset mentality. This notion has led some to caution that using the gifted label itself may make gifted children more vulnerable to this belief (Dweck, 2012). Given the popularity of mindsets and associated praise, some educators may be hesitant to tell a child they are intelligent, smart, creative, or gifted—fearing this may set up a child for risk-aversion. However, Mofield and Parker Peters (2018a) found that gifted students are not necessarily more vulnerable to developing fixed mindset beliefs about intelligence. Educators should more importantly consider *how* to talk about children's talents rather than avoid acknowledgement of their exceptional abilities. When an adult notices a child's talent or high-ability, it is important to acknowledge it, especially for students from low-income backgrounds. When students are told they have a special talent that can grow with effort, this can be inspiring and motivating (Fogarty et al., 2018). Thus, educators need not necessarily shy away from using praise that acknowledges the gift or talent (e.g., "You are gifted in math."), especially if followed with messages on how it continues to grow and develop over time and requires effort and study or practice.

Although there are mixed results regarding the efficacy of growth mindset interventions, the following considerations should be kept in mind in order to not overly simplify the concept and to encourage internalization and active application to students' lives.

> Teach students about the differences between growth mindset and fixed mindset beliefs. Explain to students that they can have varied mindset beliefs in different domains. It is inappropriate to say, "Jill has a fixed mindset" and "Jake has a growth mindset." Students need to understand that mindsets can change and relate to different content domains and contexts (Dweck, 2015).

> Interventions are more effective when they are interactive rather than passive (Sisk et al., 2018). Students should have opportunities to apply their learning about mindset beliefs through discussion and writing. For example, in Paunesku et al.'s (2015) study, the mindset intervention included students providing advice to a student who did not do well on a task and wanted to give up.

> Embed opportunities for students to reflect on mindset beliefs within the context of the curriculum. For example, encourage students to reflect on the most difficult part of a math problem and explore multiple ways to approach a solution. Explicitly model that this is an opportunity to work through a struggle in order for math skills and abilities to grow. In literature, students can reflect on characters' mindsets as they approached difficult situations, and in science and social studies, students can consider how individuals faced obstacles and persisted in the face of difficulty.

> Develop a growth mindset culture within the school by recognizing students for incremental progress. Provide opportunities for students to engage in productive struggle and learn from their mistakes. Reinforce the idea that effort leads to success. Praise students for their progress, thinking, and strategies used in a task rather than focusing only on the end result.

Explaining Failure. Seligman's (2006) concept of learned optimism is an important mechanism that can help students from low-income families sustain effort over time, even through setbacks and failures. How students experience and explain failure can affect their future pursuits of taking intellectual risks and challenges. Students who explain failure as pervasive (happening in all circumstances), permanent ("things will never change; it will always be like this for me"), and personal ("failure is all my fault") apply a pessimistic view. This frame of thinking can lead to self-doubt, anxiety, and lower persistence through difficulty (Seligman, 2006). Students, however, can be taught the "learned optimism" view. This involves explicitly teaching that (1) the failure is related directly to the *one* experience; (2) even through the failure, things can certainly change; and (3) the failure is not entirely the person's fault, as there may be some aspects of the failure experience that are outside a person's control. As a classroom teacher, I used to post a rhyme I made up in my classroom: "It's this situation, this time. Things can change, I will rise. Is this something I can control? What I cannot, I will let go." Educators can help model this thinking as failure experiences arise. Verbalizing this type of thinking can help students develop self-agency and self-efficacy even when experiencing setbacks.

Emotional Regulation. Emotions such as fear, self-doubt, and uncertainty can affect how students achieve. Indeed, emotions play an important role in talent development, especially if emotions themselves are the obstacles that prevent an individual from progressing to subsequent stages of talent development. Educators, however, can provide guidance on helping students recognize and regulate emotion. For students from low-income families, there may not be opportunities to learn how to respond to emotions in adaptive ways, and students would benefit from explicit guidance and direction. Educators can teach elements of emotional literacy by providing "emotion words" vocabulary for students to organize and sort into a continuum or categories. This can help students recognize nuances in emotion, such as anxiety and eagerness. Relatedly, students may consider emotions associated with stepping out of one's comfort zone and making a mistake (e.g., fear, anxiety, discomfort). Indeed, unpleasant emotions are associated with the popular constructs of growth mindset, grit, and resilience. When students can recognize the fear and self-doubt associated with the pursuits of challenges, the self-awareness can prompt regulation of such emotion. Educators can then help students develop appropriate coping responses to the emotion (e.g., relaxation techniques, reaching out to a friend, etc.). To further develop emotional literacy, educators can also ask students to reflect on the *purpose* of different types of emotion. Educators can teach that emotions carry messages; for example, anxiety's purpose is to prepare the body for something big, and anger's purpose is a message of protection because something important is being threatened or has been taken away (Mofield & Parker Peters, 2018b).

Managing Stress and Using Adaptive Coping. On any given day, students, especially those from low-income families, may experience stress related to competing priorities (e.g., working several hours at an afterschool job, babysitting siblings) or from typical school-related stressors (e.g., pressure to perform, overbooked schedules). Educators can help students manage stress by teaching about the role stress plays in their lives, specifically that stress is not always debilitating and can be motivating when it provides a sense of urgency to accomplish tasks. Students can learn how to be self-aware of the levels of stress they experience and identify a number of ways to manage (not necessarily eliminate) stress in their lives. Teaching students adaptive coping strategies, such as seeking support and problem solving, provides students with go-to tools for how to work through stressful situations. These can be explicitly modeled by explaining that there are two types of coping: avoidance coping and approach coping. Avoidance coping involves internalizing negative feelings (through excessive worry, crying, anxiety), externalizing feelings (through lashing out or blaming), or distancing (avoiding the problem altogether; Mofield & Chakraborti-Ghosh, 2010; Roth & Cohen, 1986). Approach coping involves applying problem solving to the situation: being able to identify the problem, consider a number of alternatives to solve the problem, and evaluating consequences to the various alternatives. Often, students see a situation one way and get overly discouraged when the problem cannot be solved. Fostering resilience includes helping students understand there is more than one approach to tackling a stressful situation or problem. Students can also recognize the importance of seeking support from others, including asking for help or having an opportunity to process and talk through an issue. Educators can also lead students through a discussion on how to manage stress by "distracting" in healthy ways, such as through exercise, breathing, coloring, or listening to music. It is important to acknowledge, however, that the stress associated with living in poverty may be overwhelming for some students; this is different from other types of school-based or performance-based stress because managing this circumstance is often out of a child's control. Still, teaching approach-coping strategies can help students from low-income backgrounds develop agency over many parts of their lives.

Learned Industriousness. How do educators teach students to work hard? Is industriousness a learned habit? According to Eisenberger's (1998) theory on learned industriousness, an individual learns to work hard when effort toward an endeavor leads to success. Over time, as success is linked to effort, effort itself becomes rewarding. However, if high effort does not lead to success, students may instead develop learned helplessness, or, if no effort is needed to gain success, then students miss out on learning the skill of working hard; the latter is the case for many gifted students. Educators can reinforce learned industriousness by providing challenging learning experiences just beyond a student's comfort zone where high effort, even with some struggle, eventually leads to success. Along the lines of promoting a growth mindset culture, educators should continually reinforce that success is linked to effort and strategy and ensure that learning tasks are rigorous enough for students to apply high levels of effort. In the same vein, students need to be set up for success. If they continually put in high effort without seeing the fruits of that effort, they are not likely to develop the confidence or self-agency to tackle challenges and setbacks that come their way.

Beyond Goal-Setting: WOOP. When working with students to accomplish goals, SMART goals, visualization techniques, and breaking large tasks into small tasks are popular ways to help students plan achievable routes to meeting their goals. However, these goal-setting approaches do not prepare students for obstacles that they may inevitably encounter. Oettingen's (2014) work on mental contrasting with intentional implementation highlights the importance of visualizing positive outcomes along with thinking through obstacles that get in the way of achieving set goals.

The reflective process of WOOP, a student-friendly acronym for mental contrasting with intentional implementations, begins with Wish. Students can take a few moments to reflect on a goal they desire to accomplish. It is important for this goal to be valuable and meaningful to the student. For example, a student's wish might be, "I want to prepare a high-quality short story to enter into a writing competition."

Next, one would consider the Outcomes, the positive implications of achieving the goal. This step involves a visualization process of experiencing the end result, achievement of the goal, including reflecting on the associated positive emotions of working toward and meeting the goal. In this example, the student may reflect on the outcome by thinking, "I will feel proud and accomplished when I submit my personal best work to the writing competition."

The second O is for Obstacles. This creates an important contrast of mental energy from a positive to a negative state. Both long-term and short-term obstacles can be considered, but most importantly at this stage, the obstacles should be sorted by "What is in my control, and what is out of my control?" Obstacles such as lack of resources, insufficient finances, and unforeseeable circumstances are indeed realities for students from low-income backgrounds. In the process of WOOP, however, the intention is to focus on obstacles that one can control, such as attitudes, emotions, and motivation. Oettingen (2014) suggested that individuals consider obstacles in the present reality that keep them from achieving set goals. These may include stress, time management, passive communication, anxiety, fear, procrastination, feeling unmotivated, being tired, etc. During this stage, time should be spend thinking about the obstacle and how it keeps one from pursuing and persisting toward a goal. This contrast from positive thinking to negative thinking creates a catalyst for motivation to move past the obstacle. The visualization of the negative experience in facing the obstacle poses a mental contrast that creates an emotional "angst" to overcome the potential threat that gets in the way of the goal. In the example of submitting writing to a competition, the obstacle might be "I tend to procrastinate, putting it off until the last minute."

The final part of WOOP is Plan. Creating a simple "if-then" plan can map a pathway to handle the obstacle when it happens. This preplan for the setback establishes an automated response for behavior. Obstacles can completely derail a person from achieving a goal, but if there is a plan to handle the obstacles, an individual is much more likely to persist. In this example, the plan might be "If I make excuses for not starting my writing, I will make myself write for at least 10 minutes that day to at least make some progress."

Oettingen's (2014) work has been successfully applied in educational contexts. Specifically, it has been shown to show increase student efforts in preparing students for standardized tests (Duckworth et al., 2011). Particularly among "disadvantaged" students, implementation of mental contrasting with intentional implementations increased attendance and grades (Duckworth et al., 2013). Related to the context of developing a drive to invest in long-term pursuits, in one study by Oettingen et al. (2015), participants who used WOOP were more likely to invest twice as much work on an academic endeavor than those who did not participate. Overall, the use of WOOP shows great promise toward self-directed learning, an essential component to helping students achieve set goals.

Psychosocial Skill Curriculum

The psychosocial skills of mindset, emotional regulation, perseverance, decision making, coachability, etc., can be taught directly through explicit instruction or indirectly as embedded within curriculum. These psychosocial skills are related to social-emotional competencies, but they are not entirely the same. Psychosocial skills can encompass social-emotional components (e.g., understanding and managing emotion, managing stress), but the emotional management skills are in the context of helping a student achieve personal goals. Through the lens of talent development, social-emotional competences can be taught as a way to catalyze paths toward higher levels of achievement. Psychosocial skills, however, can include broader skills, such as problem solving, deliberate practice, coachability, applying persistent effort, and dealing with increased pressure to perform as one progresses to higher levels of accomplishment (Subotnik, 2015). As educators consider curricula to deliberately teach psychosocial skills, some aspects of social-emotional cur-

253

ricula might be considered, as there is indeed some overlap. This is especially true if social-emotional curricula is viewed through the lens of helping students navigate unpleasant emotions that accompany setbacks and develop appropriate interpersonal skills that can enhance success at all levels of talent development. For students from low-income families, deliberate attention to these noncognitive skills are needed to prepare them to navigate the rigorous contexts of the academic world and beyond, especially if they are not likely to receive these kinds of supports from their parents, who may not have had opportunities to attend college themselves.

Some resources provide explicit lesson plans for teaching psychosocial skills directly. For example, *Teaching Tenacity, Resilience, and a Drive for Excellence: Lessons for Social-Emotional Learning* for Grades 4–8 (Mofield & Parker Peters, 2018b) includes targeted lesson plans for teaching students about deliberate practice, thinking through obstacles, applying mental contrasting through WOOP, developing interpersonal problem-solving skills, responding to criticism, applying learned optimism (i.e., Seligman, 2006), and understanding and managing emotions. These mini-lessons provide educators with direct guidance for introducing psychosocial skills and teaching students to apply and practice them. Other lessons include teaching students about the stages of talent development. For example, in one lesson, students study a person of eminence and trace the romance, precision, and integration stages of talent development (Bloom, 1985) as well as obstacles and sources of inspiration in that person's life. Students then reflect on what these individuals' lives reveal about the relationship between enthusiasm and endurance, and how this applies to their own lives. Another resource, *Peak Performance for Smart Kids: Strategies and Tips for Ensuring School Success* (Neihart, 2008), provides strategies for helping students navigate high-pressure competition and performances. The resource provides teachers and parents guidance on helping students with managing the need to belong, handling stress and anxiety, using mental rehearsal, setting goals, and managing emotions while working on the edge of one's competencies. For example, a section of this resource focuses on helping students tolerate stress and anxiety by guiding self-awareness about their fears and worries and teaching specific types of breathing exercises.

Other resources offer ways for teachers to embed the teaching of these skills within the curriculum. For example, the *Affective Jacob's Ladder Reading Comprehension Program* (e.g., Stambaugh & VanTassel-Baska, 2018; VanTassel-Baska & Stambaugh, 2018) provides scaffolds of supports through questioning that guides students to understand emotions, make plans for obstacles, engage in productive-risk taking, understand the role of identity in advancing toward a goal, develop empathy, manage stress, assess strengths for use toward long-term learning, and develop plans for long-term goals. Through thinking about a given text or media, students can internalize and relate the psychosocial concepts to their own lives. For example, students read a short story, poem, short biography, or watch a film clip, and through this medium identify, relate, and engage in some way (e.g., action plan, reflection) to apply the related psychosocial skills. Each ladder builds toward personal application or reflection. For example, in Ladder G, students learn to identify and calculate risks, consider multiple perspectives, and then engage in productive risk-taking, followed by a reflection on their decision. Additionally, the biographies are reflective of a variety of individuals so that students have opportunities to see others' successes, failures, and intra- and interpersonal skill sets, and how these made a difference in their trajectories. For example, students read a short biographical text about Michael Phelps and identify the challenges he faced as a person with ADHD. As they move up the ladder of questions, they analyze how he overcame these barriers and consider how he pushed himself to continue to compete at high levels. Then, students reflect on strategies they may use in their own lives to continue to improve performance, even if they already achieve at high levels (Stambaugh & VanTassel-Baska, 2018).

Psychosocial skills can be thoughtfully embedded within classroom instruction in other ways as well. Students can reflect on the obstacles they encountered after completing an assignment or project, especially reflecting on the "hardest part." Through reflection about the various strategies used to handle the obstacles, they can see that they were able to move forward toward completion. This type of reflection can enhance self-efficacy and build resilience, especially if students can recognize that readjusting strategies and exploring multiple options are the means to persisting through difficulty. Educators can also build in opportunities for students to reflect on their emotions and the purpose of those emotions within their instruction through student self-reflection. For example, while students are in the process of working on a long-term assignment or project, educators can provide frames, such as "I felt___ because___. This emotion is telling me___." For example, "I felt nervous because I was starting to feel like I can't tackle such a large project. It feels overwhelming. This emotion is telling me that I am facing a big challenge, and I may need to consider breaking this down into small steps. Making this plan will help me deal with my anxious emotion." The teacher can take a moment to reflect on positive ways to cope and manage these emotions. This builds resilience by helping students understand that unpleasant emotions often accompany persistence through difficulty, but they serve a purpose. Self-awareness of emotion can help students learn that feeling frustration does not have to stifle their efforts in persevering. Additionally, in various content areas, teachers can find models of individuals who persevered in the face of adversity. By studying the life of a scientist, author, or historical figure, especially from similar economic and cultural backgrounds of students, students can identify the challenges that they faced, how they responded, and how they persevered. These examples can help students see that failure is a normal part of achieving success.

The Roles of Mentors and Caring Adults

Mentors and caring adults can provide support in helping students from low-income families develop positive habits of achievement. It is especially useful if mentors with expertise in a given domain share insights into the competitive nature of gaining entry into a field, the possible educational and career trajectories, and the challenges of handling pressure, rejection, and criticism associated with high performance in that field. Mentors can provide valuable insights into navigating social dynamics and insider information related to accomplishment and advancement within a talent domain. For example, if a female high school student is interested in pursuing a major in STEM in college, a female mentor could provide support in discussing stereotype threats, strategies to overcome setbacks, and personal encounters with difficulties that inevitably led to success. Students from low-income families would benefit greatly from learning from adults who came from similar backgrounds.

Educators, mentors, and parents can provide supports for helping students think about their overall goals and how to handle the obstacles. When students encounter a disappointment or setback, the mentor can guide students through various parts of reframing their thinking through the use of Reframing Thinking Model (see Figure 10.2; Mofield & Parker Peters, 2018b). Working along the top row, the coach, mentor, or parent can help students examine the issue, asking, "What has happened?" Then, they can guide students to filter what is in their control and what is out of their control. Then, the adult can encourage a focus on immediate next steps and plans. This builds a sense of self-agency in moving forward toward an endeavor students can control. Working across the second row, the adult can ask, "What are your thoughts about this situation? What assumptions are you are making?" If the thoughts are related to self-doubt or self-criticism, the adult may ask "How can you challenge those thoughts? What would a friend tell you about those thoughts? How can you replace negative self-talk with positive self-talk?" Again, this can lead to "What are your next immediate steps?", which can alleviate anxiety in the situation by giving students a sense of control. Moving across the last row, the coach, mentor, or parent might ask, "What emotions are linked to those thoughts and this situation? What are your feelings? What are those feelings

Figure 10.2

Reframing Thinking Model

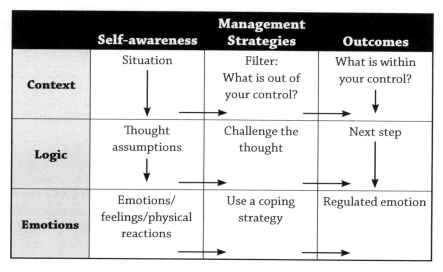

	Self-awareness	Management Strategies	Outcomes
Context	Situation ↓	Filter: What is out of your control?	What is within your control? ↓
Logic	Thought assumptions ↓	Challenge the thought	Next step ↓
Emotions	Emotions/ feelings/physical reactions	Use a coping strategy	Regulated emotion

Note. From *Teaching Tenacity, Resilience, and a Drive for Excellence: Lessons for Social-Emotional Learning for Grades 4–8* (p. 8), by E. Mofield and M. Parker Peters, 2018, New York, NY: Routledge Copyright 2018 by Taylor & Francis. Reprinted with permission.

telling you about the situation? What are some ways to handle this emotion? Do you need to vent, go for a walk, or take some time to breathe?" Considering these questions can lead to regulated emotion.

Extracurricular and Precollegiate Programs

Psychosocial skill training can also be especially relevant to extracurricular or precollegiate programs, which can help provide development of the psychosocial variables within a particular domain of talent. Such programs might embed the psychosocial skill training as described throughout this chapter. Further, opportunities in extracurricular and precollegiate programs for students from low-income backgrounds can open doors of possibility for them to experience an early sense of belongingness within the domain, which can mitigate stereotype threats. These programs also provide opportunities for students to explore their interests and talents. More information on extra- and cocurricular programs and the impact for students from low-income families can be found in Chapter 8.

These programs provide the opportunity for discovery of strengths and interests in various domains. Such organized extracurricular activities and programs can facilitate identity development, time management skills, problem solving, and emotional skills (LeMoine & Labelle, 2014). In regard to developing supports that foster resilience, these types of activities can build social capital and foster connectedness with the community, enabling access to information, resources, and assistance.

Conclusion

Ability alone does not lead to success. Motivation alone does not lead to success. Both must be nurtured within supportive environments. The deliberate cultivation of psychosocial skills can ignite the interaction of ability and motivation, propelling a student toward a trajectory of high levels of talent development. Students from low-income families may well have the ability and motivation to succeed, but they need the boost of support and know-how from other caring individuals who can help them navigate opportunities through the adversities of facing obstacles, including financial restraints. This chapter presented several ways educators and others can provide such support to help students develop agency and persistence that empowers them to see themselves as individuals with potential for future success. Educators or adults working with students from low-income families can foster resilience by providing "outer support" through challenging learning environments accompanied with high expectations. They can also directly or indirectly teach various psychosocial skills (e.g., mindset, agency, persistence) as *malleable* qualities that change and grow, not stable "have or have not" qualities that individuals possess. In doing so, educators enlarge students' capacity to cultivate inner strengths that unleash students to break into the next levels of their talent paths.

References

Blackwell, L., Trzesniewski, K., & Dweck, C. S. (2007). Implicit theories of intelligence predict achievement across an adolescent transition: A longitudinal study and an intervention. *Child Development, 78*(1), 246–263. https://doi.org/10.1111/j.1467-8624.2007.00995.x

Bloom, B. S. (Ed.). (1985). *Developing talent in young people.* Ballantine Books.

Clifford, A., (2019). *Teaching restorative practices with classroom circles.* Center for Restorative Process, San Francisco Unified School District. https://youthtoday.org/wp-content/uploads/sites/13/2017/04/Teaching-Restorative-Practices-in-the-Class room-7-lesson-Curriculum.pdf

Croizet, J., Despres, G., Gauzins, M., Huguet, P., Leyens, J., & Meot, A. (2004). Stereotype threat undermines intellectual performance by triggering a disruptive mental load. *Personality and Social Psychology Bulletin, 30*(6), 721–731. https://doi. org/10.1177/0146167204263961

Davies, S. L., Thind, H. R., Chandler, S. D., & Tucker, J. A. (2011). Enhancing resilience among young people: The role of communities and asset-building approaches to intervention. *Adolescent Medicine: State of the Art Reviews, 22*(3), 402–440.

Duckworth, A. L., Grant, H., Loew, B., Oettingen, G., & Gollwitzer, P. M. (2011). Self-regulation strategies improve self-discipline in adolescents: Benefits of mental contrasting and implementation intentions. *Educational Psychology, 31*(1), 17–26. https://doi.org/10.1080/01443410.2010.506003

Duckworth, A. L., Kirby, T. A., Gollwitzer, A., & Oettingen, G. (2013). From fantasy to action: Mental contrasting with implementation intentions (MCII) improves aca demic performance in children. *Social Psychological & Personality Science, 4*(6), 745– 753. https://doi.org/10.1177/194855061347630726

Dweck, C. (2015). *Carol Dweck revisits the "growth mindset."* Education Week. https:// www.edweek.org/ew/articles/2015/09/23/carol-dweck-revisits-thegrowth-mind set.html

Dweck, C. S. (2012). Mindsets and malleable minds: Implications for giftedness and tal ent. In R. F. Subotnik, A. Robinson, C. M. Callahan, & P. Johnson (Eds.), *Malleable minds: Translating insights from psychology and neuroscience to gifted education* (pp. 7–18). University of Connecticut, National Research Center on the Gifted and Talented.

Dweck, C. S. (2016). *Mindset: The new psychology of success.* Ballantine Books. (Original work published 2006)

Eisenberger, R. (1998). Achievement: The importance of industriousness. *Behavioral and Brain Sciences, 21*(3), 412–413. https://doi.org/10.1017/s0140525x98281234

Fogarty, R. J., Kerns, G. M., & Pete, B. M. (2018). *Unlocking student talent: The new sci ence of developing expertise.* Teachers College Press.

Frey, N., Fisher, D., & Smith, D. (2019). *All learning is social and emotional: Helping students develop essential skills for the classroom and beyond.* ASCD.

Good, C. (2012). Reformulating the talent equation: Implications for gifted stu dents' sense of belonging and achievement. In R. F. Subotnik, A. Robinson, C. M. Callahan, & P. Johnson (Eds.), *Malleable minds: Translating insights from psychol ogy and neuroscience to gifted education* (pp. 37–54). University of Connecticut, National Research Center on the Gifted and Talented.

Harrison, L. A., Stevens, C. M., Monty, A. N., & Coakley, C. A. (2006). The consequences of stereotype threat on the academic performance of White and non-White lower income college students. *Social Psychology of Education: An International Journal, 9,* 341–357. https://doi.org/10.1007/s11218-005-5456-6

Johnston, P. H. (2012). *Opening minds: Using language to change lives.* Stenhouse.

LeMoine, K., & Labelle, J. (2014). *What are effective interventions for building resilience among at-risk youth?* Community Health Initiatives, Region of Peel. https://www.peelregion.ca/health/library/pdf/rapid-review-resilience-at-risk-youth.pdf

Masten, A. S. (2014). *Ordinary magic: Resilience in development.* Guilford.

Mehta, J. (2015). *The problem with grit.* Education Week. https://blogs.edweek.org/edweek/learning_deeply/2015/04/the_problem_with_grit.html

Mofield, E., & Chakraborti-Ghosh, S. (2010). Addressing multidimensional perfectionism in gifted adolescents with affective curriculum. *Journal for the Education of the Gifted, 33*(4), 479–513. https://doi.org/10.1177/016235321003300403

Mofield, E., & Parker Peters, M. (2018a). Mindset misconception? Comparing mindsets, perfectionism, and attitudes of achievement in gifted, advanced, and typical students. *Gifted Child Quarterly, 62*(4), 327–349. https://doi.org/10.1177/0001698621875440

Mofield, E., & Parker Peters, M. (2018b). *Teaching tenacity, resilience, and a drive for excellence: Lessons for social-emotional learning for grades 4–8.* Prufrock Press.

Neihart, M. (2008). *Peak performance for smart kids: Strategies and tips for ensuring school success.* Prufrock Press.

Paunesku, D., Walton, G. M., Romero, C., Smith, E. N., Yeager, D. S., & Dweck, C. S. (2015). Mind-set interventions are a scalable treatment for academic underachievement. *Psychological Sciences, 26*(6), 784–793. https://doi.org/10.1177/0956797615571017

Oettingen, G. (2014). *Rethinking positive thinking: Inside the new science of motivation.* Penguin.

Oettingen, G., Kappes, H. B., Guttenberg, K. B., & Gollwitzer, P. M. (2015). Self-regulation of time management: Mental contrasting with implementation intentions. *European Journal of Social Psychology, 45*(2), 218–229. https://doi.org/10.1002/ejsp.2090

Olszewski-Kubilius, P., & Calvert, E. (2016). Implications of the talent development framework for curriculum design. In T. Kettler (Ed.), *Modern curriculum for gifted and advanced academic students* (pp. 37–54). Prufrock Press.

Olszewski-Kubilius, P., & Clarenbach, J. (2012). *Unlocking emergent talent: Supporting high achievement of low-income, high-ability students.* National Association for Gifted Children.

Roth, S., & Cohen, L. J. (1986). Approach, avoidance, and coping with stress. *American Psychologist, 41*(7), 813–819. https://doi.org/10.1037/0003-066X.41.7.813

Seligman, M. (2006). *Learned optimism: How to change your mind and your life.* Vintage Books.

Sisk, V. F., Burgoyne, A. P., Sun, J., Butler, J. L, & Macnamara, B. N. (2018). To what extent and under which circumstances are growth mind-sets important to academic achievement? Two meta-analyses. *Psychological Science, 29*(4), 549–571. https://doi.org/10.1177/0956797617739704

Stambaugh, T., & VanTassel-Baska, J. (2018). *Affective Jacob's ladder reading comprehension program: Grades 6–8.* Prufrock Press.

Steele, C. M., & Aronson, J. (1995). Stereotype threat and the intellectual test performance of African Americans. *Journal of Personality and Social Psychology, 69*(5), 797–811. https://doi.org/10.1037/0022-3514.69.5.797

Subotnik, R. F. (2015). Psychological strength training: The missing piece in talent development. *Gifted Child Today, 38*(1), 41–48. https://doi.org/10.1177/1076217514556530

Subotnik, R. F., Olszewski-Kubilius, P., & Worrell, F. C. (2011). Rethinking giftedness and gifted education: A proposed direction forward based on psychological science. *Psychological Science in the Public Interest, 12*(1), 3–54. https://doi.org/10.1177/1529100611418056

Subotnik, R. F., Stoeger, H., & Olszewski-Kubilius, P. (2017). Talent development research, policy, and practice in Europe and the United States: Outcomes from a summit of international researchers. *Gifted Child Quarterly, 61*(3), 262–269. https://doi.org/10.1177/0016986217701839

VanTassel-Baska, J., & Stambaugh, T. (2018). *Affective Jacob's ladder reading comprehension program: Grades 4–5.* Prufrock Press.

CHAPTER 11

Tapping Into Family Resources to Support Gifted Learners From Low-Income Backgrounds

Natalie Rodriguez Jansorn

>) "In our school system, if you are an accelerated learner, you are not encouraged to bloom. You are encouraged to blend in."
>) "The teacher can only do so much. They need support from their parents. If it doesn't come from the parents, the teacher is left to do it all."
>) "As a single mom, I don't have nobody for support to help me raise my daughter. So, I ask the teacher for help."
>) "In our rural area, where we got a Habitat for Humanity house, there's nothing serving the high end of students. You get to a point where there's that wall."
>) "I thought I was really smart at math at one point in time, but now I look at her homework and I say, 'I can't help you.'"

› "There's nobody there to listen to you or pose questions to and then your concerns spiral into nothing."

› "Parents need empowerment—give us information for how to guide our gifted child, to know about the resources out there."

These are the voices of parents. They come from all reaches of this country, living in rural, suburban, and urban communities, and everywhere in between. They are Black, White, Asian American, Latinx, Native American, multiracial, immigrant, and U.S.-born mothers, fathers, grandparents, and other familial caretakers. They are single parents, married parents, stay-at-home parents, dual-employed parents, parents with disabilities or terminal illnesses, artists, teachers, truckers, pastors, small business owners, farmers, dry cleaners, receptionists, housekeepers, social workers, and supreme champions of their children. What brings them together is that they are all part of the Jack Kent Cooke Foundation's Young Scholars Program that supports high-achieving students who have financial need. This chapter explores how educators can strengthen partnerships with families to support gifted students from low-income households by listening to families' experiences, connecting their stories to the salient literature, and generating practical implications for education. The focus will be on partnerships to support adolescents.

I am not a researcher. I am a practitioner who has worked closely with low-income families of gifted students in middle and high school for roughly 15 years. Previously, I worked with middle and high school educators to build school, family, and community partnerships guided by the research of Dr. Joyce L. Epstein of Johns Hopkins University. Therefore, this chapter begins a conversation between and among educators about helping students fulfill the hopes and dreams that they and their families hold for their futures.

The focus of the Jack Kent Cooke Foundation's Young Scholars Program is to prepare exceptional students who have financial need to get into and succeed at the nation's top performing colleges and, ultimately, go on to fulfilling professional lives through which they make significant contributions in whatever field they choose. Over the past 2 decades, we have worked with approximately 1,000 students from 49 states, plus the District of Columbia and Puerto Rico. At the time they applied to our program in seventh grade, their families reported a median adjusted gross income of $28,000. Our team of educational advisers works with students from eighth through 12th grade to help them access appropriately challenging courses, develop their talents through enrichment opportunities, and explore their curiosities in Young Scholar community residential summer programs. We could not do our work without appreciation for, input from, and partnership with families. Therefore, we visit families in their homes, host them for a residential Welcome Weekend, call and video conference multiple times per year, and provide resources to enable parents to remain knowledgeable partners in their child's education. A little more than half of the students are the first in their family to go to college. Of those who have graduated already, the majority of Young Scholars go on to attend a highly selective college or university, with Harvard, Yale, Stanford, and Princeton being the most commonly attended.

The families' experiences shared in this chapter have all been anonymized. Their information comes from focus groups, application responses, home and school visits, and interaction notes recorded by Young Scholars Program educational advisers within the past 10 years.

School, Family, and Community Partnerships

Decades of research studies (Catsambis, 2001; Epstein, 2011; Fan & Williams, 2010; Hoover-Dempsey et al., 2005; Simon, 2004), meta-analyses (Fan & Chen, 2001; Jeynes, 2012), literature reviews (Epstein et al., 2019; Henderson & Mapp, 2002) and reports (Kreider et al., 2007; Weiss et al., 2018) confirm the positive connections between family involvement and student success. They highlight varying benefits to students as shown through improved attendance, better grades, higher test scores, and college enrollment. This is true across students from all economic backgrounds and grade levels.

As students transition to middle and high school, family involvement reportedly declines (Hill et al., 2018), with some of the steepest declines seen among low-income families (Bridgeland et al., 2008). Chaperoning field trips, volunteering in the classroom, checking homework, and other common elementary school practices become somewhat obsolete with adolescents' emerging independence. Parents of adolescents report a decrease in school information practices that they perceive are done "very well" (Vaden-Kiernan, 2005). However, parents continue to express a desire to be knowledgeable partners in their child's education, and adolescents tend to say they want the same (Bridgeland et al., 2008; Epstein, 2011). Partnering with families for student success doesn't have to decrease as students get older—schools can influence how and how much parents engage in students' education (Epstein et al., 2019).

In a review of literature on parental influences on gifted children, Jolly and Matthews (2012) highlighted the benefits conveyed to gifted learners from low-income backgrounds when their parents message the importance of schooling, academic achievement, and using their talents to soar higher than their parents or grandparents. This "academic socialization" has been identified as one of the most positive influences on student achievement in middle school

(Hill et al., 2009). Even with limited financial means, families of high achievers bestow upon their children values, beliefs, and expectations for viewing "education and talent development as the key to success or the means of breaking a cycle of poverty" (Olszewski-Kubilius & Thomson, 2010, p. 4). The challenge here for school, family, and community partnerships is that family and student beliefs in the power of education must be matched by educators' beliefs in their students and their expectations for family involvement.

Partnership in support of talent development begins with acknowledging that gifted students exist in all populations (Gentry & Fugate, 2012; Hunsaker et al., 1995) and eliminating ways that inequality is perpetuated in schools (Lareau & Horvat, 1999). This means looking for strengths and building authentic partnerships rather than conducting teacher-parent interactions solely to meet basic demands mandated by the school district (Christianakis, 2011). Successful partnerships proactively invite parent involvement, welcome family input, and plan from the start to meet families' needs (Henderson & Mapp, 2002). Family support must be coupled with information and guidance about educational opportunities and how to access them (Griffin & Wood, 2015).

Inequality and Breakdown of Trust

In a *Washington Post* opinion piece, economists Doepke and Zilibotti (2019) argued that the growing gap in America between the rich and the poor is fueling intense, achievement-oriented parenting. They explained how the difference in U.S. household incomes between two college-educated earners and two high school-educated earners doubled between the late 1970s and 2010, from $30,000 (inflation-adjusted) to $60,000. Between that same time, parents reported spending twice as much time each week interacting with their children even though more mothers are now in the workforce. The growing income inequality drives concerns for access to opportunity and accumulation of resources and is spurring already-advantaged families to be even more involved in their children's education in efforts to outpace their peers. The college admissions scandals of 2019 are a prime example of this parent involvement for student success at any cost.

What does this mean for low-income families of gifted learners? As Doepke and Zilibotti (2019) pointed out:

> When parenting becomes an arms race, the rich have a clear advantage. . . . When you're holding down two or three jobs, you have less time to drill your kids on math, and you may not

> have access to tutors, test prep and private coaches . . . which
> further exacerbates inequality for the next generation. (p. B3)

This inequality means that the trust between low-income families and their gifted students' schools becomes even more critical. Relational trust between parents and teachers benefits students' academic resilience and success (Bryk & Schneider, 2004). Families have to be assured that they can trust their school to prepare their child to reach their fullest potential, and schools need to trust that families are supporting their child's learning in many ways beyond what is visible in the school building. For educators, this means: Look and listen for assets to build upon, include families in decisions, and generate solutions to challenges in order to reach your shared goal of student success. Let go of focusing on what they "don't have," "can't do," or "won't do." Shift the focus to meeting families where they are and moving forward together.

When the Young Scholars Program staff first met Austin in eighth grade, he lived with his mother in a modest home set far back from the highway in a rural Southern town. His mother had a high school diploma and had been unemployed for some time. Within this house filled to the brim with books, knickknacks, and five cats, Mom made sure that Austin's room was super organized and tidy with a desk and working computer. Austin had scored a 31 on his composite ACT and was slated to attend his large, local public high school that offered a handful of Advanced Placement courses (when there were enough students who wanted to take them) and posted a composite ACT score of 20 for graduating seniors.

Mom made it a point to talk regularly with Austin's middle school. As she put it, "I want to make sure he gets a good education, but I just don't know how to take care of some of those things." The school staff described Mom as bright, but different from the rest of the parents. Her rapid pace of speaking, punctuated by multifarious questions and worries, made it difficult to have an efficient conversation. Unlike the middle school staff, the high school staff didn't return calls requesting an appointment to talk about Austin's advanced learning needs. Perhaps they interpreted Mom's inquiries as not trusting their judgment. As Lareau and Horvat (1999) found in their research, teachers often equated parental support with acceptance of the teacher's definition of the child's performance.

Austin shared that people around town were saying he was a "spoiled brat" for looking into out-of-town schools that would take him away from his mom. So he chose to enroll in his local high school. We worked closely with the family to get the school's permission for him to take online courses to supplement its offerings. Wary of how this special treatment might look for the school, the staff permitted one course per semester so long as it was taken in addition to Austin's regularly full course load. Similar to how Griffin and Wood (2015) described other gifted students' experiences in rural settings, Austin had to manage and integrate his identity as a gifted learner within the school's mainstream cultural norms and socialization. He joined the marching band and ultimately rose to the position of drum major—at about the same time as the school flexed on scheduling and let him take his online course during study hall.

When Austin was getting ready to head off to a highly selective liberal arts college, he reflected on his mother's influence on him:

> One of my mother's biggest regrets was not going to college, and she realized that I should have a chance to pursue some of life's greatest opportunities. I never anticipated that a kid such as myself from a small town stood a chance of getting accepted, but my mom saw my potential.

School-family-community partnerships depend on trust that comes from setting aside negative perceptions in order to be more in sync in shared support for gifted learners from low-income backgrounds. In Austin's case, the school needed to trust that Austin's mom was making a sound request to accommodate his learning needs.

Epstein et al. (2019) aligned trust, caring, and respect with the framework of Six Types of Involvement that is used to capture partnership activities to support learning at home, in school, and within the community (see Figure 11.1). To build trust, educators need to seek to understand. The following sections take a closer look at the many ways that families are supporting their gifted learners' talent development within the constraints of limited financial means using Epstein et al.'s (2019) framework of Six Types of Involvement as a lens.

Six Types of Involvement

Each year the Young Scholars Program receives more than 1,000 applications from seventh-grade students. The application includes a parent section where we ask the open-ended question: "Please describe how you are involved in supporting your child's learning." I looked at the responses from 133 parents of qualified applicants (meaning they had high academic achievement and significant financial need). This subset of parents represented an ethnically and racially diverse group of families residing in 29 states, plus the District of

Figure 11.1

Epstein et al.'s (2019) Six Types of Involvement

Type of Involvement	Trust and Caring Synonyms
Type 1—Parenting Supportive home environment, including conveying the value of education	Supporting, nurturing, loving, understanding, and child raising
Type 2—Communicating Two-way communication between home and school	Relating, reviewing, and connecting
Type 3—Volunteering Help at school or on behalf of school and audience for student activities	Supervising, advising, giving, and fostering
Type 4—Learning at Home Helping with homework and engaging in a love of learning	Managing, recognizing, interacting, enriching, and rewarding
Type 5—Decision Making Leadership in school committees and advocacy on school issues	Contributing, considering, participating, and judging
Type 6—Collaborating With Community Leveraging community resources and learning by serving the community	Cooperating, assisting, developing, problem solving, and sharing

Columbia, with an estimated median family income of $33,700 and half of the parents holding a college degree. Some parents wrote a sentence, and many wrote a paragraph; most wrote in English, and some wrote in Spanish or had a family member translate their words. For this exercise—not part of the application review process—I recorded each type of involvement (Epstein et al., 2019) mentioned, with most responses tapping into multiple categories. For instance, if a parent wrote that they responded to teachers' emails, attended their child's music concerts, and took their child to the library, then I recorded a point for Communicating, Volunteering, and Collaborating With Community. This was not intended to be a scientific study but a way to organize observations of families' current practices as they felt compelled to share them.

I'll summarize the headlines and then dig deeper into each type. Very few parents (5%) reported that they held a leadership role or participated in a parent-school association (Type 5—Decision Making) as a way to support their learning. It is possible that more parents may be involved in parent-school associations but did not connect that activity with a direct benefit to their individual child's learning. One out of five respondents identified communicating with teachers, including attending parent-teacher conferences and back-to-school nights, as a means to influence students' learning. Limited direct communication between parents and middle school teachers makes sense for two reasons: Seventh graders typically have multiple teachers rather than one primary teacher, and adults are more apt to encourage students to manage communications between home and school as a sign of their emerging independence. However, this finding also raises a question about lost strength of partnership that comes from a gap in more substantial communications between parents and educators. Parents more often wrote about volunteering (40%) but mostly in the form of facilitating, attending, and driving to/from their child's academic and talent activities, rather than volunteering within classrooms or schools. Beyond the school, an equal number of the parents talked about using community resources, often libraries, to encourage a love of learning. Overwhelmingly, parents wrote about activities that take place in the home, such as their approach to parenting (71%) and engagement in learning activities at home (58%).

This high level of family involvement in learning at home and community may be missed by educators. Considering that students spend an average of 5,000 waking hours per year with family and community (Weiss et al., 2018), there is a lot of potential to leverage if schools, families, and community partners have a better understanding of what is happening in each sphere of students' lives.

Parenting—Type 1

"I came from a very poor household with 13 kids. At times, we had to choose between the bus or food. I was very hungry at times. I wanted a better life for myself and my family. I work as many hours as I need to and do whatever I need to do to give my child the amazing life she deserves."—Parent

Families with very little financially wrote about trying to provide for their child's academic success. Sometimes they gave their presence: "I can only take credit for being with him every day." An older brother writing on behalf of his parents told us, "My parents are unable to read or write. My parents always take her to school." Others wrote about meeting basic needs, like preparing breakfast every day, making sure their children get plenty of sleep, and taking children for their yearly health wellness visits. One parent highlighted safety: "I try to keep her very active and away from horrific events and nature of our violent city." This is how families support their gifted child's learning.

Many talked about providing emotional support, instilling values, and connecting education with future goals. They told us how they hold their child to high standards and encourage their child "to work hard to achieve the best grades." They coupled their expectations with caring: "She has emotional support from us at all times." And they connected their encouragement to fostering a love of learning: "I demonstrate a positive attitude about education. We try to help her love learning so she can learn better."

Parents conveyed the importance of doing well in school in order to achieve future benefit: from an altruistic view ("We have conversations about how studying hard and getting an excellent education will help us be of service to others now and in the future."), for their family ("I motivate her to be an example to her sisters and to be the first one in the family to go to a university."), and to break the cycle of hardship ("I show her examples of how the world works when education is limited."). These parenting practices reflect the academic socialization found to have the strongest influence on student achievement in middle school (Fan & Williams, 2010; Hill et al., 2009; Ong et al., 2006). Parents' beliefs and behaviors shape students' beliefs and behaviors.

Parenting Support in Latinx Immigrant Homes

Limited communication between teachers and parents has contributed to misperceptions and false beliefs about the nature of Latinx families' involvement in their children's education, especially those who immigrated to the U.S. (Quiocho & Daoud, 2006). To build strong partnerships between the Young Scholars Program, families, and their schools, we visit scholars' homes to get to know their family and the world they live in. I'd like to share glimpses into the families of three of our Latinx Young Scholars to help dispel these myths.

Alejandro lived with his mom and younger brother in the converted backroom of the barbershop where his mom worked as a hair stylist. Mom had a college degree from Mexico and had managed a local restaurant in their small Southern town until it shut down. Mom spoke limited English but spent her available time with her children while they did their homework in English. Alejandro shared the small bedroom with his brother where his mom had covered the walls with the school awards they had received over the years. In the cramped living room, the family had a secondhand keyboard that Alejandro

271

played every day, although his lessons had stopped when Mom lost her job. She told us that she loved to listen to him play.

When we met Paola on the West Coast, she and her family had just moved to their apartment from a neighborhood that was about a mile away. They said there had been a lot of "gangsters." At the new apartment, Paola and her siblings were able to play and walk outside. Paola's family of four shared the two-bedroom apartment with three other adults in order to cover the rent. The walls in the living room were covered with Paola's artwork and the children's school pictures. Paola's mom made sure she had privacy while she did her homework in the bedroom that the four of them shared. She emphasized to us that she raised her children to be polite and respectful, and to do well in school. Mom had never been to Paola's school or spoken with her teachers. She recruited a family friend, an immigration law student, to take Paola to activities and translate school materials.

In a large metropolitan city, Louis lived with his mom (a babysitter), dad (a security guard), and two siblings in their small apartment with walls covered with the children's artwork, school awards, and school and religious photos. The parents had come to the U.S. from the Dominican Republic to give their children more opportunity. Through his parents' faith and values, Louis had learned to persevere and stay positive in the face of adversity, which, in his case, had been a debilitating bout with rheumatic fever. Louis's parents monitored his homework completion, signed his homework planner, and supported him to stay after school for theater practice even when it meant he couldn't babysit his younger sibling. Their extended family, who they saw fairly regularly, celebrated Louis's accomplishments.

All three families provided a supportive home environment where they encouraged learning and talent development, modeled hard work and resilience, and celebrated their children's accomplishments. Alejandro's mom listened to his piano practice. Paola's mom gave her space and privacy to do her homework. Louis's family relieved him of babysitting so that he could pursue his acting. They all displayed school awards and pictures surrounding the children with the message that school is important. When you start with this knowledge, you can tap into this common ground to achieve greater student success. For more strategies for getting to know students' families, see Figure 11.2.

Interacting With School—Types 2 and 5

For a multitude of reasons, parents of high-achieving students from low-income backgrounds applying to the Young Scholars Program reported low rates

Figure 11.2

Get to Know Students' Families

> **Visit students' homes.** Stop by with a "welcome-back-to-school" gift (e.g., a pencil or magnet). Organize a staff community walk to greet families. Send out postcards to families announcing when you'll be saying hello at their doorstep.

> **Ask about families' hopes and dreams for their students.** Make the first homework assignment a student interview with a family member. Or, talk with families directly.

> **Host a parent-to-parent support group.** Facilitate the exchange of what's working and solutions to challenges. Share tips with families that can't attend in person.

of communication with the school (Type 2) and formal decision-making roles (Type 5) when identifying ways that they support their child's learning (Epstein et al., 2019). It might be that the application format didn't spark them to think of these aspects of school partnerships. It also might indicate changes they experienced as their children took on more independence and entered a different school structure. The work I did with Epstein and colleagues revealed that involvement with families shifted, but didn't decline, when schools designed well-planned, developmentally appropriate, partnership programs (see Epstein et al., 2019). In other words, these low rates should not be accepted as inevitable. Parents may be responding to how schools are or are not inviting their communication or input on decisions.

Parents reported communicating with teachers to varying degrees: "when necessary," "as much as possible," "all of the time," and "when asked to." Some highlighted using school technology to check grades online, receiving text reminders from teachers, and/or emailing the teachers. Although these electronic communications provide value to school-family partnerships by transferring timely information, they do little to build meaningful rapport. A few parents referenced attending parent-teacher conferences or gifted Individualized Education Program (IEP) meetings. One wrote, "Despite the English language barrier that I face, I have developed a partnership with my child's teachers and school staff." Another non-native English speaker cited "incomprehensible parent-teacher conferences" due to lack of language interpretation.

Communicating effectively with non-English-speaking parents is required by the Civil Rights Act of 1964.

Several parents talked about advocating for their child's needs. One told us, "I have meetings with the gifted teacher, counselor, and principal of this small rural school to see what we can do within the boundaries of the school's resources to give my child the additional resources she needs, even just extra time spent in gifted class." Another parent described her advocacy a bit more forcefully:

> She has been bored stiff for 7 years now. Potential LOST! It is heart wrenching. I have cried, yelled a few times, pleaded, and gone to countless meetings to try to get her opportunities. All they ever want to do is just give her more homework or let her help other students. I am there for her when they don't listen and it is more of the same. I will never give up trying.

Reflecting the parents' perspective, these responses suggest that many low-income families are not experiencing fulfilling relationships with schools to aid them in supporting their gifted child's learning.

Very few parents referenced formal decision making roles with the school. Some held a parent-teacher association leadership role in the elementary school and carried it forward to the middle school. They told us how these formal decision-making roles kept them "in the loop" on school issues, helped them raise funds for the school, and motivated their children by role modeling school involvement. Although Type 5 (Decision Making) has not been linked with student academic outcomes, there is a benefit to school leadership to listening to parents' feedback, concerns, and ideas. See Figure 11.3 for tips for working together with families.

Learning at Home—Type 4

"I'm an electrical contractor. [My daughter] helps me on weekends and a lot through the summer. One of the benefits of this situation is that I can try to show her how math really does matter in the real world. We've ended up many days laying on the ground looking up at the stars. I'm usually unable to answer the amazing questions she has about space, but I think the best thing I can do to support her is by being present."—Parent

Figure 11.3

Tips for Working Together With Families

› Seek to understand. Listen to what parents have observed and experienced.

› Ask parents about how they are supporting their child's learning at home.

› Incorporate family and community customs, traditions, and experiences into the classroom learning.

› Start parent-teacher conferences with a question to get to know families.

› Share with parents the student's strengths and talents as you've observed them.

› Invite parent involvement sincerely and enthusiastically, especially for engagement that has direct relevance for their individual student.

› Send information to parents who are unable to attend a school event in person.

› Translate materials and provide interpretation. Do not use children to interpret for their parents, as it creates an imbalance in the parent-child relationship.

› Ask about challenges that make it difficult for families to support their student's learning.

› Seek out resources from the school, community, and beyond to mitigate family involvement challenges.

The majority of parents highlighted some way that they facilitated their child's learning at home—often with the parent as an active participant. They discussed current events with children, had "dinner question competitions," and read the same books. One parent said, "I showed him how to enjoy watching documentaries and shows based on history." Another wrote, "Last night we were discussing the effect of humans on Earth's cycles and processes. My role has been to encourage my child's natural inquisitiveness." Another talked of teaching their daughter "practical skills like basic mechanics, cooking, and figuring out how to find answers when they are not right in front of her." It seems that many of these gifted learners have parents with similarly curious minds.

Parents tapped into their own assets to support their child's learning: "I teach her Arabic language on almost a daily basis so that she would have the advantage of being bilingual." Several families mentioned heritage language learning. One mother wrote: "Even though my level of education does not allow

> **Figure 11.4**
>
> *Maximizing Learning at Home*
>
> › Can you modify a homework or project assignment to prompt students to share their learning with a parent?
>
> › Can you give parents clear and simple dos and don'ts on how to support their student in your advanced course?
>
> › Can you share free or low-cost local and online resources for families to support their student's learning?
>
> › Can you give parents a "question of the week/month" that helps move the dialogue beyond "How was school?" or "What did you get on the test?"
>
> › Can you direct parent engagement to encourage student curiosity, learning and growth, and persistence to develop academic resilience?

me to help my child in many subjects, I help her with her math course." These active parent engagements in their children's learning support the research of Van Voorhis (2011) on strategies for teachers to involve parents in schoolwork (TIPS). TIPS homework directs a student to demonstrate a concept to a parent or other adult supporter without expecting the parent or adult to know anything about the subject. TIPS for middle school core subjects have been shown to benefit students' academic performance.

Some parents encouraged learning-specific skills, gave their children "free time to tinker," and provided the arrangements for learning to take place. One wrote, "I invested in WiFi for the house." Several talked about free online learning sites, like Khan Academy, and others mentioned securing full financial aid for talent center courses from Johns Hopkins Center for Talented Youth, Duke Talent Identification Program, or Northwestern Center for Talent Development. As one parent summarized, "Despite the hardships and struggle of our everyday life, I find time and take every opportunity to ask my daughter about her lessons." Family income does not define commitment to learning. See Figure 11.4 for tips on maximizing learning at home.

Involvement for the Future

For low-income families that have also experienced racial discrimination, family involvement means much more than an added boost to their child's learning. As Hill et al. (2018) found, African American parental involvement featured an "intensity and focus on keeping their children on the right track, with an assumption that any mistake or failure will derail their future" (p. 17).

The first thing Michael's mom shared with our Young Scholars adviser on their initial home visit was her stack of binders. Here in these stuffed 3-inch binders, Mom had compiled academic and enrichment opportunities sorted by interests from her extensive internet searches. She had many goals in mind for Michael when it came to school options and out-of-school programs. Michael needed to be exposed to different vocational areas so that he could narrow his focus in the next few years, and there were essential life skills that they had identified, like learning to swim, playing an instrument, self-defense, and the social business skills of golf and tennis. As a single parent of a gifted African American male in a Midwestern suburb, Mom wasn't taking any chances with Michael's talent development.

Mom had attended some college, but suffered traumatic brain injuries as a result of multiple car accidents that stripped her short-term memory capacity. She and Michael lived off of her disability benefits in a small apartment with occasional help from family. Michael would be the first male in his family to go to college.

Michael worked hard to live up to her expectations. He excelled in school with Mom's consistent monitoring of progress, her exuberant cheers at his basketball and football games, and encouragement to stick with commitments, like playing the violin when daily practice was not so enticing. With accommodations, she reenrolled in college courses, and the two talked about their schoolwork. Michael did not take much pleasure if Mom earned better grades than he did.

Michael's teacher described Mom as a pleasant and calm "guiding compass" in her son's life. Staff and parents all seemed to know her, although she struggled to recognize any of them because of her memory impairment. Mom knew what was going on in every class and was able to give other parents information about what tests were coming up, which teachers to avoid, what enrichment opportunities were available for teens on weekends, and schedules for basketball tryouts. But, when it came time for the college application process, she grew anxious about whether she and Michael had done enough. Had they successfully navigated this complex system?

Michael was accepted with a full ride to one of the nation's top-performing colleges where he graduated 4 years later with a double major. At top-tier universities, African American undergraduates account for just 6% of the student population, a statistic that has been stagnant for 2 decades (McGill, 2015). Does it really need to be this hard?

Out-of-School Time Involvement—Types 3 and 6

Unlike parenting and learning at home, which depend more on the family-child relationship and less on outside resources, participation in out-of-school-time enrichment activities requires families to have access, information, and/or funds. According to a 2015 Pew Research Center study, half of low-income families said that they were able to find affordable, high-quality enrichment programs for their children in their community. Approximately 60% of families with annual incomes less than $30,000 reported that their child participated in afterschool or weekend activities such as sports. This is consistent with the parent reports from our Young Scholars applicant subset, where 56% of the parents wrote about either volunteering (supporting participation in enrichment activities), leveraging community resources, or both.

Parents wrote about attending concerts, games, performances, competitions, science fairs, and award ceremonies. They provided moral support and encouragement: "I am her loudest cheerleader when she participates in anything." They transported their children to/from activities, and many sought out free or affordable learning opportunities. As one parent explained, "With seven kids it gets tight, but we stretched our budget to allow him to participate in extracurricular activities."

Families tapped into local community resources: museums, free concerts, wildlife exhibits, public gardens, churches and mosques, libraries, and bookstores. One parent told us, "Every weekend after she helps me finish working at my nail salon, we often go to the public library so that she can check out books to read for fun." A few took advantage of their local community college: "My child let me know he wanted to take advanced math classes, so together we worked to enroll him at the local community college."

Community assets varied by location. One Native American parent wrote, "Through time spent with our tribal communities, our son has learned about the history of our people, who we are today, and what our future holds." Another family drove 2 hours each way on Saturdays so that their son could volunteer at a fossil site and "get to practice his current dream to become a paleontologist." Another family wrote about mineral prospecting together. Many families talked about engaging in community service through food pantries, their places of worship, or scouts.

Several families highlighted the benefits for their children to participate in college or university enrichment programs. These Saturday and summer enrichment activities gave their students the opportunity to go deeper into interest areas with peers who were equally enthusiastic. They all wrote about needing financial aid to participate in these programs.

For many, accessing community resources was not easy. One parent expressed the intense persistence many have in finding community resources for their children:

> I research programs in our city, but most of them cost money. We're all over the ones that don't—like hackathons and science fairs. He participates in a rowing club that serves under-resourced kids and gives them a chance to be with a diverse groups, build rowing skills, and learn more about the college track.

But community programs play a vital role for low-income families of gifted learners: "Due to our limited education, most of the assistance our child receives is from outside programs. We provide him with transportation and moral support."

Educators can help families overcome challenges to access outside-of-school enrichment opportunities so that students can explore interests, develop talents, foster peer connections, and consider future college and career paths. Options include the following:

> ⟩ Host enrichment programs at the school directly after school and/or for full days throughout the summer. The National Summer Learning Association (https://www.summerlearning.org) provides toolkits, resources, and high-quality program examples with information on program funding sources.
> ⟩ Help reduce parents' burden of searching for programs. Identify community-based organizations that offer free or low-cost enrichment programming.
> ⟩ Put together a directory of local opportunities and national resources that offer financial aid. Share it repeatedly with families in English and their native languages, in print or electronically, generally and personally.
> ⟩ Meet one family's need. Mentor a student or pair them with a mentor, arrange transportation between families, provide lessons or tutoring at their home or school, contact organizations on their behalf to secure financial aid, and help them apply for scholarships.

Big or small, school-family partnerships can help gifted learners from low-income backgrounds leverage community resources for great support.

Expanding Community Support

Sometimes a family's situation is so strained that the definition of family must be expanded to include caring community members who can support the student's educational development.

Linh lived with her dad, who was on mental health disability and unable to work since his wife became incapacitated by a terminal medical condition. Linh and her sister slept in the garage of the modest home that extended family helped them rent. Dad expressed an unwavering belief that education was the way for his daughters to have a better life. However, filling out a questionnaire about his daughter or setting up a school appointment immobilized him. This left Linh alone to make the decisions about her education.

When absolutely necessary, Dad would drive their weary car the 2 miles to school for important events. However, Linh occasionally relied on neighbors for a ride to school, and more often walked the 2 miles through an unsafe neighborhood. Linh's piano teacher drove to her home to provide free lessons on the piano the family had purchased years ago before their health and financial decline. This piano teacher saw that Linh and her sister were becoming more isolated with less consistent support from extended family, so she started taking the girls on fun outings, inviting them to her home, and helping to pay for piano recitals, competitions, and other incidental expenses that were related to their music instruction.

At school, few staff knew Linh beyond her academic performance. She was hesitant to reach out to adults for help, whether for personal issues or for routine needs like printing schoolwork. She was a straight-A student and accomplished pianist, but not involved in any school extracurricular activities because she had no ride home.

Seeing the tension between Linh's expansive potential and limited local support, the Young Scholars Program team considered changing her context. With Dad's full support, we partnered with the middle school to help Linh apply to a boarding school that offered a full-ride scholarship. The school was within a few hours' drive from their home, and Dad agreed to drive her there for the start and end of school semesters. Linh had full access to academic and extracurricular activities beyond the classroom with no concern about daily transportation, access to food, safety, or housing security. Dorm parents and faculty members provided her a daily dose of support and encouragement.

Linh went on to be a tennis and track star in high school, challenged herself in piano competitions, mentored students in foster care, and was selected by faculty for two sought-after leadership positions. She was accepted to a highly selective small liberal arts college where she graduated with honors as a STEM major. She maintained a close relationship with Dad, and he visited her during college. Linh is now pursuing her master's degree while working at a leading medical research institution. For Linh, school-family-community support meant looking beyond the immediate vicinity to expand her caring network.

Conclusion

Students and families have much to teach educators. They are resilient, resourceful, adaptable, caring, creative, smart, and full of hope and determination for a future that matches their potential. I am hopeful that the perspectives and stories shared here inspire educators to get to know families even better and see beyond the limitations they may have been conditioned to expect. Educators must recognize the assets and strengths families bring and invite parents' input, questions, and guidance so they can create the bridge between aspirations and shared actions. When educators see the possibilities, they create a more just educational system that opens the door for all talented students to contribute significantly to the world.

References

Bridgeland, J. M., DiIulio, J. J., Streeter, R. T., & Mason, J. R. (2008). *One dream, two realities: Perspectives of parents on America's high schools.* Civic Enterprises.

Bryk, A. S., & Schneider, B. (2004). *Trust in schools: A core resource for improvement.* Russell Sage Foundation.

Catsambis, S. (2001). Expanding knowledge of parental involvement in children's secondary education: Connections with high school seniors' academic success. *Social Psychology of Education, 5,* 149–177. https://doi.org/10.1023/A:1014478001512

Christianakis, M. (2011). Parents as "help labor": Inner-city teachers' narratives of parent involvement. *Teacher Education Quarterly, 38*(4), 157–178.

Civil Rights Act of 1964, Pub. L. No. 88-352, 78 Stat. 241 (1964). https://www.govinfo.gov/content/pkg/STATUTE-78/pdf/STATUTE-78-Pg241.pdf

Doepke, M., & Zilibotti, F. (2019, February 24). The parent trap: What drives intense parenting? Income inequality. *The Washington Post,* B1–B3.

Epstein, J. L. (2011). *School, family, and community partnerships: Preparing educators and improving schools* (2nd ed.). Westview Press.

Epstein, J. L., Sanders, M. G., Sheldon, S. B., Simon, B. S., Salinas, K. C., Jansorn, N. R., Van Voorhis, F. L., Martin, C. S., Thomas, B. G., Greenfield, M. D., Hutchins, D. J., & Williams, K. J. (2019). *School, family, and community partnerships: Your handbook for action* (4th ed.). Corwin.

Fan, X., & Chen, M. (2001). Parental involvement and students' academic achievement: A meta-analysis. *Educational Psychology Review, 13,* 1–22. https://doi.org/10.1023/A:1009048817385

Fan, W., & Williams, C. M. (2010). The effects of parental involvement on students' academic self-efficacy, engagement and intrinsic motivation. *Educational Psychology, 30*(1), 53–74. https://doi.org/10.1080/01443410903353302

Gentry, M., & Fugate, M. (2012). Gifted Native American students: Underperforming, under-identified, and overlooked. *Psychology in the Schools, 49*(7), 631–646. https://www.doi.org/10.1002/pits.21624

Griffin, D., & Wood, S. M. (2015). "Mommy, I'm bored": School-family-community approaches to working with gifted, rural Black males. In T. Stambaugh & S. M. Wood (Eds.), *Serving gifted students in rural settings* (pp. 289–315). Prufrock Press.

Henderson, A. T., & Mapp, K. L. (2002). *A new wave of evidence: The impact of school, family, and community connections on student achievement.* Southwest Educational Development Laboratory.

Hill, N. E., Tyson, D. F., & Bromell, L. (2009). Developmentally appropriate strategies across ethnicity and socioeconomic status: Parental involvement during middle school. In N. E. Hill & R. K. Chao (Eds.), *Families, schools, and the adolescent: Connecting research, policy, and practice* (pp. 53–72). Teachers College Press.

Hill, N. E., Witherspoon, D. P., & Bartz, D. (2018). Parental involvement in education during middle school: Perspectives of ethnically diverse parents, teachers, and students. *The Journal of Educational Research, 111*(1), 12–27. https://doi.org/10.1080/00220671.2016.1190910

Hoover-Dempsey, K. V., Walker, J. M. T., Sandler, H. M., Whetsel, D., Green, C. L., Wilkins, A. S., & Closson, K. (2005). Why do parents become involved? Research findings and implications. *The Elementary School Journal, 106*(2), 105–130. https://www.doi.org/10.1086/499194

Hunsaker, S. L., Frasier, M. M., King, L. L., Watts-Warren, B., Cramond, B., & Krisel, S. (1995). *Family influences on the achievement of economically disadvantaged students: Implications for gifted identification and programming* (RM95206). University of Connecticut, The National Research Center on the Gifted and Talented. https://nrcgt.uconn.edu/online_resources

Jeynes, W. (2012). A meta-analysis of the efficacy of different types of parental involvement programs for urban students. *Urban Education, 47*(4), 706–742. https://doi.org/10.1177/0042085912445643

Jolly, J. L., & Matthews, M. S. (2012). A critique of the literature on parenting gifted learners. *Journal for the Education of the Gifted, 35*(3), 259–290. https://doi.org/10.1177/0162353212451703

Kreider, H., Caspe, M., Kennedy, S., & Weiss, H. (2007, Spring). *Family involvement in middle and high school students' education* (No. 3). Harvard Family Research Project.

Lareau, A., & Horvat, E. M. (1999). Moments of social inclusion and exclusion: Race, class, and cultural capital in family-school relationships. *Sociology of Education, 72*(1), 37–53. https://doi.org/10.2307/2673185

McGill, A. (2015). *The missing Black students at elite American universities.* The Atlantic. https://www.theatlantic.com/politics/archive/2015/11/black-college-student-body/417189

Olszewski-Kubilius, P., & Thomson, D. L. (2010). Gifted programming for poor or minority urban students: Issues and lessons learned. *Gifted Child Today, 33*(4), 58–64. https://doi.org/10.1177/107621751003300413

Ong, A. D., Phinney, J. S., & Dennis, J. (2006). Competence under challenge: Exploring the protective influence of parental support and ethnic identity in Latino college students. *Journal of Adolescence, 29*(6), 961–979. https://doi.org/10.1016/j.adolescence.2006.04.010

Quiocho, A. M. L., & Daoud, A. M. (2006). Dispelling myths about Latino parent participation in schools. *The Educational Forum, 70*(3), 255–267. https://doi.org/10.1080/00131720608984901

Pew Research Center. (2015). *Parenting in America: Outlook, worries, aspirations are strongly linked to financial situation.* https://www.pewresearch.org/wp-content/uploads/sites/3/2015/12/2015-12-17_parenting-in-america_FINAL.pdf

Simon, B. S. (2004). High school outreach and family involvement. *Social Psychology of Education, 7*(2), 185–209. https://doi.org/10.1023/B:SPOE.0000018559.47658.67

Vaden-Kiernan, N. (2005). *Parents' reports of school practices to provide information to families: 1996 and 2003.* National Center for Education Statistics. https://nces.ed.gov/pubs2006/2006041.pdf

Van Voorhis, F. L. (2011). Costs and benefits of family involvement in homework. *Journal of Advanced Academics, 22*(2), 220–249. https://doi.org/10.1177/1932202X1102200203

Weiss, H. B., Lopez, M. E., & Caspe, M. (2018). *Joining together to create a bold vision for next generation family engagement: Engaging families to transform education.* Global Family Research Project. https://www.carnegie.org/media/filer_public/f8/78/f8784565-4bd6-4aa3-bd80-2b98fd43380e/parent-engagement-2018.pdf

A Systems Approach to Identifying and Serving Gifted Learners From Low-Income Backgrounds

Carol V. Horn

Finding and nurturing gifted learners from low-income backgrounds requires a schoolwide, systems approach in which every member of the school community embraces a shared vision of providing equity of opportunity for every child. Schools can be powerful agents of change when they provide a context in which students are able to develop potential that might not otherwise be realized. A systems approach requires a new model that differs from traditional gifted education service models. Instead of using gifted education pedagogy with a small population of students identified as gifted, a systems model embraces the notion of a continuum of gifted services that are offered to a broad range of students in one or more areas of talent. The continuum of gifted services provides increasing levels of challenge in response to a student's performance on assessments and academic tasks. The search for talent begins in kindergarten, and the services are available through high school. Screening and identification procedures at each level are closely tied to the teaching and learning that occur in each classroom. All teachers in the school community participate in a search for talent. The curriculum and instruction are designed to challenge all learners so that gifted potential may be observed and every student who has the capacity to succeed in advanced academic programs has the opportunity to participate.

This chapter focuses on a model for creating a schoolwide, systems approach designed to identify and serve gifted students from low-income households. The model was created through an in-depth review of literature and research on the issue of underrepresentation in gifted programs. It is also based on my own experience of implementing the model in a large suburban school district.

The underrepresentation of students from poverty in gifted programs is a longstanding issue (Plucker & Peters, 2016; Yoon & Gentry, 2009), and raising awareness of this disproportionality has not lessened the inequity (Peters et al., 2019). A schoolwide systems approach has the capacity to effect long-term change that will lead to a paradigm shift regarding who receives gifted services and how they are implemented. This systems approach requires four critical elements that are implemented with fidelity (see Figure 12.1). The elements are interdependent and together create a dynamic system designed to ensure that gifted learners from low-income households are identified, served, and supported from kindergarten through graduation from high school. Each element is essential to the success of this work, and no element on its own will lead to the effective, lasting changes that are needed in order to address this important issue.

The first element is shared leadership with a unified vision. When schools are organized around a vision of the future that is created and supported by all staff members, every educator has an important contribution to make toward achieving that vision, and each individual's knowledge and expertise are valued and respected. Currently, in many school systems, teachers, regardless of their knowledge and expertise, are often left out of the picture when it comes to decision making, and the only way for them to have direct influence is to leave the classroom and pursue an administrative position. This is especially true in low-income areas where it is difficult to recruit and retain high-quality teachers. Significant numbers of those who depart from their jobs in these schools report that they receive inadequate support from the school administration, low salaries, and limited faculty input into school decision making (Ingersoll, 2004). New teachers are often assigned in high-poverty areas until they have the experience and expertise to move on. When schools are structured for success, master teachers have the same decision-making power and influence as

Figure 12.1

Model of Systemic Approach to Identifying and Serving Gifted Learners From Low-Income Households

Collaborative shared leadership among all educators in the school community	High-level curriculum and gifted education pedagogy for all students
A continuum of gifted services throughout the school year, after school, and during the summer	Ongoing professional development for all educators and parent partnerships

Finding and serving students from poverty for gifted services

administrators, and each one contributes to and informs school policy from their unique, knowledge-based perspective.

Second, high-level curriculum and instruction infused with gifted education pedagogy must be an integral part of the learning experiences provided to all children. Many of the curricula that are published for gifted learners have been implemented with a wide range of learners to determine their effectiveness. Research suggests that they not only have led to an increase in student engagement, but also have given teachers an opportunity to collect evidence of students' talents and strengths (VanTassel-Baska, 2018). Work samples, anecdotal records, and student responses to open-ended questions are just a few of the ways teachers can collect concrete evidence of a student's advanced thinking and a need for gifted services.

Third, the school must offer a continuum of gifted services from part time to full time, recognizing that students have varying levels of academic strength that develop over time in response to the nurturance that is provided. By offering a continuum of gifted services, every child has the opportunity to work at a level of challenge that is commensurate with their current performance. A continuum of services includes multiple options that are designed to nurture and develop academic talents and strengths as they are identified. These may include instructional groupings in a classroom, special time with a gifted resource teacher, advanced instruction at a higher grade level, afterschool programs, summer school, and/or flexible instructional groupings across grade levels. For example, students who are advanced in mathematical reasoning would have access to accelerated mathematics instruction. The goal is to ensure that every child has the opportunity for continuous intellectual growth in one or more academic areas.

Fourth, ongoing professional development and parent partnerships must be an integral part of this work. Professional development should include courses in gifted education and cultural proficiency. If all students are to have access to high-level curriculum and instruction, then all teachers need courses in gifted education pedagogy. Often in low-income schools, students experience instruction best described as "the pedagogy of poverty" (Haberman, 2010), where giving information and controlling behavior take precedence over thinking on a higher level, challenging ideas, and entertaining possibilities for the future. In addition, cultural proficiency training is needed to deepen an appreciation for diversity and allow teachers to make meaningful connections between the curriculum and their students' backgrounds. Courses in cultural proficiency and gifted education pedagogy provide educators with important tools and practices for finding gifted potential in students from low-income backgrounds. Finally, parent partnerships build trust between school and home and help parents become advocates for their children.

In summary, a systems approach involves the entire school community in efforts to increase access to advanced learning opportunities and talent development programs for a broad range of talented learners. For some gifted learners, this may be their only path out of poverty, and schools have a critical role to play. The following sections will provide an in-depth explanation of the model.

Collaborative Shared Leadership

Today, school systems are complex organizations that require a combination of shared leadership among many and varied professionals. New demands for collaboration and teamwork necessitate a shift in the traditional power structure. As new models of leadership are required, the emphasis on top-down power is being replaced with an emphasis on shared power and the use of power to empower others (Berry et al., 2013; Lambert, 2002; MetLife, 2013). When leadership is shared, teachers and administrators work together to build and achieve a dynamic vision that is flexible and responsive to the needs of the community. Teacher professionalism, identified as the most critical variable of school reform, necessitates an approach to leadership that originates within the culture of a school and is shared by a community of professionals. Research suggests that not only must teachers take charge of their own learning and professional development plans, but also principals must find ways to provide teachers with consistent support and continuous opportunities to grow and expand their repertoire (Berry et al., 2013; MetLife, 2013). A systems approach to underrepresentation requires a community of professionals working together with a shared commitment to find and develop talent in all children (Clarenbach, 2015). Leadership roles might include finding and sharing research on how to address the underrepresentation of learners from low-income backgrounds in gifted programs, serving as mentors to new teachers in the work that the school is doing to find and nurture potential talent, developing curriculum for summer school and special student projects, and acting as facilitators of professional development activities. At schools that are working to address the underrepresentation issue, teacher leaders organize meetings, share research-based best practices, and actively advocate for students with gifted potential who are at risk of being overlooked. When schools function as communities of leaders who listen to, value, and respect each other's ideas, increased communication, shared responsibility, and a heightened sense of ownership create a culture of learning that stimulates and nurtures motivation and achievement for all members of the school community—students as well as educators (Clarenbach, 2015; Horn, 2018).

Two essential elements play a critical role in cultivating shared leadership. First, schools must support teachers as professionals who value and desire the knowledge and expertise to work toward a shared vision and achieve shared goals. Teacher leaders are critical to a system's approach for finding and serving gifted learners from low-income backgrounds across all populations. Second, ongoing professional development is an integral part of the change process, and teachers must be given the opportunity to take charge of their learning and select the courses and professional growth experiences that they need to improve their teaching (Lambert, 2002; Wahlstrom & Louis, 2008). When the identification of talent potential in students from poverty becomes part of a school's vision, the staff creates goals, the work becomes a priority, and progress is measured, communicated, and celebrated as they work to achieve those goals. In addition, teachers select the courses and professional development experiences that will support this vision and help them achieve their goals. Identifying and serving gifted students from low-income backgrounds requires a shared leadership model that will support and sustain reform from within.

Restructuring school communities to incorporate shared leadership positions cultivates a more positive environment by placing a nonjudgmental value on providing assistance, modeling collegiality as a mode of work, providing school site opportunities for continuous learning, and encouraging others to provide leadership to their peers (Cheung et al., 2018). Teachers report that their knowledge and skills in teaching increase dramatically as a result of their involvement in leadership positions (York-Barr & Duke, 2004). Shared leadership also strengthens intrinsic motivation and supports individual growth. By sharing leadership, teachers feel more ownership of and increased confidence in the decisions they are making. They also experience greater job satisfaction accompanied by a stronger commitment to the school and their shared vision.

The principals of schools that are committed to increasing the number of students from low-income backgrounds receiving gifted services play a key role in the success of addressing this issue (Clarenbach, 2015). They are instructional leaders who meet with other principals and school leaders to collaborate, share ideas, and tackle the challenges and concerns that must be addressed as they implement a systems approach to underrepresentation. They are strong advocates for students, provide ongoing support to the teachers, and ensure that year after year students are placed with teachers who know how to nurture and develop their gifted potential.

Gifted and talented resource teachers assigned to each school, other educational specialists, and classroom teachers also play critical roles. In a systems approach of shared leadership, gifted services are provided through a collaborative model in which the gifted and talented resource teacher works with classroom teachers and other educational specialists to provide a continuum of gifted services that begins in kindergarten. The gifted and talented resource teacher meets with grade-level teams to design and implement differentiated lessons that challenge all learners to think on a higher level and study advanced content through projects, research, and extensions of the general education program. The teachers and specialists understand that finding and nurturing talent potential is dependent on their combined efforts.

Shared leadership acknowledges and builds on the contributions of the numerous professionals who work in today's schools. It is responsive to the complex demands of a changing and diverse school population. Models and theories of leadership that have been developed and researched over time can guide educators as they seek new and better ways to recruit and retain quality teachers in high-poverty schools in order to ensure that gifted learners from low-income backgrounds are identified and served.

Start Early and Build on Strengths Through High-Level Curriculum and Instruction

If current methods of identification fail to find gifted students from low-income backgrounds, and the school is committed to providing services to every child with gifted potential, then adopting practices and procedures designed to ensure that all populations have access to gifted services becomes paramount. Often in schools in low-income areas, educators focus on children's deficits (Ford, 2010; Ford et al., 2002). A schoolwide systems approach to gifted education necessitates a focus on strengths and an ongoing search for students who are able to think, reason, and problem solve at advanced levels. In this environment, teachers, principals, and school specialists collaborate, problem solve, share ideas, and work together to find and nurture the potential of every child. Conversations among administrators, teachers, and specialists ignite questions and generate discussions that lead to new ways of finding and nurturing gifted potential in gifted learners from low-income backgrounds.

One of the most critical issues to address in order to provide gifted services to high-potential learners from low-income populations is to change teacher expectations of what students are capable of achieving. These students often receive more of a rote learning and skills-based approach that does little or nothing to develop their exceptional potential (Olszewski-Kubilius & Thomson, 2010; Smith et al., 1997). Expectations must be changed in two directions. Not only must teachers believe that the students are capable of performing at high levels, but also the students must believe it themselves. Research suggests that when students are given a difficult task and are successful, their self-efficacy increases, and they are more willing to take on additional challenges (Dweck, 2006/2016). The earlier that students experience success at challenging tasks, the better prepared they will be to continue to engage in advanced learning opportunities as they move up in grade level. Numerous studies support the need for programs that identify and nurture giftedness in students from lower income backgrounds at an early age (Borland, et.al., 2000; Plucker & Peters, 2016; Scott et al., 1996; Smith et al., 1997). Beginning in kindergarten, school professionals can work together to find gifted potential, and curriculum plays an important role in the identification process.

Teacher training is critical. Ongoing assessments by educators who have been trained to provide curriculum and instruction that are designed to elicit gifted behaviors may be the most powerful means of finding and nurturing gifted learners in low-income racial and ethnic minority populations (VanTassel-Baska, 2018). Teachers who work together and design lessons that connect new knowledge and understandings to students' personal experiences gain a deeper appreciation for the backgrounds and life experiences of their students (Ford et al., 2008). Poems, stories, and plays that contain dialect, relevant role models, and varying cultural lifestyles may be integrated throughout the curriculum. Authors, artists, inventors, scientists, mathematicians, and other leaders from diverse backgrounds who have made significant contributions to society may also be infused into the entire learning experience. When students are given the opportunity to study the diverse group of leaders who have changed the world for the better, they realize that the traits and characteristics these people possess cross all lines of color, class, and culture, and their personal aspirations are enhanced.

A curriculum framework that outlines units, lessons, and resources for teachers at every grade level in every subject is invaluable to this work. Teachers do not have the time or expertise to create high-quality curriculum designed for gifted learners; however, school teams can work together to create a framework of research-based gifted curriculum and resources that provides consistency across the school and ensures that gifted services are high level and engaging. Examples include Project M^2 and Project M^3 (Gavin et al., 2006) and Engineering is Elementary (EIE; Robinson et al., 2018), as well as *Jacob's Ladder Reading Comprehension Program*, Project Athena, and Project Clarion (VanTassel-Baska, 2018). Historically, gifted curriculum was reserved for students identified as gifted. Students in high-poverty schools were neither identified nor offered the opportunity to engage in high-level curriculum and instruction. From my experience in Fairfax County Public Schools, I learned that the instructional practices and curricula designed for gifted learners could be used to challenge and engage all learners, especially students in high-poverty schools. High-level curriculum and instruction not only help teachers see potential that might be missed when using a more direct instruction approach, but also increase students' self-efficacy. As their confidence increases, they are ready and prepared to tackle additional challenges as they advanced in grade level. Research suggests that models and strategies once reserved for the gifted may be used by classroom teachers to challenge and engage all learners (VanTassel-Baska, 2018). The infusion of critical and creative thinking strategies into daily lessons is an effective way to find and nurture gifted potential. When students are encouraged to engage in learning experiences that require advanced applications of knowledge, they are challenged and motivated to reach new heights as they discover and develop their strengths and talents. Instructional strategies that require and promote higher level thinking may be used in all content areas and provide myriad opportunities for students to explore knowledge, gain understanding, and acquire skills in work that stimulates their minds and develops their potential. The problem-solving skills, thinking processes, and student products that are outcomes of these practices provide observable evidence of a student's ability to think and reason at advanced levels. The gifted and talented resource teacher can collaborate with grade-level teams to schedule classroom visits throughout the year in order to model higher level thinking strategies and discuss ways they can be integrated into classroom learning experiences. Observations, conversations, and collections of anecdotal records over time help increase the capacity of teachers to find and identify gifted potential at every grade level. These efforts to identify and build on students' strengths highlight the need to nurture the potential of all children so that gifted potential has the opportunity to emerge.

The implementation of high-level curriculum can motivate students from poverty to achieve at high levels with two positive outcomes: The students begin to understand and appreciate their own strengths, and teachers are able to collect evidence that may be used in the identification process (Horn, 2018; Robinson et al., 2018; VanTassel-Baska et al., 2002). Student performance on tasks that require critical and creative thinking and advanced problem solving can provide powerful evidence of a student's gifted potential. In a systems model, students are identified through a case study approach that examines student portfolios, performance-based assessments, ability tests, and achievement tests. The important difference is that nothing is weighted and no one piece of information may be used to find a child eligible or ineligible for gifted services. Early identification of academic strengths and talents coupled with early intervention allows the school to provide the appropriate level of challenge and increase the students' self-efficacy. The long-term goal is for gifted learners from low-income backgrounds to participate and succeed in gifted programs as they discover and develop their advanced potential.

A Continuum of Gifted Services

A systems approach requires that schools nurture continuous academic growth beginning in kindergarten through differentiation and acceleration. This provides teachers the time to work with students from low-income backgrounds on basic skills that are needed for proficiency in reading and mathematics. Teachers can also provide rich learning experiences that help learners from low-income backgrounds acquire the advanced knowledge, understanding, and skills that they will need in order to be competitive in challenging programs as they progress in grade level. Although these students have the cognitive ability to work at advanced levels, they may need additional scaffolding and support in order to succeed in gifted programs (Horn, 2018; Olszewski-Kubilius & Corwith 2018). A continuum of services provides multiple entry points and a wide variety of opportunities, which is critical for learners from low-income households, who may lack the background knowledge and experiences of students from more affluent environments. In this model, the teachers, specialists, and administrators are student advocates who provide ongoing support to students in areas of academic strength as they prepare them for the challenging curriculum and instruction that gifted and talented programs offer throughout the elementary, middle, and high school years.

By labeling the service and not the child, teachers are free to take risks and offer learning experiences (that were once reserved for a few identified gifted) to all children and then watch, observe, and record academic strengths as they begin to emerge. Having a continuum of services supports teacher efforts to ensure each child receives the appropriate level of challenge. It also promotes and supports continuous intellectual growth for every child. This approach moves beyond the notion of giftedness as a static trait and supports the notion of talent development as dynamic, evolving potential that can and should be developed in all children (Horn, 2018; Olszewski-Kubilius & Corwith, 2018; Plucker & Peters, 2016). This is especially critical for gifted learners from low-income backgrounds, who may need more time to learn English and/or strengthen basic skills.

A change in the delivery of gifted services from a stand-alone program to a collaborative model, in which the gifted and talented resource teacher works with classroom teachers and other specialists to provide a continuum of gifted services, also allows the gifted and talented resource teacher to become integrated into the total school community. This is especially important for gifted learners from low-income backgrounds, as it gives the resource teachers an opportunity to advocate for the students and support this important work with all teachers throughout the school. Multiage classrooms, looping, flexible grouping, and/or vertical teaming of teachers are examples of service delivery options that may be used to support the students. A curriculum framework that outlines resources, units, lessons, and materials that can be used to extend and enrich the general education curriculum can serve as an important guide for the implementation of high-level instructional practices. The framework should be organized by subject and grade level so that teachers will have access to lessons and strategies that will increase challenge for students who are ready. Examples of curriculum and instruction that provide advanced and accelerated learning for students from low-income households are provided in Chapter 5. When educators work together in collaborative teams that continually assess and design instruction in response to the needs of their students, they are able to overcome barriers and identify strengths in students who are at risk of being overlooked (Horn, 2018).

Because advanced learning opportunities are important for talent development, access to programs and resources is critical for students who may not have access due to financial constraints or other obstacles beyond their control (Olszewski-Kubilius & Corwith, 2018; Plucker & Peters, 2016). A continuum of services for learners from low-income backgrounds provides benefits during the school year as well as through summer school, afterschool, and weekend activities. Summer school is one example of a systems approach that extends beyond the school year and provides gifted students from low-income backgrounds with important learning opportunities that are expanded and enriched. In Fairfax County Public Schools, Young Scholars in grades 1–8 attend a 3-week summer school program each year that helps strengthen basic reading and mathematics skills while developing higher level thinking skills (Horn, 2015). The students receive specific interventions designed to develop and nurture their gifted potential. These may take the form of project investigations, problem-based learning, research, and independent study. Teachers work collaboratively to design an engaging curriculum that includes concept-based instruction, enrichment opportunities, field trips, and guest speakers. The summer school classes are often multiage, and basic skills are strengthened through learning opportunities that challenge the students to think and apply knowledge on a higher, more complex level. The ideas and problem-solving strategies that the students learn during summer school increase self-efficacy, enhance their knowledge and skills, and carry over into the school year (Horn, 2014, 2015).

As part of a continuum of services, powerful interventions may also be provided through university partnerships, such as Project Excite, developed by Northwestern University's Center for Talent Development (Olszewski-Kubilius & Thomson, 2010), and Project Promise, part of the University for Young People program at Baylor University's School of Education (Kaul et al., 2016). These programs help gifted learners from low-income backgrounds transition to high school and higher education with a high level of confidence and with intellectual peers from a similar background.

Finding and nurturing talent potential is an enormous undertaking that requires the dedication and commitment of numerous educational leaders. When school leaders work collaboratively and make a concerted effort to value the differences that children bring to school, they are able to provide multiple opportunities for students to demonstrate their academic strengths. They also ensure access to a continuum of services for all populations. Examples of models that offer a continuum of gifted services include the work of Donald Treffinger (Treffinger et al., 2004), the Schoolwide Enrichment Model (Renzulli & Reis, 2014), and Fairfax County Public Schools' continuum of advanced academic services (Horn, 2014). Each one provides all learners with myriad opportunities to engage in complex subject matter, helps them understand and value their own strengths, and prepares them for more challenging and rigorous classes as they develop their talents. Gifted learners from low-income backgrounds benefit when gifted services begin with early enrichment and offer multiple entry points for gifted services from kindergarten through twelfth grade. In Fairfax County Public Schools the continuum starts with a talent development pool in kindergarten through grade 2. Learners with gifted potential from low-income backgrounds are identified through work samples and responses to lessons taught with high-level critical and creative thinking strategies. Identified students are labeled Young Scholars and clustered with teachers who know how to develop their advanced potential. Beginning in grade 3, identified students receive enrichment and extensions to the curriculum in specific academic areas provided by the classroom teacher, part-time gifted services in one or more areas of academic strength provided by a gifted and talented resource teacher, or full-time placement in a gifted center where all subjects are taught at an advanced level. Students can move to a different level whenever there is evidence to support a need for additional gifted services. As students transition into middle school, they can take honors courses in areas of academic strength or receive full-time gifted services in the four core subjects of mathematics, social studies, science, and language arts in a gifted center. In high school, they can take honors and Advanced Placement courses, enroll in an International Baccalaureate program, or compete for admission to Thomas Jefferson High School for Science and Technology (Horn, 2015).

Ongoing Professional Development and Parent Partnerships

Ongoing professional development on multiple levels is critical to the success of a systems approach. This includes district leaders, school administrators, and school staff. Professional development opportunities include culturally responsive teaching, how to identify gifted potential in diverse populations, and how to differentiate curriculum and instruction for advanced learners. Training in cultural proficiency helps educators understand the diversity of background experiences that learners from low-income backgrounds bring to school. Teachers learn how to embed applications of cultural proficiency training into daily practice (Castellano & Díaz, 2001). They also learn instructional strategies designed to elicit high-level responses and ways to record evidence of talent and gifted potential through observations, anecdotal records, and portfolios of student work.

Principals who are committed to increasing the number of learners from low-income backgrounds participating in gifted programs at their schools also engage in professional development that supports this work. As instructional leaders, they meet with other principals to collaborate, share ideas, and tackle the challenges and concerns that surface as they address this important issue. They view themselves as leaders of leaders, and their leadership acknowledges and builds on the contributions of the numerous professionals that work in their schools. The principals are responsive to the complex demands of a diverse school population and work with school teams in order to ensure that the identified students are clustered in classrooms with teachers who know how to nurture and develop their gifted potential. They also foster a climate of respect and commitment in which every individual believes that they have an important role to play. When school leaders are able to empower and energize all staff members, the possibilities for what they can accomplish become endless (Fullan, 2003). This is especially important for learners from low-income backgrounds, who may not have opportunities or advocates outside of school to help them actualize their potential. In my work in Fairfax County, I found that principals who prioritized the work of finding gifted potential in learners from low-income backgrounds through a systems approach gained firsthand experience of the power of this model. As one principal from a Title I school shared,

> Anytime that you do something to look at a child's behavior or performance in a different way, then you're going to extend your perception of what's going on. So the more we look at children the more we're going to find out about them. I think the more enrichment opportunities we offer to students from low economic backgrounds the more potential we're going to see.

Summer institutes for teachers can play an important role in providing professional development that prepares classroom teachers to recognize and nurture gifted potential in learners from low-income backgrounds. National consultants and teacher leaders can provide training on critical and creative thinking, mathematical reasoning, historical interpretation and analysis, scientific investigations, advanced literary skills, and other practices that will not only challenge and engage these learners, but also elicit and develop their advanced potential.

In addition to summer institutes, teachers can receive additional training and support through inservices provided by the gifted and talented programs office during the school year. Classroom teachers and resource teachers can be invited to attend as school teams. They are then able to infuse the models, lessons, and strategies into their teaching practice.

Building parent partnerships and family relationships is another critical element. Schools that employ a systems approach to the issue of underrepresentation actively work to strengthen parent partnerships and the family connection. Letters, brochures, and flyers with information about activities and opportunities can be translated into multiple languages and sent home in student backpacks. Workshops for the parents can focus on what the school system has to offer and how parents/guardians can be advocates for their children. Parents may also be invited to participate in many of the learning activities to include field trips and special programs. This active involvement provides the parents with ideas on how they can work with their children at home. Parent liaisons can also be identified to communicate with the parents and provide important information on school activities and programs. As parents become partners in their child's education, they become a strong source of advocacy and support.

Data Management and Collection

Data management and collection are important on multiple levels. First, as students' strengths are identified, there must be a system for collecting evidence to support the appropriate level of gifted service. Student work samples, products, and presentations may be collected in portfolios that demonstrate a student's area(s) of talent. In addition, a systems approach requires a consistent method of data collection that allows the school district to conduct longitudinal studies as children progress through the school system. These data include test scores, services provided, courses taken, grades, and any other information that may be used as evidence of success over time. The data are also used to ensure that as students transition to different schools or grade levels, there is a method to ensure that gifted services continue without interruption. Learners from low-income households can easily fall through the cracks if there is no system in place to ensure access to gifted services and advocacy for their potential if they move to a new area or move on to middle or high school. Having a coded data system that may be accessed from a central source provides critical information that can be used to ensure that gifted services continue without interruption. Data collection also provides much-needed evidence that can be used to apply for grants and other resources to support and expand this important work.

As students' strengths and talents are identified, they may be given a code in the student information system for the level of gifted service they are receiving and when those services began. It is also important to note when and if there is a change in service for two reasons: First, it allows all educators access to this information so that they can provide continuous services and support, and second, longitudinal studies of students who are receiving gifted services provide important data on the impact of early interventions and ongoing advocacy. The service code allows the district to assess the participation and performance of students over time in order to determine whether or not they are identified for gifted services, the level of service, the courses that they take in middle and high school, their grades, and college acceptances. Some schools provide a special designation for students who need additional advocacy and support from the school district. Because students may be identified as early as kindergarten, the code provides important research on the success and impact of this systems approach over time. The data may be reported to the local school board as well as the state and federal government to enlist support for resources needed for a high-quality systems approach to gifted education that is designed to find and nurture gifted potential in gifted learners from low-income backgrounds.

A Final Note

Finding and nurturing the potential of gifted learners from low-income backgrounds is an enormous undertaking that requires the dedication and commitment of the entire school community and all of its resources. When giftedness in children is viewed as multifaceted and multidimensional potential that is ever evolving in response to internal and external catalysts, educators take a more active role in searching for gifted potential among students of varying cultural, ethnic, socioeconomic, and linguistic backgrounds. Because gifted programs are an important gateway for participation in challenging and advanced classes in middle school, high school, and higher education, access to these advanced learning opportunities must be provided to all students who have the potential to succeed. Gifted learners from low-income backgrounds are at risk of being overlooked unless a dynamic systems approach is used that includes all of the elements discussed in this chapter. A systems approach builds capacity in schools to move beyond the notion of giftedness as a static trait for only a few and support the notion of giftedness as potential that can and should be developed in all populations. The coordinator checklists in Appendix 12.1 may be used by school leaders and gifted coordinators to operationalize the four elements that support a dynamic systems approach to finding and nurturing gifted potential in learners from low-income backgrounds. The checklists are designed as a reflective tool that can be used to assess and record progress as well as identify next steps as leaders pursue this important work.

Schools that implement this comprehensive approach to the issue of underrepresentation experience changes in school culture and their perception of who is gifted. Through shared leadership, nontraditional methods of identification, a continuum of services, professional development, and parent partnerships, schools gradually move beyond a reliance on test scores to a multidimensional view of potential talent through a review of daily learning activities, performance assessments, and interactions with their students. The teachers and principals develop an invested interest in finding and nurturing gifted potential in students who have historically been overlooked. They also involve parents in the process and enlist parental support and partnerships. The changes in school culture and the multilayered structures that support change from within lead to systemic change within these schools that is more likely to endure. Because the problem of underrepresentation is complex, a multifaceted approach is needed to implement changes and practices that allow every student to have access to gifted programs and learning opportunities that promote continuous academic growth. Schools that adopt a schoolwide systems approach for finding gifted potential in learners from low-income backgrounds make a concerted effort to value the differences that children bring to school and provide multiple opportunities for students to demonstrate their academic strengths, talents, and interests. Understanding the issues that must be addressed and implementing research-based practices allow educators to create a school culture in which every child is continuously assessed and nurtured in order to reach their full potential.

References

Borland, J., Schnur, R., & Wright, L. (2000). Economically disadvantaged students in a school for the academically gifted: A post positivist inquiry into individual and family adjustment. *Gifted Child Quarterly, 44*(1), 13–32. https://doi.org/10.1177/00 1698620004400103

Berry, B., Byrd, A., & Wieder, A. (2013). *Teacherpreneurs: Teachers who lead but don't leave.* Jossey-Bass.

Castellano, J. A., & Díaz, E. I. (2001). *Reaching new horizons: Gifted and talented education for culturally and linguistically diverse students.* Allyn & Bacon.

Cheung, R., Reinhardt, T., Stone, L., & Little, J. W. (2018). Defining teacher leadership: A framework. *Phi Delta Kappan, 100*(3), 38–44. https://doi.org/10.1177/00 31721718808263

Clarenbach, J. (2015). *Expanding the view of giftedness.* The School Superintendents Association. https://www.aasa.org/content.aspx?id=37855

Dweck, C. S. (2016). *Mindset: The new psychology of success.* Ballantine Books. (Original work published 2006)

Ford, D. Y. (2010). Underrepresentation of culturally different students in gifted education: Reflections about current problems and recommendations for the future. *Gifted Child Today, 33*(3), 31–35. https://doi.org/10.1177/107621751003300308

Ford, D. Y., Grantham, T. C., & Whiting, G. W. (2008). Another look at the achievement gap: Learning from the experiences of gifted Black students. *Urban Education, 43*(2), 216–239. https://doi.org/10.1177/0042085907312344

Ford, D. Y., Harris, J. J., III, Tyson, C. A., & Trotman, M. F. (2002). Beyond deficit thinking: Providing access for gifted African American students. *Roeper Review, 24*(2), 52–58. https://doi.org/10.1080/02783190209554129

Fullan, M. (2003). *The moral imperative of school leadership*. Corwin.

Gavin, M. K., Casa, T. M., & Adelson, J. L. (2006). Mentoring mathematical minds: An innovative program to develop math talent. *Understanding Our Gifted, 19*(1), 3–6.

Haberman, M. (2010). The pedagogy of poverty versus good teaching. *Phi Delta Kappan, 92*(2), 81–87. https://doi.org/10.1177/003172171009200223

Horn, C. (2014). The Young Scholars model. In C. M. Adams & K. L. Chandler (Eds.), *Effective program models for gifted students from underserved populations* (pp. 45–60). Prufrock Press.

Horn, C. V. (2015). Young Scholars: A talent development model for finding and nurturing potential in underserved populations. *Gifted Child Today, 38*(1), 19–31. https://doi.org/10.1177/1076217514556532

Horn, C. V. (2018). Serving low-income and underrepresented students in a talent development framework. In P. Olszewski-Kubilius, R. F. Subotnik, & F. C. Worrell (Eds.), *Talent development as a framework for gifted education: Implications for best practices and applications in schools* (pp. 129–152). Prufrock Press.

Ingersoll, R. M. (2004). *Why do high-poverty schools have difficulty staffing their classrooms with qualified teachers?* Center for American Progress & the Institute for America's Future. https://repository.upenn.edu/gse_pubs/493

Kaul, C. R., Johnsen, S. K., Saxon, T. F., & Witte, M. M. (2016). Project Promise: A long-term follow-up of low-income gifted students who participated in a summer enrichment program. *Journal for the Education of the Gifted, 39*(2), 83–102. https://doi.org/10.1177/0162353216640938

Lambert, L. (2002). A framework for shared leadership. *Educational Leadership, 59*(8), 37–40.

MetLife. (2013). *The MetLife survey of the American teacher: Challenges for school leadership*. https://www.metlife.com/about-us/newsroom/2013/february/the-metlife-survey-of-the-american-teacher--challenges-for-schoo

Olszewski-Kubilius, P., & Corwith, S. (2018). Poverty, academic achievement, and giftedness: A literature review. *Gifted Child Quarterly, 62*(1), 37–55. https://doi.org/10.1177/0016986217738015

Olszewski-Kubilius, P., & Thomson, D. L. (2010). Gifted programming for poor or minority urban students: Issues and lessons learned. *Gifted Child Today, 33*(4), 58–64. https://doi.org/10.1177/107621751003300413

Peters, S. J., Gentry, M., Whiting, G. W., & McBee, M. T. (2019). Who gets served in gifted education? Demographic representation and a call for action. *Gifted Child Quarterly, 63*(4), 273–287. https://doi.org/10.1177/0016986219833738

Plucker, J. A., & Peters, S. J. (2016). *Excellence gaps in education: Expanding opportunities for talented students*. Harvard Education Press.

Renzulli, J. S., & Reis, S. M. (2014). *The Schoolwide Enrichment Model: A how-to guide for talent development* (3rd ed.). Prufrock Press.

Robinson, A., Adelson, J. L., Kidd, K., & Cunningham, C. M. (2018). A talent for tinkering: Developing talents in children from low-income households through engineering curriculum. *Gifted Child Quarterly, 62*(1), 130–144. https://doi.org/10.1177/0016986217738049

Scott, M. S., Deuel, L.-L., S., Jean-Francois, B., & Urbano, R. C. (1996). Identifying cognitively gifted ethnic minority children. *Gifted Child Quarterly, 40*(3), 147–153. https://doi.org/10.1177/001698629604000305

Smith, J. R., Brooks-Gunn, J., & Klebanov, P. K. (1997). Consequences of living in poverty for young children's cognitive and verbal ability and early school achievement. In G. J. Duncan & J. Brooks-Gunn (Eds.), *Consequences of growing up poor* (pp. 132–138). Russell Sage Foundation.

Treffinger, D. J., Young, G. C., Nassab, C. A., & Wittig, C. V. (2004). *Enhancing and expanding gifted programs: The levels of service approach*. Prufrock Press.

VanTassel-Baska, J. (2018). Achievement unlocked: effective curricular interventions with low-income students. *Gifted Child Quarterly, 62*(1), 68–82. https://doi.org/10.1177/0016986217738565

VanTassel-Baska, J., Johnson, D., & Avery, L. D., (2002). Using performance tasks in the identification of economically disadvantaged and minority gifted learners: Findings from Project STAR. *Gifted Child Quarterly, 46*(2), 110–123. https://doi.org/10.1177/001698620204600204

Wahlstrom, K., & Louis, K. (2008). How teachers experience principal leadership: The roles of professional community, trust, efficacy, and shared responsibility. *Educational Administration Quarterly, 44*(4), 458–495. https://doi.org/10.1177/0013161X08321502

Yoon, S. Y., & Gentry, M. (2009). Racial and ethnic representation in gifted programs: Current status of and implications for gifted Asian American students. *Gifted Child Quarterly, 53*(2), 121–136. https://doi.org/10.1177/0016986208330564

York-Barr, J., & Duke, K. (2004). What do we know about teacher leadership? Findings from two decades of scholarship. *Review of Educational Leadership, 74*(3), 255–316. https://doi.org/10.3102/00346543074003255

Appendix 12.1

Implementation Checklists
for Coordinators Using a
Systems Approach to Find
and Nurture Gifted Potential
in Low-Income Learners

Collaborative Shared Leadership Among All Educators in the School Community	Level of Implementation			
	Low			High
Principal and teachers meet and develop a shared vision for their school. Finding and nurturing gifted potential in learners from low-income backgrounds is a priority.				
Principal and committee of teachers plan and develop a detailed and strategic plan with timeline and goals to ensure shared responsibility and shared leadership for finding gifted learners from low-income backgrounds.				
All teachers are informed of the plan, have an opportunity to provide feedback, and meet as grade-level and vertical teams to begin implementation.				
Staff engage in frequent conversations regarding gifted education pedagogy, culturally responsive teaching practices, and nontraditional methods of identifying gifted potential.				
The principal and gifted resource teacher network and share success stories and challenges with principals and gifted resource teachers at other schools that are using a systems approach.				
Instruction and school environment are sensitive to special populations (i.e., twice-exceptional learners, English language learners, learners from low-income backgrounds) and their social-emotional needs.				
School staff and community value the diverse cultural, linguistic, economic, and ethnic backgrounds of all students.				

Strengths:

Goals for improvement (to include professional development needs):

Note. Copyright 2019 by Carol V. Horn. Reprinted with permission of the author.

High-Level Curriculum and Gifted Education Pedagogy for All Students	Level of Implementation Low			High
Students receive instruction and learn beyond the grade-level expectations. Gifted education strategies and practices are infused into the general education curriculum for all learners.				
Teachers use flexible instructional groupings at all grade levels and are committed to providing a growth mindset culture with high-end curriculum and instruction.				
Teachers and principals engage in professional development to learn models and strategies that infuse gifted education pedagogy into teaching practice for all students.				
Novice to expert assessments for growth are collected in student portfolios.				
Students are encouraged to become self-directed learners through independent study projects, project-based learning, and problem-based learning.				
Digital learning is embedded in instruction, and technology is integrated in both the process and product of curricular experiences.				
Teachers develop a curriculum framework that outlines materials, resources, and curricula that may be used at each grade level to challenge and engage advanced learners.				

Strengths:

Goals for improvement (to include any professional development needs):

A Continuum of Gifted Services Throughout the School Year, After School, and During the Summer	Level of Implementation Low			High
Beginning in kindergarten, school offers continuum of gifted services with multiple entry points and varying levels of challenge in response to ongoing assessments in reading and mathematics.				
Gifted services are offered through multiple avenues to include cluster grouping, pull-out services, push-in services, and before-school and afterschool opportunities.				
Gifted services are available to any child who has the capacity to succeed as determined through performance assessments and multiple criteria.				
As students are identified for services, the student data system records the level of service each student receives, when the service began, and when a level changes.				
Gifted services are provided through a collaborative coplanning model in which the gifted resource teacher meets with grade-level teams to plan and implement high-level curriculum and instruction that extends and enriches the general education curriculum.				
Continuum of services is guided by a curriculum framework that outlines materials, resources, and curricula that are research-based and designed for gifted learners in the four core subjects of mathematics, language arts, social studies, and science at all grade levels.				
Summer school, as well as before school and afterschool opportunities, provide ongoing enrichment and acceleration in one or more academic areas.				

Strengths:

Goals for Improvement (to include professional development needs):

Note. Copyright 2019 by Carol V. Horn. Reprinted with permission of the author.

Ongoing Professional Development for All Educators and Parent Partnerships	Level of Implementation			
	Low			High
School administrators, education specialists, and classroom teachers engage in ongoing professional development to support finding and nurturing gifted learners from low-income backgrounds. These include inservice days, graduate courses, and/or summer institutes.				
The gifted education resource teacher collaborates and plans with classroom teachers to infuse strategies and practices designed to develop critical and creative thinking and elicit higher level thinking responses.				
Teachers learn how to record evidence of gifted potential through portfolios. Evidence is collected in response to high-level curriculum and includes observations, work samples, performance assessments, anecdotal records, and test scores.				
All educators are required to take courses in cultural proficiency.				
Parents are invited to be partners in their child's education. School offers parent workshops and multiple opportunities for parents to be actively involved.				
Parent liaisons are available to help with interpretation, translations, and outreach to parents.				
School counselors are trained to provide ongoing support to gifted learners from low-income backgrounds and to ensure that they continue to receive services as they transition to middle and high school.				

Strengths:

Goals for improvement (to include any professional development needs):

Note. Copyright 2019 by Carol V. Horn. Reprinted with permission of the author.

Voices and Reflections

Tamra Stambaugh
and Paula Olszewski-Kubilius

Throughout this book, chapters have examined how poverty impacts an individual's talent development trajectory. Chapter authors highlighted the importance of domain-specific opportunities; explained how appropriate curriculum resources and instructional strategies can enable students to be successful with advanced content; emphasized the importance of equitable identification systems and assessments that take context and opportunity to learn into consideration; discussed the intersection of low income, race, geography, and other factors, and how these influence talent development; outlined psychosocial factors that enhance or impede talent development; discussed the importance of community resources and outside-of-school learning; and shared how horizontally and vertically aligned school system approaches are effective in finding and nurturing talent. Evidence-supported practices have been clearly outlined, yet educators must also remember that there are faces behind each chapter—students who will ultimately benefit from the implementation of these practices but come to educators with their own unique skill sets and contexts that must be considered.

For this concluding chapter we asked several individuals who grew up in low-income households and are at various stages in their career development to reflect on the following questions:

> How did growing up in a low-income household affect your talent development trajectory? Specifically, (a) what barriers did you face, and (b) what internal and external factors contributed to your success?

> Tell us a story about a meaningful moment in your life that related to awareness of your low-income status and how you dealt with that.

> Knowing what you know now, what advice would you provide to gifted students and their families from low-income households?

> If you could pick one factor that you believe was most critical to your success growing up in a low-income household, what would it be? Why?

> What factors coexisted with your low-income status in ways that impacted your career success (i.e., twice-exceptionality, race/ethnicity, country of origin, social capital, geographic access, etc.)?

The intent of these questions is not to conduct a qualitative study. We simply want to add voice and lived experiences to this book. We want to punctuate the evidence-supported themes found in each chapter and perhaps even highlight new ideas not previously mentioned. The respondents' backgrounds are varied in terms of geography (urban, suburban, and rural representation), ethnicity and race (Black, White, English language learner), and career level (from those just beginning their careers to those who are midcareer or retired). When reporting their income status growing up, the majority of respondents indicated that on a scale of 1–100 (with 100 being "lacking food or shelter" and 1 being "having what you needed to live adequately but without frills") most ranked their financial situations around a 60. The responses to each question were categorized and reflect seven core themes.

Theme 1: Family Support Is Important

The majority of respondents credit a family member with their success or survival. Sometimes the family member was a parent, while other times an extended family member, such as a grandparent, aunt, or uncle, served as a strong supporter. One emerita professor explained how her grandmother was a key influence:

My grandmother was a lifeline in a sea of mediocrity and boredom. My grandmother with her messages of becoming a teacher and not getting pregnant [showed that] she truly cared about me and [she] showed it daily.

Another respondent from an urban area who is now a school administrator, explained the positive impact of extended family members, given that her mother was emotionally ill:

My mother (single parent) did not have the navigational capital necessary to advocate for me or my appropriate placement in school. The disconnect between my home environment and school was extreme, so different that I spent kindergarten quiet. I was fearful of being judged and "messing up." Externally, my grandmother and uncle always believed in me. They walked alongside me as I figured out how to navigate school. They supported all of my endeavors and always pushed me to be willing to take risks. The power of belief and care were instrumental. I always knew there were two caring adults who were wildly committed to me. They made the difference.

Another respondents from a rural background acknowledged immediate family members as being supportive:

My parents did not go to college but they supported me as best they knew how. What we did not have in basic resources or necessities was made up for in support and love. My parents tried to support me—even if their support was sometimes misguided or uninformed—they wanted what was best for me. I always knew I was a priority.

Another respondent, new to the United States, explained his family's emphasis on education and outlined a recommendation for other families in his situation:

I was really lucky . . . I came to the United States to pursue a better life, so my family had a strong belief in the power of an education. For families, the biggest thing you can do for your gifted student is support them. Even if there is not someone in the family who went to college or had limited education, that is okay. What [we] need most is your emotional support and permission to make mistakes. Ask them about school. You don't have to understand the biophysics they may be interested in that day, but knowing you have made an effort, goes a long way. Having a meaningful conversation and letting your child know that they are strong and smart is free.

Theme 2: Positive and Nurturing Relationships Are Needed at All Levels of One's Trajectory

Respondents recognized the power of individuals outside of their family who served as mentors or supporters along their talent development paths. A respondent who grew up in a rural area and recently graduated with a master's degree explained:

> I was lucky enough to have met the right people at the right time, as well as built up some internal determination, that contributed to where I am now. I would not have been able to be where I am today without my support system. As a child of poverty, you learn to rely on yourself. You learn to care for others before yourself. What you don't learn is how to let others take care of you. There have been several barriers that have popped up in my journey, but having a strong network of friends who believe in you has been the key to my success. Everything from helping study for an exam to problem solving issues to keep me in school. I know that I have a network of people I can count on. This was crucial, especially when I did not have familial support—I was truly on my own. More importantly than supporting my academic endeavors, I was able to be successful because my group of people supported me as a whole person. I was in uncharted territory as a first-generation college student. Having a network of support gave me a safe place to fail.

A retired professor reflected on the mentors throughout her life, particularly influential teachers, and wrote that:

> Individual teachers took an interest in me all the way through [my career]. [I had a] high school counselor who believed in me; a dean of students who favored me; college profs in English

who thought well of me. I did not relate well to education professors. I had husbands who were supportive of my choices to pursue higher education and an associate superintendent . . . who opened doors; fellow teachers who saw talent, other supervisors . . . who promoted me. Entry into gifted education and meeting the people who were stellar in field [lists names] was impactful. I made them my mentors.

Another respondent echoed the power of mentors in her life in promoting self-confidence and supporting her career path:

I had some amazing women in my life who mentored me, supported my career endeavors and created paths that moved me to the next level. I am indebted to them for setting me on a path that pushed me to be more than I ever thought I could become. Simple words such as "you belong here" or "you can do this" or "I'll help you if you get stuck but you've got this" meant a lot. These individuals took the time to mentor me, show me the ropes, and help me with social skills, career decisions, and understanding middle-class professional values. They saw something in me that I did not see in myself at first.

The importance of belonging and relationships is also noted, as a school administrator from a low-income household offered this advice: "I encourage families to cultivate talent early, develop a network of support where relationships and resources can support the endeavors necessary for your child's growth." Another respondent, who transitioned recently from K–12 education into higher education, explained the need for leveraging relationships to gain tacit or insider knowledge and important opportunities:

It is important to know the underlying hidden rules of getting in on the inside of things that are never said aloud. Networking and knowing the right people/programs/connections are really important. Opportunity grows ability. Look for opportunities to build background and life knowledge.

In addition to mentors, a couple of respondents discussed the importance of learning how to socialize in professional settings, highlighting the value of mentoring for developing good psychosocial skills:

You also fail to see the [social] rules you have flouted, the people you have offended that control the outcomes you desire. So, the lack of social acuity is a crucial factor in limiting your ability to be successful. I often minimized this issue.

Another respondent in mid-career explained social struggles she experiences and the need for mentoring in social relationships, this way:

I am comfortable participating in academic and career endeavors now. However, social endeavors continue to be a struggle. I am still figuring out how to socially thrive in a middle and upper class world; sometimes my priorities are just not the same. I am still learning the rules of the socialization game. Those who know how to play this game seem to thrive in ways others who are equally talented do not.

Theme 3: Recognition of Talent Is Critical for Ongoing Success in a Field

Many of the respondents explained that their talents were recognized by school officials. In some instances, opportunities were provided with this recognition, as relayed by this student who is now attending an Ivy League school and preparing for a career in medicine:

My family did not speak English, I arrived in the United States at 5 years old and was having trouble with English. I was selected to transfer to a level-four Advanced Academics Program within my school. I don't know how I was selected into this program because I was still in English-as-a-second-language courses. However, this speaks to the strength of the [name] program to see potential outside of English proficiency. Through this program, I transferred from my base school to a school that had a full-time advance academic program.

Another respondent, who is a recently vetted professor, explained that the recognition of talent motivated a change in her career ambitions:

A teacher told me I could do more with my life when I told her I just wanted to grow up and sell lipstick at [a department store]. She said with my "smarts" I should apply to go to college. So,

I opened up the encyclopedia and looked up universities that were within a 250-mile radius and circled the ones I had heard of, then started applying.

Theme 4: Community and School Supports Can Provide Life-Changing Opportunities

All but one of the respondents discussed an impactful program, opportunity, or community resource that allowed them to access or at least realize the existence of opportunities beyond their immediate world. As one respondent so aptly explained: "Being poor limits your understanding of the larger world unless you force your way in to see and ultimately participate."

A student whose second language is English credited participation in his school's specialized gifted program for his admission to an Ivy League university and subsequent admission to medical school:

> Through this program I transferred from my base school to a school that had a full-time advance academic program. My first few years in this program presented difficulty as the material presented was significantly more challenging than my base school. However, when I finished this program in eighth grade, I returned to my base high school, and I excelled in honors and IB/AP courses due to the rigor of the academics in elementary and middle school. I then went on to score in the 97th percentile of the SAT and got accepted into seven Ivy League universities (I didn't apply to the eighth one), Stanford, UChicago, and even got into a BA/MD program at Brown. I am now in my final year of college at [name] University and I will be enrolling in medical school next fall. I can say that had I not been a part of [name] program, that I may not have cared as much about academics, and I would certainly not achieve as much of the success as I have achieved.

One respondent explains the importance of competitions to her recognition of her talent, but also acknowledged the financial struggle to maintain participation in such programs:

> In elementary I was on the Battle of the Books (BoB) team. I was truly an asset . . . my memory and ability to recall details was instrumental in our team successes. I remember when we

315

took our team picture for the yearbook I did not have my BOB shirt. We didn't have money for me to order one and I did not let my grandmother know in time. Despite my capacity, my ability and belonging on the team . . . I saw that I was different from the group. I was always aware of the stigma of being a free lunch kid. In high school it was overwhelming . . . I mapped out my trips through the lunch line so I would end up at the cashier who would allow me to verbally tell her my ID number, 114971. I absolutely hated it when she wasn't there or I was called to a line where one of the cashiers would pull on my ID and bring it close enough to her eyes so she could see it and enter it into the system. Those seconds seemed like eternity. I made sure to keep my eyes fixed at a point where I did not have to worry about making eye contact with anyone.

Another respondent discussed the impact of her church on access and opportunity:

Church was an important part of my life. I had opportunities there and people who cared about me and supported me. It was a community that provided me with opportunities and resources. Youth group outings and church camps were paid for by others in the church and allowed me to see beyond my tiny community.

Others recognized the importance of neighbors and friends as a resource:

[I had] a friend who had educated parents. I hung out with her at her house and learned about scholarships, the importance of extracurricular activities; [she] played the flute so maybe I should . . . her parents took us to museums, musicals, and other cultural activities I would have never done.

The role of community and neighborhood supports was recognized and acknowledged by some respondents even if these were not always available to them:

Many of my peers had parents who were educators, business owners, or other educated professions. Just the simple exposure of stimulating dinner conversation or discussing something you read in class was not possible for me. I did not always have access to basic necessities, so thinking about accessing a program, materials, technology, or other experiences that would have benefitted me in my development seemed entirely impossible but would have been impactful.

Most of those surveyed recommended that families from low-income households take advantage of free enrichment opportunities in the community, such as museums, library programs, church functions, and the like. One individual, summarized it this way:

I think the focus needs to be on the child. What interventions might feed interests, dreams, desires? Provide cultural enrichment as a baseline program (e.g., trips to museums, concerts, lectures at universities). Many . . . have never been to cultural events even though they are geographically proximate. Develop habits of regularly seeking out these opportunities, mostly free, that are of interest. Use libraries on a regular basis for reading and research. Join discussion groups organized at the library. If you do not attend church, join one for social contacts and activities that will help promote growth in spiritual and other areas. Look into college and career issues as early as sixth grade. Look for information on scholarships to participate in career activities.

Theme 5: Find Balance Between Meeting Basic Needs and Taking Advantage of Academic Opportunities

Many individuals acknowledged the benefit of community or school opportunities but also explained that these could not be taken advantage of because of the need to support the family through an outside job or take care of younger siblings. Educators must recognize these conflicts in students' lives and figure out ways to support students in both endeavors.

One recent master's-level graduate from a rural area explained the conflict in this way:

For talent development, there were a lot of difficulties in the domain of access and opportunity. Education was not valued in my house. Areas of strength or high ability were not valued

317

at my school. Pursuing opportunities beyond our town was not valued by the community. Some days, I stopped valuing my own ability. Because I came from a low-income household, I was often working late on school nights or taking care of my younger sister. I did not always have time to put forth my best effort on my school work, or I was not attentive in class. I was not offered additional academic opportunities because I was not what a traditionally "good student" looked like. Even when I was forwarded an opportunity, such as being in an AP class, I could not afford to take the AP test. When I got to college, I flipped a coin to choose my major because I did not think I had an area of strength or talent. I always felt out of place in my classes because it felt like everyone around me was so much smarter and knew so much more than I did. Being low income does not end when you move out or go to higher education. It comes with its own set of barriers. There were times that my tuition was paid, but my cabinets were empty. Even though I was at a university, I still was not on a level playing field with my peers. I had a full-time job in order to make my tuition payments, so my studies were not always priority. I had to make choices such as which books would be most important to buy or how to pay off that parking ticket . . . which I unfortunately got a lot of.

She continued to explain how she knew was poor at an early age and seemed to understand the impact:

The thought that I was the "poor kid" was always looming, and I tried my best to appear as if that was not true. The first time I can remember being truly embarrassed by the obviousness of my situation was in eighth grade. Every quarter, we had a good behavior reward activity for all of the students in the grade who exhibited appropriate behavior for the quarter. Our last quarter activity was going to be a trip to the local recreation center with pizza for lunch. The field trip cost $8. That amount of money could buy a few boxes of pasta, some eggs, some rice, but not this field trip. I remember feeling like $8 was so easy for everyone else, and I didn't understand how they just had that laying around. When the day of the field trip came, I came to school and all of my friends asked me if I was going. I told them I was not, and when they asked me why, I lied. I told them that I had gotten a detention earlier in the quarter, so I was not allowed to go. I sat in the classroom where all of the non-goers were and felt so embarrassed that I couldn't afford to go on the field trip, especially since I had good behavior. I dealt with it by lying about my situation to maintain, what I thought, was a more positive image of myself than the truth.

Another respondent explained that missed opportunities existed because of summer work.

I could not go to Governor's School because I had to work in the summer for money. I had to quit track as a sport because I had to work for money. I did not have the understanding of "what to do" to be an outstanding competitive student for scholarships (with parents not going to college they really had little guidance on the college app process).

Others wanted opportunities but knew that many times this was not possible:

The barriers of not being able to participate in lessons in any area in which I was interested [were extreme]. I once was able to take seven dance lessons but couldn't afford to be in the recital. [We did not have] a car in the family until I learned to drive at age 16. This resulted in no vacations, no weekend excursions, being trapped in an inner-city neighborhood, its schools, its establishments. Most memories are from adulthood, as when you are a child, you don't know you are poor. Lack of opportunities to participate in activities that cost money [was a barrier]. I wanted to learn to play an instrument but my mother made clear we couldn't afford it . . . I was overwhelmed the first time I went to an estate sale—how could people sell perfectly beautiful goods to buy new? I was viscerally ill. I realized that I lived in low-income areas much of my adult life, attended a fourth-rate university for four degrees, and limited my life because I grew up poor. For me, I was stuck and only appreciated my power to change some of it when I finally left [named city] at age 30. Too late to change some things but I began to develop my own way to a greater extent.

319

Another respondent reflected back on the internal struggle between making money and prioritizing impactful career decisions:

> Even now I am afraid I won't have money and will go back to the struggle I had growing up. I have consistently prioritized earning potential over publications and other choices that would get me ahead in my field. It is a constant battle, and the fear of going without drives me more times that I care to admit.

Theme 6: Recognize and Use Strengths and Childhood Experiences to Your Advantage

Even though many of the respondents explained hardships, they also added how they were able to use their hardships to their advantage and see the positive aspects of their upbringing, taking full advantage of the skills they developed in their childhood. One individual explained how she was proud that "[I had the] ability to make a financial plan and set personal goals related to budget, marrying young (at 20) to have support in my personal goals and less of a financial burden.

Another recent master's graduate credited her experiences for developing skills necessary for success in college:

> The most critical factor in my success in a low-income household was tenacity. There are a lot of days that I could not tell you why I am here. Everything was stacked against me being successful, but I refused to let that be the answer. While growing up low income definitely was not a fun experience, I accredit my success to the resiliency and grit that I developed as a result. When you have used your task commitment to pay the electric bill before it is shut off, the grit of finishing a paper or a task for work feels like nothing!

Other participants outlined how they had adult responsibilities at an early age and acquired internal skills that made them successful:

> My mother had to work night shifts so I was alone to make dinner, do homework, etc. My grandmother was committed to the state hospital for depression. She cried all day and was helpless, yet I felt the solution was wrong but I felt helpless to interfere. [I had] internal characteristics of drive and perseverance in the

face of adversity and a strong motivation to learn coupled with early independence. That allowed me to work through college to support scholarships, to drive as soon as I turned 16, to set my own schedule and rules from age 14.

Another respondent from a low-income rural area reflected on the benefits of her background and using that experience to promote a future for others of similar circumstances:

In my chosen career, being from a rural area with limited access to resources only available in the big city has been useful. I understand rural culture and societal norms, and that helps me navigate relationships, policies, and practices for gifted students in these areas. I also understand how to maximize resources and provide opportunities for those districts who may not otherwise be equipped to help their students.

Theme 7: Success Requires Motivation, Self-Confidence, Independence, and Resilience

The psychosocial strength required to succeed was acknowledged by every respondent in some way or another. Many explained how they were "adulting" well before their classmates and frequently dealt with other hardships besides poverty, which gave them the skills to cope with challenges but also took a toll on their psychological well-being. Their advice to other families in similar situations was focused on the importance of nurturing these inner strengths that they developed through hardships.

One respondent provided this advice:

A major piece of advice that I would give is to know that you are capable and don't be intimidated by perceived intelligence of others around you. You may not speak like your classmates who are the "smart kids" or be recognized by your teachers, but that doesn't mean that you are not talented. Your gifts may manifest themselves in ways that don't look like others, but that is okay. Trust me, not everyone can balance a budget in seventh grade! Keep your determination and find that area of passion that makes you happy and pursue it.

Another respondent explained how she had to be the adult of the household at times and the impact this had on her social-emotional well-being:

> My mother had an undiagnosed learning disability and was later diagnosed with depression with suicidal ideation and a couple of suicide attempts. I spent an inordinate amount of energy trying to cover for her. I did not want her to be judged for something beyond her control. Initially, she did not ask for this level of support but she eventually became dependent on my abilities. She carried immense shame for needing me in this capacity. I felt sorry that while she struggled with reading and literacy pursuits, she was amazing with math and her executive functioning allowed us to have an organized household. I wrote notes for school and she copied them so they would be presented in her handwriting. That dissonance perplexed me. Some days I was the little 8-year-old girl and moments later I was expected to help figure out adult situations. I took on responsibilities that were beyond the realm of developmentally appropriate for a child. I started to see life as a record of wins and losses. I was determined to have far more Ws than Ls. In the process my emotional well-being was compromised. Eventually, her instability was the catalyst for me to decide at 11 years old that living with my grandmother would be the best living situation for me.

Another respondent explains how she had to begin believing in herself and had to find the strength to ask for help:

> While this may sound counterintuitive to success, I am where I am because of my failures. In a low-income household, there is little to no margin of error, so I had to learn how to admit when I needed help and ask for it. One of my favorite things to say about my journey is "Everything I am doing I once thought was impossible." I thought I wasn't smart enough, good enough, or ready enough to attend college. Impossible. I have my bachelor's degree. I thought I would never be able to move away from home and make it in another state. Impossible. I have been in two different states over 6 years on my own. I thought that graduate school was out of reach and I would never make it. Impossible. I have my master's degree. I thought I would not be

able to positively impact the lives of kids like me. Impossible. I have a job that allows me to reach thousands of students to let them know that they are smart and they are deserving.

Still another respondent acknowledged the level of independence she garnered from her circumstance:

I feel that I have earned my way into being well-known in the field. No one really did it for me. I had a vision for gifted education from the beginning—creating programs and services that mattered for low-income students.

Ultimately, a school administrator best summarized the need for interpersonal skills in this way: "Show up, bring your full self (all the complexities and beauties of your identities) and believe that you are rightfully placed at the table."

Conclusion

The quotes shared in this chapter attest to the challenges that individuals from low-income families face as they try to have their talent acknowledged and developed. Their stories emphasize the powerful role that individuals—parents, grandparents, teachers—can play in helping children believe in themselves and strive to do more than their circumstances might typically allow. Recognition of potential within schools by educators was essential for most of the respondents, emphasizing the importance of equitable identification practices. The anecdotes remind educators that support is important at every step of the way; mentors from schools, churches, and communities were often the conduit for important opportunities, sources of tacit knowledge about careers, and role models for psychosocial skills. Despite stellar academic performance, students may still suffer emotionally and psychologically from the stigma of poverty and need support to manage living in what seems like two different worlds. Yet, many had strong motivation, resilience, and early maturity that enabled them to persist despite challenges and overcome difficulties. Educators need to acknowledge these great strengths and help students use them in the pursuit of their talent development paths.

About the Editors

Tamra Stambaugh, Ph.D., is an associate research professor in special education and executive director of Programs for Talented Youth at Vanderbilt University. Stambaugh's research interests focus on students living in rural settings, students of poverty, and curriculum and instructional interventions that promote gifted student learning and talent development. She is a frequent keynote speaker at national and international conferences and the coauthor/editor of several books, curriculum units, and book chapters. She has won several awards for her work, including curriculum writing awards and the Early Leader Award from the National Association of Gifted Children.

Paula Olszewski-Kubilius, Ph.D., is director of the Center for Talent Development and professor in the School of Education and Social Policy at Northwestern University. For 37 years she has developed enrichment and accelerated program models for diverse gifted learners. She writes extensively on issues of talent development. She has served as editor of *Gifted Child Quarterly* and is currently a trustee of the Illinois Mathematics and Science Academy and past-president of the Illinois Association for Gifted Children. She is past-president of the National Association for Gifted Children and received the Distinguished Scholar Award in 2009.

About the Authors

Isabella Ahrens is a graduate student studying school psychology at the University of California, Berkeley. Her interests include student athletes, parent involvement, commitment to learning, and mental health. She has contributed to research exploring Native Hawaiian mental and behavioral health as well as research examining patients receiving integrative medicine interventions.

Morgan Bessette is a graduate student in the School Psychology Program at the University of California, Berkeley. Her research interests include school discipline, at-risk youth, teacher effectiveness, reading disorders, and school-based interventions for students with Attention Deficit/Hyperactivity Disorder. She has worked as a student clinician at the University of California, San Francisco-UC Berkeley Schwab Dyslexia and Cognitive Diversity Center and has worked as an academic counselor at UC Berkeley's Academic and Talent Development Program. She is a Segal AmeriCorps Education Award recipient and is a member of the American Psychological Association and the National Association of School Psychologists.

Susan Corwith, Ph.D., is an associate director at Northwestern University's Center for Talent Development (CTD). Dr. Corwith has extensive experience in gifted program design and evaluation, advocacy and outreach. For more than 25 years, Dr. Corwith has been active in the field of gifted education, working as a K–12 educator, gifted program coordinator, administrator and researcher. Active in both state and national organizations, Dr. Corwith serves on the board of the Illinois Association for Gifted Children and chaired the National Association for Gifted Children's Professional Standards Committee.

Dante D. Dixson, Ph.D., is an Assistant Professor of School and Educational Psychology at Michigan State University. He currently serves on the editorial boards of *Gifted Child Quarterly* and the *Journal for the Education of the Gifted*. In addition, Dr. Dixson is a board member for the Roeper Institute and the Michigan Association of Gifted Children. Dr. Dixson's areas of expertise include the role of hope in the educational and psychological functioning of children and adolescents, psychosocial precursors of achievement, and the underrepresentation of youth from racial and ethnic minorities and disadvantaged backgrounds in gifted education.

Eric Fecht, Ed.D., has supported curriculum development and gifted programming for the past 8 years. He has worked as a classroom teacher, instructional coach, and professional development coordinator. Fecht coauthored a curriculum unit through Vanderbilt Programs for Talented Youth that has been recognized by the National Association for Gifted Children's curriculum network. He currently serves on the board of the Tennessee Association for Gifted and is the Director of Teaching and Learning at Harding Academy in Nashville, TN.

Maedeh Golshirazi is a Ph.D. candidate in the School Psychology Program at the University of California, Berkeley. Her areas of expertise include talent development/gifted education, at-risk children and youth, social-emotional learning, school climate, and parental involvement in education. Golshirazi is a member of several professional associations, including the American Educational Research Association, the American Psychological Association, and the Society for Research in Child Development.

Stacy M. Hayden is a doctoral candidate at the University of Connecticut studying giftedness, creativity, and talent development. She was recognized as a Javits-Frasier Scholar in 2014 by the National Association for Gifted Children and was named Outstanding Teacher of the Gifted for Region IV-E by the Virginia Association for the Gifted in 2017. Her research interests include equity, preidentification programs, and college honors programs. Prior to pursuing her Ph.D., she taught gifted elementary students and worked with the Young Scholars Program in Alexandria City Public Schools, VA.

Carol V. Horn, Ed.D., has worked extensively to develop and implement the Young Scholars model, a comprehensive approach to finding and developing talent and gifted potential in young learners from underrepresented populations. Dr. Horn was coordinator of Advanced Academic Programs for Fairfax

County Public Schools (FCPS) for 17 years and has worked in gifted education for more than 30 years. She has a master's in education in educational psychology with an emphasis on gifted from the University of Virginia and a doctorate in teacher preparation and special education from The George Washington University.

Natalie Rodriguez Jansorn is Vice President of Scholarship Programs at the Jack Kent Cooke Foundation, where she has been developing programs to support exceptional students to achieve their college goals for 15 years. A highlight of her year is meeting parents and rising ninth-grade students for a college residential experience called Welcome Weekend. Natalie has worked with schools across the country to strengthen their school, family, and community partnerships. She began her career teaching English with the Peace Corps in rural Thailand.

Joni Lakin, Ph.D., is an associate professor of educational studies at the University of Alabama. She studies educational measurement, including test validity and fairness in gifted and talented identification. She is a coauthor of the Cognitive Abilities Test (Form 8) and explores how ability tests can increase the diversity of students identified for gifted and talented programs. She also conducts research and evaluation in STEM education to promote STEM retention along the academic pipeline.

Catherine A. Little, Ph.D., is a professor in Giftedness, Creativity, and Talent Development in the Department of Educational Psychology at the University of Connecticut. Her research interests include professional learning, differentiation of curriculum and instruction for advanced learners, and classroom questioning practices. She has been the project director for Project SPARK and Project LIFT, two recent Javits-funded initiatives focused on working with schools and teachers to recognize and respond to advanced academic potential in the early grades, particularly in students from underserved populations.

Kevin H. Macpherson, Ph.D., is currently an associate director of special education at KIPP Public Schools, Northern California. His areas of interest are social-psychological interventions in schools, stereotype threat, belonging, special education, designing equitable school systems, urban education, and education policy. Dr. Macpherson was a 2012 Teach for American corps member and earned the Los Angeles nomination for the national Sue Lehmann Excellence in Teacher Leadership Award. He received his doctorate in the San

Francisco State University and University of California, Berkeley joint program in special education.

Monica C. Meadows, Ed.D., is a gifted and talented facilitator for the Pulaski County Special School District in Little Rock, AR. Monica has experience teaching various high school pre-AP and AP Science courses, and gifted and talented classes at the elementary, middle, and high school levels. Monica works closely with the University of Arkansas at Little Rock as the principal of the Summer Laureate University for Youth program. Monica holds a master's degree in gifted and talented education and a doctorate of education in educational administration and supervision with an emphasis in gifted and talented education from the University of Arkansas at Little Rock.

Franklin B. Mejía is a doctoral student in the Human Development and Learning Sciences Program at the University of California, Berkeley. A credentialed Spanish and bilingual teacher, his areas of expertise are academic talent development, education of at-risk youth, ethnic and racial identity, Latinx education, and Spanish teaching practices. Mejía's current professional affiliations include the American Educational Research Association (AERA) and three AERA special interest groups: Latina/o/x Research Issues; Research on Giftedness, Creativity, and Talent; and Talent Development of Students Placed at Risk. He is a former McNair Scholar and a recipient of the Eugene Cota-Robles Fellowship.

Emily Mofield, Ed.D., is an assistant professor at Lipscomb University where she teaches gifted education and doctoral research courses. Dr. Mofield has recently served as the National Association for Gifted Children Chair for Curriculum Studies. She has coauthored numerous award-winning advanced language arts curriculum units (with Vanderbilt Programs for Talented Youth) and is also the author/coauthor of several research publications related to achievement motivation and collaborative teaching practices. She is the co-recipient of the NAGC Hollingworth Award for Excellence in Research and Texas Association for the Gifted and Talented's 2019 Legacy Book Award for *Teaching Tenacity, Resilience, and a Drive for Excellence.*

Ann Robinson, Ph.D., is founding director of the Jodie Mahony Center for Gifted Education at the University of Arkansas, at Little Rock. She is past president of the National Association for Gifted Children and a former editor of *Gifted Child Quarterly.* Dr. Robinson received four Jacob K. Javits research and demonstration projects from the U. S. Department of Education, including three STEM-focused awards for designing and validating the STEM Starters model in elementary schools. She is the developer of Blueprints for Biography, a series of teaching guides for trade book biographies.

Nicolas Saldivar is a graduate student studying school psychology at the University of California, Berkeley. His areas of interest include hope, student civic and political engagement, and Latinx academic achievement. Saldivar has contributed to research exploring the physiological and psychological impacts of racism and heterosexism among LGBTQ and Latinx youth. He has worked in various research teams and is beginning a community internship at a local wellness center.

Carol Klose Smith, Ph.D., is an assistant professor of counselor education at Viterbo University in La Crosse, WI. She has more than 15 years of clinical experiences, which include working as a director of counseling services and working in trauma counseling. She has been a counselor educator for the past 12 years. Her current areas of research include gifted and career counseling, clinical supervision, and trauma-informed practice. In her free time, she enjoys remodeling her old house, playing the viola, and drinking coffee with friends.

Jeremy Spence is a Ph.D. student and Eugene V. Cota-Robles Fellowship recipient in the School Psychology Program at the University of California, Berkeley. His research areas include LGBTQ bullying, school experiences of queer students throughout multiple levels of schooling, self-esteem, social acceptance, and the impact of stress and stereotype threat on racial and sexual minority populations.

Susannah M. Wood, Ph.D., is currently an associate professor in the Department of Rehabilitation and Counselor Education at the University of Iowa. She is also a faculty partner with the Connie Belin and Jacqueline N. Blank International Center for Gifted Education and Talented Development, where she provides professional development opportunities for undergraduate students, graduate students, and practicing educators related to the social and emotional concerns of gifted students. Her research interests encompass preparing school counselors for practice, with a particular focus on serving the gifted population in collaboration with other educators and professionals.

Frank C. Worrell, Ph.D., is a professor of school psychology at the University of California, Berkeley. His areas of expertise include talent development/gifted education, at-risk youth, cultural identities, scale development/val-

idation, teacher effectiveness, time perspective, and the translation of psychological research findings into practice. Dr. Worrell is a fellow of the Association
for Psychological Science, the American Educational Research Association, and
five divisions of the American Psychological Association, and a member of the
National Academy of Education. He is also a recipient of the Distinguished
Scholar Award from the National Association for Gifted Children.

Mercedes A. Zapata, Ph.D., is a practicing school psychologist in the
San Francisco United School District. Her research examines disability iden-
tity among people with disabilities. Dr. Zapata is a member of the American
Psychological Association, the Association for Psychological Science, and the
National Association of School Psychologists. Dr. Zapata is a recipient of the
Eugene Cota-Robles Fellowship, the Foundation for Rehabilitation Psychology's
Dissertation Award, and the Association for Psychological Science's RISE
Award.